The Teaching of Arabic
as a Foreign Language

Issues and Directions

AL-ᶜARABIYYA MONOGRAPH SERIES
NUMBER 2

The Teaching of Arabic as a Foreign Language

Issues and Directions

Edited by

Mahmoud al-Batal

American Association of Teachers of Arabic

Al-ᶜArabiyya Monograph Series, Number 2

A Publication of

العربية

Journal of the American Association of Teachers of Arabic

Editor
Mushira Eid
University of Utah

Associate and Book Review Editor
Roger Allen
University of Pennsylvania

Assistant Editor
Tessa Hauglid
University of Utah

Production Manager
Grant Paul Skabelund
Brigham Young University

Executive Director
R. Kirk Belnap
Brigham Young University

To Our Students

whose dedication, enthusiasm and achievements
make the teaching of Arabic worthwhile.

Library of Congress Cataloging-in-Publication Data

The teaching of Arabic as a foreign language: issues and directions / edited by Mahmoud Al-Batal

    375 p.

Papers presented at the symposium, "The Teaching of Arabic in the 1990s: Issues and Directions," held at Middlebury College in Middlebury, Vermont, in June 1992.

    Includes bibliographical references and index.
    ISBN: 0–9621530–9–5

    1. Arabic language—Study and teaching (Higher)—United States—Foreign speakers—Congresses. 2. Computer-assisted instruction—United States—Congresses. I. Al-Batal, Mahmoud.

PJ6066.T43   1995
492'.78'007—dc20   95–22101
                                CIP

Distributed by American Association of Teachers of Arabic (AATA),
Brigham Young University, 280 HRCB, Provo, Utah 84602 USA

CONTENTS

ACKNOWLEDGMENTS

The papers included in this volume were presented at the symposium "The Teaching of Arabic in the 1990s: Issues and Directions," held at Middlebury College in Middlebury, Vermont, in June 1992, in celebration of the Tenth Anniversary of the School of Arabic at Middlebury. The symposium featured presentations, group discussions, and workshops and was attended by about fifty teachers of Arabic from the U.S. and abroad. The symposium provided teachers of Arabic with a much-needed opportunity to meet for an extended period of time outside their annual AATA (American Association of Teachers of Arabic) meeting at the Middle East Studies Association (MESA) and to engage in extensive discussions of issues central to their profession.

This wonderful opportunity would not have been realized without the help of a number of institutions and individuals. Middlebury College hosted the symposium and provided funding and logistical support for the symposium's various events. For this I would like to extend special thanks to Dr. John McCardell, President of Middlebury College, and to Dr. Edward Knox, Provost and Vice President for Academic Affairs at Middlebury College (then Vice-President for Foreign Languages and Director of the Language Schools), for their hospitality and the warm welcome felt by all those who attended the symposium. A number of the Middlebury Language Schools staff worked behind the scenes and logged in long hours organizing the symposium and attending to its details: Amy Barna provided coordination for all the various activities of the symposium and handled the housing needs of all participants and attendees, Beth Karnes oversaw the organization of the symposium and served as a liaison between the symposium, the Arabic School and the Vice-President's Office, Karen Andrews handled all the financial aspects of the symposium, Ernest Longey and his staff made sure that all our audio-visual needs were met, and David Herren handled all our computer technology needs throughout the symposium. To all these individuals we owe a great deal of gratitude for their efficient and professional work.

The symposium was supported in part by a grant from the Andrew W. Mellon Foundation to the School of Arabic at Middlebury College. The generous support of the Mellon Foundation over the past five years has been instrumental to the success of the Arabic School at Middlebury and to our continued efforts at developing new materials for the teaching of Arabic. On behalf of the faculty and students of the Arabic school at Middlebury, I would like to extend warm thanks to the Mellon Foundation for this generous support.

My thanks are also due to all the symposium participants who made this event possible. Their presentations, questions, and comments have made us all better aware of the issues and the challenges that are facing our field as we ready ourselves for the twenty-first century.

Also, I would like to thank all those who have helped in the production of the present volume. Professor Mushira Eid, the editor of our professional journal, *Al-ᶜArabiyya,* oversaw all phases of the production of this volume and provided valuable guidance and support. Kirk Belnap, executive director of AATA, provided tremendous support in the areas of publication, cover design and distribution. Tessa Hauglid, assistant editor of *Al-ᶜArabiyya*, handled all the details related to the typing and production of the final manuscript with great efficiency. And Karen Tucker helped in editing and proofreading the final manuscript. To all four of them I extend a heartfelt thank you.

Finally, I would like to thank Dr. Peter Abboud, the founder of the Arabic School, for his outstanding work as Director of the Middlebury Arabic School during its first nine years. His efforts during those years made Middlebury a leader in the field of teaching Arabic as a foreign language and it is my hope that the school will continue to play this leading role in the future.

Mahmoud Al-Batal

CONTRIBUTORS

Peter Abboud is professor of Arabic at the University of Texas at Austin, where he has been teaching Arabic language and Arabic linguistics courses since 1961. He is also the founder of the Middlebury School of Arabic in Middlebury, Vermont, and served as its first director from 1982 to 1990. He is the co-author of several Arabic language textbooks and a proficiency-based series of materials for reading comprehension, listening comprehension, and speaking. He has published a number of articles, reviews, and papers on language teaching, Arabic dialectology, and Classical and Modern Standard Arabic phonology and syntax. He has designed two Computer Assisted Instruction programs, one of which was co-authored with his late wife.

Mahmoud Al-Batal is associate professor of Arabic in the Department of Near Eastern and Judaic Languages and Literatures at Emory University in Atlanta, Georgia. Also, he is the current director of the School of Arabic at Middlebury College in Vermont. He has written a number of articles dealing with teaching Arabic as a foreign language and also with the cohesive role of connectives in Modern Standard Arabic and Lebanese Arabic. Currently, he is involved in the writing of two new Arabic textbooks for the elementary and intermediate levels in cooperation with Kristen Brustad of Emory University and Abbas El-Tonsi of the American University in Cairo. The two textbooks are entitled *Alif Baa, An Introduction to Arabic Letters and Sounds* and *Al-Kitaab fii Taᶜallum al-ᶜArabiyya, Vols. I & II* and are forthcoming by Georgetown University Press in 1995 and 1996.

Roger Allen is Professor of Arabic Language and Literature in the Department of Asian and Middle Eastern Studies at the University of Pennsylvania. He is a specialist in two areas: Arabic literature, with particular reference to narrative and drama, and Arabic language pedagogy. In addition to a major study on the *Arabic Novel* and an anthology of critical writings, *Modern Arabic Literature*, he has published over thirty articles on Arabic literature. He has produced a number of translations of modern Arabic narrative, including Najib Mafuz's *Mirrors* and *Autumn Quail*, Jabra Ibrahim Jabra's *The Ship* (with Adnan Haydar), 'Abd al-Rahman Munif's *Endings*, and collections of short stories by Najib Mahfuz and Yusuf Idris. As guest-editor of many journals, he has also encouraged the publication of a large number of other translations. He currently serves on the Administrative Board of the Project for the Translation of Arabic (PROTA, directed by Dr. Salma Khadra' al-Jayyusi) and is a member of the editorial boards of *Al-ᶜArabiyya*, *World Literature Today* and *the Journal of Arabic Literature*.

Professor Allen is a certified Arabic proficiency tester for the American Council for the Teaching of Foreign Languages (ACTFL) and in 1986 was asked to serve as ACTFL's national trainer of Arabic testers. Along with Adel Allouche, he has completed a proficiency-based textbook for standard Arabic using computer-assisted instructional methods, called *Let's Learn Arabic*.

M. Mahdi Alosh is assistant professor of Arabic at The Ohio State University. He is the coordinator of the Arabic Language Program at OSU and co-director of the Arabic Language and Culture Summer Institute, a three-year project for secondary school teachers of foreign languages and social studies funded by the National Endowment for the Humanities. He was the principal investigator of a project funded by the U.S. Department of Education (1990-92) to develop second-year Arabic instructional materials for college students and he was the coordinator of a similar project funded by the same sponsor (1988-1990) to develop Arabic instructional materials for first-year students. He obtained his B.A. degree in English Language and Literature from the University of Damascus, his M.A. in Linguistics from Ohio University, and his Ph.D. from The Ohio State University in Foreign Language Instruction. He is the author of *Speak and Read Essential Arabic I (Eastern)*, *Ahlan wa Sahlan* (a series of Arabic textbooks for the elementary/intermediate levels), and *Lughatuna al Hayya* (an intermediate/advanced-level series). He has written several book reviews, articles, and book chapters on Arabic and foreign language pedagogy and served on the committee that modified the Arabic ACTFL Proficiency Guidelines.

Samar Attar studied at Damascus University, Dalhousie University, Canada (M.A., English Literature) and the State University of New York at Binghamton (Ph.D., Comparative Literature). She taught English, Arabic, and Comparative Literature in Canada, U.S.A., Algeria, and West Germany. Presently she teaches

Arabic language and literature at the University of Sydney, Australia. During 1990-1991, she was a Rockefeller Fellow at the University of Michigan, Ann Arbor. She has published in both English and Arabic in the fields of literary criticism, translation, language teaching and creative writing. Her books include (1) *The Intruder in Modern Drama, A Journey at Night: Poems by Salah 'Abd Al-Sabur*, (2) *Modern Arabic For Foreign Students*, 4 volumes, (3) *Lina: A Portrait of A Damascene Girl* and (4) *The House at Arnus Square*. Her poems have appeared in anthologies in Canada, U.S.A., and England, including *The Penguin Book of Women Poets* and *Women of the Fertile Crescent*. Presently, she is working on a sequel to *Modern Arabic*, trying to integrate cultural and historical sources in teaching Arabic.

Zev bar-Lev is professor of linguistics at San Diego State University. In addition to his Hebrew program at SDSU, and while trying to introduce an Arabic program, he has taught short courses for adult education in Hebrew, Arabic, and other languages. Author of *Computer Talk for the Liberal Arts* (Prentice-Hall 1987), he has also published articles in various fields of linguistics. For the last seven years, he has been mostly involved in developing his own method for teaching foreign language.

R. Kirk Belnap is an assistant professor of Arabic at Brigham Young University in Provo, Utah. He teaches Arabic and sociolinguistics and develops educational software. He has been active nationally in promoting the teaching of Arabic: he served as acting director of the American Association of Teachers of Arabic (AATA) in 1989-90 and is now the Executive Director of AATA; he has also worked closely with the National Organization of Less Commonly Taught Languages, including serving as a member of the Data Collection Task Force.

Alaa Elgibali is an associate professor of linguistics and Arabic at the American University in Cairo. His professional interests include comparative and historical linguistics, language acquisition, and sociolinguistics. He taught Arabic as a Foreign Language in Kuwait and served as Executive Director of the Center for Arabic Study Abroad (CASA) at A.U.C.

Ahmed Ferhadi is senior language lecturer, Department of Near Eastern Languages, New York University and Executive Director of the Arabic-Speaking Academic Immersion Program (ASAIP), Jordan. He earned his M.S. in

Applied Linguistics (1979) from the University of Edinburgh, U.K.; his M.A. in TAFL (1988) and his Ph.D. in Linguistics (1989) from the University of Michigan (dual-degree program). He wrote his dissertation on Morpho-phonemics of Arbili Kurdish. His research interests include second language acquisition, sociolinguistics, interlanguage and TAFL. His publications include *Computers in Foreign Language Instruction: Enhancing the Teaching and Learning of AFL, Clitics in Arbili Kurdish, No Friends but the Mountains, The Impact of Adults and Children on the Addressor,* and *Quantifiers in the Interlanguage.*

Margaret Larkin received her Ph.D. from the Department of Middle East Languages and Cultures at Columbia University. Her research interests are Arabic literature, both classical and modern, and the teaching of Arabic as a foreign language. Among her published articles are "Two Examples of Ritha': A Comparison between Ahmad Shawqi and al-Mutannabbi" and "A Brigand Hero of Egyptian Colloquial Literature," both in the *Journal of Arabic Literature,* and "The Inimitability of the Qur'an: Two Perspectives," in *Religion and Literature.* She is an assistant professor in the Department of Near Eastern Studies at Princeton University.

Dilworth Parkinson received his Ph.D. in Arabic Linguistics from the University of Michigan in 1982. He teaches Arabic at Brigham Young University, and served as the executive director of the American Association of Teachers of Arabic for five years. He is currently working on a book about *Fuṣḥa* in Egypt.

Raji Rammuny is professor of Arabic in the Department of Near Eastern Studies at the University of Michigan in Ann Arbor. His main areas of research are methodology of teaching Arabic as a second language and Arabic grammatical theory. He has written a number of articles dealing with various aspects of teaching Arabic and has authored and co-authored a large number of Arabic textbooks, including *Advanced Business Arabic, Arabic Composition, Elementary Modern Standard Arabic, Intermediate Modern Standard Arabic,* and *Islamic Arabic Reader.* Most recently, he has developed the New Arabic Proficiency Test in association with the Center for Applied Linguistics (CAL).

Karin C. Ryding is an associate professor and chair of the Department of Arabic at Georgetown University. She received her B.A. from Middlebury College, her M.A. from The American University of Beirut, and her Ph.D. from Georgetown University. Formerly, she was head of Arabic training at the Foreign Service Institute, the training arm of the State Department, where she focussed on developing and systematizing the Formal Spoken Arabic curriculum. Her primary interests are in applied linguistics, especially methodology of foreign language teaching; history of Arabic grammar; and history of Arabic science, particularly alchemy.

Zeinab Taha is a senior Arabic language teacher in the Arabic Language Institute at the American University in Cairo. She is currently finishing a Ph.D. dissertation on "Semantics and Syntax in Ibn as Sarraj's *al-usūl fī al-naḥw*." She has taught Arabic at Middlebury College and Georgetown University during the past few years.

Munther A. Younes is a senior lecturer in Arabic Language and Linguistics at Cornell University. He previously taught at King Saud University in Abha, Saudi Arabia; the Defense Language Institute in Monterey, California; and at The University of Wisconsin-Milwaukee. He holds a Ph.D. in Linguistics from The University of Texas at Austin. His research interests focus on Arabic phonetics and phonology, sociolinguistics, teaching Arabic as a foreign language. His publications include *Tales From Kalila wa Dimna: An Arabic Reader*, "An Integrated Approach to Teaching Arabic as a Foreign Language" in *Al-ᶜArabiyya*, "Emphasis Spread in Two Arabic Dialects" in *Perspectives on Arabic Linguistics V*, and "On Emphasis and /r/ in Arabic," to appear in *Perspectives on Arabic Linguistics VI*. He is currently working on a first-year Arabic textbook that integrates spoken and literary Arabic and uses proficiency-oriented techniques.

INTRODUCTION

THE ARABIC TEACHING PROFESSION: CURRENT REALITIES AND FUTURE CHALLENGES

Mahmoud Al-Batal
Emory University
and Middlebury College

The 1980s represented a landmark in the history of the Arabic teaching profession. During this decade, important developments and transitions swept the profession, generating a momentum of change whose impact is still felt today. The most significant of these developments include the following:

1. Growth of Interest in the Study of Arabic

The growth of interest in the study of Arabic and related aspects of Arab culture during the 1980s now manifests itself in a number of recent phenomena. First, members of the profession have observed an increasing enrollment in elementary Arabic language classes and courses related to the modern Arab world at various U.S. institutions of higher education.[1] Second, a number of

---

1. Evidence of this growth remains largely anecdotal, due to the absence of detailed and reliable statistics on enrollments in Arabic language and Arabic-related courses at U.S. institutions of higher education. To the best of my knowledge, the only statistical source available is a brief article by Brod and Huber (1992) which examines enrollment trends in foreign language classes in American universities. Their data show that enrollment in Arabic classes in 1980, 1983, 1986, and 1990 remained steady, at around 3400+ students. While these figures remain the best we have at present, they do not reflect the growth reported by members of the profession.

1

universities and colleges have expanded or added full-fledged Arabic programs to their curriculum, including Brown University, The College of William and Mary, Dartmouth College, Emory University, Five Colleges in Massachusetts, The University of California at Santa Barbara, The University of Florida, The University of Virginia, and Washington University at St. Louis. Third, several universities have established new summer programs in the Arab world that aim to provide American students with the opportunity to study the language in its genuine cultural setting. Examples of such programs include the Virginia/ Yarmouk program, the Florida/Ain Shams, Egypt (now the Florida/Fez, Morocco) program, and the SUNY Binghamton/Tangiers program. In addition, a number of private institutions in various Arab countries have established programs geared in part towards American students of Arabic, such as the Arabic Language Institute in Fez, Morocco, the Language Center in San°aa, Yemen, and the International Language Institute (ILI) in Cairo. Finally, increased interest in Arabic language study is reflected in the introduction of Arabic to a small number of high schools in some of the largest U.S. cities. The effort to add Arabic to high school curricula has been greatly aided by the establishment in 1988 of the Critical Languages and Area Studies Consortium (CLASC), whose activities include the establishment of an intensive Arabic language and culture institute for high school students. The CLASC institute, whose participants come from high schools across the U.S., involves study both in the U.S. and in Egypt in cooperation with the Center for Arabic Study Abroad (CASA).

2. Introduction of New Methodologies and Philosophies

During the 1980s, developments that were taking place in the field of foreign language education in general began to influence the Arabic teaching profession. Foremost among these developments were increased interest in the communicative approach and the emergence of the proficiency movement. A number of teachers of Arabic began to address the issue of incorporating communicative competence in the Arabic curriculum and paying greater attention to the teaching of the speaking skill. *Al-°Arabiyya*, Journal of the American Association of Teachers of Arabic (AATA), devoted an entire section of its 1985 volume to the issue of teaching the oral skills in Arabic. Also indicative of this new emphasis was the establishment of the first total immersion language program at the School of Arabic at Middlebury College in 1982. The continuous expansion of the school since then reflects the interest of students in Arabic as a living language, and the field's recognition of the importance of promoting communicative competency in the language.

During the second half of the decade, the proficiency movement emerged as the most influential new philosophy in the field, beginning with the publication of the first Arabic Proficiency Guidelines in *Al-ᶜArabiyya* in 1985. The guidelines, written by Roger Allen et al. and revised in 1989, are modeled after the ACTFL Proficiency Guidelines and include descriptions of norms for proficiency in Arabic in the areas of speaking, listening, reading, and writing (see Allen 1985 and ACTFL 1989). The development of these guidelines has generated much discussion about issues such as defining instructional objectives and goals, dealing with the diglossic split in the classroom, testing, examining the place of grammar within the curriculum, and promoting cultural proficiency. One need only glance at the articles published in *Al-ᶜArabiyya* over the past five years (see, for example, Attieh 1989, Allen 1990, Heath 1990, Rammuny 1990), the chapters in the present volume, and the topics of panels at recent professional conferences to find ample evidence of the decisive impact of the proficiency movement on the field.

Finally, the 1980s witnessed unprecedented expansion in incorporating technology in the teaching of Arabic both inside and outside the classroom. A number of computer programs have been developed that aim at supplementing classroom instruction in drilling, and the use of video materials is on the rise as well. Although this technology component remains in its infancy, the level of activity in this area underscores the new direction the field is taking.

3. **Development of New Textbooks and Teaching Materials**

The application of new philosophies and approaches to the teaching of Arabic has been coupled with the development of new textbooks and teaching materials that are currently in use at American universities. Among these new textbooks are Ḥardān et al.'s *mina al-Khalīj ilā al-Muḥīṭ* [From the Gulf to the Ocean] (1980), El-Saᶜīd Badawī et al.'s *Al-Kitāb al-Asāsi*, Parts I and II (1983 and 1987), Roger Allen and Adel Allouche's *Let's Learn Arabic* (1986), Samar Attar's *Modern Arabic* (1988), Mahdi Alosh's *Ahlan wa Sahlan* (1989), Peter Abboud et al.'s new version of *Intermediate Modern Standard Arabic* (1991), Raji Rammuny's *Advanced Standard Arabic* (1994), and Brustad et al.'s *al-Kitāb fī Taᶜallum al-ᶜArabiyya* (1994).

In addition to these textbooks, a number of supplementary books and materials have been developed to promote proficiency in certain areas and/or to supplement other existing textbooks. Among these are Raji Rammuny's *Programmed Arabic-Islamic Reader* (1983) and *Advanced Business Arabic, Part I* (1987), Belkacem Baccouche and Sanaa Azmi's *Conversations in Modern Stan-*

dard Arabic (1984), Abbas El-Tonsi and Nariman Al-Warraki's *ʿArabiyyat wasāʾil al-iʿlām* (1989), Munther Younes' *Tales from Kalila wa Dimna* (1989), Karin Ryding's *Formal Spoken Arabic* (1990), and Peter Abboud and Attieh's Middlebury series *Let's Read with the Arabs, Let's Speak with the Arabs,* and *Let's Speak Fuṣḥā* (1991).

Beyond these Modern Standard Arabic (MSA) materials, a number of colloquial teaching materials have been developed, including El-Tonsi et al.'s *Intensive Course in Egyptian Colloquial Arabic* (1987), Margaret Nydell's series *From Modern Standard Arabic to the (Arabic) Dialect* (1992),[2] and Lutfi Hussein's *Levantine Arabic for Non-Natives* (1993).

On the testing front, two major efforts are underway to develop standardized tests that aim to gauge the proficiency of learners. An Arabic version of the ACTFL-designed Oral Proficiency Interview (OPI), which tests oral skills, has been developed, and training workshops for testers are held periodically in various locations. The number of OPI testers certified by ACTFL has been growing steadily. In addition, Raji Rammuny has developed the New Arabic Proficiency Test (NAPT) in collaboration with the Center for Applied Linguistics. This test, which aims to assess levels of competence in the four language skills, is also in use in a number of Arabic programs.

4. Growth of Professional Organization and Activities

Expansion in the field of Arabic during the 1980s also touched the organizational aspects of the profession. Our professional organization, the American Association of Teachers of Arabic (AATA), has experienced a significant increase in its membership both at the institutional and individual levels. The Association continues to sponsor panels that deal with issues related to the teaching of Arabic, and the Association's journal, *Al-ʿArabiyya,* has played an important role in reflecting the new directions of the profession and addressing its major issues. Most recently, the Association has been working closely with the National Foreign Language Center (NFLC) and other organizations of the less commonly taught languages to coordinate efforts and share ideas. One example of such cooperation is a project funded by NFLC and the Ford Foundation in which AATA has been invited to construct a Language Learning Framework for Arabic. The proposed framework will attempt to set a common core of objectives, functions, vocabulary, and grammatical structures to which various programs can subscribe.

---

2. Dialects included in this series are Egyptian, Gulf, Iraqi, Levantine, Moroccan, and Libyan.

These developments provide clear testimony to the dynamic nature of the Arabic teaching profession and to the new directions it is taking. Nevertheless, the profession faces a number of challenges that will further shape its future as it readies itself for the twenty-first century. These challenges include:

1 *Providing better responses to students' changing needs*

Among the significant changes that have taken place over the past ten years is the increase in the number of undergraduates taking Arabic and the growing interest among all students in learning Arabic as a means of understanding Arab culture and communicating with Arabs. Similarly, the desire to learn Arabic solely as a tool for reading texts has begun to recede, and we see more and more graduate students developing their communicative skills alongside their reading skills. These trends are documented in a survey of students taking Arabic at the college level [conducted by Belnap (1987)]. The survey shows communication with Arabs to be the most important objective for students, followed by reading. The survey also indicates that a great majority of students are interested in studying colloquial Arabic alongside MSA. In the present volume, Belnap reports the results of a more recent survey whose results include a surprising statistic: the overwhelming majority of students who take Arabic do not continue their study of the language beyond the second year.

The findings of these surveys raise some serious questions about the extent to which existing Arabic programs and materials fulfill students' needs and goals. They also raise questions about whether what we offer in our programs corresponds to what students want to learn. If students' main concerns are communication and learning about the culture and if most of them stay with us for only two years, then what type of curriculum would best suit these realities? The majority of Arabic programs in the U.S. serve a constituency of graduate students who are committed to careers in Arabic or Middle Eastern studies and thus place heavy emphasis on reading texts and developing certain grammatical skills at early stages of instruction. The main challenge that these programs face now is how they can respond to the increased demand of their new clientele for basic communicative skills while at the same time continuing to serve the needs of those committed to long careers with Arabic. These two distinct demands are not necessarily incompatible; however, to accomplish both of them will require clearly defined goals and efficient methods.

2 *Development of curriculum and materials*

Meeting the challenge of responding to students' changing needs requires that we carefully reexamine our curricular objectives and that we set priorities for the various levels of instruction. It also requires that we choose teaching materials and adopt teaching and testing methods that are compatible with these perceived goals and work to achieve them efficiently. While important strides have been made in this area over the past ten years, curricular and materials development continues to be one of the greatest challenges facing the Arabic teaching profession.

3 *Incorporation of the teaching of colloquial in our programs*

The question of how to address the diglossic nature of Arabic in the classroom has been debated for a long time. Despite the fact that a number of approaches have been formulated (for a detailed presentation of these approaches, see Al-Batal 1992), very little progress has been made towards putting these ideas into practice, and the profession is no closer to consensus on this issue now than when the debate began. Moreover, the debate has taken on new dimensions and urgency with the push towards more communicative-based programs and the call for greater incorporation of culture in the curriculum. To continue to avoid confronting this issue because of the sensitivities and complexities it involves would be to admit defeat in the face of the goals we have set for ourselves. If we agree that the ultimate model of proficiency we want to develop involves knowledge of a colloquial variety of Arabic, then it becomes incumbent upon us to develop approaches and materials that work towards achieving this model. Ideally, the formulation of such approaches should involve a great deal of sociolinguistic and pedagogical research. The argument made by a number of teachers that we should restrict the focus of teaching Arabic to the standard or classical language does not provide a viable answer to this challenge because it ignores two essential components of a modern language program: communicative competency and cultural proficiency.

4 *Enhancment of the cultural component of our curricula*

The push towards communicative-based teaching in foreign language education over the past few years has resulted in a growing interest in promoting culture as an active component of foreign language curricula. Cultural proficiency has regained prominence as a primary objective of language teaching, in part because students place cultural understanding among their primary reasons for studying the language. However, current curricular goals and teaching materials in many Arabic programs do not address the teaching of culture appropriately. Developing cultural proficiency in Arabic is still largely left to the discretion of the teacher, and while many teachers manage to fulfill their students' needs in this area, the lack of a systematic approach to the integration of language and culture costs time and energy, and results in inefficient programs and curricula. Developing such an integrated approach remains one of the most pressing challenges which the profession faces at the present time.

5 Incorporation of technology in teaching

The incorporation of technology in teaching has had a tremendous impact on foreign language education over the past ten years. In particular, videos, computers, and multimedia materials are becoming essential components of language teaching programs. Although some individual efforts have contributed to the utilization of technology in the Arabic teaching profession, they have been sporadic and limited, and have barely begun to explore the full potential of these media. As we head into the twenty-first century, we face the challenge of incorporating into our curricula the technological revolution that has touched every aspect of our lives. Our future students will be increasingly computer literate and visually oriented and will expect programs that make use of their technological skills.

6 Expansion of the research base of the profession

Finally, the above-named challenges cannot be adequately met without a solid research base that would enable us to further our understanding of the various linguistic, psychological, and cognitive aspects involved in teaching languages. Development of curricular objectives and teaching materials and methods cannot be adequately realized without research focusing on areas ranging from processes of acquisition and learning to native speakers' models of competence to the sequencing of grammatical structures. Also needed in this respect are periodical surveys of students, faculty, and programs that would put us in touch with the state of the field and allow us to monitor changes.

Within this context of realities and challenges, the present volume aims to further the debate on issues of concern to teachers of Arabic and to help chart future directions for our profession. The chapters herein are grouped into six thematic sections related to the challenges outlined above. The first section, which includes Chapters One, Two, and Three, explores several general issues pertaining to the profession and to the institutional settings of Arabic programs. In Chapter One, Peter Abboud examines the state of the Arabic teaching profession in the U.S. over the past three decades and presents an assessment of the directions in which it is heading. In Chapter Two, Kirk Belnap addresses the institutional setting of Arabic language programs in the U.S. and reports the results of an extended survey involving a number of Arabic programs. In Chapter Three, Alaa Elgibali and Zeinab Taha present an overview of the teaching philosophy of the Arabic Language Institute at the American University in Cairo and point out a number of challenges as seen from the perspective of an in-country Arabic program.

The second section, the largest in this volume, contains Chapters Four through Nine and deals with the teaching of the various skills in Arabic. In Chapter Four, Roger Allen addresses some of the issues and challenges involved in the teaching of Arabic at the advanced levels and proposes future directions for curricular planning for the advanced levels. In Chapter Five, Mahmoud Al-Batal examines the status of the speaking and writing skills in the present Arabic curriculum and the problems they pose for future curricular development. In Chapter Six, Zev bar-Lev explores an approach to the teaching of the reading and listening skills to elementary level students. Among other things, this approach aims at teaching students how to "skim-read," "skim-listen," and, more importantly, how to develop more spontaneous and realistic language use.

In Chapter Seven, Margaret Larkin also addresses the teaching of reading but focuses on close reading. She notes that the push toward functional use of the language has caused some programs to overlook close reading and argues that close reading deserves a place in the Arabic curriculum, especially at the elementary level. In Chapter Eight, Zeinab Taha deals with the grammar "controversy" that has occupied teachers of Arabic for the past few years. Her discussion touches upon issues such as the sequencing of grammatical structures for the various levels of instruction, coping with grammatical errors, and dealing with the structural variants used by native speakers and the implications of these variants for the teaching of grammar. In the final chapter of this section, Samar Attar suggests strategies based on intercultural communication for the teaching of culture in advanced Arabic classes.

The third section is devoted to the different varieties of Arabic and their relevance to the Arabic language classroom. In Chapter Ten, Karin Ryding presents a discussion of the problems involved in the use of MSA as the means of communication in Arabic classrooms. She proposes that a different variety of Arabic, namely Formal Spoken Arabic (FSA), be used at the basic and intermediate levels in order to ease students into interactive skills without detracting from the students' command or study of MSA. In Chapter Eleven, Munther

Younes argues for the simultaneous introduction in the classroom of both MSA and an Arabic dialect and presents theoretical as well as practical evidence in support of his proposal. He also presents samples of teaching materials based on this simultaneous approach and intended for students at the elementary level.

The fourth section explores the use of technology in the Arabic classroom and consists of three chapters. In Chapter Twelve, Mahdi Alosh examines the current status of computer-assisted language learning (CALL) in Arabic and discusses CALL's potential as a research tool. He also discusses some fundamental principles pertaining to the design and development of CALL programs. In Chapter Thirteen, Dilworth Parkinson considers the potential role computers can play in the Arabic classroom and examines some of the computer programs that have already been developed in Arabic. He cautions, however, that teachers should have realistic expectations of what computers can do, and calls for efforts to match the strengths of computers to our expectations. In the last chapter of this section, Ahmad Ferhadi discusses ways of incorporating the use of video in the Arabic classroom. He demonstrates how to use video presentations interactively and how to enhance class participation based on the methodological principles of the communicative approach.

The fifth section, devoted to testing, includes a chapter in which Raji Rammuny discusses the design of the Arabic Speaking Test (AST), which represents a component of the New Arabic Proficiency Test developed in conjunction with the Center for Applied Linguistics (CAL). Rammuny explains the rationale behind the AST, its administration and scoring, and the implications it has for the teaching of Arabic.

The opinions expressed in the present volume do not, in any way, represent definitive answers to the challenges facing our profession today. Rather, they are attempts to advance the debate on these issues and to help us reach consensus on the directions the profession should be taking as we head into a new century.

REFERENCES

ABBOUD, PETER ET AL. 1991. *Intermediate Modern Standard Arabic, Revised Edition.* Ann Arbor, MI: Center for Near Eastern & North African Studies.

_____ and Aman Attieh. 1990. *Taᶜalaw Naqraʾ maᶜa al-ᶜArab* (Come Let's Read with the Arabs); *Taᶜalaw Nastamiᶜ maᶜa al-ᶜArab* (Come Let's Listen with the Arabs); *Taᶜalaw Natahaddath al-Fushā* (Come Let's Speak Fusha). Middlebury, VT: School of Arabic, Middlebury College.

ACTFL. 1989. ACTFL Arabic Proficiency Guidelines. *Foreign Language Annals* 22:4.373-392.

ALLEN, ROGER. 1990. Proficiency and the Teacher of Arabic: Curriculum, course, and classroom. *Al-ᶜArabiyya* 23:1-30.

_____ 1985. Arabic Proficiency Guidelines. *Al-ᶜArabiyya* 18:45-70.

_____ and Adel Allouche. 1986. *Let's Learn Arabic, A Proficiency-Based Syllabus for Modern Standard Arabic.* Philadelphia: University of Pennsylvania.

ALOSH, MAHDI. 1989. *Ahlan wa Sahlan: An introductory course for teaching Modern Standard Arabic to speakers of other languages.* Columbus: The Ohio State University Foreign Language Center.

ATTIEH, AMAN. 1989. Istrātijiyyāt li-Tanmiyat Mahārat al-Qirāʾah al-Muwassaᶜa li-al-Marhala al-Mutawassita [Strategies for the Development of the Extensive Reading Skill for the Intermediate Level]. *Al-ᶜArabiyya* 22:107-137.

ATTAR, SAMAR. 1988. *Modern Arabic (1 & 2): An introductory course for foreign students.* Beirut, Lebanon: Librairie du Liban.

BACCOUCHE, BELKACEM AND SANAA AZMI. 1984. *Conversations in Modern Standard Arabic.* New Haven, CT: Yale University Press.

BADAWI, EL-SAᶜID AND FATHI YOUNES. 1983. *Al-Kitāb al-Asāsī fī Taᶜlīm al-ᶜArabiyya li-Ghayr al-Nātiqīn bi-hā, Part I* [The Basic Book on Teaching Arabic to Non-Native Speakers]. Tunis: The Arab League Education, Culture and Science Organization (ALECSO).

_____, MOHAMMAD HAMASAH ABD EL-LTIF, AND MAHMOUD AL-BATAL. 1987. *Al-Kitāb al-Asāsī fī Taᶜlīm al-ᶜArabiyya li-Ghayr al-Nātiqīn bi-hā, Part II* [The Basic Book on Teaching Arabic to Non-Native Speakers]. Tunis: The Arab League Education, Culture and Science Organization (ALECSO).

AL-BATAL, MAHMOUD. 1992. "Diglossia Proficiency: The need for an alternative approach to teaching." *The Arabic Language in America*, ed. by Aleya Rouchdy, 284-304. Detroit: Wayne University Press.

BELNAP, KIRK. 1987. Who's Taking Arabic and What on Earth For? A Survey of Students in Arabic Language Programs. *Al-ʿArabiyya* 20: 29-42.

BROD, RICHARD AND BETTINA HUBER. 1990. Foreign Language Enrollments in United States Institutions of Higher Education. *ADFL Bulletin* (Association of Departments of Foreign Languages) 23:3.6-10.

BRUSTAD, KRISTEN ET AL. 1994. *Al-Kitāb fī Taʿallum al-ʿArabiyya* [The Book on Learning Arabic]. Middlebury, VT: School of Arabic, Middlebury College.

ḤARDĀN, JARJŪRA ET AL. 1980. *Mina al-Khalīj ilā al-Muḥīṭ (1 & 2)* [From the Gulf to the Ocean]. Paris, France: Librairie A. Hatier.

HEATH, PETER. 1990. Proficiency in Arabic Language Learning: Some reflections on basic goals. *Al-ʿArabiyya* 23:31-48.

HUSSEIN, LUTFI. 1993. *Levantine Arabic for Non-Natives: A proficiency-oriented approach.* New Haven, CT: Yale University Press.

NYDELL, MARGARET. 1992. *From Modern Standard Arabic to the (.....) Dialect.* Arlington, VA: Diplomatic Language Services, Inc.

RAMMUNY, RAJI. 1994. *Advanced Standard Arabic through Authentic Arabic Texts and Audiovoisual Materials, Part I.* Ann Arbor: University of Michigan Press.

_____. 1990. Modifying EMSA Using the Proficiency Orientation. *Al-ʿArabiyya* 23:49-74.

_____. 1987. *Advanced Business Arabic, Part I.* Troy, MI: International Book Center.

_____. 1983. *Programmed Arabic-Islamic Reader.* Troy, MI: International Book Center.

RYDING, KARIN. 1990. *Formal Spoken Arabic: Basic course.* Washington, DC: Georgetown University Press.

EL-TONSI, ABBAS ET AL. 1987. *An Intensive Course in Egyptian Colloquial Arabic.* Cairo: The American University in Cairo.

_____ and Nariman Naʾili Al-Warraki. 1989. *ʿArabiyyat Wasāʾil al-Iʿlām.* Cairo: Arabic Language Institute, The American University in Cairo.

YOUNES, MUNTHER. 1989. *Tales from Kalila wa Dimna: An Arabic reader.* New Haven, CT: Yale University Press.

1

THE TEACHING OF ARABIC IN THE UNITED STATES: WHENCE AND WHITHER?[*]

Peter Abboud
University of Texas at Austin

Focusing on three components of language teaching—manpower, materials, and methodology—this chapter assesses the shape, direction, and impact of the progress made by the Arabic teaching profession in the last thirty years or so and gives the author's views of where the field is heading and what issues it will be addressing in the future. This chapter finds that the profession's progress so far has been characterized by its drive towards professionalization, where it has achieved a good measure of success, by collegiality and by teamwork, and that while its concern, the teaching of Arabic at the college level, has found a secure place in academe, its practitioners, as language teachers, maintain a precarious position there. Among other things, this chapter addresses the need for more empirical research and study, for more involvement and communication with other foreign language organizations, and for the increased sharing of findings and concerns with them. The chapter also presents an agenda of projects that need to be undertaken and issues and areas that need to be discussed. Throughout, it tries to describe the role that the Middlebury College/School of Arabic has been playing in the Arabic teaching profession in the U.S. since it was founded in 1982, and the role it can play in the future.

In trying to answer the two questions posed in the title of this chapter—whence and whither—I intend, as one who has been intimately involved in the Arabic teaching profession in the U.S. for thirty years, to assess the form and

---

[*]Text of the keynote address given by Peter Abboud at the Middlebury Symposium.

13

direction of the progress it has made, as well as to give my own view of where it is heading and ought to be heading, and what issues and problems it faces. Also, since this particular conference is being held on the occasion of the tenth anniversary of the establishment of the School of Arabic at Middlebury College, I will try, as the one who was privileged to found it and direct it for nine years, to address the contributions the school has made to and the role it can play in the future of Arabic language teaching. In order to bring the discussion into focus, I will center it around three important components of language teaching, what I call the three M's: manpower, materials (and tools), and methodology (and curriculum). I used these same rubrics in a report published by the Center for Applied Linguistics some twenty-five years ago (Abboud 1968); they can thus be used for easy reference and comparison. The chapter will end with a summary of suggestions concerning issues and topics that should occupy us in the coming years.

1. Manpower

In assessing the quality of the instructors involved in the Arabic teaching profession in the U.S., three areas readily come to mind: professionalism, collegiality, and teamwork.

1.1 *Professionalism*

What I mean by this term is not only that we have a professional organization founded in the early sixties to foster the professionalization of Arabic language teaching, the American Association of Teachers of Arabic (AATA), and that we have a respected journal, *Al-ᶜArabiyya*, of which we are all proud, but that we also have among those who teach Arabic in this country a number of language-teaching professionals. These are individuals who not only know the language (millions of native speakers do) but also have acquired some understanding of the processes of language learning. They are individuals who are well trained and equipped with knowledge to do their job as professionals, individuals with a solid commitment to and a genuine pride and enthusiasm for language teaching, individuals with deep involvement in the profession and the students, to whom Arabic teaching is at the core of their academic enterprise, not a sideline, a peripheral activity or a stepping stone to "better things." You need only to look at the contributors to this volume and speakers in conferences, panels, and workshops and observe the intensity, seriousness, commitment, interest, and pride in making a success of teaching Arabic as a foreign language (a far cry from the times when some have been known to say that they taught Arabic under their breath), to realize that we have been able to attract and retain people of a high caliber, and that we really have come a long way in achieving professionalism in the teaching of Arabic.

I take great pride in having been a participant in this effort to recruit, train, equip, and launch careers of young and energetic people of this caliber, and so, I think, can the School of Arabic at Middlebury College. We can, in addition, count among these professionals in our ranks experienced and equally dedicated teachers of very long standing. It is a mark of professionalism and maturity that people who have been active in a profession for a long time choose not to rest on their laurels nor live off their previous successes, but remain engaged and productive. Furthermore, I also see an important development in the constituency of Arabic instructors. Twenty-five years ago, most college instructors engaged in Arabic language teaching were linguists, litterateurs, area specialists, etc., people whose graduate work, training, and research activities were not related to the processes of learning, pedagogy, curriculum development or education, and who mostly acquired their pedagogical training on the job, through experience, reading, or attending training sessions (Abboud 1968). Since then we have added to our ranks specialists in education, foreign language education, curriculum and instruction, educational psychology, testing, applied linguistics, and the like, whose training and research interests are exactly in those fields. These are people who will revitalize our field and be our future theoreticians, experimenters, curriculum innovators, trainers, and researchers.

This is a welcome and timely development. I say this as one who belongs to the field of linguistics, which has provided personnel and leadership in Arabic language teaching (and in other foreign languages) in this country since the days of the Second World War, but whose prevailing mood is an exclusive preoccupation with theory. I must hurry to add that I still maintain that the services of the linguists who are well trained in the more "traditional" research tools and methodology of Arabic scholarship will continue to be needed, and that in these days of accelerating emphasis on inter-disciplinary endeavors and communication among the natural and the human sciences, where old artificial walls between disciplines are tumbling down, the input of all is needed to unfold the workings of the human brain which processes that supreme vehicle of communication, language. I also need to point out that the whole question of what the profile (academic training, expertise, etc.) of the ideal college Arabic language scholar/teacher is needs to be addressed and pondered.

Finally, another mark of professionalism is that in those years we have amassed expertise of the highest caliber to share with those outside our profession in government and in the private sector, both here and overseas. These are resource people who are knowledgeable and have served in a planning and policy-making capacity, and who have sat on councils at the highest levels to advise on issues pertaining to Arabic and foreign language teaching.

1.2 *Collegiality*

What I mean by collegiality is the sense that we have with others in our chosen profession that we are "in this thing together," sharing new ideas, sharing discoveries, sharing new knowledge, and working together for a common cause and for the common good. Collegiality is something that we have enjoyed to a great extent in the Arabic teaching profession in the U.S. Our enterprise has not been isolationist, cliquish, or provincial, the domain of an exclusive club. We have been successful in involving many of those engaged in teaching Arabic from academe of all persuasions. We have, in the spirit of collegiality, also involved colleagues from various government agencies in our activities and in our projects; we have benefited from their wide experience over the years, including here at Middlebury, in areas such as testing and task-oriented teaching, and we in turn have contributed our expertise to their programs and curriculum.

At Middlebury, we have developed excellent working relations with our colleagues in the Center for Arabic Studies Abroad (CASA) at the American University in Cairo, a partnership that has been fruitful and productive. We were there when CASA was conceived and born, giving guidance and direction, and have been there all along, providing knowledge, know-how, expertise, and personnel. They have enriched us with their experience, and I think they will agree with me that their work with us here in Middlebury and in the U.S. has been very beneficial to them and has contributed to their development and growth. We have established contacts with our colleagues in the Arab world and have been involved in the joint programs with Arab institutions such as the Bourguiba Institute, the Yarmouk University, and others. It was our policy here at Middlebury to invite people from these programs every summer for teaching and training and have over the years had people from various Arab countries— Morocco, Tunisia, Egypt, the Sudan, Lebanon, Syria, Palestine, Jordan, Iraq, Saudi Arabia, and Somalia. I think the School of Arabic at Middlebury has served a very important function in this way.

However, here a lot more needs to be done to establish channels of communication, exchange ideas, and find ways to benefit from the accrued experiences on both sides, in the Arab countries and the U.S. AATA should take the lead in putting us in touch with our colleagues in institutions not only in the Arab world, but also in the new Eastern Europe, in Western Europe, and elsewhere. Several of our members have actively participated in international conferences on teaching Arabic, which are excellent arenas for making these contacts, and it is a pleasure to note that this conference brought together people from various parts of the world, including the U.K. and Australia. I want to say in this regard that we can point with pride at our profession's international outlook, which goes as far back as 1968, when we boldly, or should I say presumptuously perhaps, organized a panel at the International Congress of Orientalists held in Ann Arbor, Michigan, on "Teaching Arabic in the World"!

It is certainly worth pointing out, while on the subject of collegiality, that we have been singularly fortunate in avoiding the fractiousness and tribalism of American culture today. This is especially significant because most of us who are from Arab backgrounds come from societies that have been badly smitten with and afflicted by this disease and its divisiveness. That is not to say that we do not have our differences, but for the most part I believe I am right in saying these have been issue-, not person-oriented and that they have been mostly handled in a civil and collegial manner. We have also, to a large extent, avoided the rift between young and old; for the most part, people of all ages have continued to work together actively and productively.

Finally, I do want to mention the pride that we who are native speakers of Arabic have had in welcoming in our midst our American colleagues. These are people who not only have had sound training in Arabic and Arabic language teaching, but who have lived in the Arab world and are familiar with the Arab scene. The dream of training Americans to achieve near-native control of Arabic has come true in quite a few cases, and it has been gratifying to have some of them join our ranks as professional teachers of Arabic and play a dynamic part in our endeavor. We have worked for this for a long time. Again, Middlebury can take pride in having trained and launched successful careers in language teaching.

1.3 *Teamwork*

The third point I want to elaborate on is teamwork, by which I mean the ability to work together in a profession and as groups of individuals. Efforts to get people together started way back in the late fifties, thanks to the work and vision of Charles Ferguson, formerly of the Center for Applied Linguistics and presently of Stanford University. These efforts came to full bloom when a group of fifteen to twenty college teachers of Arabic got together for about two weeks in 1965 and 1966, with Ferguson directing the first session and I the second, at the initiation of the Subcommittee on the Teaching of Middle Eastern Languages of the ACLS-SSRC Joint Committee on Middle Eastern Languages and with support from the Inter-University Summer Program Committee; these teachers for the first time reached a consensus on what teaching Arabic at the beginning and "intermediate" levels should consist of, agreed on an interpretation of the very ambiguous and confusing term "intermediate," drew up documents spelling out in detail the objectives, content, and methodology for each level, specified the projects that were needed (which included the preparation of two textbooks, one for each level), and proceeded to specify in detail the content of each and the principles they should be based on and the methodology they should implement. Papers on each of these aspects of teaching were drawn, collected, and published in preliminary editions (*Papers* 1965 and Abboud 1966).

These were ambitious undertakings, but unquestionably landmarks and pivotal points in the teaching of Arabic, for they showed beyond doubt that the teachers of Arabic had indeed come together and a profession was coming of age. Subsequently, between 1967 and 1975, several teams were assembled to implement the recommendations of these teachers' seminars. They drew blueprints for and wrote the two textbooks, a beginning (Abboud et al. 1968) and an intermediate (Abboud et al. 1971), and revised the elementary textbook in 1975, which was later published as Abboud et al. (1983). They also produced the first Arabic Proficiency Test as early as 1967, as well as three revised versions following field-testing and item analysis. This is even more remarkable in that a concerted effort was made to include as many people and institutions as possible, and participants from all colors of the spectrum in terms of persuasion.

Also, in preparing the blueprints for the textbooks, every shade of the spectrum was included: the medievalist and the modernist, the linguist, the litterateur, and the social scientist, all of whom had input into the project, either through actual participation in the various teams or through comments elicited by mail from every accessible instructor of Arabic at the college level in the country, to whom were sent all the documents we prepared. The two textbooks themselves were undertaken by teams of scholars from various disciplines and included native speakers of both Arabic and English. These team projects immensely enriched the experience of the profession and of the individuals involved, and resulted in successful experimentation in collective work, which was to serve as model for our sister languages and which, more than anything else, fostered the spirit of collegiality referred to above.

The advantages of teamwork are too obvious to need comment: in addition to ensuring wider acceptability and interest, the collective talents and experience in a team can never be matched by one individual. This tradition of teamwork is a legacy of great value that I trust we will continue to treasure, and it is my earnest hope that we will continue to work together in this framework for the projects ahead. In this connection, I would like to point out that every single recommendation of the aforementioned symposia has been implemented, giving the profession a reputation of a can-do organism.

It is a pleasure to note, too, that Middlebury adopted in the past and continues to adopt this ideal of teamwork. I will mention here, as an example, the series of reading, listening, and speaking materials that were prepared for the first four levels of instruction at the School of Arabic here at Middlebury, between 1987 and 1990, with Aman Attieh as Project Coordinator and me as Project Director. These involved a number of individuals and extensive text samples which were distributed to many instructors of Arabic in this country who requested them for comments. More about this series will follow later. We are very fortunate to have people with so many talents and such diverse expertise to draw on, which makes teamwork eminently feasible and productive. One of the greatest sources of pleasure and pride I have experienced in my career is the privilege to work with outstanding teachers and scholars who are also outstanding team players.

In summary, we can say that in the last thirty years we have seen development in the Arabic teaching profession of a cadre of well-trained individuals who have been able to organize and work together, and who have met the challenges that teaching Arabic in this country presents. We have also seen Arabic become a well-recognized component of a college curriculum in many places across the land, due in no small measure, I might add, to strong support from the national government as well as the private sector, with the funding and prestige that this support brings.

I would be less than honest, however, if I were to leave you with the impression that all is rosy, and grievously remiss if I were to leave this subject without pointing out the ominous fact that academe on the whole has been unable and/or unwilling to find a permanent, recognized, and respected niche for the language instructor *as language instructor* in its scheme of things. This is due to cultural and academic bias but mostly to the lurking feeling among administrators at various levels (and with some practitioners, sad to say) that language teaching is an activity that requires no special expertise, that it, especially at the lower levels, lacks intellectual and academic rigor and is merely a

means to an end, the goal being either to help students meet language requirements (requirements whose existence some continue to resent), or to prepare
them for the "real intellectual stuff," i.e., literature, linguistics, area studies and
disciplines, etc. Most often these perceptions stem from a total lack of understanding of the nature of language learning, which is often thought of as a matter of acquiring mechanical skills through rote memorization and pattern practice, easily undertaken by any teaching assistant or native speaker.

It is sad but true that most people responsible directly or indirectly for
language programs, including Middle East Center directors, hold such views in
their hearts. The results are regrettable, if not pernicious. It is not an uncommon
practice to recruit scholars in some field of expertise and ask them to teach
Arabic without any consideration given to the degree or extent of their competence in the language, or, in the case of native speakers, without any requirement of training in language teaching. Even where the need for the well-trained
language teacher is realized, his or her work is not properly recognized when it
comes to his/her evaluation for merit increases, promotion, etc., and is not considered equal in worth, prestige and academic value to that of colleagues in
other disciplines. For those of us who wear more than one hat, so to speak,
recognition has come for our contributions in our disciplines, be it linguistics,
literature, or what have you, but not for our equally demanding and meritorious
contributions to language teaching output, e.g., testing, curriculum development, material development, classroom experimentation, and the research and
publications related to these endeavors.

It must be noted that the issue is not whether research and publication are
desirable in a university; they are not only desirable but essential. The issue is,
on the one hand, whether ways can be found to reward and appreciate the immensely demanding and time-consuming efforts of the language teacher/scholar;
and, on the other hand, if academe is prepared to recognize the output and scholarship of the language teacher/scholar in applied linguistics, education, second
language teaching, and foreign language education, as well as the scholarship
related to language teaching of the language teacher/scholar who wears two
hats. Unless and until we find ways to persuade academic administrations to
change their attitude and their entrenched resistance to looking at language learning and teaching as intellectual challenges, and to give the language professional equal rights as a full-fledged, and not a second-class citizen and colleague, our enterprise and gains will continue to be threatened and those Arabic
language programs will continue to suffer, as some institutions are finding but
only after paying a heavy price.

It is worth noting—and this should come as no surprise—that the most successful language instruction programs are those that have teachers/scholars who are also language professionals running them. This has certainly been the case with the success story of the School of Arabic at Middlebury. Let me also say that the attempts at some institutions to avoid facing these issues—whether by lowering the qualifications of the key language program people they hire, by not encouraging and valuing the professional development and research capabilities of their faculty, or by hiring transients or temporary help on "soft money"—are not, in my opinion, likely to put their language programs on a sound basis.

To the institutions that want to build first-rate language programs, I would say: turn them over to a trained, professional teacher/scholar, and once you are fortunate enough to locate such a gifted individual, hold on to him/her for dear life and treat him/her with the dignity and respect he/she deserves. To our professional organization, I would say: we need to mount a massive campaign to educate our administrators, starting at the departmental and center levels, as to the nature of our enterprise and its intellectual and academic undergirding. We have allies in our sister programs in the more commonly taught foreign languages and in the national foreign language organizations with whom we need to seek common action.

To my younger colleagues here considering careers in language teaching, I want to say in all candor that they need to be fully aware of what they are getting into, that all too often the commitment to a professional language teacher/scholar is too shallow, and that a pharaoh who knows and appreciates a Joseph will often be succeeded by or turn into a pharaoh who "knoweth not Joseph," and they need to plan ahead and be prepared for such times. To this gloomy picture I should perhaps add that there are some encouraging trends on the horizon; with the breakdown of walls among the disciplines of the humanities, the contributions that language people bring to our understanding of learning, and foreign language learning in particular, may start to be recognized soon.

2. Materials and Tools

By any standards, the volume of materials we have produced—textbooks, dictionaries, texts, readers, grammars, programmed courses, computer programs, proficiency-based materials and tests, etc.—has been impressive. In fact, at this moment I know of four or five ongoing materials projects at varying stages of development. This is, of course, not the place to evaluate these efforts nor to weigh their impact or contribution to our field. I will merely point out that, though teamwork is fortunately not absent, solo works by individuals seem on the rise. This highlights the fact that updated bibliographical data, with brief descriptive and evaluative annotations of the materials used in teaching Arabic in the U.S., are missing.

I do want, however, to pose and try to answer questions that I consider of special import. In all the work that we have done, have we made a contribution to foreign language teaching? Is what we are doing merely an imitation of what people are doing in the more commonly taught languages? Have we had an impact on our sister foreign languages (commonly or not-so-commonly) taught in the U.S.? You might recall that a similar question was once addressed to Taha Husayn, one of the great Arab writers and literary critics of the twentieth century. He was asked whether he subscribed to the notion advanced by some critics that Arabic literature did not really contribute anything original or produce anything that could be considered world caliber, but was basically an imitation of the works of others. His immediate response was that he did not believe this to be the case, but that after going through the stages of first reading Western literature and then imitating it, the Arabs did produce a literature that was original, that got translated into Western languages, and that did, in his opinion, have an impact.

I am, of course, not Taha Husayn, and it is with a great deal of trepidation that I tread this area of briefly assessing our contribution to foreign language instruction. Because of my intimate involvement in Arabic language instruction in general, and in the projects I will be talking about in particular, my remarks will sound immodest and self-serving. However, I will tell you frankly what I think. What are some of our contributions? First, we in the Arabic profession have been pioneers in producing sophisticated Arabic computer-assisted instruction programs (see Victorine Abboud 1971 and 1978), going back to the late sixties and early seventies, long before the word computer became a household term. People from outside our field who have researched available computer programs have noted the high degree of design sophistication and creativity, coupled with the uncanny ability to capitalize on the capabilities of the computer that these programs reflect.

Secondly, we produced textbooks, (Abboud et al. 1983 and 1971) mentioned earlier, whose sales continue to increase year after year, both within the United States and world-wide (I wonder whether any American textbook in any one of the more commonly taught languages is used to teach that language as a second language overseas, e.g., French in France?). These textbooks have spawned other books, which, though different in various degrees, still bear their clear imprint on them, as well as an innumerable array of supplements, including computer programs and computer-based materials, such as the recently produced ArabCard developed at the University of Durham in the U.K., and teaching aids, such as flash cards, etc.

Finally, I will mention that we produced here in Middlebury between 1988 and 1990, a series in three levels each, of reading, listening, and speaking materials (Abboud and Attieh 1991), respectively, that I think are unparalleled among the foreign languages that are taught in this country in terms of range, breadth of coverage, sheer amount of authentic texts, including a large number of audio and video tapes, and the full implementation of a sophisticated, pedagogically-sound design, and other features too many to mention. Two of the most distinguishing characteristics of these materials are the feature of gradation in the Middlebury materials and the feature of vocabulary recycling in *Modern Standard Arabic, Intermediate Level (IMSA)*.

2.1 *The Feature of Gradation in the Series* "Come Let's Read/Listen/ Speak Fuṣḥā with the Arabs"

These Middlebury materials, completed in 1990 and referred to earlier, will "revolutionize the teaching of Arabic in this country," according to an evaluation committee of two of our colleagues. The materials take students from the novice all the way to the superior level and are graded (a) by level, with each level determined by the kinds of tasks the students are required to perform, together with the nature and complexity of the texts, from the novice task of extracting simple information from a table or a schedule, to the superior task of comparing arguments and "reading between the lines" in a sophisticated argumentative essay; (b) by topic, in the case of the advanced level, e.g., handling texts with historical content and politically-oriented texts before literary and socio-cultural texts, and by complexity of style and "density" of argument presentation from lesson to lesson within the same topic; and (c) by task within the same lesson, forming, e.g., for the advanced level, a progression from determining the main argument, to pinpointing details, and all the way to answering inferential questions, and, for novice level, from extracting information from a table to comparing items to extrapolating data from the same table. To my knowledge, no such thorough application of this principle of gradation has been implemented to this extent and range anywhere. We have proved it can be done and have used it successfully in our classrooms. Incidentally, the Michigan readers anticipated this principle of gradation in that "they [the five readers] form a progression from less to greater difficulty in terms of style and content, and may effectively be used in the order presented" (McCarus and Yacoub 1962:v).

2.2 *The Feature of Recycling Vocabulary in* Modern Standard Arabic, Intermediate Level (IMSA)

It is a well-established principle, and one that has been amply validated by empirical research, that vocabulary retention is a function of recycling and re-insertion and reiteration. One of our colleagues at the Middlebury conference referred to a recent study which reported that in order for students to be able to retain vocabulary, they have to be able to see it some twelve or so times. This principle was actually implemented in the 1971 version of *IMSA*, where a vocabulary item was re-introduced at least once in the lesson following the one in which it was first introduced, then again in one of the next two lessons, then at least once in one of the three succeeding lessons, and thereafter never less than once in one of the following three lessons. How was this accomplished? We used an admittedly primitive (by today's standards) computer program that tracked vocabulary items all over the place! This was 1971! This principle was also applied when *EMSA* was revised in 1975. I know of no such attempt on this scale being done anywhere else. In this connection, I am pleased to announce that we are now undertaking a thorough revision of *IMSA* (actually this is a revision of the 1980 revised *IMSA,* which has been circulating in mimeographed form in a number of places since that time) and we are hoping that the revised edition, which introduces a number of innovative features, including a total revamping of the grammar drills, will continue to serve our community.

From the brief survey that precedes, and this is only a very partial list of works with which I am most familiar and which I mention only by way of example, you can see that I strongly believe we have made contributions to foreign language instruction. The question remains: have we had any impact, and are our sister languages and language professions aware of our work? I have already alluded to some impact on our sister Middle Eastern languages and on some materials in the Arab world. For the rest, though, I am less sure. Why? The answer is, of course, quite complex. It is certainly partly due to the fact that we have not been expansive nor have we had a good public relations campaign to "spread abroad" what we have done through publications in the official organs of foreign language instruction. But, to be honest with you, I have the feeling that it may have something to do with the Euro-ethnic bent in our culture. After all, is it not the essence of scholarship to acquaint oneself with all that has been done in the field? So why not in Arabic?

Quite immodestly but truthfully, let me say that when we set out to write the above-mentioned materials, we searched for and consulted all available works we could lay our hands on. (I remember we bought and distributed to every participant in our 1965 and 1966 seminars copies of the most widely-used textbooks in French, German, Spanish, and Japanese in the U.S.; I do not mean to sound self-righteous here, seeing that even among our own colleagues in our own small circle there are some who have been remiss in this regard.) Lest my remarks be misunderstood, I would like to say that this is not an attempt on my part to help us find a place in the sun through the hateful process of victimhood, which is prevalent in the U.S. and elsewhere, too, today, nor am I trying to imply that we have been victims of the "system," that we have been discriminated against, and so on. I mean these remarks to be a call to what my fellow countryman Edward Said has called "worldliness," but which I would much rather (betraying my religious reform bias against that term) call "universality" or "globality," i.e., openness of mind and awareness of the world outside. I would like to invite our colleagues from other languages and urge them to inquire about what we and others have done. I do think it would be worth their while.

To my own colleagues here and elsewhere, I would like to say that we need to be more aggressive in our research and publication efforts and make sure we communicate more with our colleagues outside our own circle in other foreign languages, through participation in national workshops, seminars, annual meetings of appropriate societies, and through the medium of publication. In this regard, I would like to refer to one instance where involvement of some colleagues has resulted in their having some impact beyond our borders. Those among us who have been active in the American Council of Teachers of Foreign Languages (ACTFL) circles have effectively made the point that the generic proficiency "guidelines" that were developed and seemed to work for the "commonly taught" languages did not really fit Arabic and the other "exotic" languages, and that for these languages "specific" guidelines were needed. I think we have gained reluctant or willing acceptance from our other colleagues in the commonly taught languages as far as that is concerned. Quite frankly, I still wonder whether they understand the full implications of why there are specifics, and how these specifics might just impact them.

3. Methods and Curriculum

I derive my own use of these terms from the aphorism that the best methodology is one which seeks to understand the ways students, a given set of students about whom certain presuppositions related to their backgrounds, goals, programs, etc., are made, learn, and then seeks to use them. Here, there is no question that we have made a lot of progress and have shown that, for the most part, we have been aware of the learning theories that have been advanced, and have been able to assimilate them with varying degrees of commitment and success. But it is also an area where excesses of our culture tend to be most obvious, namely, bandwagonism, rigid orthodoxy, as well as "political" correctness to name a few. Time will only allow me to briefly comment on "methodological" correctness which academicians are specially susceptible to, before moving on to discuss some of the methodological issues that we face. Methodological correctness implies that there is only one way and one route to solving problems or realizing goals, that you can be right only if you subscribe to this route or method, and that it is politically wise to be perceived as taking that party line, whatever the "line" is that is generally held to be correct.

However dangerous it is to reject this stance, it is a dangerous and divisive stance to take. This must not be taken to mean that I am advocating methodological anarchy—and I have already referred to its existence to a greater extent than I would like to see—where everything goes. It is interesting to note that our colleagues who got together in the sixties to chart a path for the future for themselves did not at any point presume that that path was the one and only path to follow, though they clearly and unequivocally stated that given their reading of students studying Arabic in the U.S. at that time, the path they were embracing and recommending seemed to make the most sense. They never claimed that that methodology was for everybody either. What they did declare implicitly was that individual circumstances and different objectives may dictate other ways, but they insisted that whatever the persuasion (including that of the so-called grammar/translation, which they rejected), those objectives, methodologies, and curricula had to be clearly spelled out and mapped out in a well-articulated integrated sequence, not in terms of pages covered or books used, but in terms of clearly spelled out tasks and activities. I think this was wise and a worthy example to follow.

Now, here are a few of the issues related to methodological and curricular matters that need to be addressed in the future.

3.1 The Need for Clearly Articulated Goals

It is sad to note that after all these years there are still Arabic programs, and they seem to be the rule rather than the exception, that do not have clearly articulated objectives for their sequential language courses. Students complain that when they move from year to year or even semester to semester in these programs, they often are turned over to instructors who are unaware of what they did in previous courses and who often prescribe materials and methods that have nothing to do with previously used materials or methods. This was a matter of great concern to us at Middlebury, administration, faculty, and students alike, at both ends of the summer. First, it was difficult to assess at the beginning of the summer what the students had done in their home institutions in order to place the students in the class they were most suited for, since number of years of study did not seem to have any cumulative effect; the problem was partly alleviated when we began to administer oral proficiency tests and other available tests for the other skills. Our concern at the end of the summer was to ascertain that the students would be able to build on their painstakingly acquired skills once they left Middlebury.

The reasons for this sad state of affairs are many. It is almost a given that some instructors would resist the attempt to develop clearly stated objectives to which they would commit themselves, on the basis of their freedom to teach what they want to teach and the idea that "nobody tells me what to do in my classes," which strikes me as odd in view of the damage it inflicts on students. But more surreptitious is the low esteem with which language teaching is held, which I referred to earlier. What is unthinkable in other areas in academe is allowed to exist in language programs, where of course the situation is much more serious, since language teaching is not a one-semester or one-year deal, but a set of sequential courses where each builds on what precedes it, much like mathematics or the natural sciences. The upshot: it is absolutely essential in language teaching to define our goals and state how we hope to achieve them. It is worth stating that these objectives and curricula need to be realistic, and this is achieved through a process of continual evaluation and refinement in light of student performance, objectively determined through a longitudinally-conducted series of validated tests in the various skills that we purport to teach. Once again, who can do this but the professionally trained instructor.

Some of us here have been concerned about the curriculum and methodology of a terminal two-year program. I have already stated that objectives and methods need not be uniform everywhere. Even where there is concurrence in point of view with respect to methodology and approach, it is not unreasonable to accept the premise that the content and goals of such a program and those of one which goes beyond the two years—and envisages preparing students for graduate courses and research—could take different paths. It would be a mistake in my opinion to impose the methodology of the former and its rationale on the latter and vice-versa.

In this connection, there is a need in programs with graduate components that go beyond a two-year sequence to work out goals with input from colleagues in literature, linguistics, and other disciplines, who have a vital interest in having students with sound language training, and to harmonize expectations on both sides. Also, I would like to state that it is my firm conviction that it is time to begin to fully Arabicize our graduate course offerings in areas that are the domain of departments of languages, literatures and cultures, i.e., to require not only that the readings and sources for these courses include readings and sources in Arabic, but also that the actual teaching and class discussions be in Arabic. With very few exceptions, and I am glad to note there are a few, we are lagging behind our sister departments of the more commonly taught languages, where it is inconceivable to teach those courses in English (Spanish literature or French civilization in English?). We in the Arabic teaching profession have been timid and diffident in stating this. It is high time that we work towards that end.

3.2 *The Place of Grammar in the Curriculum*

This is an issue that deserves more serious thought and one for which the commonly taught languages cannot provide too much guidance, given the radically different derivational nature of the Arabic language. Several issues are involved: what form, at what point, for what purpose (immediate and long range), what approach, how much, the role of mechanical drills, what form of presentation, etc. Even when we accept the premise that our activities should be task oriented and not grammatically driven, most of us have been concerned with how grammar is to be dealt with at the novice and intermediate levels and rarely address what is beyond. Are there structures that are to be studied in greater depths or that have not been introduced? What are they, where and how are they to be introduced, and how is that to be done effectively? I once made a suggestion, which I am sure was made by others, that we carefully distinguish for certain levels passive control of certain structures, on the one hand (i.e., ability to "understand" them, in the receptive skills such as in reading comprehension), from active control, i.e., the ability to use them in the productive skills, on the other. I do not imply that there have not been discussions around "grammar"; however, my observations are that these discussions have often been rather vague and conducted without the benefit of an overall context, in which grammar is considered part of the whole, not merely what grammar is appropriate to be presented at, say, the elementary level.

To make these discussions meaningful, we need to look at clearly articulated curricula not for one semester's work but for a whole program, and not for one activity but rather together with other activities, speaking, reading, etc.

Some people have been criticizing the *EMSA* approach (and you are looking at one who has), but to make the criticism meaningful we need to look at carefully articulated courses and see what possible alternatives there are. In this regard, an approach for dealing with grammar was suggested in 1988-1990, in conjunction with the Middlebury materials referred to above, for the first four levels of instruction there, that incorporated these ideas of active vs. passive control. Also, in the revised version of *IMSA* we do make some statements in the grammar drills, which incidentally have been completely rewritten and revamped in that regard.

3.3 *Medieval Prose Literature*

The necessity of learning to handle medieval texts in graduate programs of Arabic is hardly a subject of disagreement (and here we part ways with our sister foreign languages where such an issue never arises), but the method of training students to handle them has, to my knowledge, not been fully addressed. Thus, there is an unspoken assumption that the skills of reading for gist, as well as other well-known reading strategies, work only for Modern Standard Arabic. When it comes to older texts we go back to an inordinate reliance on vocabulary (i.e., dictionaries), word-for-word grammatical and morphological analysis, translation, etc. I find that hard to understand. As far back as 1971, medieval texts were provided to be read for the gist, or "extensively" as the term in vogue then was (Abboud et al. 1971). Also, at Middlebury we conducted an experiment (1989-90), and I believe successfully, in incorporating in the curriculum of the upper advanced level pieces from medieval Arabic literature, which showed that we could use the same reading for comprehension principles and strategies for them as well. We need to talk about this issue.

4. **Summary**

In this presentation, I have discussed our achievements and where we stand now (whence?) and the work that lies ahead (whither?). The following is a brief summary of some of the issues which I believe should occupy our thinking in this decade and into the twenty-first century:

1. The need for empirical studies. On a number of occasions in this chapter, the almost total absence of empirical studies and of carefully controlled experiments on various aspects of learning and teaching Arabic has been implied or pointed out. I personally know of one study that was made at the University of Texas a couple of years ago where one of our students tried to determine experimentally whether one could learn Arabic faster at the beginning level by

starting with vocalized texts rather than unvocalized texts; my late wife also conducted a study a number of years ago comparing the acquisition of the Arabic sound and writing systems through a computer program and through more traditional methods. There are others, I am sure, but it seems obvious that in this area we are found lacking. This may be a function of the training that most of us have had, which did not involve this kind of experimentation, or of lack of research interest. Some of our assumptions are based on impressions that need to be tested, as are some of our practices, and even well-established tenets of foreign language research need to be validated for Arabic. That is where our colleagues trained in the methods of educational empirical research can come in and render a tremendous service to our profession. I call upon them and all of us who are so inclined to give urgent attention to this matter; not only will empirical research help clear up and provide information on some of the issues that confront us, but it will also be an important contribution to the mounting body of studies on issues of interest to the whole field of learning theory and foreign language education.

2. The need for concerted and affirmative action to educate administrators on the nature of the work and contributions of the language teaching specialist—as a professional and as a scholar—and on their intellectual undergirding.

3. The profile and future training of the college teacher of Arabic.

4. The need to inform our colleagues in the sister foreign languages of our work, and to share our contributions, research, and insights in national and international forums and publications.

5. The clear delineation of our goals and objectives of each Arabic language program, and articulation of how they are to be achieved.

6. The evaluation of all existing Arabic as a second language teaching materials and tools of access, including those produced in the Arab world and elsewhere, and, in the light of what we have, the determination of present and future needs.

7. The need to determine the place of grammar in our curricula.

8. The need to determine the place of medieval materials in curricula.

9. The articulation of objectives of advanced language courses, in programs with graduate components, in cooperation with colleagues in literature, linguistics, and other disciplines.

10. The Arabicization of our linguistics, culture, and literature graduate courses.

11. Underlying all of these, the need for teamwork.

The nature of these issues and suggestions is such that a concerted, profession-wide action needs to be undertaken. I strongly recommend the format of the one- to two-week group discussion sessions or "workshops" that proved to be so overwhelmingly successful in the past. As in the past, a task force needs to study these issues and determine priorities. Experience has taught that these activities may be sponsored and supported by groups or organizations, but it is the initiative of energetic individuals with some stature in the field that will get them going.

In this chapter I have not touched on the issue of diglossia. This was purposefully done because I believe that with our present state of knowledge, which is mostly based on impressions and recycled information, discussions of it are more likely to produce heat than light. It is my personal opinion, and that of a number of colleagues here and elsewhere, judging from conversations with them, that we should call for a moratorium for the time being on further discussion of it. There is so much that still remains to be done that we cannot afford to spend our energies on this single issue. This is not that it is not important; it is, and critically so. However, full-blown discussions of diglossia in Arabic language teaching should await more data, new insights, and the results of further and more widespread experimentation.

It is the privilege and, indeed, the responsibility of each generation to question and reexamine the assumptions of a previous generation, and to reassess stances vis-à-vis issues. However, in my opinion, it is sheer waste to throw away hard won grounds, hard earned experience, and carefully obtained consensus, except after alternatives are thoroughly discussed and weighty consideration has been given to the implication of that which we are about to do. Wisdom cautions against throwing away the landmarks that have been placed along the road by our predecessors. Those landmarks that have guided the way must not be destroyed or removed without seasoned and careful study of the alternatives first. I hope you do not interpret this to mean that what was done before is necessarily right just because it has become tradition. It is not. But neither is it necessary to reject it because it was done before our time.

I would like to end this chapter with two parting thoughts. First, on this occasion, I know you will join me in wishing the School of Arabic great success in its prime tasks of teaching students Arabic, in serving as a training ground for future teachers of Arabic, in experimenting with materials and methods, in enhancing the dialogue among the practitioners of Arabic instruction, and in serving as a beacon for our profession in the future. Second, I would like to leave you with an adage that you will find engraved above the stage in Ewart Memorial Hall at the American University in Cairo. It is one that I looked at many times when I was a student there and have had occasion to ponder often then and over the years. It contains much wisdom, wisdom in the Arabic sense of the word, which involves the domains of the mind, the heart, the intellect, good judgment, tact, and savoire faire, close to the French word *sagesse*. The saying reads, "Let knowledge grow from more to more." I certainly look forward to the years ahead when our knowledge of Arabic and of teaching and learning Arabic will be greatly enhanced by what you are doing and what you are planning on doing. Then the saying continues, "and more of reverence in us dwell." This reverence refers to reverence for others, for their work, for ourselves, for our work, for our limitations, for how little we know, and yet for what we are capable of achieving. Thus, "Let Knowledge Grow from More to More, and More of Reverence in Us Dwell."

REFERENCES

ABBOUD, PETER. 1968. *The Teaching of Arabic in the United States: The State of the Art.* Washington, D.C.: ERIC Clearinghouse for Linguistics.

_____, ED. 1966. *Papers of the Arabic Teachers' Workshop on Intermediate Modern Standard Arabic Instruction.* Austin: Middle East Center, University of Texas.

_____, ET AL. 1968. *Elementary Modern Standard Arabic.* Ann Arbor: University of Michigan Press.

_____, ET AL. 1971. *Modern Standard Arabic: Intermediate level.* Ann Arbor: University of Michigan Press.

_____, ET AL. 1983. *Elementary Modern Standard Arabic*, Parts 1 and 2. Cambridge: Cambridge University Press.

_____ AND AMAN ATTIEH. 1991. *Taᶜālaw Naqraʾ Maᶜal-ᶜArab* [Come Let's Read with the Arabs] (4 volumes). *Taᶜālaw Nastamiᶜ Maᶜa al-ᶜArab* [Come Let's Listen with the Arabs] (4 volumes), and *Taᶜālaw Natahaddath al-Fushā* [Come Let's Speak Fusha] (4 volumes). Middlebury: School of Arabic, Middlebury College.

ABBOUD, VICTORINE C. 1971 and 1981. *Barnāmaj Taᶜlīm al-Kitāba al-ᶜArabiyya* [Computer Assisted Instruction Program for The Arabic Writing System], Mainframe, 1971, and IBM PC Implementation, 1981.

_____. 1978 and 1982. *Barnāmaj al-Mufradāt wa-Fahm al-Nuṣūṣ li-al-ᶜArabiyya al-Muᶜāsira. al-Marhala al-Mutawassiṭa* [Computer Assisted Instruction Program for Vocabulary and Reading Comprehension for Modern Standard Arabic. Intermediate Level]. Mainframe, 1978, IBM PC, 1982.

McCARUS, ERNEST N. AND ADIL I. YACOUB. 1961. *Contemporary Arabic Readers* (5 volumes). Ann Arbor: The University of Michigan Press.

Papers of the Arabic Teachers' Workshop. 1965. Washington, D.C.: Center for Applied Linguistics.

2

THE INSTITUTIONAL SETTING OF ARABIC LANGUAGE TEACHING: A SURVEY OF PROGRAM COORDINATORS AND TEACHERS OF ARABIC IN U.S. INSTITUTIONS OF HIGHER LEARNING*

R. Kirk Belnap
Brigham Young University

Principled program and policy decisions depend on adequate information. A recent survey of students in Arabic Language programs in the U.S. and Canada provides a picture of student priorities and attitudes about Arabic and how it is taught in their respective institutions (Belnap 1987). However, this is only one side of the issue: curriculum, materials, resources, instructors, and program administrators all figure in the process of the teaching and learning of Arabic.

This chapter reports the results of a telephone survey of coordinators and teachers of Arabic from a stratified random sample of institutions of higher learning in the U.S. It provides a representative view of: 1) the types of institutions offering Arabic and the distribution of students across and within these institutions; 2) the types of instructors found in the various institutional categories and their training and participation in the Arabic Language teaching field; 3) textbooks and other teaching materials in use; 4) teacher and student priorities; 5) the role of the American Association of Teachers of Arabic.

*I would like to thank Richard Brod, Elyse Burt, John Caemmerer, Jose Madrigal, and the National Center for Higher Education Management Systems (NCHEMS) for their assistance in designing, conducting, and reporting this survey. I express particular gratitude to the teachers and administrators who responded to this rather lengthy survey, as well as the secretaries, administrators, roommates, and spouses who helped us contact them.

The survey results underline a number of important issues the profession needs to address in order to move forward. Three areas stand out in particular: the needs of programs at smaller institutions, the need for increased cooperation between teachers and between programs, and the importance of the first two years of instruction.

1. Introduction

In 1987, we surveyed Arabic students at twenty-four North American universities (Belnap 1987). That survey provides a revealing picture of students of Arabic and the reasons why they take Arabic, including information on their backgrounds and priorities and how they feel about the process of learning and teaching Arabic and how it could be improved. Since we have so recently examined the learner in addressing the issue of Arabic in the 1990s, we felt it would be helpful to examine the other side of the teaching/learning equation: the teacher and the instructional environment. As a result, we conducted a survey which examined the institutional setting of Arabic language teaching in institutions of higher learning in the United States. This survey complements and updates some of the information on Arabic contained in Clark and Johnson's survey of materials development needs in the less commonly taught languages at institutions of higher learner in the U.S. (1982).

Our primary goal in conducting this survey was to describe as accurately as possible the present state of Arabic language teaching in the United States in response to questions such as: Who teaches Arabic? What types of institutions offer Arabic and what are their programs like? What is the distribution of students according to institutional type and level of study? What texts and other materials are used? What are instructors' priorities in teaching Arabic and how well do they match students' priorities in learning Arabic? What role does the American Association of Teachers of Arabic (AATA) play and what more could it do to further the teaching of Arabic? The answers to questions such as these are important; in order to know where we should go from here, we need to know where we are. We have attempted in this paper to present information which will aid us in knowing where we are as a profession and, we hope, challenge us to assess our situation and move forward.

Section One of the chapter deals with the construction of the survey. Section Two addresses the types of institutions offering Arabic and the distribution of students across and within these institutions. Section Three examines the instructor variable, including the types of instructors found in the various institutional categories and their training and participation in the Arabic language teaching field. Section Four focuses on texts and materials, including recommendations for improvement. In Section Five, teacher and student priorities are compared and contrasted. The issues include the relative importance of the sub-skills of reading, writing, listening, and speaking; objectives in teaching/study-ing Arabic; and attitudes toward studying a colloquial variety. Section Six dis-cusses AATA's role and how it could further serve the profession by dissemi-nating information, promoting teacher training, and encouraging the develop-ment and wider distribution of materials. Section Seven summarizes the results of the survey, emphasizing efforts that might be undertaken with maximal yield and minimal cost.

1.1 *Methodology*

This chapter reports the results of a telephone survey of coordinators and Arabic teachers selected on the basis of a random sample of Arabic language programs in the U.S. We adopted a telephone survey format primarily because it would be extremely difficult to construct a mail survey which would be valid for all of the types of institutions we planned to survey; on more than one occa-sion we found it necessary to adapt the survey to the teacher or institution. In short, a telephone survey allowed for greater freedom. If it was apparent from a response (or a direct request for clarification) that the respondent did not under-stand a question, the person conducting the survey was able to explain it. The telephone format allowed for greater latitude in exploring issues, including is-sues the researcher overlooked in designing the survey. This format correspond-ingly allowed for corrections and revisions in the survey instrument in the course of collecting data, and for relatively easy follow-up at a later date, when neces-sary. The telephone format did impose certain restrictions on the types of ques-tions one could ask: questions could not be too difficult. For example, ques-tions involving complex scaling were rather taxing for respondents without the benefit of graphics to ease comprehension. While a telephone survey is gener-ally costlier and more time-consuming, a higher response rate may offset these considerations. Of the coordinators and teachers we were able to initially con-tact, all eventually responded to our survey. A 100% response rate is virtually unheard of in written surveys, and even in telephone surveys.[1]

Table 1 gives an overview of the institutions included in the random sample. Our purpose was to obtain a representative sample of the broad range of institu-tions with Arabic Language programs. We arrived at this sample as follows: From the Modern Language Association (MLA), we obtained a list of those

---

1. Our 100% response rate of those contacted may have been a matter of mere chance. Two things suggest this was not the case: First, Jose Madrigal, a statistician who consulted with us on

Table 1.

Type and number of institutions and individuals included in the survey

Institution type	Institutions with Arabic programs	Institutions sampled	Number of surveys administered
Research Universities	38	4	6
Research Universities/AATA	14	2	6
Doctorate-Granting Universities	17	2	2
Comprehensive Universities & Colleges	18	2	2
Liberal Arts Colleges	18	2	2
Two-Year Colleges and Institutions	20	2	2
Specialized Institutions	11	3	4
Total:	136	17	24

institutions which reported Arabic Language programs in the MLA's 1990 survey of U.S. institutions of higher learning.[2] With the assistance of the National Center for Higher Education Management Systems (NCHEMS), we then divided these 136 institutions into the Carnegie categories.[3] We determined that

developing the survey and on our sampling technique, warned us that we needed to cut our survey down substantially in size; people are rarely willing to respond to a long survey. We cut a few questions from the survey but decided not to cut any more, as we did not want to further limit the issues we would explore. John Caemmerer, a fellow at the National Foreign Language Center in Washington and the director of a number of surveys of Russian students, teachers and programs, also consulted with us on the construction of our survey. He related to me that one of their mail surveys was longer than our survey but they still had a good response rate. He attributed this to the dedication of the rank and file teacher to the profession and to improving it. We, too, were impressed with the dedication to the teaching of Arabic of those who responded to our survey, whether they were full professors or engineering students hired on a part-time basis to supervise independent study courses. Of course, our persistence and the more personal nature of a telephone conversation no doubt figured in our high response rate. In contrast, Clark and Johnson's mail survey of department chairs and instructors of less-commonly taught languages received a 23% response rate (1982:13).

2. The Modern Language Association conducts this survey every three years in the fall. Surveys are mailed to each institution's registrar. See Brod and Huber 1992 for a detailed report of the MLA's 1990 survey of foreign language registrations in U.S. colleges and universities. Of particular interest in that report, Arabic language enrollments increased dramatically from 1960 to 1980 (from 541 to 3466) but remained surprisingly constant between 1980 and 1990 (3436 in 1983, 3417 in 1986, 3475 in 1990—but see footnote 5 concerning the 1990 enrollment figure) (1992:8). From 1980 to 1990, the other languages among the top twelve foreign language enrollments showed at least 5% increases (Chinese, French, German...) or 25% decreases (Ancient Greek and Hebrew).

3. The Carnegie classification system groups institutions into categories on the basis of the level of degree offered and the comprehensiveness of their missions. This system is widely used in

AATA institutional members constitute a class of institutions with a particularly high commitment to Arabic language instruction and should therefore not be grouped with other institutions not evincing this commitment. Of the eighteen U.S. AATA member institutions sampled in the MLA survey, 78% fall into the category of research universities. As a result, we divided the research university category into those which are AATA institutional members and those which are not. Following an established sampling formula, we determined the number of institutions we would need to sample from each class of institutions in order to have a 95% confidence level that our results were representative of the population from which they were drawn.

Research universities offer a full range of baccalaureate programs and are committed to graduate education through the doctorate degree, and give high priority to research. They receive annually at least $12.5 million in federal support for research and development and award at least fifty Ph.D. degrees each year (most of the universities in our sample received far more federal funding). The category of doctorate-granting universities differs from the research university category in that there is not as high a commitment to research. In addition, they award fewer Ph.D. degrees annually (at least twenty in one discipline or ten or more in three or more disciplines). Comprehensive universities and colleges offer baccalaureate programs and generally graduate programs through the masters degree. More than half of their baccalaureate degrees are awarded in two or more occupational or professional disciplines (such as engineering or business administration). They enroll a minimum of 1500 students, though most enroll over 2500. Liberal arts colleges award more than half of their degrees in liberal arts fields or are too small to be considered comprehensive; these institutions tend to be highly selective undergraduate colleges. Two-year colleges and institutions offer certificate or degree programs through the associate of arts level. Specialized institutions include professional schools, theological seminaries, bible colleges, and military colleges; they offer degrees ranging from the bachelors to the doctorate. While specialized schools are generally smaller, they may be affiliated with sizable institutions, such as research universities. We decided to sample three of the specialized category—instead of the two required by the sampling formula—in order to provide a better picture of this very diverse category.

---

research on and discussions of higher education; for an example of a foreign language application see Huber 1993:6. We used only the major Carnegie categories (most of these categories are subdivided into types I and II—according to the amount of federal research funding they obtain, the number of graduate programs they have, or the selectivity of the institution).

Our goal was to survey all of the individuals directly involved in teaching Arabic at each institution. This was interpreted as meaning all who taught Arabic during the 1991-92 academic year, including student instructors and teaching assistants if they actually taught students in the classroom or supervised students in independent study programs (but not if their responsibilities were essentially restricted to grading homework or tests or functioning as occasional tutors). Program coordinators responded to a longer form of the survey which included questions relating to the Arabic program and to the institution in general (a copy of the coordinator's survey form is included in the appendix). Both the coordinators and other teachers responded to the same set of questions addressed to individuals. In a few cases where the coordinators were not Arabic teachers, we gathered information regarding the program from the coordinators and from a teacher in order to complete the long form of the survey. In other words, we administered one long form to the coordinator at each institution; in the event that there was more than one teacher, we administered shorter forms of the survey to these other teachers. We obtained the names and telephone numbers of these individuals from department secretaries or program coordinators. In some cases, we were not able to contact all of the individuals at an institution because they had moved or were out of the country.[4] In every case, however, we sampled a proportion of the teachers that would allow us to draw reliable conclusions about Arabic language teaching at that institution.

2.   Institutional Overview

The MLA survey gives the distribution of undergraduate and graduate students by individual institutions; these are listed by state and are subcategorized according to whether they are two-year or four-year institutions. Thus, from the MLA survey we learn that Georgetown University reported the largest enrollment of Arabic students in the U.S. (142). Not surprisingly, it has the largest number of undergraduate students (121)[5]; the University of Chicago, however, reported the largest number of graduate students (forty-two) enrolled in Arabic

---

4. The MLA survey, from which our list of institutions was drawn, was conducted in the fall of 1990. We were unable to contact the coordinators of some institutions initially selected for the sample. Between the MLA survey and our survey, one two-year college had discontinued its Arabic program. Another two-year college said that Arabic was seldom offered. A doctorate-granting university reported that Arabic was not offered every semester. We were further unable to contact the part-time instructor from a third two-year college. As a result of our not being able to contact the coordinators and teachers of these programs, we randomly selected other institutions from the same categories to replace them.

5. The MLA survey actually lists Brigham Young University as having the largest under-

courses.[6] As for the state with the largest Arabic enrollment, New York led with 410 undergraduates and fifty-eight graduate students for a total of 468; twenty-one institutions in the state of New York reported Arabic enrollments.

Table 2 gives the distribution of undergraduate and graduate students from the 1990 MLA survey of U.S. institutions of higher learning according to the Carnegie classification of their institutions. Nearly two-thirds of all Arabic students are enrolled in research universities. Research universities which are also AATA institutional members have by far the largest programs in terms of enrollment (61.4 students per institution). What table 2 fails to reveal is the stability, or lack thereof, of programs in the different types of institutions. Larger programs are more stable, that is, they are less likely to be discontinued than smaller programs. As noted in footnote 4, one institution (a two-year college) we attempted to survey had discontinued its Arabic program and others reported that they offer Arabic only sporadically. In the course of the survey, a coordinator at a liberal arts college mentioned in frustration that his institution had decided to no longer offer Arabic in the future.

The instability of smaller programs is evident in comparing the MLA survey with the institutions that responded to Clark and Johnson's 1982 survey and reported Arabic programs. One-third (6/18) of the Arabic programs responding in 1982 did not respond to the MLA survey in 1990. We contacted these institutions to determine the fate of their programs. Five of the six (a liberal arts college, a comprehensive university, two doctorate-granting universities, and a theological seminary) reported that they no longer offer Arabic. The sixth institution (a two-year college) reported that they do not offer Arabic for credit (this would account for the fact that the MLA survey does not include it); they do

---

graduate enrollment—129 students. We are not sure how they arrived at these figures. We checked with our registrar's office and they reported forty-seven undergraduate students. BYU sponsors a study abroad program at its Jerusalem Center for Near Eastern Studies. Students there elect to take either a one-credit-hour course in Arabic or Hebrew; during the Fall of 1990, seventy-one students took the Arabic class. The forty-seven who took Arabic at the Provo campus added to the seventy-one in Jerusalem totals 118—closer but still not the 129 reported by the MLA. However, we are not at all sure that this is how the MLA arrived at this figure (our registrar's office normally does not report Jerusalem Center enrollment as part of the regular BYU enrollment figures): the figure may represent an error on the part of our registrar's office in reporting the statistic to the MLA, or an error on the MLA's part. We corrected the error for the purposes of this survey. For this reason the totals reported here will be slightly lower than in other reports or publications based on the MLA survey data.

6. With the exception of the specialized schools, the University of Chicago was the only school with more graduates (forty-two) than undergraduates (nine); many specialized insitutions admit only graduate students.

offer a one-day-a-week evening Arabic class which they referred to as a "sampler" class. Research universities are notably absent from the list of institutions no longer offering Arabic. The lack of stability and continuity in smaller programs no doubt affects the quality of their programs.

Table 2.

Undergraduate and graduate students enrolled in Arabic courses

Institution type	Institutions with Arabic programs	Under-graduate students	Graduate students	Total students enrolled	Average number of students per institution
Research	38	1113	148	1261	33.2
Research/AATA	14	705	155	860	61.4
Doctorate-Granting	17	290	8	298	17.5
Comprehensive	18	230	0	230	12.8
Liberal Arts	18	98	0	98	5.4
Two-Year	20	423	0	423	21.5
Specialized	11	169	54	223	20.3
Total:	136	3028	365	3393	24.9

Three institutions in the sample (a two-year college and both comprehensive universities) were members of the National Association of Self-Instructional Language Programs (NASILP). NASILP's members constitute a consortium of institutions that do not have full-fledged programs in uncommonly taught languages; they offer such languages on a self-instructional basis. Students work with materials (texts and tapes) specifically designed for self-instruction; at some institutions they meet weekly with a native speaker tutor, as was the case at one of the two-year colleges and one comprehensive university in the sample. At the other comprehensive university, from one to three students met together with a tutor; although the class was technically not self-instructional, they did do more work outside of the classroom than is usually the case. Student progress in NASILP member institutions is generally evaluated by a professional contracted from outside the institution (usually a specialist at another institution in the region). Outside evaluation provides a quality check on programs and helps to maintain some common standards. NASILP provides a valuable service to smaller programs without full-time instructors in that it provides a coherent curriculum and a framework for evaluation. Few two-year institutions, however, are members of NASILP.

Uncommonly taught languages at NASILP institutions constitute a category the MLA is only partially successful in surveying. The MLA survey asks registrars for enrollments by the name of each language. NASILP programs are generally listed under "critical languages" or "self-instructional languages"; since the MLA survey contains no such category, a number of these language enrollments are not reported. Thirty member institutions responding to the 1992 NASILP annual program inventory reported Arabic enrollments.[7] We found that 37% (11/30) of these institutions did not report Arabic enrollments in response to the Fall 1990 MLA survey, although each of them had reported other foreign language enrollments. In order to determine why these institutions did not report their Arabic enrollments, we attempted to contact each by telephone. Of the eight contacted, two did not offer Arabic in the fall of 1990. The six that did offer Arabic were listed under the following categories: "critical languages," "self-instructional languages," "less commonly taught languages," "World Language Institute," "foreign languages," and "Evening and Weekend Classes." In other words, registrars probably did not report them on the MLA 1990 survey because of the way they were listed.

Table 3 presents the distribution of students in institutions in our sample according to their level of study. Students are not evenly distributed among the different levels of instruction. Over half of those enrolled in the Arabic programs we sampled were first-year students; a total of 86% (508/588) of the students at these institutions were in their first two years of Arabic study. This pattern is evident in every institutional type in the sample.[8] The high attrition between first- and second-year in the specialized category is largely due to one institution which has a one-year foreign language requirement; this institution reported sixty students in the first year, fifteen in the second, and eight in the third year.

Throughout this chapter we use the common terminology of "first year, second year, third year..." in reference to students' level of study. First- and second-year Arabic usually consist of approximately four or five classroom

---

7. The breakdown of NASILP members reporting Arabic programs according to institutional type is: four research (none of which were AATA institutional members), two doctorate-granting, ten comprehensive, eleven liberal arts, and three two-year institutions. The NASILP two-year college in our sample was not one of the three two-year colleges that responded to NASILP's program inventory. The NASILP approach clearly appeals most to smaller four-year institutions.

8. Richard Lambert, director of the National Foreign Language Center, observed that the consequence of minimal foreign language requirements in the U.S. "is what can almost be called a natural law: in both high school and college, 50% of the students at each level drop out at the next level" (1992:13). In other words, the rate of attrition found in table 3 is not peculiar to Arabic.

Table 3.
Distribution of students according to level of Arabic study[9]

Institution type	1st year	2nd year	3rd year	4th year
Research	103	49	23	8
Research/AATA	36	22	15	-
Doctorate-Granting	35	18	5	15^{10}
Comprehensive	38	18	-	-
Liberal Arts	28	10	-	-
Two-Year	31	25	-	-
Specialized	70	25	-	-
Total:	341	167	57	23

hours per week for two semesters or three quarters. Of the institutions surveyed, 71% (12/17) reported that first-year students spend four or five hours in class per week (this figure includes one two-year school which reported that students spend five to eight hours per week working under the supervision of a tutor). Of the schools reporting less than four classroom hours per week, one comprehensive university reported three hours per week and the other reported that students spend two hours per week with a tutor (both of these institutions are NASILP members). At a doctorate-granting university, students spend one and a half hours in class per week. A specialized institution reported three classroom hours per week. Only one institution, also from the specialized category, reported more than five hours per week in class: students are in the classroom eight hours per week for the first year of instruction and six hours in subsequent years. Most institutions reported that the number of classroom hours decreases as the students progress. Third- and fourth-year students generally spend three hours in the classroom each week.

All but one institution (doctorate-granting) reported that at least some of their students go on to pursue their Arabic studies elsewhere: thirteen coordinators mentioned that their students transfer to other institutions, ten mentioned study abroad programs, and four mentioned summer programs (all but one program mentioned that they encourage their students to participate in summer

---

9. The figures given in table 3 are estimates of enrollment provided by program coordinators. As such, they are not precise measures of enrollment in any given institution; they are important because they give us a picture of the relative distribution of students according to levels.

10. The professor indicated the increase in enrollment in the fourth year was due to native speakers enrolling in these classes.

programs[11]). The number of students who do pursue the study of Arabic elsewhere is probably few. One coordinator at a two-year college estimated that only 5% of his students transfer to another school and continue studying Arabic. Some of the attrition documented here is students who leave the public educational system and go on to participate in government or military Arabic language training programs; however, again, the number is probably quite small.[12]

Only two institutions reported fourth-year programs. This, however, does not mean that Arabic is not available beyond the third year of study, only that there is not a clearly articulated four-year sequence of courses. In fact, we are aware of Arabic literature and other classes available for more advanced learners in at least one of the institutions not reporting a fourth-year level. From table 3, we can also see that few of the smaller institutions offer more than two years of instruction. Students who wish to pursue Arabic must transfer elsewhere. In order for students to make a smooth transition between programs, the need for coordination between programs is evident.

3. Instructors

This survey revealed a broad spectrum of types of instructors. They range from full professors with thirty years' experience teaching Arabic to an electrical engineering student who has been a part-time instructor for a year. table 4 presents the distribution of the instructors surveyed. (The numbers in parentheses in table 4 indicate the actual number of instructors we were able to contact if all were not available.) The research universities have the larger programs, with professors, lecturers, and graduate assistants often teaching in the same department. These professors and lecturers tend to hold Ph.D.s in literature or linguistics; the graduate assistants are also from these two fields. The doctoral-

---

11. Summer programs and study abroad programs constitute important categories not addressed in this survey.

12. Nazih Daher, then chairman of the Department of Asian and African Languages at the Foreign Service Language School, observed that only two or three students have significant prior Arabic language exposure of the approximately one hundred students who participate each year in the FSI's intensive Arabic programs. He estimated that fifty to sixty students participate annually in the lengthier programs (as long as forty-four weeks) and thirty to forty participate in the the eight-week course only. He, too, thought that very few students in the intensive Arabic training programs of the Defense Language Institute (DLI) in Monterey, California, had prior Arabic experience. In fact, the flow of students seems to go in the reverse direction. In our experience, few students leave Arabic programs at colleges and universities to enter DLI; after leaving DLI, however, a few do pursue their Arabic studies at academic institutions.

Table 4.

Distribution of Arabic teachers by title and institutional type

Institution type	Institutions sampled	Professorial	Lecturer	Student instructors
Research	4	2	3	5 (1)
Research/AATA	2	2	2	2
Doctorate-Granting	2	2*	-	1 (0)
Comprehensive	2	-	-	2
Liberal Arts	2	1	-	-
Two-Year	2	-	-	2
Specialized	3	4 (3)	2 (1)	-
Total:	17	10	7	8

*One of these two is a part-time professor; he holds a B.A. and teaches Spanish in the public schools.

granting institutions tend to have smaller programs, usually one professorial rank instructor per institution (in this case, one linguist and one literature specialist). Comprehensive universities tend to have even smaller programs and only a part-time instructor; in the survey, there was one dentistry student and one computer science graduate student who were part-time instructors. Two-year institutions were essentially the same, the part-time instructors being a graduate student at a local university and a math teacher from a local high school.[13] In the liberal arts college category, one instructor, a professor, divides his time between teaching Arabic and another foreign language; the other, a lecturer, is primarily an Arabic instructor. The specialized institutions tend to have more full-time Arabic teaching faculty; their specializations correspond to the type of institution in which they teach, for example, instructors at a religious studies institution came from the field of Islamic studies.

While there may be considerable diversity among the instructors surveyed, one common thread links them: a high degree of commitment to the teaching of Arabic. Nearly every individual surveyed impressed us with the desire to improve the programs. One might be tempted to think that the part-time instructors from unrelated fields—dentistry, for example—might be less likely to take language teaching seriously. We found the opposite to be the case. These individuals, all native speakers of Arabic, relished teaching Arabic and saw in it an

---

13. This part-time instructor was quite exceptional: he reported that he has taught Arabic for twenty-five years, seventeen at the same two-year institution. Other part-time instructors have considerably less experience.

opportunity to share knowledge of their often misunderstood culture with American students. These part-time instructors eagerly asked for advice on matters such as textbook choice and how to find teaching materials.

Four of the five program coordinators of the research universities, including the AATA member research universities, held the title of lecturer. At the two research universities (one being an AATA institutional member) where there were more than one full-time Arabic instructor, lecturers functioned as the language program coordinators—even though professorial-rank teachers of Arabic were members of the faculty. This raises the issue of power. Because the coordinators of the larger programs tend to be lecturers, they are potentially at a disadvantage since lecturers do not wield the same degree of power and influence as professorial-rank faculty. In short, when it comes to the push and shove of department or college politics, the lecturer is likely to lose; when the program coordinator is powerless, the program is bound to suffer.

The problem of the relative powerlessness of lecturers is not confined to the case of an Arabic program competing for resources with other departmental or college programs or priorities. The lecturer or junior faculty member coordinators may find some of their efforts blocked by their own Arabic-teaching colleagues of higher status. In discussions with teachers from a variety of programs, and from the ranks of both lecturer and professor, we have heard the comment that senior faculty members often dictate the content and emphasis of the lower levels of instruction. Their most frequent comment was that some senior faculty members complain that the students coming to them after two or three years of Arabic are not prepared for their courses. A typical example would be that of the senior professor who demands that students come to him prepared to read unpointed texts with full voweling.

On the other hand, senior faculty enjoy experience from which junior faculty stand to benefit. The situation of a coordinator who enjoys the full support of senior faculty is perhaps ideal: He or she can concentrate fully on providing the best learning environment possible, being free from many of the concerns which distract those of professorial rank, and at the same time not suffer from the powerlessness decried by coordinators who are not so fortunate. Problems emerge when a senior faculty member does not consider the needs of all concerned and insists on a curriculum which caters to his or her special interests, a curriculum which may not be in the best interest of the majority of students. For example, to follow up on the example cited above, we can see that if a teacher's goal for first- and second-year students is to "have access to the modern Arabic media" and "to communicate orally with native Arabic speakers" (and most teachers responding to the survey said these were their priorities), then the time invested in developing the highly specialized skill of reading a text fully voweled may not be time well spent for the majority of students, who will not proceed beyond the second year.

Of course, a program coordinator with a personal agenda could also easily make decisions which are not in the best interest of the students as a whole. This is perhaps less likely for a lecturer to do as the lecturer is generally in closer contact with lower-level students, and therefore more likely to be sensitive to their concerns and goals. On the other hand, the senior faculty member, who teaches only specialized courses in his or her field, might be less sensitive to the broad range of needs of entry-level students, since the few students who reach the intermediate or advanced level are hardly likely to be representative of the class with which they began studying Arabic. (This is an argument in favor of senior faculty at least periodically teaching introductory-level courses, or at least being closely involved with introductory-level students.) Naturally, in designing the curriculum one need not ignore the needs of those few students who will pursue advanced studies in Arabic, any more than one needs to ignore the vast majority of students who will take only one or two years. Students can only hope that those in positions of responsibility will design the curriculum in such a way that neither type of student is slighted.

In larger programs, differing priorities might be accomplished through separate tracks. For most programs, however, this is not practical—nor necessarily desirable. An alternative approach to addressing priorities which differ according to level might be to provide a special mini-course for students who plan to continue on into courses taught by traditionally-minded professors (those who, among other things, feel strongly that students should be able to read a text with full vowelling). In such a course, students would concentrate, for example, on developing the special skill of reading a text fully voweled, as well as on other skills not necessarily crucial to general reading and speaking ability. This is not to say that first- and second-year students should know nothing of these specialized skills, but priority would not necessarily be placed on the active ability to perform these tasks. Some have expressed concern that failing to stress such skills early in a student's contact with Arabic will result in "abominably fluent" students or "terminal 2's" (students whose output is agrammatical speech and writing). To be sure, the profession is in need of solid research to determine whether there is reason to fear such an outcome if the active mastery of some skills whose functional load is not so great (such as voweling) are not stressed until the third or fourth year of study. On the other hand, it might be that a pragmatic approach would encourage more first- and second-year students to pursue Arabic further, resulting in the end in increased numbers of students—as compared to present levels—eventually learning the kinds of skills that initially might have dissuaded them from pursuing Arabic.

Naturally, an institution's program cannot be all things to all people. While instructors can tailor their programs somewhat to help individuals realize their personal goals, their students must realize there is only so much they can do. Instructors need to be honest about what they can reasonably provide. Just as teachers should understand their students' needs and goals, students, too, should clearly understand what they can expect of a program and how well that program will help them in achieving their goals. Instructors need to be candid about their goals and priorities in order that students understand precisely what is expected of them so that they can make informed decisions.

Table 5 indicates that 75% of non-student instructors have participated in seminars on the theory and practice of teaching Arabic or some foreign language. Most instructors also reported that they regularly read books or journal articles on foreign language teaching methodology or language acquisition research. In no case did an instructor, student or otherwise, reply in the negative to both of these items. In other words, all instructors in the survey reported that they had either had TAFL, other FL or ESL teacher training, or they regularly read books or journal articles in the field. Most answered affirmative to both questions. Student instructors (largely found at comprehensive and two-year institutions) were most likely to answer no to one of these questions, and usually to the question about training. Table 5 also shows that approximately the same number of people who have some kind of training are also members of AATA. In fact, every AATA member in the survey indicated that they have participated in some kind of training (and many have taken related coursework). Two AATA members, however, replied that they do not regularly read books or journal articles in the field.

In table 5 we see that 75% of the non-student instructors also indicated that they are active in developing materials for their Arabic courses (supplementary reading exercises, computer programs, drills, etc.). Of these instructors, however, only one-third indicated that they seek to coordinate their efforts with others in the field. This suggests duplicated effort—that few are taking full advantage of what others are doing. Those who responded that they were active in materials development were asked whether these efforts were rewarded, in terms of promotion or tenure decisions. Only one instructor—at a doctoral-granting institution—responded that his materials development efforts were

Table 5.

Arabic teachers' (excluding student instructors) training and involvement in the field

Institution type	FL training yes	FL training no	AATA member yes	AATA member no	Materials develop-ment yes	Materials develop-ment no	If develops materials, then coordinates with others yes	If develops materials, then coordinates with others no
Research	4	1	4	1	4	1	2	2
Research/AATA	4	0	4	0	3	1	1	2
Doctorate-Granting	2	0	1	1	1	1	0	1
Comprehensive	-	-	-	-	-	-	-	-
Liberal Arts	1	1	1	1	1	1	0	1
Two-Year	-	-	-	-	-	-	-	-
Specialized	1	2	1	2	3	0	1	2
Total:	12	4	11	5	12	4	4	8

rewarded; on the other hand, an instructor at a research university went so far as to say that his efforts were punished.

Table 5 indicates that teachers at larger institutions are far more likely to be AATA members than those elsewhere.[14] As for part-time teachers (not included in table 5), only one of nine was a member of AATA. Five of these eight non-AATA members were not acquainted with AATA, including one graduate student who taught at a research/AATA university with three faculty members who were all AATA members. A number of these part-time instructors expressed enthusiastic interest in AATA. Apparently, there is a segment of the Arabic teaching population that, given the opportunity, would like to participate but are not aware of the option. This group consists largely of individuals at smaller institutions who have little training or experience; these marginal members of the field would probably benefit a great deal from a closer association with others in the field through membership in AATA.

4. Texts and Materials

Elementary Modern Standard Arabic (EMSA) (Abboud, McCarus et al. 1983) is by far the most widely used textbook for the first two years of instruc-

---

14. The liberal arts college professor who was not an AATA member at the time of the survey was a member as recently as 1989. All of the full-time instructors had at least heard of AATA. A professor at a specialized institution mentioned that he felt he should be a member.

tion.[15] Although respondents were not specifically asked, a number mentioned that they supplement this textbook with materials developed by the Middlebury College School of Arabic group. *Modern Arabic, Book 1: An introductory course for foreign students* (Attar 1988) was the only other textbook mentioned more than once. As for those textbooks mentioned only once, one research university in the sample used *Ahlan wa sahlan* (Alosh 1989) and another uses *From the Gulf to the Ocean* (Hardane et al. 1979). *Conversations in Modern Standard Arabic* (Baccouche and Azmi 1984) was used at one of the liberal arts colleges. In the "specialized" category, one institution used *Formal Spoken Arabic* (Ryding 1990); another used the Qur'an as a text in conjunction with *EMSA*. One AATA/ research university used *Let's Learn Arabic, Part 2* (Allen and Allouche 1986) for second year.

To give an accurate picture of the situation, we stress that this survey provides a snapshot of Arabic programs at one moment in time, as it were. For most aspects of the programs involved this poses no real problem; that is, there is enough stability over time that the survey gives an accurate overall view of the nature of the people and programs involved. In our opinion, this is not the case with textbook choice. In discussing the matter of textbooks, teachers—at all levels—talked again and again about their uncertainties as to what textbook to use. *EMSA* is, and has been for some time, the most widely used text. What this survey does not readily reveal is the widespread searching evident in the field. We are personally aware that programs in the sample (research universities) have changed textbooks a number of times in the past few years. The

Table 6.

Textbooks used in the first two years of instruction

Institution type	EMSA	Modern Arabic	Other
Research Universities	2	0	2
Research Universities/AATA	1	1	0
Doctorate-Granting Universities	2	0	0
Comprehensive Universities & Colleges	2	0	0
Liberal Arts Colleges	0	1	1
Two-Year Colleges and Institutions	2	0	0
Specialized Institutions	2	0	2
Total:	11	2	5

15. The NASILP Arabic program is based on *EMSA*; the first ten chapters have been rewritten especially for a self-instructional context.

coordinator of one program switched from *EMSA* to a second textbook six years ago; two years ago he switched to a third textbook. In the first year of using this third textbook he found that it does not provide sufficient grammatical explanations, so he now requires students to purchase a pedagogical grammar to supplement it. This example is not uncommon; coordinators at other research universities have had similar experiences. If we had conducted this survey just two years ago we would have found a different set of textbooks being used (though *EMSA* would still have been the most commonly used textbook). If we were to administer this survey in two years, we suspect the landscape would again be different. Most of the "other" textbooks being used at the present have either recently been published—or they are being circulated in pre-publication form. Clark and Johnson reported that *EMSA* was the overwhelming favorite (15/20) in 1982; none of the other four beginning textbooks mentioned then were mentioned by respondents to this survey (1982:J-12). Other textbooks are currently in preparation and are eagerly awaited by some; their arrival will probably change the scene again. New textbooks tend to reflect the transition to a more functional approach.

EMSA was also the most frequently named third-year textbook (mentioned three times), followed closely by its sequel, *Modern Standard Arabic: Intermediate level* (Abboud et al. 1971). The institutions mentioned as using *Formal Spoken Arabic* (Ryding 1990) and *From the Gulf to the Ocean* (Hardane et al. 1979) use them through third year. One specialized institution uses عربية وسائل الأعلام [*Arabic of the Media*] (Al-Tonsi and Al-Warraki 1979) for its third-year text. A number of teachers mentioned supplementing their first- and second-year textbooks with authentic materials (unedited materials originally meant for native consumption, e.g., advertisements in magazines, recordings of news broadcasts, menus from restaurants, train schedules, newspapers, and novels). The tendency to use increasingly more authentic materials builds through third year to the point that these are the only materials mentioned for fourth year.

Toward the end of the survey we asked, "What do you see as the most pressing need facing the Arabic language teaching profession?" At least half of the respondents' replies can be clearly interpreted as requests for more and/or better materials. One of the most common responses (7) was "improved textbooks." In response to questions about teaching materials, four more instructors mentioned the need for better textbooks. Some suggested revising and updating current texts. One person called for high quality "proficiency" textbooks with color pictures (such as those used in French, German, and Spanish). The desire for a better textbook is almost universal, and perhaps more so among teachers of less commonly taught languages. Clark and Johnson's survey of instructors of uncommonly taught languages included the question: "What is the *greatest current need* that you have with regard to suitable and effective instructional materials *for this course?*" For beginning courses, "textbook" was the most common answer for all of the less commonly taught languages except one (44% of Arabic instructors, 46% of Chinese, 40% of Japanese, 29% of Russian...) (1982:32).

Some teachers may see in a better textbook a panacea for all their pedagogical problems. No textbook is likely to deliver everything teachers would wish. Only a third of full-time instructors (5/15) called for improved textbooks as compared to two-thirds of the part-time instructors (6/9); this may indicate that experience tempers the tendency to see a new textbook as the final solution. In the 1987 survey, 4% of the students suggested that their textbooks needed to be improved; a far higher priority for students (23%) was "more speaking in class" (Belnap 1987:36). In no way do we intend to suggest that there is not a great deal of room for improvement, only that the temptation to blame the textbook is great and that other areas may be in equal or greater need of attention.

Six teachers (all full-time) mentioned computer programs for teaching Arabic among their greatest needs in the area of materials. One suggested that more software is needed for advanced levels; two others called for "more software for all levels." One instructor at a liberal arts college specifically asked for software for the Apple IIe computer. The fact that part-time instructors did not mention software among their material needs probably stems in part from their ignorance of what is available; availability of computer labs may also play a factor. The part-time instructors in our sample were largely at smaller institutions. Two institutions reported that they did not even have a language lab; both are smaller schools (a two-year college and a specialized institution). Only large universities reported actually having computer programs available to help students learn Arabic (both "AATA/research," two of the four "research," and one of the three "specialized" institutions).

The same caveat applies to computer programs as textbooks: some seem to feel that computer-assisted language learning (CALL) can solve all their problems. Long experience with "high tech" developments in language teaching (beginning with the language lab of the sixties) suggests caution. Without reservation or critical examination, many otherwise intelligent souls wholeheartedly embrace new technological developments as the promised messiah. "Multimedia" is often nothing more than flash without substance; "high tech" can be synonymous with an outlandishly expensive and short-lived fad. CALL is not likely to be the final answer; however, it has the potential of being a powerful tool.[16] Hardware and software developments are making the storage of high quality audio and video more practical. Near instantaneous access to such materials greatly enhances interactive educational materials. However, the total cost of such learning aids can be prohibitive. Financially strapped institutions balk at providing the necessary hardware for a computer lab of reasonable size. Often ignored are the far greater costs—in both time and money—of software development. As a result, high quality programs with more than limited application are rare.

One teacher at a specialized institution summed up the situation by saying that the profession "needs a good basic course integrated for all basic skills, more computer programs, and a variety of integrated materials for all levels, especially at the intermediate level." The idea of better integration of materials was voiced by more than one experienced teacher. This, of course, is a task far beyond the abilities of an individual. Those who suggested better integration of materials into the curriculum recognized this and called for increased cooperation between teachers.

Seven respondents named audio-visual materials among their greatest needs. Six of these mentioned specifically the need for video tapes; three mentioned the need for audio tapes or for better tapes. Five of the seven who mentioned audio-visual materials were part-time teachers; this suggests that smaller programs lack even the basic resources available at larger schools.[17] Of course, every program, regardless of size, would benefit from increased availability of high quality audio and video materials. Such materials have the advantage that the necessary equipment to use them—at least in the classroom—is probably available at every institution.

---

16. Unfortunately, infatuation with dazzling new technologies leads language teachers-turned-computer enthusiasts to set aside their better pedagogical sense and use the computer for its sake, because it *can* be used, and not necessarily because it is advantageous to use. Just because something can be done with a computer does not mean it should be done. Too often, CALL programs are expensive page turners. Pages are best left in books where they are easier to read. The ideal is to capitalize on the strengths of the computer (or any technology or method) in a way that is most beneficial to students and teachers.

17. This was confirmed in our discussions with teachers at smaller institutions. Many of them asked us about materials others use. When they realized what was available, many desperately wanted to obtain such materials.

5. Teacher and Student Priorities

Respondents were asked to rank the language sub-skills of listening, speaking, reading, and writing according to their priority for first- and second-year students. Some respondents said they preferred not to rank them but rather to rate them (that is, for example, instead of assigning only one skill a "3," all or none of the skills could be assigned this rating); as a result, instead of ranking these skills they rated them on a four-point scale. For example, four respondents (three full-time and one part-time) chose a rating of "1" for all four skills and others ranked or rated two of the skills as a "1" and the other two skills as a "2" (this accounts for the uneven distribution in table 7). One respondent declined to rank the skills at all, saying he was not comfortable doing so. Table 7 indicates that the instructors consider the reading, listening, and speaking skills most important and the writing skill considerably less so for students at the beginning levels.

In our 1987 survey, students were also asked to rank the four sub-skills according to their relative importance for them. Their responses are reproduced here as table 8. A direct comparison between tables 7 and 8 is not possible because a greater proportion of the students followed the written instructions on the survey to rank the skills in order of importance (rather than to rate them); like the one teacher mentioned above, some students did not respond to this item at all. Nevertheless, tables 7 and 8 do give us some idea of teacher and student priorities. Students ranked speaking and reading highest but listening was also a clear priority, with a third of the students ranking it second. Writing, on the other hand, was not a high priority for the students as a whole: nearly half of the them ranked it fourth.

Full-time and part-time instructors essentially agreed in their priorities— with the exception that the part-time instructors rated writing much lower than did the full-time faculty. Only part-time instructors gave a "4" rating to the

Table 7.

Instructors' assessment of the importance of the four sub-skills for first- and second-year students.

Importance	Listening	Speaking	Reading	Writing
1	13	13	14	7
2	7	5	6	7
3	3	3	2	4
4	0	2	1	5

Table 8.

Students' assessment of the importance of the four sub-skills (Belnap 1987:34).
Total N=568.

Importance	Listening	Speaking	Reading	Writing
1	12.7%	31.0%	30.1%	4.4%
	(72)	(176)	(171)	(25)
2	31.2%	17.6%	15.3%	16.0%
	(177)	(100)	(87)	(91)
3	18.1%	16.7%	28.5%	14.4%
	(103)	(95)	(162)	(82)
4	16.4%	12.7%	5.5%	44.0%
	(93)	(72)	(31)	(250)

writing skill. This correlates with the students in the 1987 survey who also ranked writing as a low priority. Part-time instructors, who are mostly students themselves, apparently are more in tune with their students' priorities (and sympathize with them) than are the full-time instructors.

Not every student or teacher, of course, ranked speaking and reading as their highest priorities and writing as a lower priority. For example, one professor who teaches classes on the Qur'an at a specialized institution ranked reading as his first priority, then writing, then listening, then speaking. Clearly, one's purpose in teaching Arabic will figure significantly into one's priorities.

5.1 Instructors' Priorities for Reasons to Study Arabic

Teachers were asked to rate as high, medium, or low priority four different reasons for studying Arabic, according to their "personal goals in teaching Arabic to first- and second-year students." Table 9 displays their responses. "To communicate orally with native Arabic speakers" received the highest rating, followed by "to have access to the Arabic media." "To read modern Arabic

Table 9.

Instructors' priorities in teaching Arabic to first- and second-year students

Priority rating	Read modern literature	Read medieval texts	Access to the modern media	Communicate orally with Arabs
High	11	2	15	19
Medium	7	4	4	2
Low	3	18	2	2

Table 10.

Students' 1987 ranking of reasons for taking Arabic

	Ranked among top three		Total times chosen	
	%	N	%	N
Literature & culture	36.8	209	56.3	320
Want to travel/live in Middle East	36.6	208	57.0	324
To talk to Arabs	29.2	166	51.1	290
Research: original sources	20.2	115	34.9	198
Like languages	19.2	109	44.7	254
To read Qur'an/religious texts	16.7	95	29.8	169
General education requirement	14.3	81	25.4	144
Have Arab friends	12.7	72	25.4	144
For fun	12.0	68	23.4	133
To prepare for a career	8.8	50	19.9	113
Heritage	8.1	46	14.4	82
Linguistic research	2.3	13	7.0	40

literature" also received high ratings. "To read medieval texts" was a low priority for most. One part-time instructor at a comprehensive university and a full professor at a specialized institution rated "to read medieval texts" as low and medium, respectively, but said that reading the Qur'an was a high priority.

In the 1987 survey, students were asked "Why did you start to study Arabic?" They were presented with a list of possible reasons, as well as the possibility of adding their own. They were asked to rate them in order of importance. Table 10 presents the results (Table 6 from Belnap 1987:33).

Direct comparison of tables 9 and 10 is not possible because the responses were gathered using different techniques. However, there is clear agreement among students and instructors that most students are learning Arabic to function in the modern Arab world. Unfortunately, the list of options presented to students in the 1987 survey was not worded as specifically as that presented to the instructors in this survey; in the 1987 survey there was no option directly addressing the importance of gaining "access to the modern media."

5.2 Attitudes on the Importance of Studying a Dialect

Students in the 1987 survey were asked, "How important is a colloquial Arabic dialect to your future plans involving the Arabic language?" Instructors were asked how important it was to them that beginning students study a colloquial variety of Arabic (when asked, "beginning" was defined as first- and second-year Arabic students). Both groups' preferences are given in table 11. Once again, the results obtained from the two surveys are not directly comparable: In this case, the two groups responded to different questions. If we bear this in mind, the results can nevertheless be useful for comparison. Approximately half of the students and teachers felt positively about studying a colloquial. At first glance, it appears that the students feel more strongly about this than the teachers. However, we must not forget that the instructors were asked if studying a colloquial variety is desirable for beginning students. Many, if not most, of those who did not reply favorably to this question do feel students should study a colloquial; however, they prefer that a student wait some time before beginning with colloquial Arabic. For example, one who responded with "undesirable," a teaching assistant in a large program at a research university, felt that "Middle Arabic"—which he defined as "simplified *fuṣḥā*"—should be the language spoken in the classroom during the first two years of instruction and that colloquial instruction should wait until the third year. Later in the survey, however, when asked about his priorities in teaching Arabic to first- and second-year students, he responded that using Middle Arabic for oral communication—a high priority for him—"sounds funny" and that the learner needs to "switch to dialect."

Somewhat more than half of the instructors felt that *fuṣḥā* (this category includes the responses MSA, Modern Standard Arabic, Classical, and Literary

Table 11.

Importance of a dialect for students and instructors

Importance	Students (1987)	Importance	Instructors (1992)
very important 1	30% (159)	very desirable	20.8% (5)
2	18.7% (106)	desirable	29.2% (7)
3	19% (108)	does not matter	25% (6)
4	6.7% (38)	undesirable	12.5% (3)
unimportant 5	8.1% (46)	very undesirable	8.3% (2)
no response	19.4% (110)	no response/ "depends"	4.2% (1)

Table 12.

Variety first- and second-year students should be taught to speak

Preferred variety of Arabic	Part-time teachers	Full-time teachers
fuṣḥā (MSA, Classical, Literary)	7	6
Formal Spoken Arabic	1	4
Educated Spoken Arabic	0	1
Colloquial and more formal variety	0	2
Colloquial variety	1	2

Arabic) should be the variety students are taught to speak in the first two years of instruction (see table 12). Others preferred a "hybrid" or intermediate variety such as Formal Spoken Arabic or Educated Spoken Arabic. There did not seem to be a clear concept of what these varieties are in the minds of at least some of the respondents: some apparently see them closer to *fuṣḥā,* while others see them closer to colloquial.[18] For example, one professor at a research institution was careful to define FSA as "not *fuṣḥa,* elevated colloquial." On the other hand, some not likely to be familiar with the term probably felt it to be a conversational *fuṣḥā.* A few felt that students should be using colloquial, or colloquial along with some more formal variety.

We note again in table 12 a marked difference between the full-time and part-time instructors. Part-time instructors strongly preferred *fuṣḥā,* while the majority of full-time instructors preferred something else. We suspect ideological factors figure heavily in these preferences. (See Milroy and Milroy 1991 for a detailed discussion of the ideology of standard languages.) Nearly every speaker of Arabic, native or non-native, is socialized into accepting the notion of the supremacy of *fuṣḥā.* Having grown up in a culture that officially recognizes *fuṣḥā* as the only legitimate variety of Arabic, native speakers tend to feel this way more than non-natives.[19] With one exception, the part-time instructors, who strongly preferred *fuṣḥā,* were native speakers. Moreover, they, being largely students, are younger. They also have less experience teaching Arabic. Those at smaller institutions come from fields not typically associated with language

---

18. This should come as no surprise, as the same confusion can be seen even in the literature on Educated Spoken Arabic. Mitchell subdivides ESA into two types, formal and informal, one closer to *fuṣḥā* and one closer to the vernacular (1986:17). Others, however, have not been so precise.

19. In zeal for traditional values and attitudes of the target language culture, some nonnatives do become more native than the natives, so to speak.

study (electrical engineering, math, dentistry, and computer science). As a result of these factors, they have less experience in critically examining their language and their attitudes toward it and are consequently more likely to reflect traditional prejudices against the vernacular. This, of course, is a tendency and not a natural law. One part-time native speaker instructor at a community college felt that it would be "very desirable" to introduce colloquial in the first year of instruction and that it should be the variety students are taught to speak.

The three part-time, native speaker instructors at larger institutions (research universities, two of which were AATA institutional members) also preferred *fuṣḥā*. These students reported their fields of specialization as Arabic literature, Arabic linguistics, and Arabic language and literature. (The Arabic linguistics student was the student who felt that beginning students should be taught to speak Middle Arabic, a "simplified *fuṣḥā*.") The preferences of these student instructors may have been influenced in part by the attitudes of the Arabic coordinators who were their supervisors. Two of these coordinators preferred *fuṣḥā* and felt that studying colloquial in the first two years was "undesirable" or "very undesirable." One coordinator preferred Formal Spoken Arabic and chose "doesn't matter" concerning the importance of studying colloquial during the first two years (he felt colloquial study should begin in the third year).

The one part-time instructor who taught at a medium-sized institution (doctorate-granting) felt that Modern Standard Arabic should be the variety first- and second-year students are taught to speak. However, only moments before, he had mentioned that the study of colloquial was "desirable" and should begin in the first year. His and others' responses can be seen as inconsistent. Contradictions between language attitudes and actual usage abound in speech communities across the world. We should not be surprised to find inconsistencies in instructors' replies as they attempt to consider their students' needs from a practical perspective and try to reconcile these with deeply ingrained prescriptive attitudes.

Few, if any, of the teachers surveyed believed that students should never learn to speak a colloquial variety of Arabic. Timing is the issue. For the professional student this is not a problem, but for most students time is a major concern. Less than 20% of all Arabic students continue beyond the second year. In light of the instructor preferences shown in table 12, this means that over half of the students who take Arabic and do not continue beyond the second year of instruction will not be exposed to a variety of spoken Arabic in the classroom. However, students and teachers alike clearly indicated that their highest priority for first- and second-year students is to learn to "communicate orally with native Arabic speakers."[20] Table 11 further indicates that far more students and teachers feel positively about the importance of studying a colloquial than negatively. Nevertheless, most students' primary purpose in studying Arabic—and their instructors' expressed primary purpose in teaching Arabic—appears to be only marginally addressed. In spite of the claim that conversation is a high priority, few beginning Arabic students are taught normal conversational Arabic.[21] Perhaps instructors should ask themselves how students would react if they were told this at the beginning of their first Arabic class.

Proponents of teaching beginning students to speak *fuṣḥā* argue that doing so is actually in the students' best interest. Reasons commonly cited include one or more of the following: 1) teaching students to speak a dialect first—or at the same time they are learning *fuṣḥā*—will only confuse them; 2) as there are so many dialects, it is difficult to settle on which dialect to teach; as a result, learning *fuṣḥā* is preferable since it (many say) is the origin of the modern dialects and it is therefore easier to learn any given dialect knowing *fuṣḥā* than it is to move from one dialect to another; 3) *fuṣḥā* is the only variety worthy of study. Teaching beginners to speak *fuṣḥā* may, in fact, be in students' best interest. However, evidence cited in support of this approach continues to be anecdotal. Which approach is best—for a given set of goals—is an empirical question and one that will require a good deal of research, research that should not be postponed.[22] Tradition notwithstanding, the burden of proof is upon those

---

20. In fact, all twelve instructors who stated that *fuṣḥā* is the language beginning students should be taught to speak also rated "to communicate orally with native Arabic speakers" as a "high" priority for these students.

21. Fifty-four percent (320/588) of the students in the sample were studying Arabic at institutions where instructors insisted that *fuṣḥā* be the language of classroom conversation for first- and second-year students. Twenty-three percent (132) of the students are at institutions where instructors prefer ESA or FSA; the remainder—also 23% (137)—are at institutions where the instructors favor a colloquial variety. Given the confusion about the terms Educated Spoken Arabic and Formal Spoken Arabic, many of these students at institutions in this category may not actually be exposed to a variety similar to natural conversational speech. We also question whether all of those at institutions claiming that colloquial, ESA, or FSA should be the language of instruction actually do teach a variety close to vernacular speech. In other words, when asked about the option, respondents may have thought it a good idea but their responses do not necessarily reflect practice (as we have seen, practice and attitudes may be quite different). Unfortunately, the survey was not constructed to explore this issue further.

22. Immediately after one coordinator told us she did not find AATA useful, she expressed her frustration at the lack of second language acquisition research pursued in the field. She feels AATA should do more to encourage more and better quality research bearing on teaching Arabic as a second language.

who argue that an indirect approach (teaching beginners to converse in *fuṣḥā*) is preferable to a direct approach (teaching students to converse in the same manner Arabs converse).

One experienced Arabic teacher and national figure in the profession stated that "the most pressing need facing the Arabic language teaching profession" is to develop a strategy to solve the problems arising from "multi-glossia." Hot debate continues to characterize this topic. Instructors' and students' interests will be served best by constructive debate. Whatever the outcome of this particular issue (if there ever is an end to the debate), the profession must focus careful attention on the beginning levels of instruction if it wants to be responsible to its clientele. In other words, while we do not want to neglect those who will pursue the study of Arabic beyond the second year, we should beware of overlooking the needs and wants of the majority of our students who will be with us only a short time.[23] This is not to suggest that student wishes should be the sole factor in determining the curriculum: learners do not necessarily know what is best for them. On the other hand, teachers have the tendency to teach as they were taught; critically examining one's teaching and one's curriculum demands openness, energy, and time. Coordinators and instructors would probably do well to re-examine their priorities and their students' priorities and consider their timetable and their students' timetable. This certainly applies to far more than the issue of which variety of Arabic first- and second-year students should be taught to speak.

6. AATA's Role

Eighty-eight percent (21/24) of the respondents felt that AATA is useful to them. When asked how AATA could better serve them, two-thirds of the coordinators and instructors provided suggestions. Four suggested that AATA should organize more conferences and workshops and that these should be more accessible. One coordinator at a research institution stressed the importance of making workshops accessible to both graduate students and teachers. Another suggested greater emphasis on culture and literature conferences and workshops; he also stressed the need for financial aid to enable more instructors to attend these meetings. Three professors felt AATA should do more to promote the study of Arabic by calling attention to its political importance and by communicating its importance and the difficulties of running an Arabic program to

---

23. Morahg (1991) contains discussion of the time/priorities problem facing teachers of Hebrew and presents excellent suggestions which could be applied to other foreign language learning contexts.

the administrations of institutions where Arabic teachers are found. Three, including one instructor who responded that AATA is not useful to her, suggested that AATA should do more to promote communication and contact between members. Another suggested it should participate more actively in the various institutions' Arabic programs.

6.1 *The Dissemination of Information*

Four of the five part-time instructors/coordinators suggested that AATA help them with their textbook and material needs. One asked specifically for materials to help teach culture. One suggested that AATA send him examples of texts and curriculum. In the course of the interview with these instructors, we were impressed that AATA could help these marginal members of the profession in a significant way. The idea of AATA as a clearing house for ideas, information, and materials has been discussed for some time. It already fills this function to some degree and is moving toward doing so even more by building a database of programs and materials. Ideally, it would be the repository of a large stock of supplementary materials, including audio and video tapes, computer programs, and various types of "authentic materials." In fact, AATA is staffed by an executive director, who must perform his AATA responsibilities in addition to the responsibilities of his full-time faculty position, and by a part-time administrative assistant. These people are quite busy with the present role of AATA (largely consisting of organizing the annual meeting, collecting dues, publishing the newsletter, and helping with the publication and distribution of the association's journal, *Al-ᶜArabiyya*). Without additional help, volunteer or paid, AATA is not likely to expand its services markedly.

One thing AATA could realistically do, which would benefit smaller programs in particular, would be to provide information on options available to instructors and coordinators. As mentioned, many of the part-time instructors had never heard of AATA, and many of them were anxious to know about the types of textbooks and other materials available. At relatively little expense, AATA could make a difference in the quality of many Arabic programs around the country merely by providing basic information on textbooks, tapes, and other materials and where to get them. A critical evaluation of materials would be especially useful to newcomers to the field. For example, in cooperation with textbook authors, AATA could coordinate the assembly of a curriculum evaluation packet. This packet might contain sample chapters from a variety of textbooks, short statements from the authors summarizing the goals and merits of their books, and an additional list of comments, pro and con, assembled from those who actually use each book. Sample curriculum outlines representing the considerable variety of programs found across the country might be included in such a packet; the names of individuals willing to serve as curriculum consultants might also be included. Such an evaluation project would be of worth to far more than the marginal members of the profession.[24]

Reaching out to such programs means reaching out to a good portion of the country's students. The results from our sample indicate that the students at two-year colleges and comprehensive colleges and universities and half of the students at doctorate-granting universities have access only to part-time instructors with little familiarity with the field. This means that nearly a quarter of the college-level Arabic students in the country are enrolled at these smaller institutions.[25] Anything AATA could do to help these programs—particularly those that are not NASILP members with self-instructional programs—would affect large numbers of students previously beyond its reach. Such efforts would help to improve the quality of their programs and possibly increase the likelihood that they would be more stable (less likely to be canceled). Stability, in turn, provides the opportunity for continued improvement.

One problem noted in the survey is the lack of coordination between programs. Lambert (1992) identifies this characteristic as one of the greatest weaknesses of foreign language education in the United States. With few exceptions, each program in the sample was essentially an island; only one program mentioned having an arrangement (informal) with another program to coordinate the transfer of students. AATA could facilitate contacts between institutions by apprising institutions in geographical proximity—or having common goals—of each other's existence. Coordinators of larger programs might not be doing only the smaller schools a service if they established a relationship with them: smaller programs, such as those at two-year colleges, could serve as feeder schools for the larger program. The coordinator of the larger program could serve as a curriculum consultant to the smaller schools; many smaller programs would no doubt welcome the opportunity to adopt a well-organized curriculum

---

24. We were surprised to find that even some long-time members of AATA did not know where to find some common texts and materials. Their inability to keep abreast of developments probably results from the time demands of their other responsibilities, such as their research agenda and committee or administrative assignments.

25. We arrive at this figure (802/3393) by calculating the number of students enrolled in Arabic classes at each type of institution listed in table 2 characterized by having only part-time instructors. Since one of the two instructors at the doctoral-granting institutions was a full-time instructor who was a member of AATA, we estimated that half of the students at such institutions are taught by part-time instructors.

which would streamline the transition of students from one program to another and thereby encourage more students to continue studying Arabic after leaving the institution where they began. AATA could help to establish these links, but the real work would be done by those with a vested interest in the success of such links.

6.2 *Encouraging Teacher Training*

A number of respondents felt that AATA should assume a more prominent role in teacher training. Most of the teacher training AATA currently conducts—if it can be called that—is done at its annual meeting. This is largely attended by teachers who are already active in the field; most AATA members already have some degree of training (see table 5). None of the four part-time teachers at the smaller institutions had formal training in teaching Arabic.[26] AATA could considerably expand the types of teachers served, and broaden its membership base, by promoting regional teacher training.[27] Again, AATA does not currently have the funding or personnel to assume much responsibility for such an undertaking; however, it could help to coordinate regional efforts. In-house training seminars for teaching assistants at larger universities could be expanded to provide training opportunities for part-time teachers from schools in the region. This could help to increase the quality of such seminars, as well as grant opportunities for wider service and recognition.

A more aggressive approach to teacher training would be to establish one or more national teacher training centers. This would require a truly massive effort. A well-organized program sponsored by a consortium of universities could probably secure federal or other funding for the first few years of operation. Such a training center might be organized somewhat on the model of Eleanor Jorden's Bryn Mawr College summer program for training native Japanese

---

26. At first glance, many might be horrified at the thought that a quarter of the country's Arabic students have only untrained teachers who are largely ignorant of available texts and materials. The situation is not as bad as that: every part-time teacher in the sample had at least something to recommend him or her as a teacher. The dentistry student who taught at a comprehensive university had some training in teaching English as a second language; the computer science graduate student, also at a comprehensive university, had participated in seminars on teaching foreign languages. At the two-year college level, one instructor had experience teaching high school, another reported that he regularly reads from the foreign language teaching literature. At the next higher level (doctorate-granting universities), both part-time instructors had two or more years of formal training in teaching foreign languages.

27. This survey leads one to wonder how representative AATA is of the Arabic teaching profession. Table 5 indicates that AATA members tend to be instructors at larger institutions. Broadening the membership base would strengthen AATA's claim to represent the profession.

speakers with no prior experience to teach Japanese as a second language. A scaled-down version of this might be held in tandem with one (or more) of the summer Arabic programs. The six coordinators who reported that they hire student instructors were asked if they would be willing to send their part-time instructors to a regional or national training seminar or workshop. All responded affirmatively but only two felt that institutional funds might be available, though probably limited. Funding students to attend such a workshop would be problematic. Jorden's teacher training program might serve as a model here, too.

As a facilitator, AATA could also help to reduce the amount of unnecessary duplication of materials development efforts. Again, ultimately, the success of this effort will depend on individuals taking the initiative to inform AATA of what projects they have completed and what they are presently working on. AATA could serve as a bulletin board. This could be done in various ways, such as through the newsletter, a central database, or an electronic bulletin board (or any combination of these). An electronic bulletin board would provide a forum for speedy interaction but, at least for some time, this approach would no doubt exclude a large segment of the population it aimed to serve.

6.3 *Encouraging the Development and Dissemination of Materials*

AATA is in the process of building a database, but at present few have responded to the survey forms sent out with the newsletter. A database is only as good as its contents. If developers do not keep AATA informed, the database will be of limited use. If it is of limited use, people are not likely to use it. If people are not likely to use it, developers are less likely to go to the trouble of contributing to it. Clearly, something needs to be done to make the database both an attractive source of information and a desirable place to cite one's work. It will be an attractive source if it actually proves to be helpful to instructors. This necessitates that it be both easy to use and convenient to gain access to the materials. It will be a desirable place to cite one's work if there are some awards attached. For some, the recognition and appreciation of their peers will be sufficient. Other developers would contribute religiously if their materials were somehow seen as contributions which could be cited, that is, that they were somehow referenced and given official recognition, not as scholarly publications but as the professional products of material developers. More colleges and universities are beginning to acknowledge such contributions as legitimate contributions worthy of consideration in the promotion and tenure decision-making process. Such an award system opens the doors for misuses, of course. A peer review board could function to assure that only quality work is recognized; in addition, this would add legitimacy to the professional nature of the endeavor. Designating AATA awards to be given annually for the best materials development projects in various categories would further encourage participation; such awards could be as simple as the designation "best public domain computer program of the year."

The newsletter already serves the function of informing the profession of major new developments in the materials area. To emphasize the potential of the database, and to encourage regular submissions and inquiries, the newsletter could feature a regular column devoted to announcing new materials which have been developed and new projects in process. This would help to ensure that the database and opportunities for cooperative work are not forgotten.

The problem of disseminating materials remains to be addressed. As mentioned, access to materials must be convenient or there will be little sharing. No developer wants to be inundated with requests for copies of materials unless the interchange is somehow profitable. Programs generally have limited budgets and AATA does not have the staff nor the facilities to presently undertake a major distribution effort which would involve preparing packets, duplicating audio and video tapes, copying computer programs—not to mention billing and mailing. The issue dealing with potential copyright violations comes to mind. On the other hand, AATA is not a large organization; further, the profession does not share a common curriculum. From a practical perspective, AATA can be seen as an umbrella for a number of groups with special concerns. Not every member in the profession is likely to want every new development. For example, those who promote the use of *fuṣḥā* in the classroom will not be interested in many of the materials developed by those promoting the use of a colloquial variety in the classroom. AATA could serve the modest but useful function of putting people with common interests in touch. AATA could help to inform instructors of who is working on what so that they can get in touch with developers themselves.

7. Conclusions

This survey of a representative cross-section of Arabic programs provides a rare bird's-eye view of Arabic language teaching at institutions of higher learning in the United States. The results indicate where we are as a profession and underline a number of important issues the profession needs to address in order to move forward. Three areas stand out in particular: the needs of programs at smaller institutions, the need for increased cooperation between teachers and between programs, and the importance of the first two years of instruction.

The results of this survey suggest numerous ways the field could improve. Some things can be done easily, others not so easily. Reaching out to smaller institutions—which up to the present have basically been ignored—is one step that would not require a great deal of time or resources. It is a step that could immediately affect a considerable segment of the profession and, therefore, a large number of students. All of the respondents in the survey from these smaller institutions were anxious to have increased contact with others in the field. Some asked how they could join AATA. These instructors were particularly concerned to learn more about the textbooks and materials that are available. Providing even the most basic information would be a real service to many of them.

Reaching out to these programs can be seen as one step toward increased contact and cooperation between teachers and between programs. Individual programs stand to benefit a great deal from increased communication between members of the field. Such contact could result in increased efficiency, in that there would be less duplication of effort in materials and curriculum development. Increased sharing of ideas, such as methods for teaching particular concepts, would also improve the quality of programs. These are not the only advantages, however; increased contact helps to avoid stagnation and the perception of isolation (a feeling common to many instructors since they are the only Arabic instructor at their institution). Some segments of the teaching profession are in constant contact but we suspect that this is exceptional. (Table 5 indicates that only a third of those active in materials development coordinate their efforts with others.) Both the degree and frequency of contact could be greatly increased.

The high rate of student attrition is cause for concern. High attrition is typical of foreign language programs in general, but taken in consideration with other factors it is of greater concern to teachers of Arabic (and probably teachers of other "truly foreign languages"). Arabic takes longer to learn than French, German, or Spanish. All else being equal, Arabic students will not attain the same degree of proficiency after two years as they would have if they had been studying Spanish. In spite of this, they are not likely to study Arabic longer. This places a greater burden on Arabic instructors and coordinators to determine what is in the students' best interest to learn, given that 80% of them will not proceed beyond the second year. Both students and instructors have indicated that communicating orally with Arabs is their highest priority in learning or teaching Arabic. However, more than half of the instructors surveyed prefer to teach their first- and second-year students to speak a variety of Arabic which is rarely used by Arabs for conversational purposes. This particular example is only one of many concerns. If instructors are serious about considering the needs and wishes of their students, they would do well to re-examine what they do during the first two years of instruction. In spite of the apparent contradictions, present practices may turn out to be in the students' best interests—as some have argued; however, this should be verified through careful research and testing. In any case, those who set the curriculum need to bear in mind student and teacher priorities and the facts of enrollment trends.

Finally, the survey highlights the variety found in the field. Instructors ranged from part-time student instructors with little training or experience to lecturers and professors with over twenty years' experience. While the majority agreed that learning to converse with Arabs and to read modern Arabic is their primary goal, there were others teaching Arabic for special purposes. The survey makes clear that the profession is not likely to settle on a common curriculum. An attempt to do so would tear AATA apart. In fact, a common curriculum would be a mistake in light of the varied goals and abilities of members of the profession. There is more than one way to teach Arabic and more than one set of legitimate goals. Members of the profession can be united in their commitment to teaching Arabic and in acknowledging that there are many reasons students learn Arabic and no one right way to address all of those goals. Although the profession as a whole will probably never settle on a common curriculum, this must not prevent those with common interests from working together to develop high quality programs and materials. As long as it takes place in the spirit of mutual respect, open dialogue, and cooperation between those sharing common interests and philosophies—and between those who differ—it will go far towards realizing the improvements yearned for by dedicated teachers and students of Arabic.

APPENDIX

AATA Telephone Survey of Arabic Language Teachers
(Coordinator's Form)

This is (name) from the American Association of Teachers of Arabic (AATA). We are conducting a telephone survey of Arabic language teachers in institutions of higher learning in the United States. We would appreciate your participation in our survey; your individual responses will be held in strict confidentiality. That is, we will not, under any circumstances, release your name and your responses without your prior consent. The results of the survey will give us a clearer picture of the nature of the Arabic language teaching profession. This, in turn, will help us know what needs and strengths there are so that we can more effectively serve the profession at large. This information will help us, for example, in our fundraising efforts. The survey will take approximately twenty minutes of your time. May we begin the survey now? (If not: When can I call back?)

Name of institution: _____

Instit. type: AATA/Research/Doctorate/Comp./Two-yr/Liberal Arts/Religious/Special

Name of teacher: _____   Phone Number: _____

               male / female   Best time to call: _____

Questions for designated program coordinator (person in charge of Arabic language instruction):

How many levels (years) of Arabic do you offer? _____

How many students are currently enrolled in the following levels? (estimate if need to)

        1st year _____

        2nd year _____

        3rd year _____

        4th year _____

Do you offer an undergraduate major in Arabic? yes / no

Do you offer an undergraduate minor in Arabic? yes / no

Do you offer a graduate degree in Arabic? yes / no

    If so, what is the highest degree offered? Certificate / M.A. / Ph.D. / other

What department is Arabic language instruction housed in: _____

Are your students mostly: undergraduates or graduates (other: _____)

Approximately what proportion are undergraduate:

      no undergraduates 1/4 1/2 3/4 all undergraduates

Is there a sizable expatriate Arab community in your area? yes / no

Is there a sizable Muslim community in your area? yes / no

In your first- and second-year courses, approximately what percentage of your

      students are: Ethnic Arabs? _____

                    Muslims? _____

Do some of your students who have completed their Arabic studies at your institution

      pursue Arabic elsewhere each year? yes / no

      If yes, where do they go? locally available / transfer to other school /

            summer programs / study abroad / other _____

For 2-year programs: Do you have a formal agreement with another institution for

      your students who want to pursue Arabic studies beyond your program? yes / no

      If yes, what? _____

Do you encourage your students to go to summer programs? yes / no

Does (*name of institution*) have a federally funded Middle East Center? yes / no

Do you have other external funding for Arabic language study? yes / no

      From what source?_____

Would you find it helpful to you and your program if the American Association of

Teachers of Arabic (AATA) offered sample curriculum outlines and suggestions? yes/no

      In what other ways could AATA be of service to you and your program?

_____

_____

Do you regularly employ student instructors? yes / no

      If yes: Do student instructors participate in an organized in-house training

            seminar on teaching a foreign language?

      If yes: Would you be willing to send your student instructors to a regional or

            national training seminar or workshop? yes / no

      Are funds available at your institution for such training? yes / no

Have you made institutional decisions about curriculum and textbooks for the first

      three years of Arabic instruction, or do you leave it to the teachers to decide?

      institutional decision / teacher decision

      If institutional decision, what textbooks have you decided on:

      1st year: EMSA / Allen & Allouche / Alosh / Badawi / Saudi / other _____

      2nd year: EMSA / Allen & Allouche / Alosh / Badawi / Saudi / other _____

      3rd year: EMSA / IMSA / Allen & Allouche / Alosh / Badawi / Ziadeh / other _____

Is a language lab available at (*name of institution*)? yes / no

Questions for each Arabic instructor:

How many years have you been teaching Arabic _____

What is your major field or discipline: literature / linguistics / language teaching /
    social science or area studies / other: _____

Within this field or discipline, is your primary area of interest in Arabic? yes / no

Is your position at (*name of institution*) full-time? yes / no

    If yes: Is it tenure-track? yes / no

        If yes: Are you tenured? yes / no

What is your official appointment or professional rank: teaching assistant / graduate
    assistant / student instructor / adjunct instructor / lecturer / assistant prof. / assoc.
        prof. / full prof. / other: _____

What is the highest degree (or equivalent) you hold? High School / A.A. / A.S. /
    B.A. / B.S. / M.A. / M.S. / Ph.D. / D. Ed. other _____

How many years have you been at (*name of institution*)? ____

Were you hired primarily to teach Arabic or was teaching Arabic a secondary
    consideration? Arabic / other

What textbook(s) do you use and at what level?

    1st year: EMSA / Allen & Allouche / Alosh / Badawi / Saudi / other _____

    2nd year: EMSA / Allen & Allouche / Alosh / Badawi / Saudi / other _____

    3rd year: EMSA / IMSA / Allen & Allouche / Alosh / Badawi / Ziadeh /
        other ____

    4th year: IMSA / Allen & Allouche / Badawi / Ziadeh / no textbook (lit.,
        newspaper...) / other text: _____

    other: level _____ : textbook(s): _____

    other: level _____ : textbook(s): _____

Other than the materials presented in the textbook, do you provide special materials
    for teaching Arab culture? yes / no

Are Arabic videos available to students? yes / no

Are computer programs for learning Arabic available? yes / no

Do you feel you have adequate materials? yes / no

What do you feel is your greatest need in this area (materials)?

    printed materials / audio tapes / videos / computer programs / other:

_____

Which skills do you consider more important for your first- and second-year students?
    Please rank the listening, speaking, reading, and writing skills in order of
    importance (1 being most important and 4 least). If two or more are of equal
    importance you may rank them equally.

        listening _____

        speaking _____

reading _____

writing _____

What Arabic language extra-curricular activities do you provide your students?

videos / lectures / socials / conversation hour / other _____

How important is it to you that beginning students study a colloquial dialect of Arabic:

very undesirable / undesirable / doesn't matter / desirable / very desirable

If in favor of dialect study or doesn't matter: In your opinion, at what level should

students begin studying a colloquial?

1st year / 2nd year / 3rd year / 4th year / other: _____

Which colloquial dialect would you prefer your students study: Levantine / Egyptian /

North African / Gulf / Iraqi / (other: _____)

What variety of Arabic do you think students should be taught to speak in the first two

years of instruction? *Fuṣḥā* / Formal Spoken Arabic / a colloquial / other: _____

Are you a native speaker of Arabic? (Is Arabic your first language?) yes / no

If yes: What is your native dialect: Syrian / Lebanese / Palestinian / Jordanian / Su-

danese / Egyptian / Libyan / Tunisian / Moroccan / Algerian / Iraqi / other: _____

If no: Are you a native speaker of English? yes / no

If no: What is your native language? _____

These questions are for non-native speakers of Arabic:

What dialect(s) of Arabic do you speak? _____

How did you learn this dialect (these dialects)? _____

_____

In total, how many years have you lived in an Arabic-speaking country? _____

How many years has it been since you were last in an Arabic-speaking country? ____

How long do you expect it will be until the next time you go? _____

Are you familiar with the 0-5 scale used by Foreign Service Institute? yes / no

If yes: Have you ever been rated by an official FSI or ACTFL examiner?

What rating were you given for speaking? 0 0+ 1 1+ 2 2+ 3 3+ 4 4+ 5

OR: novice low / novice mid / novice high / intermediate low / intermediate

mid / intermediate high / advanced / advanced plus / superior

Would you say that this rating accurately reflects your present abilities? yes / no

In which broad ranges would you place your current command of Arabic? (0-5, incl.

plus or ACTFL ratings) (Provide explanation of 0-5 rating scale if unfamiliar

with the scale.)

speaking _____

listening _____

reading _____

writing _____

Resume questioning natives (as well as non-native speakers) here:

Have you had formal training in the theory and practice of teaching a foreign
  language? yes / no

   If yes: How many semesters? _____

Have you participated in seminars on the theory and practice of teaching a foreign
  language? yes / no

Do you regularly read books or journal articles on foreign language teaching methodology or language acquisition research? yes / no

Are you or have you recently been involved in the production of Arabic Language
  teaching materials? yes / no

   If yes: Are such efforts awarded, in terms of promotion or tenure decisions?
     yes / no

Have you or are you currently coordinating your efforts or cooperating with others in
  the field to produce materials? yes / no

There are many reasons for students to study Arabic. Consider your personal goals in
  teaching Arabic to first- and second-year students; rate the following as either
  High priority / Medium priority / Low priority.

  ____ to read modern Arabic literature

  ____ to read medieval Arabic texts

  ____ to have access to the modern Arabic media

  ____ to communicate orally with native Arabic speakers

  ____ none of these, rather to:

  _____

Are you a member of the American Association of Teachers of Arabic (AATA)? yes / no
   If no: Are you familiar with it?

Do you find AATA useful to you? yes / no

In what ways could AATA serve you better? _____

_____

Are you a member of another language teaching association: ACTFL / MLA / other:

_____

How familiar are you with the ACTFL Proficiency Guidelines?
   very / somewhat / not at all

What do you see as the most pressing need facing the Arabic language teaching
  profession? materials development / teacher training / improved textbooks /
  improved means of evaluating student performance / increased access to
  authentic materials / better informed administrators
  other:

_____

_____

Are there any other comments or suggestions you would like to make?

_____

_____

Thank you very much for your cooperation. If you have any questions, you may
    contact us at (801) 378-6531.

OUR NOTES (impressions from the survey, circumstances of note):

Program coordinators' responses to the question: **"In what other ways could AATA be
    of service to you and your program?"**

Instructor responses to the question: **"What do you feel is your greatest need in this area
    (materials)? printed materials / audio tapes / videos / computer programs /
    other:____ "**

Instructor responses to the question: **"In what ways could AATA serve you better?"**

Instructor responses to the question: **"What do you see as the most pressing need
    facing the Arabic language teaching profession? materials development /
    teacher training / improved textbooks / improved means of evaluating student
    performance / increased access to authentic materials / better informed ad-
    ministrators / other: _____ "**

REFERENCES

ABBOUD, PETER F., ET AL. 1971. *Modern Standard Arabic: Intermediate level (parts 1-3).* Ann Arbor: Department of Near Eastern Studies, University of Michigan.

ABBOUD, PETER F., ERNEST N. McCARUS, ET AL. 1983. *Elementary Modern Standard Arabic,* vols. 1 & 2 (2d ed.). Cambridge: Cambridge University Press.

ALLEN, ROGER AND ADEL ALLOUCHE. 1986. *Let's Learn Arabic.* Philadelphia: University of Pennsylvania.

ALOSH, MAHDI. 1989. *Ahlan wa sahlan.* Columbus: Ohio State University Foreign Language Publications.

ATTAR, SAMAR. 1988. *Modern Arabic, Book 1: An introductory course for foreign students.* Beirut: Librairie du Liban.

BACCOUCHE, BELKACEM AND SANAA AZMI. 1984. *Conversations in Modern Standard Arabic.* New Haven and London: Yale University Press.

BELNAP, R. KIRK. 1987. Who's Taking Arabic and What on Earth for? A survey of students in Arabic language programs. *Al-ᶜArabiyya* 20.1 & 2: 29-42.

BROD, RICHARD AND BETTINA J. HUBER. 1992. Foreign Language Enrollments in United States Institutions of Higher Education, Fall 1990. *ADFL Bulletin,* 23.3: 6-10.

CLARK, JOHN L. D. AND DORA E. JOHNSON. 1982. *A Survey of Materials Development Needs in the Less Commonly Taught Languages in the United States. Final Project Report.* Washington, DC: Center for Applied Linguistics.

HARDANE, JARJOURA, ET AL. 1979. *From the Gulf to the Ocean (Du Golfe a l'Océan).* Paris: Didier-Librairie Hatier.

HUBER, BETTINA J. 1993. The MLA's 1987-89 Survey of Foreign Language Programs: Institutional contexts, faculty characteristics, and enrollments. *ADFL Bulletin* 24.2: 6-38.

LAMBERT, RICHARD D. 1992. *Foreign Language Planning in the United States.* National Foreign Language Center Occasional Paper, October 1992.

MILROY, JAMES AND LESLEY MILROY. 1991. *Authority in Language: Investigating language prescription and standardisation.* London and New York: Routledge.

MITCHELL, TERRY F. 1986. What is Educated Spoken Arabic? *International Journal of the Sociology of Language* 61:7-32.

MORAHG, GILEAD. Hebrew on Campus: Student motivations and expectations. *Shofar* 9.3: 55-69.

RYDING, KARIN C. 1990. *Formal Spoken Arabic: Basic course.* Washington, DC: Georgetown University Press.

AL-TONSI, ABBAAS A. AND NARIMAN N. AL-WARRAKI. 1989. عربية وسائل الأعلام [*Arabic of the Media*]. Cairo: American University in Cairo.

3

TEACHING ARABIC AS A FOREIGN LANGUAGE: CHALLENGES OF THE NINETIES[*]

Alaa Elgibali
Zeinab Taha
The American University in Cairo

This chapter addresses some of the challenges facing the Teaching of Arabic as a Foreign Language (TAFL) in this decade. To illustrate these challenges, the Arabic language programs at AUC are examined in order to elaborate the framework envisaged for an integrated, culturally-sensitive approach to language learning and teaching.

We argue that the distribution of language skills must be presented authentically to the learner, for if the ultimate goal of foreign language learning is to emulate one's peers, programs should provide learners with the opporunity to try to achieve just that. Hence, in designing programs and syllabi, one must take this distribution of skills into consideration.

Accordingly, we advocate establishing a realistic order of priority of tasks for the learners to master, based on their needs. We would serve our students better if we concentrate on the skills that are actually used and on how they are proportionally distributed in relation to each other, rather than on attempting to teach non-Arabs skills that Arabs themselves might like to have but do not. In doing so, the legitimate call for authenticity would not be limited only to the content or form of the materials used but would also extend, and perhaps more crucially, to the more fundamental selection of the skill to be acquired.

[*]The authors are grateful for valuable input from their colleagues Ahmad Taher Hassanein, Nariman Al-Warraki, Nadia Harb, Laila El-Sawi, Ragia Effat, and Mona Kamel.

1. Introduction

Teaching Arabic as a foreign language has come a long way in the last twenty years. Nonetheless, professionals in the field are aware that in this decade, serious and basic research has to be done on second language acquisition, teaching methodology, materials development, and standardized testing. As an example, we venture in this paper to discuss those issues in general and what we attempt to achieve in that respect at the American University in Cairo.

The American University in Cairo (AUC) has been in the business of Teaching Arabic as a Foreign Language (TAFL) for over fifty years. Currently, the teaching of Arabic as a foreign language is offered at AUC under the auspices of the Arabic Language Institute (ALI) which houses the Center for Arabic Study Abroad (CASA), runs its own intensive full-time program in the Arabic Language Unit (ALU), provides requisite credit and remedial non-credit courses for AUC's non-Arabic-speaking learners, and trains new teachers in its masters program in TAFL. With twenty-two full-time teachers and over two hundred learners, ALI is perhaps the largest professional organization of its kind in the business of providing training in Arabic and related area studies to high school seniors, college undergraduates, graduates and professors, as well as other professionals from over twenty different countries.

Marking its twenty-fifth anniversary at AUC, CASA inaugurated a series of biennial teacher training seminars in cooperation with ALI. The first was held in the summer of 1991 at AUC for five weeks and included trainers and trainees both from the U.S. and Egypt. The goal of that seminar was to provide TAFL professionals in the U.S. and Egypt with an appropriate forum to exchange ideas and share experiences. Moreover, the seminar was aimed to encourage ALI faculty to examine closely and better define the overall approach of the Institute to the issues most pertinent to TAFL now and in the future.

In the following overview, we plan to outline that approach and briefly delineate how we envisage to carry out this mission in the next decade. We hope that the following discussion of our operational model will be of interest and value to similar programs; conversely, we hope to receive feedback and suggestions from colleagues in the field as to how we can improve our teaching and learning strategies.

2. Modus Operandi

Benefiting from its unique location in Egypt where Arabic is the native language, ALI increasingly views itself as a learning, rather than teaching, institution. This perception entails that learners at all levels of competence from novice to superior have an opportunity to acquire the language while using it in its natural context. Our goal is for the learners to acquire at the Institute those linguistic tools and skills that enable them to form working hypotheses which they can then instantly test and modify in their interaction with a real language environment. To help the learners accomplish this task, teachers attempt to assume a less dogmatic role and play instead the role of facilitators. Their main job, then, is the planning and coordinating of formal and informal activities that reinforce and reward effective learning strategies. In that framework, learning becomes a dynamic process in which the learners play an active role and immerse themselves in the language community, aiming at becoming fluent through natural and meaningful interaction with the environment.

3. Medium of Instruction

The issue of whether to use a non-target medium, English, to teach a foreign language such as Arabic to foreign learners is still controversial. ALI constantly strives to minimize the use of any language other than Arabic as the language of either instruction or interaction. There are practical and theoretical motivations for this approach. First, our student body is multi-lingual; therefore, we cannot possibly provide instruction in the native languages of all of our learners. Actually, being housed at an American university, we want to avoid a situation where our learners who are not native speakers of English end up learning more English than Arabic. Second, it is more realistic now to try to achieve the goal of minimizing the use of a non-target language because there are more teaching materials written exclusively in Arabic: those are either locally produced at ALI or commercially available. Third, we believe that eliminating the use of non-target media is theoretically sound because it creates for both the learner and the teacher a demanding situation in which the need for communication presents a meaningful challenge; overcoming this challenge gives both interlocutors a sense of achievement.

4. Target Model

A learner does not interact with the target language in a vacuum. Therefore, we must present the learner with a target linguistic model, i.e., an idealized model of a native speaker whom the learner should strive to emulate. Any society has a multitude of social strata intertwined with a horde of language varieties, codes, and jargons. Egypt, of course, is no exception. Consequently, we have to make a conscious choice as to which type of speaker we should pick for our idealized model. In the words of Badawi (1985:15):

> Apart from those who seek in foreign communities mainly the weird and exotic aspects of the lower strata in society, learners of foreign languages expect to acquire the type of speech which enables them to communicate freely with at least their peers in the communities whose language they are learning.

The majority of our learners are in academe. The other minority, while not academically-oriented in their relationship to Arabic, still need to function mainly in the circles of the educated. Accordingly, our idealized target model has to be one of the learner's peers, an educated person. In fact, we argue that, regardless of which geographical dialect is chosen, only the model of an educated speaker should be presented to the foreign learner. Having the sociolinguistic properties of the speech of an educated person as a learning model gives the foreign learners an added benefit in that it broadens their scope of communication with other educated speakers in the various dialect areas (see El-Hassan 1980).

5. Language Skills

If the learners are to interact effectively with the environment, they must be aware of the reality of its language situation. Ferguson's (1959) classic article on diglossia formally recognized the existence of (H)igh and (L)ow forms in modern Arabic. Since then, several descriptions have been proposed to characterize, in whole or in part, the current language situation in the Arab world including Egypt (see Kaye 1972, Badawi 1973, Schmidt 1974, Zughoul 1980, and Elgibali 1985). While differences among these varying descriptions abound, one theme can be found in common: Arabic has at least two varieties, each with a definite set of social functions. In the context of this well-recognized diglossic nature of the language, its two varieties (*fuṣḥā* and colloquial) have different functional distribution of skills among native speakers of Arabic. Predictably, intra-societal communication makes use of all four skills, albeit without necessarily assigning them equal weight. In the following sections we will outline our perspective of the functional domains in which these forms and skills are used by an educated speaker. *Fuṣḥā*, be it classical or modern, has three skills: reading, writing, and listening. Egyptian colloquial has mainly two: speaking and listening, and possibly reading and writing. We must point out that in the following presentation a discussion of the learning of grammar is deliberately missing. We believe that knowledge of grammar is an indispensible tool to a good and accurate language performance. Grammar is learned and taught at ALI. However, instead of being taught separately, it is taught as part and parcel of every language activity and of every language skill. We will now proceed to summarize our perspective on the functional distribution of those skills and illustrate how we go about enabling the learners to acquire them.

5.1 *Reading and Writing*

Reading is an essential language activity for the literate native speaker; it is even more so for the non-native learner. Belnap (1987:34) reports that learners usually consider reading as one of the most important skills in Arabic. Accordingly, reading is an integral part of the core curriculum at the ALI. Simply put, we hold that one learns how to read through the process of reading itself. Carell et al. (1988:269) convincingly argue that "written material, as a source of linguistic data, promotes the growth of general language competence; increased language competence in turn enhances reading ability." Hence, our learners are continually exposed to challenging amounts of reading material. Our task as facilitators is reflected in what we do in the process of selecting and grading the material as well as in preparing pre- and post-reading activities.

In selecting the material, we believe that the content and quantity of texts in the reading program are the most important elements in developing the reading skill. Content determines whether the topic is intellectually stimulating and of interest to the learner. Quantity, on the other hand, is a crucial factor in providing the learner with the opportunity to accumulate vocabulary and reinforce learned material. Both are indispensible requirements of successful language acquisition. At the ALI, a wide variety of authentic reading materials is introduced to the students. The materials presented consist of both fiction and non-fiction works covering historical, political, economic, and cultural topics. The reading materials, especially at the intermediate and advanced levels, are TOPIC-DRIVEN: they revolve around a specific topic like orientalism, women's status, or terrorism. The advantages of a topic-driven syllabus are that it tends to make the content of the texts more accessible for the learners and indirectly enhances their repertoire of vocabulary. The more one reads about a certain topic, the wider one's background knowledge becomes and the greater the probability that one would encounter the same kind of vocabulary again. Accordingly, the texts become more comprehensible and the cumulative effect of vocabulary learning can occur even though the learner's primary focus is not directed to vocabulary building (see Carell 1988:86). The following, for example, is a partial reading list on the topic of "Orientalism":

1. Hasan Hanafi. 1991. *Muqqadima fī ᶜilm al-istighrāb* [Introduction to Occidentalism]. 22-35.

2. Fouad Zakaria. 1984. Thaqāfatuna al-muᶜāṣira bayna al-taᶜrīb wa-al taghrīb [Arabization and Occidentalization in Our Contemporary Culture]. *Al-ᶜArabī* 302:30-35.

3. Fouad Zakaria. 1986. Al-istishrāq wa azmat al-thaqāfa al-ᶜarabiyya al-muᶜāṣira [Orientalism and the Crisis of Contemporary Arab Culture]. *Fikr* 10:32-41.

4. Yahia Haqqi. *Qindil umm haashim* [The Lamp of Um-Hashim]. 135 pages.

5. Tawfiq al-Hakim. *ᶜUsfūr min al-sharq* [A Bird from the East]. 186 pages.

6. Al-Tayyeb Salih. *Mawsim al-hijra ilā al-shamāl* [The Season of Migration to the North]. 171 pages.

As can be seen from the above list, learners are exposed to different styles of well-known novels, plays, and short stories from different Arab countries. Students are indirectly involved in the process of choosing the reading materials as we always endeavor to make the materials relevant to the needs and interests of our learners; accordingly, our reading lists are ever changing with the continuously changing needs and interests of the learners. Every assigned text is accompanied by guiding questions and a list of vocabulary items including synonyms, antonyms, definitions, and sentences illustrating the use of idiomatic expressions.

In grading the reading material, we take into consideration three elements: the linguistic complexity, the background knowledge included in the texts, and the sophistication of the tasks required from the learner. Thus, we start with linguistically accessible texts dealing with familiar topics and limit comprehension activities to answering the five *wh-* questions (who, what, when, where, and why). As we proceed in the course and as the learners' reading experiences increase, they are expected to perform more sophisticated tasks, such as making informed evaluations, giving personal opinions, or making inferences.

In our attempt to help the learner become a proficient reader, we plan a series of pre- and post-reading activities. It is felt necessary that before assigning any text, it is the teacher's role to inject his/her personal interest and enthusiasm into the material. Pre-reading activities should reassure the learners and facilitate the task of reading for them. The learners are encouraged to read for comprehension and enjoyment of the content and they are discouraged from resorting to dictionaries unless they absolutely have to (see Chastain 1976:314). The pre-reading activities include clarification and comments by the teacher on what s/he considers to be unfamiliar key concepts, expressions, and vocabulary items. The number of pages assigned is usually large: for a two-day assignment, we routinely assign no less than thirty pages if the reading material is fiction and no less than eight pages if it is non-fiction. Such large reading assignments make it impossible for the learner to accomplish the reading assignment while looking up every unfamiliar word. Pre-reading activities also draw upon audio-visual stimuli such as video films (e.g., documentaries, movies), slides, and audio materials (e.g., interviews, talk shows, and lectures). For example, the films are shown to the learners to provide background knowledge necessary for the comprehension of a text, especially if this text happens to have unfamiliar cultural information or context, along with a sophisticated style like those of Naguib Mahfuz, Yahia Haqqi, and Yusuf Idris. Pre-reading activities help facilitate the task for the learners and provide them with confidence.

Reading classes meet three times a week. In class, learners are encouraged to ask questions or comment on any difficulties they encountered while preparing the reading assignment at home. The content of the text is then discussed and the learners are encouraged to answer each others' questions in an attempt to enhance group activity and improve class dynamics. In discussing novels and short stories, the cultural aspect is always brought into light, for we deal with the literary work assigned not only as a source of linguistic data of a certain style, but also as a source of cultural information. Once a week, we have our learners read aloud in class for pronunciation accuracy. This activity has been found most useful as the teacher can identify individual weak points (in grammar, pronunciation, vocabulary, or reading strategies) and thus can help the learners overcome them. The learners also read silently (for comprehension) a short passage or an article in a few minutes and then answer certain questions summarizing the content; with time, this activity enhances the reading speed and encourages learners to abandon the word-by-word decoding approach (see Carell et al. 1988:230). These class activities also offer teachers a good opportunity to observe the learners carry out the task of reading. It is in class that the teacher can train learners not to panic at the occurrence of an unfamiliar word by recommending certain strategies for guessing meaning through the use of morphological, syntactic, and semantic clues (see Wallace 1988:135).

Concerted efforts are exerted to integrate the writing and reading skills. So, in addition to answering content questions in writing, learners are asked to utilize new vocabulary and unfamiliar idiomatic expressions in meaningful sentences. They are also expected to write commentaries on certain novels or articles. In addition, there are also separate writing classes. There, the teacher tries to extract useful materials from the reading assignment for use as samples of the various writing styles such as descriptions, comparisons, commentaries, etc. Eventually, learners can move on from this mode of controlled writing to creative written expression.

5.2 *Content-Based Instruction*

At a later stage in our program, we incorporate the content-based reading and writing approach into the curriculum. Content-Based Instruction (CBI) is employed at the Institute to approximate life-like learning situations for advanced learners. Specifically because the content has to be of immediate relevance to a particular group of learners, CBI courses are offered as electives. These electives are determined by a process of voting and consensus building. The course topics range from medieval historical texts to contemporary political thought. Areas of religion, culture, literature, economics, political science, and arts are well represented in the choice of the courses.

Since the CBI courses are designed to give the learners a chance to excel in their areas of interests, they are expected to approach the learning process from an angle that is different from that which they adopt in the other regular reading and writing courses. This is done by guiding the learners to develop certain learning strategies. Therefore, class time is usually employed to increase the learners' understanding of the subject matter as well as its cultural implications.

In CBI courses, Arabic is dealt with as the medium of teaching, and the focus of class activities and assignments is on the content. The learners, therefore, read texts and concentrate mainly on the message. Discussions in class concentrate on the texts that are read by the learners. Problems posed by the language are dealt with whenever they arise and only when they impede understanding of the content. Excessive linguistic explanation is avoided since the goal of CBI is to concentrate on the content rather than the form. However, a balance between attention paid to form and content is a goal that we try to achieve, especially in courses requiring focus on both, such as literature, Qur'anic studies, Arabic syntax, and translation.

In an attempt to further prepare the learners to deal with Arab society, some CBI courses are offered in national universities where the learners are completely immersed in the culture and are expected to perform at the level of their native peers. The level of the language used in national universities assumes a native or native-like proficiency on the part of the students; therefore, only advanced students attend such classes.

The level of the language used is in fact a delicate problem in CBI courses and many decisions have to be made every year depending on the type and level of learners we get. The first problem constitutes a challenge to CBI courses in general: should a language teacher or an area specialist teach a CBI course? This is an important question to ask since area specialists may be authorities in their fields but fail to respond adequately to the learners' linguistic needs. At AUC, we have tried both options with various degrees of success. After many semesters, we have come to believe that our best bet is to employ a specialist with a background of teaching foreign students. The best results come from courses taught by such teachers. Our language teachers have been successful in handling courses like Arabic syntax, literature, translation, history, and women's issues, since a number of them have formal training in these disciplines.

The second problem is more specific, and its acuteness usually changes in degree from year to year: how do we offer *enough* courses to cover *all* the interests of the learners? This is more of an administrative problem that we manage to solve by achieving a balance between the different interests of the learners and the maintenance of a good-sized classroom. Electives, then, are taught as courses, rather than tutorials with one or two students in each class. From the results and feedback obtained from our learners, we truly feel that CBI is the culmination of all the linguistic gains which our learners accumulated during the early months of studying Arabic at ALI. CBI provides the learners with an appropriate forum to interact with the Egyptian society on firmer ground and through wider channels.

5.3 *Listening*

Listening activities are integrated in all courses. However, ALI offers specialized listening comprehension courses as a matter of focus to guarantee that the learners actually enhance their listening skills. A wide variety of audio and video tapes, both authentic and simulated, are used in listening comprehension courses to provide learners with systematic aural comprehension training on how to decode acurately, in a culturally appropriate context, what they listen to, both in *fuṣḥā* and colloquial. The materials used aim to enhance learners' listening skills at the levels of phonology, word structure, sentence, language style, and global message. These various levels are briefly illustrated below:

a. Phonology. Here learners work on discriminating between sounds in predictably problematic areas such as ḥ (voiceless pharyngeal fricative) vs. ʕ (voiced pharyngeal fricative), ḥ (voiceless pharyngeal fricative) vs. h (voiceless laryngeal fricative), and ʕ (voiced pharyngeal fricative) vs. ʔ (glottal stop). In such exercises, the learners have a copy of the text they listen to with paired choices, one of which they must identify as the correct sound.

b. Word structure. Here learners deal with whole words and liaison problems across word boundaries at the phrase level. Dictation, both spot and of whole passages, is a useful training tool which encourages the learner to concentrate, at least momentarily, on the form. Structures like prepositional and noun-adjective phrases or *idāfas* serve as clues to understanding the sentence as a whole. Exercises aimed at recognizing words using the definite article are an example. Another exercise which serves the development of the listening skill on both the phonological and structural levels is to ask the learners to write the content of a taped program (usually one or two minutes long) word for word. Although frustrating, this exercise has proven to be very successful in helping the learners distinguish word boundaries.

c. Sentence. Here the learner focuses on decoding the meaning at the sentence level. This is a further step in developing the listening comprehension skill where learners decode what they hear for retention. The learners are given true/false questions to test their understanding of complete ideas in complete sentences rather than fragments of sentences.

d. Language style. In order to prepare the learner to understand people outside of the classroom, we use natural dialogues that expose the learners to language data where native speakers naturally coalesce colloquial and *fuṣḥā* features. Dialogues and authentic materials, both from radio and television, are presented at all stages. At the beginning stages, the learners are given shorter dialogues than students at the higher levels. Both the activities carried out in class and the teachers' expectations from the learners vary according to the learner's level. Comprehension questions may be presented here either in the MSA variety or in spoken colloquial to check the learners' understanding of the message when speakers mix *fuṣḥā* and colloquial features.

e. Global message. Here learners deal with the overall message, inferential information, and shades of meaning and innuendos of style. At the beginning stages, the learners need not remember nor concentrate on the details of the material. They are only required to get the gist of what they are listening to. As the learners' listening skills develop, the listening materials become longer and the learners are expected to concentrate on the global message as well as on some important details. In order to do so, the learners are encouraged to take notes, in Arabic or in any other language, in order to be able to write a summary or an outline of the material they listen to.

To help the learners develop their note-taking skill *while* listening, they carry out activities which are graded in complexity. In the early stages, learners are given completed outlines with which they may follow a program or a lecture. Later, they are given outlines that are partially complete, and they are asked to fill in the missing parts. At the advanced stages, learners take notes and write their own outlines. It is worth mentioning that note-taking while listening is usually introduced at the intermediate level and learners are encouraged to go through all the stages throughout the course. The teachers assist the learners in following the lectures and in writing outlines by providing them with symbols that can be used for abbreviations and some common rhetorical devices and expressions which native speakers usually use in organizing their ideas.

5.4 *Speaking*

For the non-native learner, learning to speak Arabic is perhaps the most problematic aspect of the language, for s/he immediately discovers that the word "Arabic" is no more than a term of convenience with no specific designation. Then, there is always the question of which Arabic (dialect area) to learn. Once this question is resolved, the learner is then faced with the dilemma that even within this "specific" dialect area, Arabic has several inertwined layers or levels of which the learner must first become aware and then master, either actively or receptively. In Egypt, according to the widely-accepted description of Badawi (1973), five such levels exist: *fuṣḥā al-turāth* (Heritage Classical); *fuṣḥā al-ʿaṣr* (Contemporary Standard); *ʿāmiyyat al-muthaqqafīn* (Educated Spoken); *ʿāmiyyat al-mutanawwirīn* (Literate Spoken); and *ʿāmiyyat al-ummiyyīn* (Illiterate Spoken). We will begin with a discussion of those issues relevant to the learning of Egyptian colloquial(s).

5.4.1 *Colloquial*

Colloquial is the active medium of oral interaction in the Egyptian society. Accordingly, it is used in a wide range of situations, ranging from the mundane (e.g., shopping) to the abstract (e.g., ethics and aesthetics). By colloquial, we refer to the linguistic repertoire and social contexts covered by the two levels Badawi (1973) calls *ʿāmiyyat al-muthaqqafīn* (Educated Spoken) and *ʿāmiyyat al-mutanawwirīn* (Literate Spoken). It must be noted that, at every opportunity, those social contexts of relevance to the learning situation are incorporated into the classroom techniques and strategies described below.

The general approach for classroom activities is to focus on those activities that are learner-centered rather than teacher-centered (see Eckard and Kearny 1981). This means that the learners should be encouraged to speak to each other and not only with their teacher. In order to achieve this, the teacher should present activities such as role-play, questions and answers, discussions, and games. These activities facilitate speaking in the "real" language and approximate natural communication contexts. They are also graded from controlled activities, to semi-controlled, to free activities. Teaching conversation effectively requires the choice of a suitable direction of the speaking activities by consensus between the learners and the teacher. The degree of control of the speaking activities depends on the grammatical structures and vocabulary as well as the social functions that the teacher wishes to introduce to the learners. The teacher should keep in mind that class activities have to match the general proficiency level of the learners as well as the structures and vocabulary to which they have been introduced. Otherwise, these activities become aimless and above or below what should be done in class. For example, if the teacher wants his/her learners to practice the perfect tense, the teacher should introduce a conversation based on questions such as: tell us about your own experience when you first went to school as a young child! If the teacher wants to reinforce the present habitual tense, questions like "what do you do when you take a taxi" would be the base of the conversation. The more grammatical structures and vocabulary the learners learn, the freer class activities there can be.

The success of class conversations depends, to a great extent, on establishing well-defined terms for both the teacher and learner. Thus, each one knows exactly what is expected of him/her; otherwise the teacher would wait patiently (or impatiently) until the learners start to talk, or s/he would keep on talking until the learners find something to say. In both cases, there is no conversation.

Speaking is also a skill that requires guidance and practice; it is the teacher's responsibility to provide the learners with guidance and give them suitable opportunities for practice. Typically, the teachers choose the conversation activities, explain them, make sure that all learners participate, answer any questions and provide the structure and vocabulary items the learners need. They should also make sure that they talk less and the learners talk more (see Eckard and Kearny 1981). To facilitate this process, some pre-conversation activities should be introduced such as:

1. Introducing new vocabulary and practicing using them in meaningful sentences.
2. Introducing pattern drills based on certain structures.
3. Introducing directed listening where the learners listen to real recorded conversation on different topics such as renting an apartment, buying a car, answering a telephone call, etc.
4. Introducing questions, expressions, and compliments, and training the learners to answer them.
5. Using pictures for different purposes, such as teaching or reviewing certain grammatical structures, pronunciation, intonation, vocabulary, etc.

6. Practicing the creation of imaginary dialogues from pictures including two or more persons.
7. Presenting reports on certain topics or articles.

As for correction, the teacher should not stop the flow of speaking activities for correction unless the error seriously impedes comprehension. Instead, s/he should record the conversations on an audio or video tape for a general remedial session in which all learners participate. Stopping the learners at every occurrence of an error would discourage them from talking fluently and with confidence or they might even stop talking completely (see Paulston and Bruder 1976). In general, the teacher should strive to create a classroom atmosphere that is conducive to free expression and where the learners are not inhibited to use new structures and vocabulary items even if they make mistakes in the interim. To create such an atmosphere, the teacher might:

1. introduce meaningful activities and make learners interested in them;
2. make the learners feel that their personal experiences are valuable and related to the culture such as getting a driver's license at the Department of Motor Vehicles;
3. encourage the learners' interest in each other;
4. be close to his/her learners, for the closer a teacher is to the learners, the more successful the class is;
5. confirm that the purpose of classroom activities is learning and practicing, not examining the learners' performance;
6. give the learners confidence in themselves and in their ability to achieve greater progress in the language;
7. introduce what is called "conversation strategies" to the learners to help them keep a conversation going, e.g.:
    a. When asked a question, answer it and then ask another one, e.g., "How are you?" "Fine, thanks. And you?"
    b. When asked a question, answer it giving extra information, e.g., "Are you a student?" "Yes, I'm studying history. How about you?"

In a colloquial conversation class, then, the learner is an actively participating member in a dialogue, not a passive listener or note-taker. The learners thus find themselves forced to think in Arabic and to remember the structures and vocabulary they practiced before in pattern drills or have been exposed to elsewhere. Instead of answering in previously memorized answers, they are expected to use the language in real situations as native speakers do outside the classroom. Constant participation in class activities helps most learners lower their inhibitions and develop their feelings of confidence and achievement when they find themselves able to use real language in the classroom as they would in the real world (see Eckard and Kearny 1981).

5.4.2 Fuṣḥā

All the classroom activities described earlier (5.3.1) for teaching collo-quial are also followed in teaching spoken *fuṣḥā*. However, there are some dif-ferent and/or additional activities that are pertinent only to the domains of *fuṣḥā;* these are described here. In Egypt, spoken *fuṣḥā* is a specialized skill; it is a target of those who are both willing and able to reach it. Though limited, it has an important role in the society and is presumed to be used in certain formal domains such as public speeches, university lectures, sermons, and the like. In the words of Badawi (1992:55):

> As Arabs, we welcome speaking *fuṣḥā* in all situations. It represents a social demand that fosters intellectual interaction among different segments of soci-ety. However, we currently do not see this as a realistic social phenomenon. There is a big difference between the demand or hope and what actually takes place. [Our translation]

Seen in these terms, we look at spoken *fuṣḥā* exactly as we would at translation or paleography: a specialized skill that is offered as an elective to those who wish to master its intricacies.

Typically, a spoken *fuṣḥā* course is offered to advanced learners whose exposure to spoken *fuṣḥā* has so far been either simply receptive or, if active, limited only to controlled situations. The goal of this course is to use the oral/ aural approach to train the learners in using spoken *fuṣḥā*, and only *fuṣḥā*, accu-rately in a wide range of socially appropriate situations. When the speaker uses *fuṣḥā* in these situations, s/he is held in high esteem by the audience. As we can see here, the language situation has to do with social appreciation.

The spoken *fuṣḥā* class is divided into three stages, each with its own seg-ment of the syllabus. In the first stage (one month), learners are urged to talk about familiar topics like their own biographies and familiar public events. In so doing, we expect them to talk without hesitation. In a typical session, each learner is assigned ten minutes to give a presentation to the class on a chosen topic. Another ten minutes are devoted to general discussion. Then the teacher's feedback on the use of language starts. The presentations are recorded on cas-sette tapes, and before the end of the day, each learner is able to take his/her own copy to listen again to all the presentations at home.

At this stage there are some typical problems we face: poor listening comprehension ability, slowness of expression, and misuse of words found in the dictionary. Learners often rely on English/Arabic dictionaries as vocabulary sources but inadvertently select the Arabic word arbitrarily. Another problem, we should admit, is created by us as teachers of Arabic. CASA students, for example, first study literary Arabic, then come to AUC to study colloquial. In colloquial classes, they are trained to change *q* to *ʔ* or *j* to *g*. Then we ask them again in the spoken *fuṣḥā* class to reverse the process, which they find initially difficult. For the sake of fluency, we do not force learners to use case endings. However, we sometimes come across some learners who insist on vocalizing everything fully, and as teachers, we endeavor to guide them to the easy and more realistic track.

In the second stage (second month), learners are exposed to both live and recorded materials, mainly lectures or cultural programs. Each learner listens to the recording at home before s/he briefs in *fuṣḥā* his/her peers on its content in class, giving his/her point of view, analysis, evaluation, criticism, etc. Discussion usually starts on the topic at hand and then extends to other related matters. All discussions are carried out in *fuṣḥā*.

In the third and final stage, which lasts for six weeks, learners become able to hold more sophisticated discussions related to their fields of specialization or to some other topic. Here, we enrich their language output with vocabulary, technical terms, and high frequency idioms and expressions. We also comment, when necessary, on the major issues associated with a particular topic, introducing authors and writers, traditional or modern, and inviting guest speakers.

In the second and third stages, many of the problems that were encountered in the first stage disappear, but new ones appear. This is due to the learners' legitimate ambition to express themselves in a way that is more precise and more specific. This ambition usually slows them down a little bit, but gradually they speed up once more. To create strong motivation among learners, we sometimes have them participate in debates on interesting topics. Our task in these two stages, where the problems diminish, is to show the learners the distinction between what is linguistically and stylistically good, better, and best so that they become familiar with more than one way of expressing an idea or thought.

Before the end of the semester, we give learners the opportunity to have two or three rehearsals, just to train them on what they will be required to do in real life. We list several topics on cards, one topic per card, and ask each learner to select one card, read the topic carefully, then start talking about it in *fuṣḥā* and record their speech on a cassette tape. In the rehearsals, we try to show the learners the weak points that they should avoid. The progress of learners can be seen when they compare their first and last recordings.

5.5 *Cultural Dimension*

In our attempt to enable the learner to interact effectively with culturally authentic language input, we strive to go beyond grammatical correctness and develop the learner's ability to produce culturally appropriate forms. Accordingly, those culture-specific or cross-cultural aspects that are of relevance to the learners in their new environment are incorporated at all stages of learning and discussions. Discussions, most importantly, aim at creating a consensus and awareness between the learner and the teacher that such differences exist and provide a forum for them to explore jointly those areas of cultural similarities or differences. In so doing, we hope to build between the learners and the target culture at large empathetic bridges[1] that are based on an attitude of tolerance, perhaps even appreciation, of differences. This attitude is not meant necessarily to lead to the assimilation or even the acceptance of the different cultural norms. Rather, it is meant to promote an awareness of the Self and the Other and to facilitate interaction by minimizing the likelihood of cross-cultural misunderstanding and increasing the level of cultural sensitivity.

Misunderstandings due to cross-culture difference are a likely possibility for the non-native learner, especially when immersed in the native culture of the language. Indeed, violations of culturally expected norms of appropriateness can be costly. In a meeting conducted entirely in Arabic with a group of foreign visitors, a respected Azhar scholar got gradually irritated as the visitors kept addressing him in the intimate *inta* (informal you) instead of the expected *ḥaḍritak* (formal you) which he, predictably, used when addressing any of them. Finally, the scholar turned to the Egyptian escort and openly expressed his displeasure at the seeming arrogance of his visitors. Shortly after, he ended the meeting. Another learner (a man) almost got into trouble when, with all the good intentions in the world, he told the wife of an Egyptian acquaintance, whom he had just met, that she was very beautiful. Of paramount importance, then, is the transmission of the language to the learner consumed in its culture. Performance that meets only the criterion of grammatical correctness falls short of our, and the learner's, target.

---

1. The term "empathetic bridges" was used by Nadine O'Conor during a presentation at the 1992 Georgetown University Round Table.

As teachers and curriculum designers, we realize that the teaching of culture has its special difficulties and, therefore, try to incorporate cultural capsules in all our materials, be it oral or written. In doing so, we encounter two major problems. The first is related to maintaining a balance between the learners' linguistic level and the complexity of the texts involving the cultural elements. There is always a mismatch between the linguistic ability of the students and what they want to learn through listening and reading about Egyptian culture. Teachers attempt to overcome this difficulty by controlling the level of the cultural materials introduced in class and by explaining some of the cultural subtleties. For expediency, explaining could take place in English, especially at the elementary levels. If the learners are left to make hasty generalizations about what they hear and see, they may end up enlarging the amount of misconceptions which they already had before arriving to the native environment. The learners are given cultural tasks to carry out outside of the classroom, such as shopping, asking for directions, attending social events, and getting reactions from Egyptians towards certain issues of interest. In class, the learners report the information; then a discussion takes place to clear up any misunderstandings that may have been formed. Such activities are done mainly in speaking and listening classes because they lend themselves naturally to the types of cultural discussions that take place. Another technique which we have started to use recently is to pair English-speaking students of Arabic with Egyptian students who are learning English as a foreign language. Both groups of students meet outside the classroom and engage in conversations in both languages (e.g., they speak Arabic for fifteen minutes, then English for another fifteen minutes). This technique has proven to be extremely successful because it provides the foreign learners with an opportunity to closely interact with Egyptians, opening up the door to learning intensively about the culture.

Another problem that we face, when dealing with cultural issues, is related to the diversity of Arab culture, both in general and in any given dialect such as those of Egypt. Typically, we face a situation where even inside the city of Cairo one finds various degrees of traditionalism, on the one hand, and westernization on the other. This fact constitutes a big challenge in the teaching of Arab culture in general (Al-Batal 1988). The teacher is therefore expected to introduce to the learners various forms of what is and what is not accepted in Egyptian culture. More importantly, the teacher's task becomes more that of a guide who makes sure that the learners know what is out there. As mentioned earlier, our task is not to make the learners accept or even agree with what they see and hear but rather to help them become aware that differences exist and that the people of the host culture expect them to understand these differences, if not to appreciate them.

Whether the problem is that of the language level of the learners or the diversity of the Egyptian culture and the difficulty of the learners in avoiding making false generalizations, it remains a question of tolerance on the part of everyone concerned in the learning/teaching process. Our philosophy continues to emphasize that culture should be introduced from the very beginning stages. Hence, what goes on outside the classroom goes hand in hand with what goes on inside the classroom, minimizing the likelihood of cultural misunderstanding.

5.6 *Integration of Skills*

In the previous sections (5.0-5.4), we have presented our approach and techniques in dealing with each of the various language skills separately. In reality, however, we do not see the skills as separate; rather, we endeavor to present them encapsuled in their cultural context, cohesively, and in an integrated fashion. The integration of skills is essentially a way to make up for the artificial division of the language into its various modes of reception and expression. It is also an approach to presenting language to the learner cohesively and in a fashion that reflects the natural distribution of its skills. In addition, the integration of skills, in our view, is thematically or functionally driven and NOT structurally or grammatically oriented. To illustrate, the learner learns to shop in colloquial, to discuss nuclear armament in a mixture of *fuṣḥā* and colloquial, but to read, write, or listen to a talk about Muhammadan Sunnah in *fuṣḥā*.

Language is often artificially divided for teaching purposes into four equal skills: reading, writing, speaking, and listening. In teaching Arabic as a foreign language, reading was traditionally emphasized at the expense of the three other skills which were more or less neglected. Therefore, in our attempt to remedy the longstanding neglect of writing, speaking, and listening, we must not create a fictitious, teacher-concocted language situation where all skills are given equal weight in both codes. We also want to avoid falling into the classic trap of arbitrarily imposing an alien model that may fit other languages, but not Arabic.

6. **Language Authenticity**

We argued earlier that the choice of topic not only determines which skill(s) will be focal and which will be peripheral, but also dictates which level of language is appropriate. We argue here that this distribution must be presented authentically to the learner, for if the ultimate goal of foreign language learning is to emulate one's peers, programs should provide learners with the opportunity to try to achieve just that. Hence, in designing programs and syllabi, one must take this distribution of skills into consideration. For example, it is useful and realistic for all learners to master speaking in colloquial, a language variety used naturally and effectively in a large set of social situations ranging from the food market to university lecture halls. In addition, learners cannot do without being able to read for comprehension. Similarly, it is useful to train all learners in all levels from novice to superior on reading *fuṣḥā* aloud since it is a task that the learners might be called upon to perform in the same fashion that their native peers do.

Conversely, if offered to all learners, a course entitled spoken *fuṣḥā*, while having a nice ring to it, in the final analysis would be deceptive and misleading since it promises to divest the learners' energy into developing a skill which, no matter how noble, is nonetheless a skill that their native Arabic-speaking peers do not have, except as a specialized skill. Several arguments, in fact, can be made here against directing our AFL learners to invest in learning the skill of speaking *fuṣḥā* except as an advanced, specialized skill. First, the discourse tasks requiring performing orally in *fuṣḥā* are often too complex for any learner below superior to execute successfully. Second, any attempt to use *fuṣḥā* in mundane situations (like shopping) would immediately provoke social ridicule. Moreover, discourse, by definition, is a two-way channel of communication using a mutually intelligible code(s). Language reality shows that oral communication involving *fuṣḥā* is more often than not a multi-code affair: an Azharite sheikh, for example, may deliver his sermon in one code (*fuṣḥā*) but his audience will almost certainly direct their questions in a second code (colloquial). Undoubtedly, AFL learners are not routinely called upon to play the role of an Azharite sheikh, but will frequently be in situations where they have to listen to and comprehend *fuṣḥā*. Consequently, it is more worth their while to be trained in listening to *fuṣḥā* than to speaking it.

Finally, a major argument for mastering the skill of speaking in *fuṣḥā* is that *fuṣḥā* serves as a unified, and unifying, pan-Arab language variety for the Arabs themselves. This, to a great extent, is true. In the case of the non-native speaker, however, it is reasoned that *fuṣḥā* is a language variety that the non-native speaker can use and be understood in wherever s/he goes in the Arab world. Again, taken at face value, this argument may hold true especially when communication involves an Arabic speaker who is capable of producing *fuṣḥā*. But, alas! Those are few and far between. More likely, the non-native speaker will take part in a rapidly disintegrating conversation where s/he might be understood but is also being gradually tuned out as that native speaker progressively loses his/her ability and/or interest in sustaining this conversation in *fuṣḥā*. Worse still, the fact that that non-native speaker is using an unnatural language code may decrease the effectiveness of his/her attempt to accomplish the purpose of his/her discourse (have you ever seen a *fuṣḥā* speaker haggle over a price and successfully bring it down?).

What we advocate, then, is to establish a realistic order of priority of tasks for the learners to master, based on their needs. We would serve our learners better if we concentrate on what and how skills are actually used and proportionally distributed in relation to each other, rather than on attempting to teach non-Arabs skills that Arabs themselves might like to have but do not.[2] In doing so, the legitimate call for authenticity would not be limited only to the content or form of the materials used but would also extend, and perhaps more crucially, to the more fundamental selection of the skill to be acquired.

7. Proficiency and Testing

Interest in the concept of "proficiency" and "proficiency-oriented instruction" began in 1979 when the Carter's Commission on Foreign Language and International Studies recommended the adoption of a national U.S. standard for measuring language proficiency. Omaggio (1986), discussing the teaching of foreign languages in general, argues that "the concept of teaching for proficiency is not really new at all. It has, in fact, been the central issue in language teaching all along" (p. xi). This may well have been the case of commonly taught foreign languages like French or German or even the case of teaching Arabic in its natural environment, as in Egypt. However, in the case of Arabic in the United States, this interest in proficiency was needed, along with the initiatives it sparked, to expand the scope of skills taught as well as to improve the quality of teaching. We feel, however, that because this interest in proficiency is originally conceived as a testing technique, not enough work has been done to facilitate the learning or acquisition process.

In addition to our local achievement and pro-achievement tests, it is evident that we, and the whole field at large, need a standardized measure of language ability. To our knowledge, the Arabic Proficiency Test which was developed by the Center for Applied Linguistics is the only one of its kind that attempts to test all four skills. It is, however, still at the field-testing stage. In that

---

2. In this regard, we commend the recent step taken by the Middlebury Arabic School in introducing colloquial into the program.

respect, there is also the commendable contribution offered by the 1989 ACTFL Guidelines for Arabic (henceforth, the guidelines) in refining the techniques and expanding the scope of the FSI evaluation tool. The authors of the guidelines call upon "teachers and academic programs to continue to refine and update the criteria... so as to reflect the needs of users...". In response to this call, we would like to point out that if the ultimate goal of the learner is to perform language tasks in the same way a native speaker does, the basic distribution of the speaking and listening skills must be reconsidered in terms of whether the tasks performed are to be in colloquial or in MSA. All the speaking and listening behavioral tasks designated by the guidelines as characteristic of the Intermediate and Advanced levels or even the Superior level appear, to us, to fall clearly in the domain of dialect and not in the domain of MSA. This entails reversing the dialect versus MSA specification in the guidelines, i.e., that, for example, at the Advanced Plus level the learner can perform all the tasks described in a dialect (not MSA) and show an increasing familiarity with the lexicon and syntax of MSA (not of a dialect).

By this, we are not suggesting that the acquisition of Arabic as a second/ foreign language does or should mimic or replicate its acquisition as a first language. Instead, we appeal to the concept of authenticity which, we argue, does not only mean that we use materials not prepared specifically for teaching purposes but also that we teach our learners to communicate in the fashion and modes native speakers actually use to communicate among themselves. We realize the logistical problems inherent in our proposal (e.g., which dialect to choose, number of testers, funding and nature of programs in the United States, etc.) but, again, we do so while keeping the language reality in mind.

8. Conclusion

In the previous discussion, we have tried to delineate the main issues that we believe represent the challenges for teaching Arabic as a foreign language in the nineties, both in the United States and elsewhere. It is evident that we cannot teach Arabic successfully without incorporating in our teaching approaches the reality of that language and those traits that are particular to it. One cannot, for example, adopt a model of four skills at large without adapting it to factor in the relevant and proportionate distribution of one skill to another. The concept of authenticity, we argue, should be extended, beyond using authentic teaching materials, into the larger framework of authentic language input and authentic cultural context. Teaching for proficiency is a legitimate goal, but a major challenge of the profession in the nineties remains the need for an accurate definition of the characteristics of a proficient Arabic speaker. Our teaching materials, approaches, techniques, and procedures should serve as tools to transmit those characteristics to the non-native speaker.

REFERENCES

BADAWI, EL-SAID M. 1973. *Mustawayāt al-ᶜarabiyya al-muᶜāṣira fī miṣr* [Levels of Contemporary Arabic in Egypt]. Cairo: Dār al-Maᶜārif.

_____. 1992. "Muqtaḍayāt al-kafāʔa fī taᶜallum al-ᶜarabiyya ka-lugha iḍāfiyya" [Proficiency Requirements in Learning Arabic as a Second Language]. In *Teaching Arabic as a Foreign Language: Issues and experiences*. Tunis: ALECSO.

AL-BATAL, MAHMOUD. 1988. "Towards Cultural Proficiency in Arabic." *Foreign Language Annals* 21:5. 443-453.

BELNAP, R. KIRK. 1987. Who's Taking Arabic and What on Earth for? *Al-ᶜArabiyya* 20:29-42.

BOWEN, DONALD AND HAROLD MADSEN. 1985. *TESOL Techniques and Procedures*. Cambridge, MA: Heinle & Heinle.

CARELL, PATRICIA, DEVINE JOANNE, AND DAVID ESKEY. 1988. *Interactive Approaches to Second Language Reading*. Cambridge: Cambridge University Press.

CHASTAIN, KENNETH. 1976. *Developing Second Language Skills: Theory to practice*. Chicago: Rand McNally College Publishing.

ECKARD, ROLAND and MARY ANN KEARNY. 1981. *Teaching Conversation Skills in ESL*. Washington, DC: Center for Applied Linguistics, ERIC Clearinghouse on Languages and Linguistics.

ELGIBALI, ALAA. 1985. *Towards a Sociolinguistic Analysis of Language Variation in Arabic: Cairene and Kuwaiti dialects*. Ph.D. dissertation, University of Pittsburgh, Pittsburgh, PA.

FERGUSON, CHARLES A. 1959. Diglossia. *Word* 15:340-352.

EL-HASSAN, SHAHIR. 1977. Educated Spoken Arabic in Egypt and the Levant: A critical review of diglossia and related concepts. *Archivum Linguisticum: A review of comparative philosophy and general linguistics* 8:112-132.

KAYE, ALAN S. 1972. Remarks on Diglossia in Arabic: Well-defined vs. ill-defined. *Linguistics* 81:32-48.

MCKEOWN, MARGARET AND MARY CURTIS, eds. 1987. *The Nature of Vocabulary Acquisition*. Hillsdale, NJ: Lawrence Erlbaum.

OMMAGIO, ALICE. 1986. *Teaching Language in Context: Proficiency-oriented instruction*. Boston: Heinle & Heinle.

PAULSTON, CHRISTINA AND MARY BRUDER. 1976. *Teaching English as a Second Language: Techniques and procedures*. Cambridge: Winthrop.

SAVINGNON, SANDRA. 1984. *Initiatives in Communicative Language Teaching*. Addison-Wesley.

SCHMIDT, RICHARD W. 1974. *Sociolinguistic Variation in Spoken Arabic in Egypt: A reexamination of the concept of diglossia*. Ph.D. dissertation, Brown University, Providence, RI.

WALLACE, CATHERINE. 1988. *Learning to Read in a Multicultural Society: The social contest of second language*. Englewood Cliffs: Prentice Hall.

ZUGHOUL, MOHAMED. 1980. Diglossia in Arabic: Investigating solutions. *Anthropological Linguistics* 22:201-217.

4

Higher Level Language Skills in Arabic: Parameters and Issues

Roger Allen
University of Pennsylvania

This chapter addresses itself to some of the issues that face Arabic programs, particularly in the area of articulation between levels and the criteria that should govern the bottom-up and top-down processes that affect decisions regarding the content and methodology of upper-level courses. The chapter investigates traditional methods through which the goals of courses at different levels in Arabic programs have (or have not) been determined, and suggests that the challenge of implementing competency- (or proficiency-) based teaching and learning forces program coordinators to face in more realistic ways than in the past decisions about modes of sequencing types of language and content-materials. The chapter concludes that, as the Arabic teaching profession addresses itself to the theoretical and applied research involved in these issues, the changes that have already been implemented will come to be viewed as merely the start of a wholesale transformation in teaching and learning goals and strategies.

1. Introduction

Being an Oxford graduate, I can never tire of making use of the possibly apochryphal story concerning the early phases of Arabic language learning at Cambridge in former times. The professor, so the story goes, would instruct would-be incipient Arabists to purchase William Wright's translation of Caspari's grammar and study it carefully, since at the same time next week he proposed to commence a reading of *Al-Kāmil* by al-Mubarrad. Within a pedagogical frame of reference, what we see here is a linkage of the processes of language acquisition and academic methodology, what might be termed perhaps the "sink or swim method." If this narrative is indeed apochryphal, then a narrative of my own experiences at Oxford may be slightly less so, although thirty-one years may color the memory to a certain degree. By now (1961), the abruptness of the Cambridge initiation seems to have been acknowledged, since the process began with eight weeks of the Reverend Thatcher's *Grammar*. It continued with a three-course load (in my case, after a summer vacation during which, in a classic case of language attrition, I managed to forget most of the verb forms that I had begun to acquire). That fall, the selection happened to be: the Qur'an, Ibn Khaldun's *Al-Muqaddimah*, and the *Maqāmāt* of al-Hamadhani and al-Hariri. I still retain the foot-high pile of vocabulary lists that resulted. While undergoing this initiation in England, I can still recall the combined sense of amazement and liberation I felt upon buying copies of Ernest McCarus's Michigan readers and eagerly devouring their contents and vocabulary while attempting to unravel the complexities of al-Jahiz's *Risālat al-Qiyān* (another set-text at Oxford).[1]

2. Levels of Instruction: Variations in Goals and Content

These remembrances of a different system from several decades ago are included here, not merely as personal reminiscences, but because they point to what seems to me, in the context of the topic of this chapter, to be one of the larger ironies: I can hardly complain about not being exposed to authentic materials from an early stage, something that those who support the principles of proficiency-based teaching advocate with some vigor. Those of you who have taught your way through that "slough of despond" which is the second-level course in Arabic (however it is termed) will probably recognize the sense that most students seem to have at that stage: the end of an exciting first-year experience is followed by a course characterized by little apparent progress, full of seemingly never-ending vocabulary and grammar. That sensation was never part of my experience in the second year; it was a constant from the outset. I have a suspicion that we may be able to draw some corollaries from such a difference, and I will certainly suggest later on that there *is* something in the use of authentic materials, albeit in a completely different learning context.

In coming to the United States, I found that the one week or eight weeks of initiation into the language-system of Arabic to be found in the older British system was expanded into a much longer period. This was partly due, of course, to the different educational systems, but there were clearly different goals and

---

1. *Contemporary Arabic Readers*, edited with notes by Ernest N. McCarus et al., vols. 1-5, Ann Arbor, Michigan: University of Michigan Department of Near Eastern Studies, 1962-66.

methods as well. The NDEA Act had encouraged concentration on modern Arabic and within a broader range of disciplines. In more recent times, that range has been further expanded to include the use of the language within professional schools and their academic contexts. These developments in Arabic teaching and learning have taken place within institutions where the instructional staff have for the most part been members of language and literature (or, at the very least, humanities) departments. Development of the reading skill has remained the predominant goal of instruction. New textbooks and syllabi have focused on other skills too, but until relatively recently their organizing principles have been grammar-based and the primary pedagogical purpose of skill activities has been the internalization of the principles of the language. Certain institutions have also offered instruction in colloquial dialects—a focus that has become increasingly important with the expansion of studies in such areas as anthropology, linguistics, folklore, and contemporary literature (especially modern fiction and drama), but few have been able to afford a full range of courses in a dialect, and it has proved difficult, if not impossible, to integrate such courses into a coherent language-study program.

3. Enrollment Trends and Advanced Language Programs

I hope that I do not either exaggerate the current situation or ignore significant trends or initiatives if I suggest that the bulk of our student enrollments in Arabic have been and continue to be at the beginning levels. This provides confirmation of the conclusions of John Carroll's rather depressing findings published in 1967 regarding the commonly taught languages; some of its corollaries regarding the less-commonly-taught languages are explored by Richard Lambert in another somewhat distressing document for language teachers, *Beyond Growth*.[2] Until recently, I would suggest that, in the American university context, the process of moving from lower- to upper-level language courses in Arabic has been one of leaving a carefully orchestrated pedagogical context, with a relative abundance of prepared curricular materials, for one in which the focus has, for the most part, been on the research methodologies of the field of the professor concerned. Let me immediately add two riders to that statement. The first is that I am not maintaining that such a shift is necessarily a bad thing, but merely that it seems to me to have resulted out of necessity in a diminished

---

2. John Carroll, "Foreign Language Proficiency Levels Attained by Language Majors Near Graduation from College," *Foreign Language Annals* 1 & 2 (1967): 131-51. Richard Lambert, *Beyond Growth: The next stage in language and area studies*, Washington: Assocation of American Universities, 1984.

focus on specific issues relating to upper-level language-acquisition *per se*. The second is that clearly the remarks do not apply to certain institutions in which the entire program has a more defined focus (as examples, I might cite the Johns Hopkins SAIS program and a Management School such as Thunderbird in Arizona). It needs also to be said that some work has been done on the preparation of materials for the upper levels of language acquisition, most notably by faculty at the University of Michigan; I have mentioned the readers prepared by Ernest McCarus and his colleagues, but I need to add a number of readers and specific skill materials prepared over the years by Raji Rammuny.[3]

Aware of the constrictions imposed on us by the givens of American society at large, undergraduate requirements, scheduling, and the difficulties that all these factors cause in bringing students to the higher levels—let alone retaining them for long enough to do so—with such facts in mind, all of us have been grateful for the opportunity to send our huddled masses yearning for upper-level language instruction to CASA. Bearing in mind the wide variety of teaching and learning scenarios that I have just described, it is hardly surprising that the CASA staff have been faced with an extremely challenging task. It needs to be stated that they have consistently done a wonderful job of adapting their program to the variety of student competences and expectations and of producing a large number of well trained and committed graduates, as any number of the current and next generation of Arabic teachers present at this conference in Middlebury can attest. The program has served as a proving ground for experiments in separate skill instruction at the higher levels and in the integration of the standard and colloquial forms of the language into a single program, an experience from which American Arabic programs have all benefitted and will continue to do so. More recently still, the Middlebury School of Arabic, whose tenth anniversary we are celebrating, has provided another venue where students can hone their skills in Arabic under circumstances different from and generally more favorable than those that their host institutions can foster during the academic year.

And into this scenario in the mid-1980s came proficiency. It needs to be reiterated that it was not and is not just another in a continuing series of new approaches to either teaching or learning, but rather a fresh and completely different approach to the rationalization of language programs as a whole—an

---

3. For example, Raji Rammuny, *Advanced Arabic Composition Based on Literary Texts and Audiovisual Materials*, Ann Arbor: University of Michigan, Department of Near Eastern Studies, 1978; *A Programmed Arabic Reader*, Ann Arbor: New Era Publications Inc., 1983; and *Advanced Business Arabic*, Troy, MI: International Book Center, 1987.

"organizing principle." Initially (in the early 1980s) there were two distinct aspects to the endeavor: one involved the preparation of Guideline descriptions, and the other training in one mode of testing one skill, the Oral Proficiency Interview. The second process was far more public than the first and aroused much interest, enthusiasm, and opposition. That was all fine and good, but I would suggest that it had two unfortunate side-effects. Firstly, a large number of language teachers and administrators leapt to an erroneous assumption that has proved very difficult to eradicate and counteract: namely that, within the curricular context, "proficiency" is to be linked or even equated with the speaking skill. The second effect was less of a perception and more of a reality, namely, that we were really working backwards, extrapolating from an assessment device all sorts of ideas and experiments about curriculum, syllabus, classroom priorities, and so on. It was in the much less public arena of Guidelines composition that the implications associated with such issues were being addressed. The history is reasonably well-known, I believe. A first set of Generic Guidelines (termed "provisional" and published in the early 1980s) was almost immediately found to be based on assumptions regarding Indo-European languages. A first set of Arabic Guidelines, entirely based on descriptions of activities in the standard language, was prepared at Penn and published in 1985. The Generic Guidelines were rewritten and published in 1986 as an ongoing area for research and revision. The ACTFL Arabic Guidelines were prepared by a national committee of Arabists and published in *FLA* in 1989.[4] In this context, it is worth noting once again that only in the area of Speaking are the assumptions incorporated in the Guidelines backed up by validation data collected over a significant period of time. The descriptors for the other three skills are essentially extrapolations deduced by analogy and supported by the best available current research on those skills. In the case of each skill, the validity of the assumed sequences of language acquisition and of the activities described has yet to be proved. Some of the issues associated with this question have been emerging from data provided by ACTFL Validation projects: the one for French and English has already been published,[5] and a second one, involving Arabic, Chinese, and Japanese is now in process.[6] In sum, it still needs to be

---

4. "ACTFL Arabic Proficiency Guidelines," *Foreign Language Annals* 22.4 (Sept. 1989): 373-92.

5. Pat Dandonoli and Grant Henning, "An Investigation of the Construct Validity of the ACTFL Proficiency Guidelines and Oral Interview Procedure," *Foreign Language Annals* 23:1. 11-22.

6. The Arabic group includes Mahdi Alosh (Ohio State), Mahmoud Al-Batal (Emory and Middlebury), and Roger Allen (Pennsylvania).

emphasized that the Generic Guidelines and all language-specific sets stemming from them are ongoing research documents.

4. Implications of Proficiency

In the context of the Guidelines for Arabic, I would like to broach three topics that impinge upon the questions posed in my title. Firstly, the Generic and Arabic Guidelines both include a new level of Distinguished for the receptive skills of Listening and Reading, thus implying a rise towards 3+ and 4 on the ILR Proficiency scale. Besides the expected references to the tailoring of language to situation—tact, negotiation, nuance, the uses of humor (the recognition of puns, for example), anger, and so on—the Arabic Guidelines for this highest level extrapolate from the other published Guidelines by making reference to a familiarity with the classical heritage of Arabic in the Reading descriptors and also by placing a developed awareness of the significance of code-switching into the Listening descriptors for this level. Both these instances allow me to identify what is, I trust, a fairly obvious point: the Guidelines cannot identify everything at every level; their illustrations are exemplary, and merely try to establish the points at which certain language behaviors become a *sine qua non* for placing a learner into that particular level of proficiency. Whether we are talking about grammatical accuracy, for example, or the ability to use more than one type of Arabic, the fact that such things are mentioned in the descriptors for the higher levels of the scale and thus given greater apparent emphasis is not intended to suggest that such factors are not to be part of the process of learning and evaluation at the lower levels. Quite the opposite. One might ask how one is supposed to display a developing language accuracy and/ or an ability to use more than one level of language at the Advanced level if the process of internalizing both has not started long before that stage. The same principle also applies to the choice of materials. Regarding the Reading skill, for example, it is certainly *not* the intention of the Guidelines that any course at the highest level that would wish to produce Distinguished-level readers would consist of a crash-diet of classical texts. I have tried to illustrate elsewhere the clear utility of both classical and modern texts in a proficiency-based classroom almost from the outset.

My second and third points are linked, since both concern the Arabic language itself and its ideal constructs, "native-speakers." Proficiency is, of course, defined as a system that uses a yardstick based on native-speaker behaviors. In Arabic, we have, I believe, something of a dilemma, in that not only do we face the complexities of a diglossic situation in which native-speakers in the many different parts of the Arab world operate along a spectrum of language-usage between their own colloquial dialect and the standard language, but also we have rather little research at our disposal concerning the actual processes whereby such native-speakers use their language in a variety of situations with complete sociocultural authenticity. Research such as that of Mushira Eid on code-switching is invaluable in this context, as is the kind of comparative study of different dialects such as that of Kristen Brustad.[7] The most recent issue of *Al-ᶜArabiyya* contains an utterly fascinating study by Dilworth Parkinson on attitudes to language types to be found in Egypt.[8] However, unless I am mistaken, we need a lot more of this type of linguistic research in the context of assessing current and future pedagogical directions in Arabic. Let me try to pose the issue in the form of the following questions: Are we to assume that, in the context of pedagogical planning for the teaching and learning of Arabic, we can construct a single model for the language behavior(s) of native-speakers of Arabic? Are we to organize a curricular model on the basis of a particular dialect region? If so, which region are we to adopt and for which reasons: that of Egypt, for example—clearly the most frequent choice thus far and for a variety of reasons— where the President and popular preachers will deliver speeches and sermons in the colloquial dialect, or that of the Gulf states where, if I understand sociocultural norms correctly, such behavior would be regarded as a solecism of some proportion? I should emphasize here that I am not attempting to assign relative *value* to the behavior of native speakers from one region of the Arab world or another, but merely to suggest that there is a difference between the various models. I might illustrate this on the basis of my own personal experiences. I have been interviewed by Moroccans who described their attitudes to the languages in which they function by saying that Berber was their first language, French their second, and standard Arabic their third, and who eventually requested that we move from Arabic to French because they felt more comfortable (I am sure they were also being tactful); by Egyptians who, because in recent times I have rarely stayed in the country long enough to eradicate the blend of standard and colloquial with which I usually communicate, themselves

---

7. Mushira Eid, "The Non-Randomness of Diglossic Variation," *Glossa* 16 no. 1 (1982): 54-84; "Principles for Switching between Standard and Egyptian Arabic," *Al-ᶜArabiyya* 21 (1988): 51-80; "Directionality in Arabic-English Code Switching," in *The Arabic Language in America*, ed. Aleya Rouchdy, Detroit: Wayne State University Press, 1992, pp. 50-71; Kristen Brustad, "The Comparative Syntax of Four Arabic Dialects: An Investigation of Selected Topics," Ph.D. diss., Harvard, 1991.

8. See Dilworth Parkinson, "Searching for Modern *Fuṣḥā*: Real-Life Formal Arabic," *Al-ᶜArabiyya* 24 (1991): 31-64.

made use of a blend of the colloquial and standard; and by Iraqis and Kuwaitis who seemed prepared to operate throughout the interview in the standard language without comment or apparent malaise. I am, of course, aware that their behavior towards a foreign professor of Arabic can hardly be considered typical and that my own impressions may be simply that—impressions; my only point is to note the variety of possible communicative situations that native-speakers of Arabic may *potentially* use. I must assume that there are a large number of native-speakers of Arabic who are quite capable of conducting an interview in the standard language at the Superior level on the ACTFL-ETS scale. The question that I am trying—somewhat stumblingly—to raise here is: quite how socially appropriate is that as native-speaker behavior and does it differ from one region of the Arab world to another? This question is not posed simply as a sort of abstract linguistic conundrum. For, when we move to the Arabic Guidelines themselves, we discover that they suggest that a Superior level rating in Speaking will no longer be given for one type of Arabic alone. At the Advanced level the descriptors for the oral skills begin to mention the need to "adjust language use to situation." For a Superior level rating, a Superior level competence in standard and colloquial is expected. Two brief points should be made immediately: first, the Guidelines make no judgment as to which type of language is learned first; and second, that, as some of you who have attended more recent OPI Workshops with me will know, we are still experimenting within the interview structure itself with the implications of this description of Superior level proficiency in speaking.

5.   Future Directions

I am acutely aware that Pandora's box has just been opened very wide. I will finish by pointing to just a few of the issues that we may wish to address here and into the future. Perhaps the most obvious area of research concerns the prioritization of teaching and learning of the colloquial and standard languages. There have been and are experiments in combining the two, initiatives that are bound to raise a number of issues regarding materials selection that may not be new but will nevertheless need to be addressed. Perhaps the most obvious issue is that of precisely which criteria are to be used in selecting the colloquial dialect to be taught and learned in combination with the standard language and indeed who is to make such a choice. How are beginning students supposed to know which area of the Arab world they wish to adopt as a focus of study and thus which dialect they need to acquire? One might even ask whether it is important for them to be able to make such a choice or whether instead the very combination of the standard language with the colloquial of any region (or perhaps a sampling of different regions) is sufficient to illustrate the diglossic situation in the Arab world. A counter argument might point out that if it is our goal to foster authentic language use, what purpose will have been served if an American student who has learned the Arabic of Lebanon, for example, along with the standard language decides to conduct research in Egypt or Morocco and tries to use the colloquial with which s/he is familiar in those countries? As an alternative, should we at this juncture acknowledge the potential value of preparing a syllabus that makes use of an essentially "generalized" colloquial such as that used as the Foreign Service Institute in Washington and found in Karin Ryding's recently published *Formal Arabic*?

Beyond these considerations regarding the choice of types of language to be adopted, the adoption of a rigorous four-skills approach, coupled with the introduction of more than one type of language into the beginning levels of Arabic instruction, will surely illustrate further the old adage: "less equals more." Senior colleagues only in search of readers of advanced-level texts and already suggesting that students today do not know as much as... [fill in the blank with the idealized era in question], will probably have even more complaints of that kind, perhaps not yet realizing that the students now emerging from language classes constitute an entirely new product with different sets of skills *and* expectations. Beyond this central question, others also suggest themselves: the comparative merits of a four-skills approach as opposed to skill-specific courses, and at which levels and in which circumstances each type is most appropriate; the relative value of content-based instruction with particular topical or disciplinary focus as opposed to more topically generalized courses, the relative value of study abroad and internships in the target culture as opposed to skill-specific upper-level courses, content-based instruction, socio-culturally appropriate language use, necessary pragmatic skills for business and other areas— these issues and many others promise us a future full of research and experiment as we assess our own curricula and the student language acquisition patterns that actually emerge from them against the parameters that the Guidelines invite us to test and, if necessary, to adjust.

6. Conclusion

I believe that it is fair to say that the advent of proficiency as an organizing principle in language programs within academe has encouraged a situation in which language teachers are taking the realities of the Arabic language and its use more into account in the making of curricular and pedagogical decisions.

That in turn has revealed the urgent need for more research on the behavior of native-speakers on the one hand and for more experiments in materials preparation, classroom teaching and learning, and testing on the other. However, adherence to the principle of authenticity that proficiency advocates forces us to acknowledge that no single model that purports to reflect what native-speakers do can cover the variety of language situations to be found across the breadth of the Arab world. When this variation in source material is added to the different teaching and learning strategies that are available to develop competences in learners, it surely becomes clear that, as teachers of Arabic, we need to embark upon a whole series of experiments in the teaching and learning of Arabic, approaching the process of curricular planning and innovation with enough flexibility to incorporate within our goals the wonderfully varied features of the Arabic language that should serve as a constant challenge to our own pedagogical creativity.

REFERENCES

ACTFL Arabic Proficiency Guidelines. 1989. *Foreign Language Annals* 22:4. 373-92.

BRUSTAD, KRISTEN. 1991. *The Comparative Syntax of Four Arabic Dialects: An investigation of selected topics.* Ph.D. dissertation, Harvard, Cambridge, MA.

CARROLL, JOHN. 1967. Foreign Language Proficiency Levels Attained by Language Majors Near Graduation from College. *Foreign Language Annals* 1 & 2: 131-51.

DANDONOLI, PAT AND GRANT HENNING. 1990. An Investigation of the Construct Validity of the ACTFL Proficiency Guidelines and Oral Interview Procedure. *Foreign Language Annals* 23:1. 11-22.

EID, MUSHIRA. 1982. The Non-Randomness of Diglossic Variation. *Glossa* 16:1. 54-84.

_____. 1988. Principles for Switching between Standard and Egyptian Arabic. *Al-ᶜArabiyya* 21:51-80.

_____. 1992. "Directionality in Arabic-English Code Switching." In *The Arabic Language in America,* ed. by Aleya Rouchdy, 50-71. Detroit: Wayne State University Press.

LAMBERT, RICHARD. 1984. *Beyond Growth: The next stage in language and area studies.* Washington: Association of American Universities.

McCARUS, ERNEST N., ET AL., eds. 1962-66. *Contemporary Arabic Readers,* vols. 1-5. Ann Arbor: University of Michigan Department of Near Eastern Studies.

PARKINSON, DILWORTH. 1991. Searching for Modern *Fuṣḥā*: Real-life formal Arabic. *Al-ᶜArabiyya* 24:31-64.

RAMMUNY, RAJI. 1978. *Advanced Arabic Composition Based on Literary Texts and Audiovisual Materials.* Ann Arbor: University of Michigan, Department of Near Eastern Studies.

_____. 1983. *A Programmed Arabic Reader.* Ann Arbor: New Era Publications Inc.

_____. 1987. *Advanced Business Arabic.* Troy, MI: International Book Center.

5

Issues in the Teaching of the Productive Skills in Arabic

Mahmoud Al-Batal

Emory University
and Middlebury College

The teaching of the speaking and writing skills in the Arabic curriculum has traditionally been overshadowed by an emphasis on the teaching of the reading skill and the development of grammatical accuracy. Recent interest among teachers in Arabic in developing overall proficiency, however, has led to a reexamination of these two skills and their role within the Arabic curriculum.

This chapter discusses some of the issues involved in the teaching of the writing and speaking skills in Arabic and suggests approaches to teaching them in a communicative-based Arabic curriculum. The chapter is divided into two main sections. The first section examines the current status of the speaking skill in Arabic programs, including the problems it poses to the teaching of the language, and recommends a new approach for dealing with these problems. The second section presents an overview of the status of the writing skill in Arabic curricula and provides a discussion of the pedagogical importance of writing as a means of reinforcing vocabulary, grammatical structures and organizational skills. It also offers several principles for making the teaching of writing an integral part of the Arabic curriculum.

1. Introduction

The present chapter addresses some of the basic issues involved in the teaching of the two skills of speaking and writing in Arabic. These two skills have been referred to in the literature of foreign language education as "the productive skills" in comparison with the skills of listening and reading, which have been termed "the receptive skills"[1] (Byrnes 1985, Krashen et al. 1984b, Omaggio 1986, Terry 1986).

The teaching of the speaking and writing skills in Arabic has long been relegated to a position of secondary importance, due on the one hand to the prominence given to the reading skill and the mastery of grammatical forms and structures and, on the other, to particular difficulties associated with teaching these skills (see further below). The goal of teaching students to read analytically remains primary in many Arabic classrooms and textbooks; while speaking and writing have made inroads, they are generally treated as supportive skills rather than communicative ones. Thus, speaking is mainly used to discuss what has been read, and writing is employed as a means of reinforcing grammatical structures.[2] The neglect of these skills in the classroom is mirrored by a serious lack of appropriate teaching materials that are specifically intended to teach these skills.

The present chapter will examine speaking and writing in terms of their current status in the Arabic curriculum and in terms of the problems each poses to the curriculum. It will also discuss future directions for the teaching of these skills in light of recent developments in foreign language education and the changing needs of our students.

2. The Teaching of the Speaking Skill

2.1 The Status of the Speaking Skill in Arabic

Interest in the teaching of the speaking skill in Arabic is a relatively recent phenomenon. The spoken component of the language began to receive emphasis in the early 1970s and the 1980s, inspired by new developments in foreign language education such as the communicative approach and the proficiency movement.

Prior to the 1970s, the teaching of Arabic was, by and large, dominated by the Grammar-Translation method, which gave prominence to reading and translation and which placed primary emphasis on the learning of grammatical struc-

---

1. The use of the term "productive skills" here, however, should by no means be taken to imply that some language skills are more active than others. In fact, Byrnes maintains that all language skills involve production in one way or another; she states that while the productive language skills require that the language user *produce meanings* that are communicated either orally or in writing, the receptive skills center on *producing understanding*, taking as the input oral and written language forms (1985:78).

2. While the importance of integrating all language skills cannot be denied, it is equally important for the learner to receive special training in the productive skills in order to speak and write fluently.

tures and forms. Arabic was dealt with as a "text-language" rather than a living language, and students learned much *about* the language but rarely had the opportunity to practice the language orally or even hear it. Furthermore, the texts often used were Classical Arabic texts rather than Modern Standard Arabic (MSA). This approach produced students who were capable of analyzing texts but were unable to function communicatively in an Arabic-speaking environment.

This dominant trend in teaching Arabic began to change in the 1970s due to the influence of the Audio-Lingual Approach to language teaching. An important outcome of this change was the appearance of new Arabic textbooks and a growing interest in applying new methods to the teaching of the language. The new textbooks were *Elementary Modern Standard Arabic I* (first published in 1968 and revised in 1975) and *II* (first published in 1968 and revised 1976) and *Modern Standard Arabic: Intermediate Level* (1971; revised edition forthcoming), all by Abboud et al. Influenced by the Audio-Lingual Approach, these books signaled an important shift in the philosophy of teaching Arabic and in the kind of Arabic taught. The books placed more emphasis on Modern Standard Arabic, the language of the written and spoken media. Although not ignoring grammatical accuracy, these books did pay more attention to listening and speaking. However, while the Audio-Lingual approach adhered to the primacy of the spoken language through the use of pattern practice, *EMSA* used the concept of pattern practice without concentrating primarily on oral Arabic. Thus, in a way, *EMSA* represented a kind of reconciliation of the Grammar-Translation and the Audio-Lingual approaches. Speaking as a separate skill did not receive great emphasis and the books did not provide opportunities to practice conversation on its own. Most drills were mechanical, and the oral drills were very controlled and were meant to reinforce the grammatical structures learned. This was true of *IMSA* as well.

Another important development that occurred in the 1970s was the emerging interest among some teachers of Arabic in applying new teaching approaches that stressed the oral skill. In 1978, Karin Ryding published an article in which she presented the principles of the Community Language Learning approach and explained how this approach could be applied to Arabic. One of the central activities involved in this approach was conversation (1978:13). At the same time, Raji Rammuny called for a greater emphasis on the teaching of speaking, beginning with the elementary level, and for the inclusion of audio-visual materials that would facilitate students' acquisition of the language (1978:90-1).

The 1970s also witnessed the publication of a number of books that were aimed at teaching Arabic dialects. Some of these books dealt with the Egyptian

(Abdel-Massih 1975), Moroccan (Abdel-Massih 1970), Gulf (Qafisheh 1977), and Saudi (Omar 1974) Arabic dialects. These books reflected the growing interest in spoken Arabic; however, like their MSA counterparts, they emphasized grammatical structures rather than the speaking skill. In addition, they treated these dialects as something completely separate from MSA, rather than as an integral part of the Arabic language. For example, their use of phonetic transliteration reflected the perception that spoken Arabic and written Arabic were two distinct languages rather than two levels of one language (see further 2.2.1 below). The fact that the dialects were taught in separate courses also underscored this thinking.

In the 1980s, the teaching of the speaking skill became the center of attention of a sizable body of Arabic language teachers. In 1985, *Al-ᶜArabiyya*, the Journal of the American Association of Teachers of Arabic, devoted a whole section to the issue of teaching the oral skills in Arabic. The section included five articles by Thurayya Haddad, Gerald Lampe, Dilworth Parkinson, Raji Rammuny, and Wafaa Wahba that dealt with different aspects of the teaching of speaking in Arabic. All five articles were unanimous in calling for the establishment of speaking as an integral component of the teaching of MSA.

One of the most important events in the evolution of the Arabic teaching profession's thinking about the speaking skill occurred when the Arabic Proficiency Guidelines were first published in *Al-ᶜArabiyya* in 1985. The guidelines, written by Roger Allen et al., were modeled after the ACTFL Proficiency Guidelines and included descriptions of norms for proficiency in Arabic in the areas of speaking, listening, reading, and writing (Allen 1985:52-70). The development of these guidelines had a positive impact on the profession in general and the teaching of speaking in particular, in that it renewed debate over the teaching of speaking. The guidelines, revised by Allen et al. and published by the American Council on the Teaching of Foreign Languages (ACTFL) in 1989, have become a central focus of the discussion about the problems of teaching the speaking skill (see Allen 1990, Heath 1990, Younes 1990, Al-Batal 1992).

2.2   Problems in the Teaching of the Speaking Skill

2.2.1 *The diglossic nature of Arabic*

The Arabic language is one of the few world languages that are characterized by the phenomenon of "diglossia,"[3] a term which refers to the coexistence, side by side, of two (or more) varieties of the same language. Originally, diglossia

---

3. For a detailed definition and discussion of diglossia in Arabic, see Ferguson (1959:325-340).

in Arabic was defined as the existence of two mutually exclusive language varieties: *al-Lugha al-fuṣḥā* "the literary language," also referred to as "Modern Standard Arabic" (MSA), and *al-Lahajāt al-ᶜāmmiyya* "the colloquial dialects."[4] Most past and present approaches to teaching spoken Arabic find their rationale in this view. Despite the fact that our understanding of the concept of diglossia and its manifestation in Arabic has evolved considerably since this definition was proposed, the original view continues to have direct impact on how Arabic is taught.

Recent studies indicate that MSA and the dialects do not represent distant and separate entities but rather the two ends of a continuum along which mixed varieties exist (see Badawi 1973, Mitchell 1978, Meiseles 1980). These varieties display substantial degrees of overlapping and continuity. Native speakers of Arabic combine and shift among these varieties based on the context of the situation in which the language is used. Rarely do educated native speakers use only one variety at a time. Yet most classrooms not only keep MSA and the dialects separate, they do not even introduce the concept of mixing. In addition, the relationships among the various Arabic dialects show a considerable number of shared features. While much research is still needed to reveal the extent of similarity between the dialects and MSA, on the one hand, and among the dialects themselves on the other, there is growing evidence that the dialects have much in common, especially in their syntax (see Brustad 1991). The Arabic teaching profession has neglected this area of inquiry despite its obvious implications for the classroom.

Dealing with this diglossic nature of Arabic in the classroom is perhaps the most formidable challenge that faces the teaching of the speaking skill. This challenge has become more acute in the past ten years with the rise of the proficiency movement and the emphasis it has placed on the teaching of functions. Among the functions specified for the novice and intermediate levels of proficiency are those related to daily life (describing one's family, daily routines, shopping, ordering a meal, etc.). While the teaching of such functions was not an issue for most teachers of Arabic fifteen or twenty years ago, it is now be-

---

4. Modern Standard Arabic is a mainly written, literary, and formal variety that functions as the official language in all Arab countries and is learned mainly through formal education. The dialects, on the other hand, are mainly spoken languages which vary widely along geographical and socio-economic lines from one Arab region to another and from one community to another within the same region. These dialects provide the vehicle of most oral communication and oral literature and are occasionally used in written contexts as well, such as dialogue in novels and short stories, advertisements, cartoons, and personal letters.

coming a relevant matter for many of them. Consequently, these teachers are becoming increasingly concerned with the question of which variety to use for the teaching of these particular functions and how this variety is to be introduced in the classroom. Many have opted for the use of MSA or a simplified version thereof at all levels, despite the fact that native speakers of Arabic invariably use a colloquial variety for these functions. Others have chosen to introduce these functions via colloquial, which they perceive as a more natural means of teaching daily-life situations. These two approaches will be examined in detail later in this chapter.

2.2.2 Teaching toward real proficiency

The interest in the concept of proficiency and the need for producing guidelines for speaking has made the challenge of diglossia a more pronounced one. One of the main challenges facing the profession today is how realistic speaking proficiency guidelines can be produced, reflecting the model of the native Arabic speaker and the sociolinguistic levels and contexts in which the language is actually used. The question was first tackled in 1985, when the first version of the Arabic Proficiency Guidelines was published. In that version, the speaking guidelines were based solely on the use of MSA, which meant that the descriptions of the speaking situations presented in the guidelines were not totally accurate. It also meant that the descriptions provided for the higher levels of proficiency (Advanced and Superior) in particular did not replicate native-speaking situations. The arguments for adhering exclusively to MSA were: 1) that there is a question of which dialect(s) to choose for teaching and for the descriptions, and 2) that it would not be feasible to offer courses in Arabic that would allow for the combination of MSA and one of the dialects (Allen 1985:48-49). The 1985 Speaking Guidelines completely avoided the issue of diglossia, except for a brief mention of the difficulties which might be faced by an Advanced Plus student in dealing with everyday situations which native speakers themselves find troublesome to deal with in MSA (55). Avoiding the diglossia issue resulted in speaking guidelines that focused primarily on grammatical competence and ignored other important aspects of communicative competence as presented by Canale and Swain (1980), such as sociolinguistic competence and strategic competence. These two important components of communicative competence are closely connected to the question of which Arabic to use in which situation.

The revised version of the speaking guidelines (ACTFL 1989:375) represented a remarkable change in philosophy vis-à-vis the diglossic situation in

Arabic. First, while the old guidelines were based on MSA alone, the new speaking guidelines state that the descriptions are predicated on the assumption that MSA and/or any colloquial dialect is acceptable. Second, instead of avoiding the whole issue of diglossia, as was the case in the old guidelines, the new guidelines make an attempt at dealing with diglossia and reflecting it in the descriptions. The new guidelines state that "at the higher levels of proficiency (Advanced High and Superior) the learner must show the ability to comprehend and to communicate in both MSA and a dialect, with at least partial awareness of appropriate choice depending on the situation involved" (374). The revised guidelines go as far as listing colloquial words such as *ma^{c}lēsh* "never mind," *kīfak* "how are you?," *bukra* "tomorrow," *^{c}āyiz* "I want," and *baddī* "I want" in the descriptions provided for the novice-low and novice-mid levels of proficiency (375).

While the new revised guidelines indicate that there is progress towards dealing with the challenges of teaching the speaking skill, there remain a number of significant problems. The committee (headed by Roger Allen) that undertook the task of writing these revised guidelines acknowledges these problems and maintains that the new guidelines are in further need of refining and revision. Perhaps the main problem of the present speaking guidelines is that they present an "upside-down" model of oral proficiency. Normally, proficiency in a foreign language develops in a gradual manner, starting with the ability to talk about everyday situations for students at a lower level of proficiency and progressing to the ability to speak on more abstract topics at a higher level of proficiency. Rather than reflecting this sequence and including the ability to function in the dialect in the lower levels of proficiency, the guidelines define this ability as characteristic of students at the higher levels. While the speaking guidelines may undergo further changes in the future, the way in which they have evolved thus far points to the degree of complexity involved in determining oral proficiency in Arabic. It also indicates that the profession is still uncertain on how to define norms for the speaking skill.

2.2.3 *Lack of appropriate speaking materials*

Lack of materials is a problem that is characteristic of all skills in Arabic; however, materials that are especially designed for speaking activities are scarce at best. The reasons for this scarcity were discussed above; they include the perception among many teachers that the main objective of teaching Arabic is to prepare students to read texts and to understand the grammar of the language, as well as the complex problems of diglossia which discourage some teachers from dealing with the speaking skill at all. Despite the fact that some new textbooks for Arabic (e.g., Allen and Allouche 1986, Badawi et al. 1987, Alosh 1990) make efforts to include speaking activities, these activities remain sporadic at best, and they account only for a small fraction of the entire activities included in these textbooks. In these books, there is a lack of systematic and gradual presentation of speaking activities associated with the various levels of proficiency. Examples of such activities include: at the novice level, activities whose goal is to develop accurate and intelligible pronunciation, such as students dictating to each other; at the advanced level, giving formal presentations; and for all levels, guided one-on-one conversation with specific communicative goals (as opposed to the goal of reinforcing vocabulary and structure).

2.3 *Future Directions for the Teaching of the Speaking Skill*

The discussion above indicates that the teaching of the speaking skill has become a subject of interest of the profession in the past few years. It also shows that one of the driving forces behind this interest is the proficiency movement. This movement has forced the Arabic profession to reexamine its perceptions of the speaking skill and its importance to the Arabic curriculum, as well as to rethink its approaches to dealing with the problems of diglossia in the classroom. Despite the fact that this rethinking has not yet yielded concrete classroom solutions to the problem, it has helped the profession shape two main directions for the teaching of the speaking skill.

One direction is to focus on developing students' oral proficiency in all functions and contexts in MSA alone, with the hope that students will later become proficient in an Arabic dialect and thus achieve overall proficiency in the language. The achievement of proficiency in the dialect may be realized by taking some dialect courses at the students' home institutions—wherever such courses are offered—or by traveling to an Arab country in which the study of a dialect can be pursued. In fact, this seems to be the case currently for a large percentage of our students who take two or three years of MSA and then travel to the Arab world for a summer or one academic year, where they continue their study of MSA and begin their study of the dialect.

This direction is the one favored by the majority of teachers of Arabic in the U.S. mainly because it shields them from dealing with the problems of diglossia in the classroom. The rationale that is usually advanced in support of this direction is that the introduction of all functions (including those related to daily-life) in MSA, albeit unrealistic sometimes, serves to reinforce the overall level of proficiency of students and help them internalize its vocabulary and structures. Additionally, using MSA as the sole medium of speaking in class would spare instructors from making a decision as to which Arabic dialect(s) to teach. Such a decision can be a difficult one for many teachers given the political realities of the modern Arab world and the questions posed by many educated Arabs about the legitimacy of teaching the dialects.

While this direction may have its merits and may be worthy of pursuit for some teachers, it has some serious limitations. First, it creates a fake model of oral proficiency by presenting the students with an artificial variety that is not used by the native speakers since no one uses MSA for daily-life situations. Oftentimes, students who have learned MSA for two years or more cannot perform the simple tasks of checking into a hotel or ordering a meal in the Arab world using the same language that a native speaker would use in these situations. Creating such an artificial language raises some serious questions about the true proficiency-based nature of our Arabic syllabi. Second, it is not in tune with the concept of proficiency and the proficiency guidelines. If we accept the current guidelines' depiction of the advanced student as someone who is capable of comprehending and communicating in both MSA and a dialect, then how can we base our language teaching on one variety without the other? How can we state that the ideal level of proficiency for which we aim is a level that includes both MSA and a dialect and then leave it to students to develop their proficiency in some dialect on their own? Third, it creates an impression that MSA and the dialects are distinct entities rather than overlapping varieties within the same linguistic system. Fourth, it does not fulfill the needs of most of our students; it does not prepare them to survive in an Arabic-speaking environment. The Arabic which they will have learned will not enable them to function in a natural manner. According to a national survey in which five hundred students of Arabic participated, most students stated that they are interested in developing their oral skills in the language and are interested in the study of colloquial (Belnap 1987:36).

The second direction would be to develop a system that incorporates the teaching of MSA and a dialect within the same course. The concept of integrating the teaching of MSA with a dialect is not entirely new and was applied at a limited scale in the Arabic programs at the Foreign Service Institute and the Army Language School (today's Defense Language Institute) in the 1950s and the 1960s (see Mansoor 1959 and Said 1959). Recently, this concept has gained momentum among some college teachers of Arabic as a necessary step to make the Arabic programs truly "proficiency-based." Inspired by this concept, Heath

(1990:45) states that the development of students' proficiency in the dialects should not be relegated to the role of afterthoughts or supplements to the "regular" courses but should be made part of an integrated and gradual approach that aims at teaching all the strains of Arabic (Classical Arabic, MSA, and the dialects) and the strategies of interplay among them. In his view, the pressing question facing teachers of Arabic now is not which of these three strains to teach, but how they all can be taught effectively (45).

Similarly, Younes (1990) has proposed an approach to the teaching of Arabic that would start with a spoken Arabic dialect, build a dialectal foundation in listening and speaking, then gradually introduce MSA materials (113-114). The focus of the dialectal foundation, Younes maintains, is to build the skill to communicate in situations in which the colloquial is typically used, such as personal identification, family, weather, work, etc. (114). MSA materials would be introduced in the form of texts to be read and listened to but discussed in the dialect. The teaching of the dialect continues after the introduction of MSA materials, and the two varieties are used side by side.

Guided by the same principles, Al-Batal (1992) has proposed the adoption of an approach that would reflect in the Arabic classroom the diglossic situation (with its different varieties) as it exists in the Arab world today. The proposed approach introduces MSA as a variety that is mainly written but that is also spoken in a variety of situations. It also introduces an Arabic dialect as a variety that is used mainly for daily-life communications and as a vehicle for some forms of literary expression. In addition, the proposed approach introduces students at higher levels of proficiency to a third variety, a mixture of MSA and a dialect, which characterizes the speech of educated native speakers in most contexts.

The integration of the teaching of MSA and the dialects in the Arabic classroom would represent a major step forward in the direction of improving the quality of our Arabic programs and responding to the needs of our students while, at the same time, reflecting the latest thinking in foreign language pedagogy. One should not, however, underestimate the challenges that would be associated with the adoption of such an integrated approach. Pedagogical questions related to the way in which the integration can be carried out and to the way in which syntactic and morphological differences between MSA and the chosen dialect should be handled, need to be answered. In addition, sociolinguistic research is needed in order to determine the features of an educated native speaker's discourse and to understand the way Arabs from different dialectal backgrounds communicate with each other. Moreover, adopting such an integrated approach would require a whole new set of textbooks and supporting instructional materials that reflect its philosophy. Efforts to produce such textbooks are currently underway. An elementary textbook in which Levantine Arabic is introduced in conjunction with MSA is being developed by Munther Younes at Cornell University. Another elementary textbook that focuses mainly on MSA but which has an Egyptian colloquial supplement is being developed by Brustad, Al-Batal, and Al-Tonsi at Middlebury College. The availability of such materials will facilitate the shift into this new direction in the teaching of the speaking skill and will allow teachers of Arabic to work towards a more realistic model of proficiency.

3. Teaching the Writing Skill

3.1 *Status of the Writing Skill in Arabic*

While the speaking skill has started to receive more attention in the last decade, writing has not been as fortunate. Writing is perhaps the most neglected language skill in Arabic. Arabic programs and textbooks, by and large, do not treat writing as a meaningful act of communication but rather as a supportive skill that serves mainly to reinforce vocabulary and grammar and to test comprehension of reading materials. Time spent on writing activities in Arabic classrooms is minimal compared to time spent on grammar explanation and manipulation activities, reading, and even speaking and listening. The relative importance of writing in Arabic can also be seen in the attitudes of students towards writing. In a national survey that included over five hundred students of Arabic, the majority of students surveyed ranked writing as the least important skill to them (Belnap 1985:34).[5] The status of writing can also be seen in our students' overall level of proficiency. The majority of students who have spent two or more years with the language experience great difficulties in producing writing that is genuine in terms of style and cohesion. While their writing may be grammatically correct, it tends to resemble English style, making their writing an English composition written in Arabic words (Al-Batal 1989:137-8).

This neglect of the writing skill is not exclusive to Arabic programs alone but seems to characterize other foreign language programs as well. In a study conducted on twenty middle and high school teachers of French, German, and Spanish in Wisconsin, Nerenz (1979) pointed out that writing activities accounted for only two percent of the total available class time (84). Similarly, Rivers

---

5. Forty-four percent of the students surveyed ranked writing as the least important, 14.4% ranked it as the third most important, 16.0% ranked it as the second important, and 4.4% ranked it as the most important skill.

states that college students with four, five, and even six or more years of study of foreign language are still unable to express themselves in a clear, correct, and comprehensible manner in writing (1981:291).

A number of factors have contributed to the neglect of writing in Arabic. First of all, materials that are specifically designed to teach the writing skill are extremely scarce. One of the few textbooks that deals specifically with writing is *Advanced Arabic Composition Based on Literary Texts and Audio Visual Materials* by Raji Rammuny (1980). The aim of this book, as explained by the author, is to help students at the advanced level develop fluency and ease in the use of literary Arabic for both oral and written communication (iii). It provides teachers and students with texts that are intended for reading and discussion; writing activities follow based on the content of the texts and the discussions. Although the book provides useful discussion of common errors in writing as well as stylistic hints on the writing of letters, it does not deal with the mechanics of Arabic writing nor does it deal with the cohesive elements of an Arabic text.

Another book that deals with some aspects of writing is *Adawāt al-Rabṭ fī al-ʿArabiyya al-Muʿāṣira* [Connectors in Modern Standard Arabic] by Al-Warraki and Hassanein (1984). The book is designed for intermediate-level students, and as its title indicates, it focuses on the use of connectors and their syntactic and semantic characteristics. The book is very useful in that it addresses the semantic features of the various connectors[6] and provides numerous examples and exercises to help students use them correctly in writing. A major shortcoming of the book, however, is that all the explanations it provides are limited to the sentence level; the functions of some of the connectors at both the paragraph and the discourse levels are overlooked.[7]

The teaching of Arabic as a foreign language, then, suffers from a severe shortage of materials that deal with the mechanics of Arabic writing and the characteristics of Arabic style. Likewise, the teaching of Arabic as a first language suffers from a similar shortage of materials. There are very few materials that explain to Arab students what the characteristics of good style are or how the development of ideas should proceed. In the same way, the study of cohesion is very limited and connectives, which are major contributors to cohesion, are presented as syntactic elements rather than text-building elements. Native

---

6. This is an important aspect of the book, given the fact that the classification of connectors in Arabic grammar is syntactically-based, and thus fails to reveal the significant semantic and textual functions which connectors perform.

7. For a detailed discussion of the connectors and the various levels at which they function within the text, see Al-Batal (1990).

speakers of Arabic seem to become good writers in an almost unconscious way; they acquire the writing skill by extensive exposure to written texts through reading and by memorizing great numbers of essays and compositions written by their language instructors or printed in composition textbooks. This extensive exposure to texts is similar to what Krashen (1984a) refers to as comprehensible input. This input includes language with structures that are slightly beyond the student's current level of competence, but which is comprehensible through the use of context and knowledge of the world.

This lack of materials in both Arabic as a first language and Arabic as a foreign language has a direct impact on the teaching of Arabic as a foreign language. Most teachers of Arabic largely overlook the stylistic and cohesive aspects of the writing process and focus their attention on the syntactic errors of the students. The end result of this is that students of Arabic seem to be transferring their writing styles and strategies from their first languages into Arabic.

3.2 *Making Writing Part of the Arabic Curriculum*
3.2.1 *Why writing is important*

The past two decades have witnessed a growing interest among foreign language educators in developing the writing component of foreign language curricula. The teaching of writing can serve a dual purpose. It can be perceived as a form of communication with other people and as an important pedagogical tool that is capable of facilitating students' learning of the target language. As a support skill, Raimes (1983:3) points out that writing is important because it: 1) reinforces the grammatical structures, idioms, and vocabulary which we teach the students, 2) provides the students with the chance to be adventurous with the language, to go beyond what they have learned to say, and 3) makes students more involved with the new language through the effort to express ideas and the constant use of eye, hand, and brain. Another important aspect of writing is that it makes students more relaxed and confident with the new language because it allows them to work at their own pace and to make changes and revisions without the pressure to perform on the spot that is associated, for instance, with speaking (Al-Batal 1989:138). In addition, written work, as Byrne points out, serves to provide the learners with tangible evidence that they are making progress in the language, and it also provides them with some variety in classroom activities (1979:7).

While the supportive function of writing is very important, especially at the lower levels of proficiency, it should not obscure the fact that writing is also an act of communication and an avenue for self expression. A useful discussion of the supportive and communicative functions is included in Rivers (1981) and Dvorak (1986). Rivers draws a distinction among three different types of writing: notation, writing practice, and composition.[8] Notation, she explains, includes copying and reproducing something which has been read or heard and is aimed at developing the students' ability to use the writing system of the target language. Writing practice is the type that is involved in grammatical exercises, the construction of simple dialogues, uncomplicated translation exercises, dictation, and the cloze procedure. And composition or expressive writing deals with the conveying of information or the expression of original ideas in a consecutive way in the new language (294). While notation and writing practice represent the supportive functions of writing, composition represents its communicative function. Similarly, Dvorak distinguishes between transcription which involves writing that focuses primarily on the conventions of language form (grammatical or lexical structure) and composition which refers to the skills involved in effectively developing and communicating an idea (145).

An understanding of both these functions is crucial for the development of a well-rounded writing program in Arabic. At lower levels of proficiency, writing exercises of the notation or writing practice exercises can help make students more comfortable with the new script and sound system and can enhance their grasp of grammar and vocabulary. At higher levels of proficiency, however, writing activities should be concerned with how ideas are communicated in the language and how texts are formed. This entails work on the various aspects of cohesion in Arabic such as the use of connectives, repetition, and substitution.

The place of the writing skill within the Arabic curriculum needs to be reexamined so as to make writing an integral and active part of the curriculum. The Arabic Proficiency Guidelines provide a good starting point towards achieving this goal. They present teachers with descriptions of the possible content and contexts for writing activities as well as norms of writing accuracy for each level. In addition to the guidelines, there are a number of basic premises that can be useful in any attempt to improve the writing content of the Arabic curriculum.

3.2.2 Premises for designing writing materials and activities

Since communication is normally driven by the need or desire to communicate, writing activities should attempt to create needs which students can satisfy by writing. This makes writing both more challenging and interesting, and

---

8. Rivers also lists a fourth type, translation, which I consider to be a form of writing practice.

encourages students to be more creative with it. "It is difficult for students and teachers to think of writing as a purposeful or communicative exercise if the goal of the writing activity, whether stated or unstated, is grammatical accuracy" (Dvorak 1986:157). An example of how routine writing activities in Arabic can be made goal-oriented may be found in Al-Batal (1989:140). Instead of asking the students to write a few paragraphs in which they talk about themselves and their study, family, or city, the activity can be placed within an authentic communication context. The teacher can provide the students with names and addresses of Arab friends (taken from pen pal pages in Arabic newspapers or magazines) and ask the students to write letters to these new friends talking about themselves. Following the activity, students can be asked to mail these letters to the friends they have chosen. Making writing activities goal-oriented helps the students think of the content and structures of the language, the context within which the language is being communicated, the audience to whom they are writing, and the appropriateness of the level of the language used.

Another premise that should be considered in designing writing materials in Arabic is the idea that writing involves continuous revision. This is an aspect that is usually overlooked in writing activities in Arabic. Teachers often assign a writing activity and then collect students' papers for correction and grading without giving students the chance to revise what they have written. This is in contrast to what happens with native speakers whose writing involves a series of revisions and drafts. Native speakers who are good writers spend more time planning their writing before they begin, constantly reexamine their writing to maintain a sense of the whole composition and line of argument as they write, and revise aspects of the content and the argument more than poor writers do (Omaggio 1986:224). Revision should also be an indispensable part of the writing process for non-native speakers and should be presented as such in the classroom. Students should be encouraged to think of writing as a multi-phased process that entails outlining, drafting, editing, and rewriting.

A third issue that should be considered in the design of writing materials in Arabic is the interaction between a writer and a reader. In most cases we write because we want other people to read what we write. Very often, however, writing activities in the classroom limit this interaction to the teacher and student. Even in this case the interaction is not real because the teacher tends to serve as a judge of what is written and to focus on how the material is written rather than on what is written. In designing writing tasks for our students, we should try to create readers who can share with them their ideas and provide feedback for what is expressed. One easy way to create readership is to have students exchange their writings with their classmates. The classmates can read them and give feedback on both the content and the style. Such feedback is crucial to the revision process. The teacher can also assume the role of a reader and provide comments on the content of the student's writing rather than correcting the grammatical errors only. Focusing only on the grammatical mistakes, as Dvorak points out (1986:156) will make students focus on producing error-free writing rather than on the content of what they are writing.

4. An Overview

The teaching of the productive skills in Arabic is entering an important new phase. Arabic is no longer seen as merely the language of classical texts. As more and more students of the language express their desire to be able to communicate in Arabic at all levels, in formal contexts as well as informal ones and in writing as well as speaking, the field of Arabic teaching will be forced to meet these new student needs. Reading and grammar will continue to be essential to the study of the language; however, writing and speaking will continue to become increasingly important. New approaches and teaching materials in the areas of speaking and writing, that reflect the realistic communicative needs of our students, will be desperately needed.

REFERENCES

ABBOUD, PETER ET AL. 1983. *Elementary Modern Standard Arabic* (2 parts.) London: Cambridge University Press.

_____. 1971. *Modern Standard Arabic, Intermediate Level* (3 parts.) Ann Arbor: Department of Near Eastern Studies, University of Michigan.

ABDEL-MASSIH, ERNEST. 1970. *A Course in Moroccan Arabic*. Ann Arbor: Center for Near Eastern & North African Studies, University of Michigan.

_____. 1975. *An Introduction to Egyptian Arabic*. Ann Arbor, MI: Center for Near Eastern and North African Studies.

AL-BATAL, MAHMOUD. 1989. Nashāṭāt Waẓīfiyya li-tadrīs Mahārat al-Kitāba [Functional Activities for the Teaching of the Writing Skill.] *Al-ʿArabiyya* 22:137-156.

_____. 1990. "Connectives as Cohesive Elements in a Modern Expository Arabic Text." In *Perspectives on Arabic Linguistics II*, ed. by Mushira Eid and John McCarthy, 234-268. Amsterdam: John Benjamins Publishing Company.

_____. 1992. "Diglossia Proficiency: The Need for an alternative approach." In *The Arabic Language in America*, ed. by Aleya Rouchdy, 284-304. Detroit: Wayne University Press.

ALLEN, ROGER. 1985. Arabic Proficiency Guidelines. *Al-ʿArabiyya* 18 (1&2): 45-70.

_____ AND ADEL ALLOUCHE. 1986. *Let's Learn Arabic: A proficiency-based syllabus for Modern Standard Arabic*. Philadelphia: University of Pennsylvania.

_____. 1987. "The Arabic Guidelines: Where now?" In *ACTFL Proficiency Guidelines for the Less Commonly Taught Languages*, ed. by Charles Stanfield and Chip Harman. Washington, DC: The Center for Applied Linguistics & ACTFL. American Council on the Teaching of Foreign Languages (ACTFL). 1989. "ACTFL Arabic Proficiency Guidelines." *Foreign Language Annals* 22:4. 373-392.

_____. 1990. Proficiency and the Teacher of Arabic: Curriculum, course, and classroom. *Al-ʿArabiyya* 23 (1&2): 1-30.

ALOSH, MAHDI. 1990. *Ahlan Wa Sahlan, II: An introductory course for teaching Modern Standard Arabic to speakers of other languages*. Columbus: The Ohio State University Research Foundation.

AMERICAN COUNCIL ON THE TEACHING OF FOREIGN LANGUAGES (ACTFL). 1989. ACTFL Arabic Proficiency Guidelines. *Foreign Language Annals* 22:4. 373-392.

BADAWI, EL-SAID. 1973. *Mustawayāt al-ᶜarabiyya al-muᶜāṣira fī miṣr* [Levels of Contemporary Arabic in Egypt]. Cairo: Dār al-Maᶜārif.

_____ ET AL. 1987. *Al-Kitāb al-asāsī fī taᶜlīm al-ᶜArabiyya li-ghayr al-nāṭiqīn bi-hā, Part II* [The Basic Book in Teaching Arabic to Non-Native Speakers]. Tunis: The Arab League Organization for Education, Culture, and Sciences.

BELNAP, R. KIRK. 1987. Who's Taking Arabic and What on Earth for? A survey of students in Arabic language programs. *Al-ᶜArabiyya* 20 (1&2): 29-42.

BRUSTAD, KRISTEN. 1991. *The Comparative Syntax of Four Arabic Dialects: An investigation of selected topics.* Ph.D. dissertation, Harvard University.

BYRNE, DONN. 1979. *Teaching Writing Skills.* Essex, U.K.: Longman.

BYRNES, HEIDI. 1985. "Teaching Toward Proficiency: The receptive skills." In *Proficiency, Curriculum, and Articulation: The ties that bind,* ed. by Alice C. Omaggio, 77-108. Middlebury, VT: The Northeast Conference on the Teaching of Foreign Languages.

CANALE, MICHAEL AND MERRILL SWAIN. 1980. Theoretical Bases of Communicative Approaches to Second Language Teaching and Testing. *Applied Linguistics* 1:1-47.

DVORAK, TRISHA. 1986. "Writing in the Foreign Language." In *Listening, Reading, and Writing: Analysis and application,* ed. by Barbara H. Wing, 145-167. Middlebury, VT: The Northeast Conference on the Teaching of Foreign Languages.

FERGUSON, CHARLES. 1959. Diglossia. *Word* 15:325-40.

HADDAD, THURAYA. 1985. Taᶜlīm al-Mahārāt al-Shafawiyya: Mawqif Jadīd [Teaching Oral Skills: A new outlook]. *Al-ᶜArabiyya* 18 (1&2): 15-21.

HEATH, PETER. 1990. Proficiency in Arabic Language Learning: Some reflections of basic goals. *Al-ᶜArabiyya* 23 (1&2): 31-48.

KRASHEN, STEPHEN. 1984a. *Writing: Research, theory and applications.* Oxford: Pergamon Press.

_____ ET AL. 1984b. A Theoretical Basis for Teaching the Receptive Skills. *Foreign Language Annals* 17:4. 261-75.

LAMPE, GERALD. 1985. Tadrīs al-Mahārāt al-Shafawiyya fī al-Lugha al-ᶜArabiyya [Teaching the Oral Skills in Arabic]. *Al-ᶜArabiyya* 18 (1&2): 11-14.

MANSOOR, MENAHEM. 1959. Arabic: What and When to Teach. *Georgetown University Monograph Series on Languages And Linguistics* 12:83-96.

MEISELES, GUSTAV. 1980. Educated Spoken Arabic and the Arabic Language Continuum. *Archivum Linguisticum* 11:1.118-43.

MITCHELL, TERRY. 1978. Educated Spoken Arabic in Egypt and the Levant, with Special Reference to Participle and Tense. *Journal of Linguistics* 14:227-258.

NERENZ, ANNE. 1979. "Utilizing Class Time in Foreign Language Instruction." In *Teaching the Basics in the Foreign Language Classroom: Options and strategies,* ed. by David Benseler. Skokie, IL: National Textbook Company.

OMAGGIO, ALICE. 1986. *Teaching Language in Context, Proficiency Oriented Instruction.* Boston: Heinle & Heinle Publishers, Inc.

OMAR, MARGARET. 1974. *From Eastern to Western Arabic.* Washington, DC: Foreign Service Institute, Department of State.

PARKINSON, DILWORTH. 1985. Proficiency to Do What? *Al-ᶜArabiyya* 18 (1&2): 11-43.

QAFISHEH, HAMDI. 1977. A *Short Reference Grammar of Gulf Arabic.* Tucson: University of Arizona Press.

RAIMES, ANN. 1983. *Techniques in Teaching Writing.* New York/Oxford: Oxford University Press.

RAMMUNY, RAJI. 1978. "Tadrīs al-Lugha al-ᶜArabiyya fī al-Jāmiᶜāt al-Amrīkiyya" [Teaching Arabic in American Universities]. In *Seminar on the Present and Future of Arabic and Islamic Studies: Final report,* ed. by Abdul-Mola Baghdadi and Raji Rammuny, 77-92. Ann Arbor: Department of Near Eastern Studies, The University of Michigan,.

_____ AND HAMDI QAFISHEH. 1978. *A Course in Levantine Arabic.* Ann Arbor, MI: Department of Near Eastern Studies, The University of Michigan.

_____. 1980. *Advanced Arabic Composition Based on Literary Texts and Audio-Visual Materials.* Ann Arbor: Department of Near Eastern Studies, The University of Michigan.

_____. 1985. Istrātijiyyāt taᶜlīmiyya nājiḥa li-tanmiyat al-mahārāt al-shafawiyya fī tadrīs al-ᶜArabiyya al-faṣīḥa [Effective Instructional Strategies for the Teaching of Oral Skills in Modern Standard Arabic]. *Al-ᶜArabiyya* 18 (1&2): 29-54.

RYDING, KARIN (LENTZNER). 1978. The Community Language Learning Approach to Arabic: Theory and practice. *Al-ᶜArabiyya* 11 (1&2): 10-14.

RIVERS, WILGA. 1981. *Teaching Foreign-Language Skills.* Chicago: The University of Chicago Press.

SAID, KAMIL T. 1959. The Arabic Language Course, Middle East Slavic Language Division, U.S. Army Language School. *Georgetown University Monograph Series on Languages and Linguistics* 12:97-100.

TERRY, ROBERT. 1986. Testing the Productive Skills: A creative focus for hybrid achievement tests. *Foreign Language Annals* 19:6. 521-8.

WAHBA, WAFAA HASAN. 1985. Al-mahārāt al-shafawiyya bayna al-naẓariyya wa al-taṭbīq [Oral Skills between Theory and Practice]. *Al-ᶜArabiyya* 18 (1&2): 69-90.

AL-WARRAKI, NARIMAN NAILI AND AHMED TAHER HASSANEIN. 1984. *Adawāt al-Rabṭ fī al-ᶜArabiyya al-Muᶜāṣīra* [The Connectors in Modern Standard Arabic]. Cairo: Center for Arabic Studies, American University in Cairo.

YOUNES, MUNTHER. 1990. An Integrated Approach to Teaching Arabic as a Foreign Language. *Al-ᶜArabiyya* 23 (1&2): 105-122.

6

TEACHING SPONTANEITY
IN ELEMENTARY ARABIC*

Zev bar-Lev
San Diego State University

The present chapter is an attempt to enhance more natural use of Arabic as a foreign language among students from the very beginning of study. It begins by outlining and exemplifying proposals to teach skim-reading from the very beginning of the elementary level. Then it describes how these techniques can be applied in aural work, to impart skills of "skim-listening." Finally, it comments on the teaching of skills of spontaneous, realistic language-use in conversation. Realistic language-use is thus developed as a primary goal of elementary curriculum with the help of the present proposals.

While these techniques have emerged in a special program and have been developed specially for use within specific workbooks, they are presented here in such a way as to allow teachers to use them in any curriculum. Indeed, their efficiency is such that they can be used even in curricula that might otherwise offer little time to practice speaking and listening.

1. Background

The present chapter explores an approach to enhancing more natural use of Arabic as a foreign language, as applied to the goal of receptive use of language: reading-comprehension and listening-comprehension. A unique feature of the approach is that it teaches natural use of language (albeit on a specially reduced scale) from the very beginning of study. Thus, in receptive skills, it proposes specific techniques to teach SKIM-READING—techniques that can and

*The research described here was funded in part by the National Language Resource Center of San Diego State University, under a grant from the U.S. Department of Education, Center for International Education.

should be used from the first weeks of study; similarly, it teaches skills of "SKIM-LISTENING," and, more generally, skills of spontaneous, realistic language-use, all from the very beginning of the elementary level.

Many teachers of Arabic are concerned about the hurdles that students will have to jump at later levels if their initial study fails to teach some particular structural aspect of the language. For example, it is often thought that if students do not learn Modern Standard Arabic, with its case-endings, and even if they do not learn to read traditional texts aloud, then they will have difficulty when they must speak and write formally in later years, or, still more, if they use Arabic for religious purposes or decide to study medieval literature. The result of all this concern is that many hurdles that might otherwise be distributed over three or four years end up piled all together at the beginning of many elementary programs.

This mountain of hurdles has its benefit: students who are not capable of the most demanding study of Arabic are eliminated from the beginning, before they start. But it has a disadvantage, too: many other students with more modest abilities and goals are eliminated, for example, those who might later develop an ability to converse at an intermediate level and read practical materials such as newspapers, although not medieval literature.

Since, in fact, most students do not go on beyond two years of study, many courses seem to be aimed, from the very beginning, at a small minority of their students. One might wonder whether this is a good tactic, even for the goal of motivating students into higher and more specialized study: Is it really motivating to learn the difficulties of a field so long before one has learned its attractions? Perhaps some students who would later be capable of, and interested in, more sophisticated study are simply not ready for it in the very beginning.

Thus, the opposite assumption is taken in this paper, as in some work that I have been doing on Arabic and a number of other languages for some seven years. Starting as a psycholinguistic experiment with a few students, I have developed, taught, and revised workbooks, called "Mini-Courses," in more than ten languages with the specific goal of clearing away as many hurdles as possible from the initial stages of study, while at the same time attempting to develop maximum spontaneity of speaking, with a small vocabulary and the absolute minimum grammar needed for basic communication.

The Mini-Courses have been specially appreciated by students with limited, non-academic goals, e.g., people about to travel or marry. But others have used the Mini-Courses to get a good start on traditional academic study, and it is this application that is most significant for ordinary curriculum.

The Arabic Mini-Course (bar-Lev 1993a) has a special benefit (for example, as against the French or Russian Mini-Courses) of being parallel to the Hebrew Mini-Course, which begins my longest program, consisting of three semesters. In view of the very close parallels between the languages, many innovations invented for Hebrew are applicable, at least somewhat directly, to Arabic. For example, the teaching of the alphabet is closely parallel in the two languages.

As described in bar-Lev (1991a), the Arabic Mini-Course teaches a generic vocabulary of about 250 words within about twenty class-hours, along with the most basic grammar, such as gender and main persons of the present tense. Like other Mini-Courses, it uses a simplified phonetic spelling to bypass any problem with the alphabet at the beginning. (Such phonetic spellings are common in Spoken Arabic courses such as Rice and Sa^{c}id (1979); for tourists, they have long been accepted in all languages.) Spoken Arabic can thus be learned in the Mini-Course without the alphabet, although a separate supplement (bar-Lev 1992) can also be used to learn the alphabet concurrently or subsequently. (The only major change in the Arabic Mini-Course from the description in bar-Lev (1991a) is that it now begins with the imperative, instead of the past tense, for a more direct introduction to the present tense; the alphabet course, however, still uses the past, for its direct representation of the root.)

2. Curricular Goals

The underlying assumption of both the Mini-Courses and the present proposals, especially for regular curriculum, is that students generally cannot study with a predominantly grammatical focus for a year or more, and subsequently switch to natural use of the language, in which grammar is only one of many components.

In Arabic, specifically, I suggest that we cannot expect most students to read letter by letter, with vowels, and to pay close attention to grammatical endings for a year or two, and then expect them to skim-read a year or two later, and suddenly interact with speakers—who themselves may not use some of these endings, and in any case speak more quickly than will allow morpheme-by-morpheme processing, use more vocabulary than can possibly have been learned, and exhibit a range of dialectal variations far too wide to be specifically prepared for.

Even courses with a strong communicative component may not prepare students as well as is actually needed. For example, even if students are reading authentic texts such as newspaper articles, and even if they can read without special preparation, the very use of a dictionary makes this reading unrealistic, since one cannot generally access a dictionary whenever one reads a newspaper. Similarly in listening comprehension, the most authentic oral texts do not guarantee realism of use, for example if they are read twice, since most real-world oral texts (e.g., news broadcasts) are not repeated.

In conversation, the most open-ended classroom activities often exhibit a predictability of topic that is totally unrealistic. Students may discuss time of day for twenty minutes or more in class, in a lesson devoted to this topic, whereas in reality (e.g., in the street) one may often have to "discuss" the time for a mere second, without any time to prepare oneself psychologically.

Can there really be anything controversial about trying to enhance more natural use of Arabic, or of any foreign language? It seems strange to proclaim the 1980s as the decade of oral proficiency, as do Harlow and Caminero (1990:489), on the grounds that fifty voluntarily responding university departments of Western European languages test oral proficiency once per semester, for an average 10% of the course grade! But is the situation in Arabic classrooms better than in these Spanish and French and German classrooms?

Krashen and Terrell's (1983:37-39) recommendation to "lower the affective filter" in the classroom so as to enable students to acquire language skills more easily, and Young's (1990:551) implied suggestion to avoid forcing students to speak in front of the class, in a sense miss the point, if the goal is natural use of language. After all, if students are not comfortable enough in the language to talk in front of their classmates, will they be confident enough to approach a group of native-speaker strangers, interrupt them, and initiate communication with them? If even the scariest teacher intimidates them into bashfulness, will they be able to bargain and even argue with taxi-drivers or others they may encounter in the street?

What may be most surprising in the present approach is the assumption that naturalness should be taught from the very beginning of study. But if teachers worry about teaching the case-endings of MSA or reading aloud out of concern to prepare their students for later challenges, would it not be even more appropriate to think about preparing these students from very early in curriculum for spontaneous, realistic use of the language? Sample conversations (which must necessarily be fixed, since they are presented in the textbook and/or tape), even with small variations, may be closer to realistic language-use than verb tables, but they do not really guarantee realistic abilities—in fact, they guarantee the very opposite. (In fact, I will argue below for the priority of authentic

SKILLS over authentic TEXTS: Specially prepared texts allow authentic skills to be taught earlier, and this is a tremendous advantage.)

Abstractly, would it not seem more logical to teach any needed skill from the very beginning, rather than to assume the possibility of a later switch? What, logically or methodologically, can justify deferring truly natural use of language for a year or more?

More generally, it is impossible to acquire a complete knowledge of a second language after the "critical period" of approximately thirteen years. (For the specific application of the classic concept of critical period to second-language acquisition, see Johnson and Newport 1989.) Adult learners will never be confused for a native speaker, and will never be in command of the vocabulary and grammar of a native speaker (although it is possible, with extreme artificiality, to put them in command of some aspects of grammar that many native speakers do not usually use).

What selection of the whole language, then, is optimal? How much of the vocabulary and grammar can be taught, and to what level of spontaneous use? The present approach recommends a higher level of spontaneity, with whatever lessening of lexical and grammatical range can fit into this spontaneity. I am not arguing for native-like spontaneity, but only for a level of spontaneity that will allow the language to be used by all or most of the students actually studying it, or likely to study it—including the vast numbers of students who do not relate well to verb-tables!

3. The Problem of Comprehension

Various "pre-reading" activities are commonly used in the classroom, as recommended, for example, by Chastain (1988:225-226), to evoke the appropriate background knowledge, as well as ensure the necessary linguistic background. The present suggestion, however, is that such "helpful," "teacherly" devices are in fact counterproductive, since they create a greater distance between the classroom and reality.

How many classroom readings are presented without a vocabulary, and then are read without a dictionary and made to serve some information-gathering goal, all in a reasonable time? How many listening comprehension exercises contain a significant portion of unknown words and forms, and are presented at a natural speed—and only once? These are outlines of reading and listening comprehension as they must generally be practiced in the real world.

How many teachers model authentic conversation in class? I do not mean authentic language, but authentic pace—including, of course, large numbers of unknown words: Ordinary native speakers may try to speak more simply for the sake of a foreigner, but they will generally target the known vocabulary very badly, if only for the simple reason that they do not know which textbook the given student has studied. As teachers, we automatically learn what words our students know when we use a given textbook twice or so, but the comfort that we can thereby provide our students is artificial.

Students will have to gather the news from a newspaper in a few minutes, almost invariably without a dictionary, if they are going to read a newspaper at all. They can read article after article with the help of the teacher or dictionary, and be completely unprepared for the very next article, unless we teach them much more flexible skills than we can presently teach. Students cannot ask the newscaster to repeat or explain individual words, nor do the radio and television stations pass out vocabularies even for their planned productions. Even TV Guide does not preview specific news stories! People in the street may repeat or explain an occasional word, but repeated requests for help will alienate them—or, still worse, turn them into teachers.

"Not to let a word get in the way of its sentence, nor to let a sentence get in the way of its intention, but to send your mind out to meet the intention as a guest; THAT is understanding." So Richards (1987:161) begins his definition of listening comprehension. But he notes that "there is little direct research on second language listening comprehension." Perhaps we can look for a more definite idea of the possibilities for comprehension in the specific question of vocabulary.

Nation (1990) suggests that some twenty thousand words occur in ordinary undergraduate reading, but that only some two thousand are frequent enough in all types of text to warrant teaching them to all students. But Fox (1987) had already shown the folly of aiming at either the higher or the lower vocabulary estimate; he recommends about seven thousand words as adequate for comprehension at a comfortable level, i.e., providing for recognition of thirty-nine out of every forty words. (These figures must all be regarded as estimating orders of magnitude, rather than specific quantities. Perusal of Landau's (1959) list shows that these orders of magnitude may be roughly applicable to Arabic as well.)

But how many years of university-level study of Arabic are needed before the average student will know seven thousand words well enough to read and comprehend—much less to listen and comprehend—in "real time" (i.e., without a dictionary, or even long cogitation)? It is my suggestion that even two thousand words are beyond the limits of most students of Arabic within two years of study.

This leads us to the "radical" but inevitable conclusion that comprehension must be redefined if it were to become achievable for foreign students of Arabic. Very little natural language-use can be integrated into ordinary courses—*unless* a radically different starting point is taken to comprehension. It is, therefore, my purpose here to outline the techniques used in the Mini-Courses, in the hope that they can be used by interested teachers on their own.

The various techniques of written and spoken language are separate. They are presented here in a logical order, but they could be discussed independently. For example, section 2 begins by discussing an innovation, called "glyphs," which are the starting point for reading comprehension as taught in the alphabet workbook in Arabic (as in Hebrew), although not a necessary starting point, and not the starting point in the spoken-Arabic workbook. Thus, readers should feel free to ignore any single section, but adopt the innovations of any subsequent section if they so desire.

4. **Readings and "Glyphs"**
The starting point of the teaching of all written language, in the Arabic (and Hebrew) alphabet-supplement to the Mini-Course, is the acquisition of a vocabulary of "sight-words": words recognized as wholes. This method provides a direct (although only partial) access to the content of written texts.

These sight-words are taught along with the alphabet, to optimize learner flexibility; thus, students are taught both to "decode" unknown words phonetically, and also to recognize words (especially cognates, such as names of countries) by key letters. Thus, students will be capable of recognizing words as wholes, or by some of their letters, or by letter-by-letter decoding—whichever is most appropriate to the specific situation as well as their own preferred learning style. (This approach is apparently unique in allowing for different learning styles in the study of the alphabet.)

Reading comprehension along the lines to be suggested could be taught in any framework that teaches whole-word recognition, whether sooner or later. But, I believe, sight-words, as well as the alphabet, are taught especially effectively via special illustrations, called "glyphs." Glyphs are first presented as ordinary pictures (figure 1), to cue the pronunciation of spoken Arabic words, so that these spoken Arabic words can be practiced without their English translations (figure 2).

Figure 1
Pictures & Pronunciations

Learn to say each word when you see its picture:

"water"	"door"	"pen"
a waterfall	two swinging	a hand holding a pen
with a rock	doors	on a page

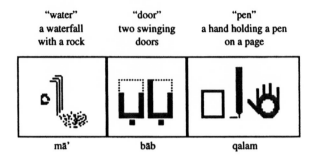

| mā' | bāb | qalam |

Figure 2

Pronounce rapidly:

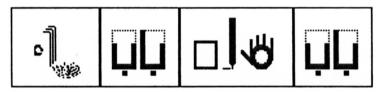

(In the workbook, a more student-oriented phonetic spelling is used.)

Although so far used simply as illustrations of the objects or actions represented by the Arabic words, the glyphs are subsequently also revealed to be visual clues to the Arabic spelling (figure 3).

Figure 3

The above words are spelled as follows:

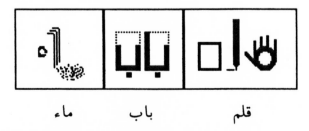

| ماء | باب | قلم |

Can you still see the pictures in the spellings? For example, can you see the hand (ة), the pen (ل), and the page (م)? ...

Figure 4

Translate rapidly:

4. ...　　　3. قلم　　　2. ماء　　　1. باب

These short steps allow all students to learn Arabic sight-words within a few minutes (Figure 4). The effectiveness of glyphs can be measured by the fact that hundreds of students have learned thirty or more sight-words in Hebrew with the help of glyphs, including approximately five students with diagnosed learning disabilities, and a number of others as well who were unable to learn any written Hebrew at all with ordinary methods. Similarly positive results have been seen with Arabic, although necessarily on a smaller scale.

The only students unable to benefit from glyphs are some of those who had previously studied the alphabet. Teachers, too, are generally not able to "see" them—even after they teach with them and see their benefits for their students. (And indeed, perhaps it takes a special teacher to use some technique that he or she does not appreciate, however much students may seem to benefit from it.)

The goal of teaching sight-words is not just to teach rapid recognition of useful words, but, more important, to teach the alphabet in context. The advantage of teaching letters in context is that students will not have any difficulty putting letters together, as they sometimes do in ordinary methods. Cognates and names, as noted, are read phonetically with the help of matching exercises, to ensure that students use key-letters, rather than letter-by-letter analysis. (Vowels are also presented, for exercises in pronouncing.)

Some fifty sight-words are sufficient to teach the whole Arabic alphabet. While it is possible to teach twenty or more sight-words without letters, letters are actually introduced concurrently to allow each student to learn with his or her own preferred learning style, as noted earlier. A variety of word-recognition strategies is thus taught explicitly, where most programs address reading as if it were decoding only. Also, by teaching letters in the context of whole words, whole-word recognition is emphasized, even for the words that must be recognized on the basis of key-letters.

Putting aside the alphabet, we can now focus on sight-word recognition, which is more relevant to skim-reading. After all, skim-reading requires rapid recognition of words—not necessarily at the pace of native speakers, but rapidly enough to preclude word-for-word reading, much less decoding or sounding out whole texts word by word.

5. Skim-Reading

Whether a teaching program uses glyphs or not, it can teach skim-reading well enough as long as it teaches sight-word recognition. Moving from letter-by-letter "decoding" to flash card practice can also provide the basis from which skim-reading can also be taught. Flash cards need not be used for every word the student will ever learn, but enough practice in rapid recognition must be given to establish the principle of whole-word recognition firmly. (Compare Clarke and Silberstein 1977.)

More generally, skim-reading as taught here does not emphasize speed at all. Speed-reading, I believe, is a skill of the eye: It quickly breaks down if the mind does not operate in tandem. Also, I find that students' resistance is best overcome if they are allowed to proceed at their own pace in the beginning—as long as they are not able (because of the way the exercises are structured) to look up unknown words. Decoding should also be prevented or at least discouraged during comprehension exercises. But traditional textbooks, in which students learn every word that occurs in the readings, implicitly encourage decoding, at least as a back-up strategy; what is needed are special texts to force the students to use the desired skills.

Sight-words, in the proposed method, are used as a starting point for teaching skim-reading, via "word-search" puzzles of the same type as are sold in supermarkets (figure 5). Students readily do word-search puzzles, and move on to word-search in text, filling in the translations of verses of Qur'an and other sentences (figure 6). Associating verses with their translations is a useful activity in itself, and is culturally enriching, even if they are not read aloud or learned word for word. In spite of its game-like structure, this exercise-type does practice component skills of skim-reading, viz., recognizing known words, ignoring unknown words, and arriving at a coherent meaning.

Similar techniques are used to teach students to do "word-skimming" (or, as I prefer to call it, "root-search"): to recognize roots in spite of attached affixes (figure 7). This skill is especially easy in Arabic (although by no means as easy, for Americans, as in Western European languages), especially when it is printed without vowels.

Students also learn "skim-reading"—or, as it is called, "skip-reading": guessing the content of a whole text on the basis of a small number of recognized words (figure 8). (Learned words are emphasized here to show what students have learned, but they are not underlined in the workbooks.) Even learning disabled learners have little difficulty spotting the known words in such exercises and coming to a general idea of the content.

I still find that many students need encouragement to recognize that this is a "real" skill, at least as important as the more traditional word-for-word reading. But at least I find that students do prefer skim-reading over word-for-word reading with just a little practice.

"Intensive skim-reading" exercises (called "puzzle-stories") are built out of a skeleton of a reading that could be easily understood as a regular reading (figure 9), except that extraneous difficult words are added as purposeful distractors, to challenge students to understand in spite of them, on the basis of what they do recognize (figure 10).

Note that the original stories must be artificially simple, since students do not necessarily recognize every word that they have learned. The preference here is to allow whatever artificialities are necessary in the texts to allow naturalness of skill.

In spite of its apparent simplicity, this exercise-type is extremely challenging, since, inter alia, students will sometimes think they recognize words which, in fact, they do not know. Learning to deal with this problem is, of course, necessary for real use of language. (It should be noted again that students do not see the original simple story, or the emphasis provided here.)

The techniques exemplified are totally neutral with respect to choice of topic and varieties of language. So Arabists who prefer to avoid such cliché topics as camels and deserts, and use Modern Standard Arabic, can easily do so.

However, my students—in Hebrew as well as Arabic—enjoy local color, even when somewhat stereotypical; such topics encourage imaginative use of language within the limited abilities of the elementary student.

And my program happens to use "Written Spoken Arabic" (as evidenced by *šaaf*), which does happen to be easier and more useful for most purposes; compare the discussion in Parkinson (1991) and the references cited there. By the way, *šaaf* does occur in Landau's (1959) frequency list based on newspaper Arabic, although not as frequently as *raʔaa*.

While rising above geographical and sociolinguistic variation does make sense, the cost of "Modern Standard Arabic" to the learner, with its case endings, is simply too high, quite apart from its distance from ordinary spoken language. It is interesting that *šaaf* occurs throughout the spoken dialects, from Saudi to Moroccan.

Figure 5
Word-Search

Circle the words that you know in the puzzle:

باب يها ماء ب هع ل قلم

Figure 6
Word-Search in Text

Circle the words that you know, and fill in their meanings in the translations:

١. وانزلنا من السماء ماء طهورا

٢. الله يفتح باب الرزق

٣. قلم الحرية خالد

1. We send down pure _____ from the sky
2. God opens the _____ of the living
3. The _____ of freedom is immortal

Figure 7
Root-Search

Underline and translate each root. Ignore its affixes, as shown in the first example:

٣. ...   ٢. القلم   *door* ١. الباب

Root-Search in Text

Circle the words that you know, and fill in their translations:

الذي علم بالقلم

who taught with the _____

Figure 8

Skip-Reading

[Learned words are bolded here, but not in the workbook.]

Circle all the words and roots that you know. Make up a story that uses these roots. Compare your story with those of your study-partners.

مشى **الجمل** في الصحراء وتعب .

بحث **الجمل** عن الماء لمدة طويلة .

جاء **الجمل** الى **الجبل** وشاف ماء .

وقد **شرب** لمدة طويلة .

Figure 9

Skeleton for puzzle story (Figure 10)

[Learned words are bolded here, but not in the workbook.]

سافر تاجر الى مصر .

واحب الهرم .

اخذ سيارة ضخمة ،

وسافر طويلا في **الصحراء** .

ولم يعرف اين هو ...

Where did the merchant go? ......

Figure 10

Puzzle Story

سافر تاجر اجنبى الى مصر .

واحب الهرم الاكبر والمشهور بحماسة .

استأجر **سيارة** ضخمة ،

وسافر طويلا في **الصحراء** .

ولم يعرف اين هو يتجول ...

Where did the merchant go? ......

Teachers who think that such a reading technique is useless might ask themselves what vocabulary their students have, even after years of study, and whether the more traditional skill of reading word for word, or this technique of skim-reading, is therefore more directly applicable to real reading. Students cannot continue using a dictionary or their teacher's helpful hints when reading a newspaper; nor can they learn enough words to ever read independently, if this entails recognizing almost every word. It is traditionally assumed that students can learn to manage on their own later—but reports of students do not substantiate this assumption, even for Western European languages.

Traditional teachers (and traditional students) may be more immediately convinced of the usefulness of "intensive skim-reading" ("intensive skip-reading"). This term might seem like an oxymoron: Isn't skim-reading inherently opposite to intensive reading? Actually, not at all. In principle, after all, students are often interested in getting a fairly exact meaning out of a text, but they are not necessarily able to recognize or look up every word they do not know; in fact, I would suggest that they can almost never know all the words in an ordinary text, even if they (try to) use a dictionary.

The familiar technique of "guessing words from context" misidentifies the needed process: Exercises in guessing words from context are almost as time-consuming, and therefore as inapplicable, as dictionary search. In other words, students cannot (or at least should not) guess the meaning of all words they do not know; instead they should skip over them, and jump right to the meaning of the text. Hence, intensive skim-reading.

6. Skim-Listening

We turn now to listening comprehension. The innovations here are parallel to those discussed, in the sense that they focus on empowering the student to comprehend when a high proportion of words and forms are unknown. But they are independent, even in the Mini-Courses, since, after all, studying Spoken Arabic without the alphabet is an option.

The skeptical reader may ask why I fuss with questions of vocabulary, etc.: Isn't it enough to provide abundant "comprehensible input," as recommended by Krashen and Terrell? While of course it is the goal of all materials for comprehension to provide comprehensible input, I suggest that, in the Less Commonly Taught languages (LCTL) in particular, it is impossible for the teacher to ignore the lexical and grammatical details of comprehensible input. Thus, whatever is comprehensible to the weakest student will be too easy for the strongest;

what is appropriately challenging for the average student will leave many weaker students in the dark and cause them to be frustrated.

We must, on the contrary, pay close attention to the structure of all materials that we use to teach comprehension, and, just as important, teach our students how to comprehend more effectively, so as to broaden the range of what will be comprehensible input for them; that is, if we teach them truly effective techniques for comprehending (in preference, e.g., to "tracking" exercises in which the student reads a text while hearing it).

Transcription is used here, as in the textbook, to emphasize that these exercises are given orally. (But the transcription does also allow independent study, and also home review of aural exercises.)

Listening comprehension begins with aural word-search (figure 11—the Mini-Course uses a special "student spelling"). Analogous to recognizing roots in spite of affixes are exercises in recognizing new forms of words (figure 12), which is especially helpful in teaching recognition of Arabic verb root-vowel changes, and broken plurals.

The goal in writing stories is to achieve maximum sophistication of meaning combined with simplicity of language. While further practice will no doubt allow us to achieve these goals more easily, I have no doubt that the first efforts exemplified here fall far short of the ultimate possibilities.

Repetition of simple words is important for beginning learners. Furthermore, it is crucial to avoid the temptation to try to build stories around profound or amusing "punch-lines." These are, I believe, often fatal to elementary learners. Pedagogically, they tend to be just far enough beyond the students' real discourse abilities as to ruin their impact—especially in listening comprehension, if, as assumed here, we are "forbidden" to repeat.

Figure 11
Word-Search

Find all the words that you know in the following word-search puzzle and translate them instantly. Do not translate any words that you do not know.

šabaab	falaafil	kabaab	ruuħi
ħadd	ruzz	arwaj	ᶜaṣiir
ħaliib	la	jallab	sabaq
ħaraka	ħisaab	rajaᶜ	finjaan
...			

Figure 12
Word-Skimming

The following are new forms of words that you know. How many of them can you identify?

qaamuu, naamuu, akaluu, zaarat, axaðat, takallamuu, ᶜamiluu
yaquum, yanaamuu, yaʔkuluu, saaᶜadat, yaᶜmal, yaštarii, yuḥibbu

Words occur in many forms. (English is relatively simple in this respect.) While it may take many years to learn how to form and use them, it is relatively easy to recognize them. Do not try to learn to use forms from context alone: Keep speaking with the simpler and safer forms learned earlier. But at the same time, expand your ability to comprehend by recognizing forms beyond what you can produce. Translate:

il-malik wa-l-ᶜaskari yiju wa-yitkallamu, wa-yaaxðu il-ḥummuṣ.

Figure 13
Skip Listening

Find 5-10 words that you know in the following story, and guess the content of the story using these words....
[Learned words are not emphasized in textbook]

qaam il-muᶜallim min il-firaaš. wa-akal il-muᶜallim mišmiš, wa-maša li-l-madrasah. fii-l-madrasah huwa axað il-qalam, wa-katab kalimāt kaθiira, wa-takallam maᶜ iṭ-ṭalaba.

Skip Listening

Find 5-10 words that you know in the following story, and guess its content using these words: [Learned words are not emphasized in textbook]

qaabal il-muᶜallim il-muhandis fii-ṭ-ṭariiq wa-qaal, "marḥaba." qaal il-muhandis li-l-muᶜallim, "ahlan, kayf el ḥaal?" qaal il-muhandis, "il-ḥamdu li-l-laah." il-muᶜallim ṭalab min il-muhandis ann yajii li-s-suuq wa-yištirii mišmiš, hummuṣ, ruzz, wa-laḥm. il-muhandis qaal, "kwayyis, is-saaᶜah kam?" il-muᶜallim qaal, yumkin is-saᶜah sitta. qaal ᶜil-muhandis, "wayn is-suuq?" qaal il-muᶜallim, "qariib min ij-jabal." qaal il-muhandis, "kwayyis, nimšii."

"Skim-listening" ("skip-listening") consists primarily of getting the overall topic of a story when students hear it. These texts must be kept extremely simple, and the goals kept low: Students in the very beginning are probably not able to recognize any more of a "theme" than, say, a location, e.g., "there is something about a lot of foods, maybe it takes place in a restaurant."

Note that one of the challenges is simply hearing familiar words in a continuous text. Teachers may be tempted to overcome this difficulty by repeating the text, or emphasizing familiar words unnaturally. But the whole point of this exercise is to read it just once. The speed need not be conversational, but it should be continuous and without special hints. Of course, no special preparation should be given before it: Pre-reading activities (as mentioned earlier) actually undermine the very goals that they are intended to teach, by allowing students to guess the central point of a text without any contact with the text itself. (As soon as they hear "Now, class, what do you know about beetles? Would we be better off if there were no beetles in the world," students already know that the theme of the reading is "our friend, the beetle." They—and we— may think that they are getting this from the text, but in fact they are getting it from the teacher.)

7. Spontaneity in Conversation

The "waiter" exercise (figure 14), although it can be given in the very first lesson, is actually a complex exercise in that it also demands a pragmatic response: The student must ignore extraneous material and catch the food-orders. This response is the beginning of a series of exercises, sprinkled throughout the materials, to integrate skim-listening techniques into ordinary conversation. Further exercises (figure 15) specifically practice question-answer on the basis of partial recognition of the words in a question.

Figure 14
Skim Listening

You are a waiter; try to catch what each person orders, and write it down (in English).... (Do not try to use words or forms given here, ...)
[Learned words are not emphasized in textbook]

1. ana ᶜatšaana, jiblii kaas ḥaliib suxn, min faḏlak.
2. šu ana aḥubb? aa, biddi akul šwayyit samak.
3. ana muš juᶜaan. ṭayyib, šwayyit mišmiš.

Figure 15
Skim Listening

Listen for a person or thing that you recognize in the following questions and statements, and react by saying anything you want about that person or thing. Say two-three sentences or more about each.

[Learned words are <u>not</u> emphasized in textbook]

iš ʿamal <u>il-muʿallim?</u>

bi-eeš mašyūl <u>il-waziir?</u>

iš ḥaṣal <u>li-l-malik?</u>

The strictly "grammatical" answer may not be "pragmatic," as you can see with questions like: "Is there a good restaurant around here?"...

The traditional assumption is that students must learn "literal" (logical, hyper-coherent) communication in class, and can learn pragmatically-loose conversation (as well as talking nonsense) outside. The present assumption is the reverse. I propose (and emphasize to students: Figure 16) that natural conversation requires the ability to "hang loose"—both by being willing to participate in a conversation in which some (perhaps much) may be unclear, and to be imaginative and interesting, rather than literal, in one's own participation.

Figure 16

Don't be like the many "serious" students of foreign language, who wander the countries of the world, dictionaries open, endlessly repeating, like robots:

Do not sound like a typical foreigner, when asked a question:

Do you have an expensive house?	—What does "expensive" mean?
Big. Is your house big?	—Your house?
Your house, is it big?	—Oh, my house. Yes.

You can be a confident speaker, even if you don't exactly understand the question:

Do you have an expensive house?	—My house is nice.
	My house is big and red.
	I love my house....

Where the traditional student may hear "Do you know what time it is?" and answer "3:00 a.m." (or perhaps even "yes"!), the student who has been specifically trained to integrate pragmatic information into language use from the very beginning is more likely to notice that his stereo is blaring. Even further, especially in an LCT language, it is also vital to provide linguistic tricks for dealing with language as it occurs. For example, the recommendation of the textbook is to try to catch any word in a question, and say something interesting about it. If students hear the word "restaurant" or "bathroom," they should say whatever seems pragmatically relevant, which might include where a good one can be found, rather than focus on the question-word, which might prevent them from hearing the key word itself.

Although devoted wholly to receptive skills, this chapter cannot conclude without noting the importance of speaking: It is my claim that, even with specific exercises such as those proposed here, spontaneous interaction presupposes the ability to speak confidently, continuously, and creatively (as outlined in bar-Lev 1991a). Indeed, the main rationale for the Mini-Courses is that speaking, for most students, is the very definition of knowing a language—as well as being the skill in which useful (however limited) abilities can be acquired within a very small amount of time.

A main exercise in the Mini-Courses is the "Talkathon," in which students simply talk for as long as they can—both in their study-groups and in front of the whole class. They are not allowed to ask for help while talking, and any hesitations and self-corrections are frowned upon. This classroom exercise is, in a sense, the foundation-stone for all spontaneous conversation in the present approach, and the primary distinction of the present approach from Natural Approach and other communicatively-based modern methods: Where it is by now common to believe that acquisition emerges from "comprehensible input," it is my proposal that speaking is a more efficient key to acquisition, and even to comprehension.

More generally, teachers might try a Talkathon with their students. They may be appalled by the fumbling, or by the silence. Students may rationalize by saying that they just cannot think of topics. But thinking of topics is part of the challenge of speaking. Should not students be able to speak spontaneously for at least a few sentences?

Students who practice the above techniques become enviably comfortable with their new language. To be sure, they sometimes talk off the topic (after all, my classroom "rule" is, if you do not understand anything, talk about anything at all), but, even ignoring the fact that real people often choose to take the topic in a new direction, these students speak much more naturally and enjoyably than we are used to seeing in the classroom. Their answers are not mechanical.

As noted at the beginning, it is my hope that these and any of the other specific exercise-types can readily be used by any interested classroom teacher, even without the specifics of the whole proposed methodological framework or the workbooks.

The general claim is that natural use of language should and can be the goal of classroom instruction from the beginning—but at the same time that such goals are not likely to be achieved (or even attempted) without special "unnatural" contrivances such as those proposed here.

To review the question as posed at the beginning, and the answer as we have developed it here: In any curriculum, especially one of a mere three semesters for an LCT language (especially one with a complex morphology and a challenging writing system), a radical selection of the language must be made. This is especially so when we regard the language as a set of skills or abilities, rather than a set of structures: If we dump too many structures (vocabulary or grammar) on the student (no matter how good our intentions, or indeed how devoted the student), we will short-change the abilities, leaving students with an abstract concept of the language rather than the language itself.

Some teachers may think that they have taught language skills, because they have seen these skills operate within the context of classroom exercises: The students read a difficult story or news-article, and answered the questions (whether with the teacher's help, or in study-groups, or even "independently"— each working alone with a glossary), they comprehended and answered the oral questions (the two students who volunteered answers did quite well, with only a little help), they had a conversation on the assigned topic that showed excellent "fluency" and even, in a few cases, significant variation from the sample given in the textbook.

How close are they to reading a newspaper article on their own? Will another few thousand words make them able to read a newspaper quickly and independently enough for it to be worthwhile? And how close are they to speaking spontaneously, without an assigned topic? Will a hundred more sample conversations make them more spontaneous? How many more semesters will it take before they can use the language spontaneously? And, just as important, what if they will simply not study Arabic long enough to learn a few thousand more words, or see more sample conversations?

REFERENCES

BAR-LEV, ZEV. 1991a. Two Innovations for Teaching Arabic. *Al-ᶜArabiyya* 24:1-30.

_____. 1991b. Two Innovations for Teaching Tones. *Journal of Chinese Language Teachers Association* 26 (3): 600-612.

_____. 1992. *The Dancing Abjadiyyah.* Manuscript.

_____. 1993a. *Arabic for Scaredy-Cats.* Manuscript.

_____. 1993b. Sheltered-Initiation Language Learning. *Applied Language Learning* 4 (1-2).

_____. 1994. An 'Unnatural' Approach. *Mid-Atlantic Journal of Foreign-Language Pedagogy* 2.

CHASTAIN, KENNETH. 1988. *Developing Second-Language Skills: Theory and practice.* San Diego: Harcourt Brace Jovanovich.

CLARKE, MARK A. AND SANDRA SILBERSTEIN. 1977. Toward a Realization of Psycholinguistic Principles in the ESL Reading Class. *Language Learning* 27:1. 135-154.

EL-SADANY, TAREK A. AND MOHAMED A. HASHISH. 1989. An Arabic Morphological System. *IBM Systems Journal* 28:4. 601-612.

FOX, LEN. 1987. "On Acquiring an Adequate Second Language Vocabulary." In *Methodology in TESOL: A book of readings*, ed. by Michael H. Long and Jack C. Richards, 307-311. New York: Harper and Row (Newbury House).

HARLOW, LINDA AND ROSARIO CAMINERO. 1990. Oral Testing of Beginning Language at Large Universities: Is it worth the trouble?" *Foreign Language Annals* 23 (6): 489-501.

JOHNSON, JACQUELINE S. AND ELISSA NEWPORT. 1989. Critical Period Effects in Second Language Learning: The influence of maturational effects on the acquisition of English as a second language. *Cognitive Psychology* 21:60-99.

KRASHEN, STEPHEN D. AND TRACY D. TERRELL. 1983. *The Natural Approach.* San Francisco: Alemany.

LANDAU, JACOB. 1959. *A Word Count of Modern Arabic Prose.* New York: American Council of Learned Societies.

LONG, MICHAEL H. AND JACK C. RICHARDS. 1987. *Methodology in TESOL: A book of readings.* New York: Harper & Row (Newbury House).

NATION, I. S. P. 1991. *Teaching and Learning Vocabulary.* New York: Harper & Row (Newbury House).

PARKINSON, DILWORTH. 1991. Searching for Modern *fuṣḥā*: Real life Formal Arabic. *Al-ᶜArabiyya* 24:31-64.

RICE, FRANK A. AND MAJED F. SAᶜID. 1979. *Eastern Arabic*. Washington, D.C.: Georgetown University Press.

RICHARDS, JACK C. 1987. "Listening Comprehension: Approach, design, procedure." In *Methodology in TESOL: A book of readings,* ed. by Michael H. Long and Jack C. Richards, 161-176. New York: Harper and Row (Newbury House).

STILLINGS, NEIL A. ET AL. 1987. *Cognitive Science: An introduction.* Cambridge: MIT Press.

YOUNG, DOLLY JESUSITA. 1990. An Investigation of Students' Perspectives on Anxiety and Speaking. *Foreign Language Annals* 23:6. 539-553.

7

THE ROLE OF CLOSE READING IN THE ELEMENTARY ARABIC CURRICULUM

Margaret Larkin
Princeton University

In recent years, with the increasing emphasis on a more functional approach to language teaching, teachers of reading have come to rely more and more on techniques that used to be virtual strangers to the classroom. These include skimming or scanning, quantity reading, and fast in-class reading of short texts where the goal is to teach the students to zero in on the salient elements of meaning. With these changes, the old standby, oral reading, has suffered a concomitant loss in status. This article argues for reserving a place for oral reading in the elementary Arabic classroom, provided it is oral reading that is specifically and attentively guided by the teacher.

Through the directed dialogue set up by the teacher, students can be trained to look for syntactic units that make up chunks of meaning. As they learn to anticipate and to become good contextual guessers, they are learning precisely the strategies recommended by the proponents of "reading for meaning." Thus, the old standby, oral reading, can be manipulated in such a way as to provide not only the pronunciation training it was always seen to provide, but also valuable programming in the process of reading itself. At the same time, the student who is given the opportunity to read aloud with guidance is given the chance to experience the visceral pleasure of producing the music of the language by him/herself.

Times have definitely changed as far as Arabic teaching in the U.S. is concerned. Once upon a time, the specter of a student who had studied the language for as much as three or four years unable—or perhaps more appropriately, unwilling—to read any Arabic text without constant reference to the dictionary was not at all uncommon. Indeed, it was not uncommon for a student with this length of acquaintance with Arabic never to have read a text of more than a couple of pages.

Things have changed. The cause of this change can be traced to the efforts of several specific players in the field of Arabic teaching. The Center for Arabic Study Abroad (CASA) was the first to provide students from the U.S. with the experience so glaringly missing in their study of Arabic in the States, namely the reading of long texts at a faster rate. The generations of students educated by the CASA teachers have carried the technique into their own teaching and have gone with it far beyond the old reading-translation method.

More recently, those championing the application of proficiency standards to Arabic have been successful in influencing teachers in the direction of more functional reading. Finally, more and more students have benefited from the diverse reading methods and immersion experience afforded at the Middlebury School of Arabic. Thanks to the work of all these educators, it is much less unusual to find a student who can read longer texts comfortably, without obsessive reliance on the dictionary, and to whom the idea of "skimming" a text is not anathema.

With the welcome emphasis on techniques such as scanning and skimming and quantity reading, there has been a parallel discrediting of the method of word-by-word oral reading that was once the bedrock of Arabic teaching. Many teachers have completely abandoned the practice of having students read out loud in class at the earlier stages, claiming, quite understandably, a shortage of class hours. Others have relegated the task of listening to students' reading to teaching assistants or to the tape recorder. Still others treat reading aloud as a condiment to be done only occasionally as a change of pace, rather than as a staple of their teaching program.

While I have always been a proponent of the kinds of techniques that are now becoming more widespread in the teaching of Arabic in this country, I now find it necessary to ask whether close reading does not still have a role early in the Arabic curriculum. What I would like to do in this paper is to make the case for reserving a place for close reading in the elementary Arabic curriculum.

To start, we will need a preliminary definition of what I mean by "close reading," which I have deliberately not called "oral reading." While the "close reading" I have in mind is most certainly conducted out loud, it goes well beyond the traditional situation of having the student struggle with a word-by-word rendition of a text, with his/her mistakes being mechanically corrected at the point where the teacher deems him/her to have suffered enough, followed by a word-by-word literal translation of the text read.

The kind of reading intended here might more properly be referred to as "guided oral reading," for its purpose is not only to have the student reproduce the sounds of the text out loud, but also to allow the opportunity for inculcating a set of reading habits that will, hopefully, become habits of life for as long as the student continues with Arabic. In other words, the time spent having students read aloud is time dedicated to "programming" them in how to read Arabic. Some of the specific components of this definition will emerge over the course of our discussion.

The majority of researchers in the fields both of reading and second-language learning are in agreement that oral reading at the early stages of learning to read is not advisable. Largely influenced by the field of psycholinguistics, most agree that "reading is less a matter of extracting sound from print than of bringing meaning to print" (Smith 1982:2). The consensus is that "[w]hat takes place [in reading aloud] is really a pronunciation exercise—of questionable value though it may be—and the essential purpose of reading is totally thwarted" (Byrnes 1985:85).

That essential purpose is the attainment of meaning, comprehension, which, it is said, is impeded by the attention to detail and to phonology that goes along with oral reading. The belief is that oral reading requires the student to focus on individual letters and individual words making it impossible for him/her to realize the meaningful relationships between the words that are the stuff of understanding (Smith 1982:6, Cazden 1972, Saville-Troike 1979:26, Byrnes 1985:84, Coady 1969:6). Frank Smith furthermore points out that the mere anxiety of being made to read aloud can inhibit the student's natural efficiency in reading (Smith 1982:51).

While reading aloud certainly provides an opportunity for pronunciation check—and, in my view, a useful one—it also serves other much more crucial functions. In fact, it serves many of the very goals held near and dear by some of its fiercest critics. Let's consider the all-important issue of reading for meaning.

It is generally agreed that attaining meaning in reading is contingent on the ability to discern the meaningful connections between the words, then the phrases, then the sentences of a given text. As a person reads, his/her awareness of the meaning leads him/her to anticipate elements of the text before they come up. The same mechanism operates simultaneously on the syntactic level. For this reason Oller's term "a grammar of expectancy" is particularly a propos (Oller 1973:113). Underlying much of the bad press that grammar has recently gotten is, I believe, the misguided notion that grammar is unrelated to meaning.

There is a point at which this is true (Chomsky 1965:160-162), but there is a vast area in which the semantic and syntactic work together, and it is this territory that the language learner must find his/her way through first. It is the role of the teacher to help the student develop the ability to anticipate what is likely to come up in a text, whether on the basis of the overall meaning or the grammatical structure, which "will enable him to eliminate a broad spectrum of possibilities and allow very direct and efficient processing" (Byrnes 1985:79).

There is no way for the teacher to gain access to the decoding process that the student is employing without having him/her read aloud. Carol Hosenfeld, in her article "Cindy: A Learner in Today's Foreign Language Classroom" (1979:53-75), proposes a method of having the student decode his/her reading out loud. This consists of the student providing a running commentary of how s/he is putting the text together as s/he reads. It is noteworthy that in her list of decoding strategies that encourage contextual guessing, she includes two recommendations that focus explicitly on grammar:

> Identify the grammatical function of an unfamiliar word before guessing its meaning;
> Recognize the grammatical function of words and use the information to identify: (a) unessential words (such as articles and adverbs), and (b) words whose form must be changed before they can be found in a glossary (Hosenfeld 1979:59-60).

This is not precisely a method I would use because it relies heavily on translation and because, in its attempt to have the student become conscious of what s/he is reading, it distracts him/her from the reading itself. Instead, it is possible to get a dialogue—largely in Arabic, though not necessarily exclusively so—going with the student as s/he reads that serves the purpose of having him/her either ask him/herself the questions needed to anticipate elements of the text more efficiently, or to bring his/her awareness back to the meaning of the text if it seems s/he is becoming bogged down in the effort to produce the sounds of the words accurately.

Let's consider a few sentences from several basic texts of volume 1 of *Elementary Modern Standard Arabic* to identify some of the types of guidance/intervention the elementary Arabic teacher can offer.

حضر كريم الى امريكا من لبنان ودرس في جامعة جورجتاون . وبعد الحصول على شهادة في اللغة الانكليزية رجع الى بيروت ودرس في مدرسة ثانوية .

لقناة السويس أهمية دولية عظيمة ، فهي تقصر المسافة بين الشرق و الغرب... وقد أصبحت هاتان المدينتان بعد حفر القناة من أهم المدن المصرية .

حكم الفرنسيون مصر ثلاثة اعوام و نصف عام ، ثم رحلوا عنها فحكمها محمد علي الذي عمل على نشر التعليم بين المصريين ، فأرسل عددا من أبناء الشعب الى اوروبا للحصول على شهادات جامعية .

Consider the first sentence. After the student has read it, the teacher can re-phrase parts of the sentence to keep the meaning in mind. The phrase /min lubnān/ "from Lebanon," for example, can be changed to an equational sentence using the nisba adjective as the predicate: /yaʿnī, huwa lubnānī, alaysa ka-dhālik?/ "i.e., he is Lebanese, isn't that so?" Depending on the type of vocabulary that has been used in the classroom up to that point, the teacher may choose to uses cognates, /jāʾa/ for /ḥaḍara/ "he came," for example. Indeed, reading aloud in this manner is an aid to the perennial problem of vocabulary acquisition.

Depending on how flexible the teacher judges the student to be, forms such as the verbal noun /ḥuṣūl/ "obtaining" can be changed to the verb form with questions such as /ayna ḥasala ʿala shahāda fi-l lughati l-inkilīziyya?/ "where did he obtain a degree in English?" which can be followed up with a sentence using the verbal noun again: /wa mādhā faʿala baʿda l-ḥuṣūli ʿala hādhihi sh-shahāda?/ "and what did he do after obtaining this degree?" At a convenient pause, perhaps between paragraphs, the teacher can begin manipulating the perfect tense conjugation by asking questions using the verbs in the passage: /ana darastu fi jāmiʿat kādha—ayna darasta anta qabla al-ān?/ "I studied at the University of X—where did you study before?" To the probable answer: /darastu fī madrasa thānawiyya/ "I studied at a high school," the teacher can follow up with /mādha darasta fi l-madrasati th-thānawiyya?/ "what did you study in the high school?," and begin to manipulate the other vocabulary from the text or from previous lessons: /al-lugha al-inkilīziyya/, /al-lugha al-ᶜarabiyya/ "the English language, the Arabic language, etc."

In order to get the student used to looking a bit ahead as s/he reads, the occurrence of the noun /jāmiᶜa/ "university" without definite article or pronominal suffix should be signalled, so the student knows to glance ahead to see which of the roster of possibilities is fulfilled in the next word. Will the next word make an iḍāfa? Is it an adjective? The student should be trained to take the presence of a noun immediately following as a signal of an iḍāfa. In other words, the sequence of nouns should become a cue that sends up a red flag marked "iḍāfa" to the student.

The same point, with a differing result, can be taken up with the phrase /madrasatin thānawiyyatin/ "a secondary school" in the second sentence. Here the second possibility occurs, i.e., the article-less, suffix-less noun being followed by an adjective. If the choice has been made to have the students read with full case inflections, then this realization will signal to him/her the need to add nunation to the noun. This is something American students have difficulty getting used to. In the instance at hand, the student should be encouraged to take quick notice of the nisba ending, which marks the word as an adjective, announcing the need for nunation on /madrasatin/.

Obviously, we want all of this to take place quickly, but we have to be realistic enough to realize that students need to be trained in the process first before they can perform reading tasks that will seem second-nature to them later on. Once the student has gotten the point, s/he must be expected to read the corrected adjectival phrase as a whole, not two separate words, correctly or incorrectly inflected. In this way, the phrasing will become associated with the meaning that has now become firmly established in the student's mind.

In the first sentence in the second set of sentences, students should be helped to pick out the chunks of meaning and anticipate the filling in of certain syntactic slots: starting out with the preposition /li/, the reader knows that this sentence has begun not with the subject but with the predicate, which is the prepositional phrase, and that the subject, which we are waiting for, will be indefinite. The relationship between the two nouns /qanāti s-suways/ "the Suez Canal" can be handled as in the example above. Since the now identified iḍāfa is clearly the object of the preposition /li/, that leaves us still waiting for the indefinite subject of the sentence. The nisba ending on /ahammiyya/ "importance" might throw the student off unless s/he knows to glance quickly ahead at the two following words. Recognizing them as obvious adjectives, s/he will be able to realize that /ahammiyya/ is the awaited indefinite subject.

In the next sentence, the gender possibilities set up by the verb form /aṣbaḥat/ "it has become" must be hooked to the feminine dual subject, which should be read in phrase with its demonstrative adjective. The prepositional phrase beginning with /baᶜda/ "after" should be shelved momentarily, while the reader looks for the predicate of /aṣbaḥat/. When students are made to get used to the secondary nature of prepositional phrases, they tend to be less distracted by them from the syntactic pillars of the sentence. In this sentence, the fact that the predicate begins with a preposition will throw the student off unless the preceding phrase has been put out of the way temporarily.

Similarly, in the last sentence, the student must be guided in keeping dependent clauses from getting in the way of completing the main thought of the sentence contained in the independent clause. In this instance, a simple question such as /man arsala abnāᵓa sh-shaᶜbi ilā urubbā?/ "who sent [sons of] the people to Europe?" will make sure that the student does not lose sight of the focus of the sentence.

This process may sound very arduous spelled out in this manner, but in practice it picks up a smooth rhythm of its own. Furthermore, there are many other features of meaning and syntax that the student can be alerted to, but the methods employed in doing that are idiosyncratic and cannot be properly illustrated here.

It should by now be clear that reading aloud is by no means a solo performance by an isolated and anxious student struggling to decipher a text. On the contrary, it is a dialogue in which the student gets a great deal of suppport and guidance from the attentive teacher—and the teacher must, in fact, be very attentive indeed. The many interruptions and interjections on the part of the teacher, which might seem disruptive to some, can in fact be a relief to the spotlighted student. The insertion of related conversation using the text's vocabulary, for example, is a boost to the student because the form is usually one s/he is familiar with from classroom discussions, and this provides him/her the ego-enhancing experience of being able to respond easily to the questions asked. This, in turn, makes the content of the text more real and meaningful to him/her. It is primarily a good rapport between the participants in this reading dialogue that will make it possible, and it is on this point that rational analysis falters before the inescapable need for some instinctive know-how.

It is my view that the student, having gotten through his/her problems with the text, should be given the opportunity to read his/her portion of the text fluidly and uninterruptedly, with the sustained understanding that the preceding dialogue with the teacher has reaped. This is related to the point made above regarding the need to read words as parts of the meaningful phrases they are part of. Some critics of oral reading claim that the process of reading aloud, because it requires attention to the sounds of the language, slows down the natural meaning-making process. The natural process of segmenting or "chunking" on the basis of meaning is disturbed by focusing on the smaller units manageable first to the eye and then to the aural apparatus (Smith 1982:6).

Although I certainly cannot find fault with the basic psycholinguistic description of the process of reading, when it comes to learning a foreign language, I believe the process of reading aloud must be viewed somewhat differently. While it is certainly true that the search for meaning, or rather the expectation of meaning, is the prime mover in the process of reading, it is nonetheless true that any language offers other cues to meaning, which there is no reason to eliminate from the language student's arsenal. There are patterns of intonation and phrasing that go along with particular units of meaning. There is a rhythm to every language. There is no reason why the student should not be learning these aspects of the language—features that will only enhance performance in the other skill areas—and using them as cues to meaning in the process of reading.

Wilga Rivers is one notable exception to the roster of critics of oral reading. Happily, the view she expresses accords entirely with my own on this issue.

> Reading aloud in association with reading by the teacher (or a recorded model) also makes the passage to oral proficiency more feasible, since students develop a feeling for the sounds of the language, for intonation, and for the flow of fluent phrases (Rivers 1981:266).

I should make clear at this point that the texts I ask students to read aloud in the early stages are either texts they have specifically read first at home in private, texts that manipulate mostly very familiar vocabulary and syntactic structures, or texts from earlier lessons which they have already "mastered."

Given a good rapport between teacher and student, a first-time reading in class of the second category of texts can be very instructive: there is enough familiar material there for the student to feel more or less secure, but since the student is putting together the meaning as s/he reads, the teacher has an opportunity to witness the process being used to make sense of the text. The presence or absence of important anticipatory strategies can thereby be established and direction can be given on the spot. The last category of text offers a particularly good morale builder, since students often have difficulty perceiving their own progress.

"[P]rint cannot be read aloud in a comprehensible way unless it is comprehended in the first place" (Smith 1982:71) and assigning these types of reading allows the oral reading to become a test not only of pronunciation, but also of comprehension and the concomitant phrasing and intonation Rivers speaks of. It is for this reason, too, that the student should always be given an opportunity to read the text, however small it may be, as a whole, once all the pieces seem to be in place in his/her mind.

> In native-language reading, fluent readers look ahead to the next word group, or even further, and relate it to what preceded before reading it aloud. This determines the stress and intonation patterns they will use. . . . It is more difficult to do this with a foreign language text unless the material of which it is composed is very familiar. Students therefore need much practice in reading in "meaningful mouthfuls," never producing orally a new segment until they have identified the word grouping to which it belongs in relation to the ongoing discourse (Rivers 1981:272; 273-274).

An important element in the Arabic reader's arsenal that can be developed with the help of oral reading is a sensitivity to the morphological patterns of the language. The mine of information available to the contextual guesser from Arabic morphology is obvious: besides the semantic implications of the various verb forms, expectations regarding agency and transitivity are set up through the use of participles in a given sentence. When we neglect morphology, we are indirectly encouraging excessive, unnecessary use of the dictionary and discouraging students from becoming efficient contextual guessers. While some would claim that the patterns of the language can be internalized through their graphemic representations alone, my own feeling is that the sound of the various patterns must also be internalized and indeed that they are more easily assimilated on the phonetic level.

When we have our students read silently from the printed page, separating the visual image of the language from the sounds of the words, we are treating Arabic as if it were a logographic language such as Japanese. On the one hand, meaning is associated with the sounds of the words through listening and speaking practice which involves no printed symbols. On the other hand, when they read silently, the students are associating meaning with the graphemic representation of the language on the page. There is no opportunity to bring these two separate coding processes together—except through reading aloud. Different people remember things differently, and it defies commmon sense to deprive students of additional paths to memory when it is possible to unite the different types of stimuli the language has to offer.

There is in fact some evidence that with languages such as Arabic, where the graphemic representation can quite systematically be converted into the phonological representation, the phonological code occurs prior to the semantic code (Koda 1988:149).

> The word recognition process of phonologically highly recoverable orthographies, such as Serbo-Croatian, Spanish and Arabic, can be characterized as linear-mode processing.... [I]n word recognition of such orthographies, two coding processes—phonological coding (i.e., the process of obtaining a phonological code) and semantic coding (i.e., the process of obtaining the meaning)—occur sequentially in that respective order. Studies investigating word recognition in highly recoverable systems consistently indicate that in the reading of such orthographies, the phonological code is obtained prior to the meaning (Koda 1988:135-137).

If this is not enough to suggest that we should not deprive students learning to read of this avenue of stimulus, in two experiments, Keiko Koda was able to demonstrate a high degree of cognitive process transfer from the native language to the second language reading. This means that the manner in which language learners tended to read the second language was determined to a great extent by the orthography of their first language and the type of reading it dictated (Koda 1988:149, Green and Meara 1987).

If this is true, it means that for the majority of our students, whose native language is English, the manner in which they learned to read English will be transferred to their reading of Arabic. Whether or not they learned to read during the time when "phonics" was emphasized, all these students had one important thing in common: they were all fluent in English before they learned to read and so, inevitably, the process of learning to read involved recourse to the phonological coding they had already internalized. It makes even less sense for us to neglect the connection between the sounds of the language and its visual representation when it is the phonological coding that will, in any case, take precedence for these students.

I have claimed that reading aloud is not inimical to the goals of proficiency-oriented language teaching, and further on I will suggest some ways in which it can be combined with other reading techniques more often championed by the proponents of proficiency standards for optimal effect. Putting aside for the moment all the pedagogical considerations, it is clear that reading aloud is a most appropriate fulfillment of one of the stated goals of proficiency-oriented teaching, namely to foster through the selection of materials awareness of the culture of the target language.

It is undeniable that the ability to read standard Arabic aloud correctly is a valued skill in the Arab world and that it holds a place of importance surpassing that which comparable skill enjoys in many other cultures. Written text intended to be delivered orally is a recognized category of discourse. In her delineation of "four basic modes of speech," Byrnes includes the following: "Oral presentation of a written text, as in newscasts, more formal commentaries and lectures; oral presentation of a fixed script, such as that produced on stage or in a film" (Byrnes 1984:319).

In the Arab world, we can add to these examples, the delivery of political speeches in parliament, university lectures and seminars and, in particular, the reading aloud of newspapers and magazines—an activity that goes on regularly in even the most mundane circumstances. Oratory has a long and honored tradition in Arab culture, and the effects of this tradition can still be felt and seen today throughout the Arab world. The kind of exercise students are experiencing when they read aloud is not just one in pronunciation, but rather in the culturally cherished skill of delivering standard Arabic discourse.

There are, I believe, some serious losses we would suffer were we to banish reading aloud from our Arabic classrooms. The first of these relates directly to the most widely-recognized goals of oral proficiency.

Hackneyed though the statement may be, it is important for us to remember that students learning Arabic are always, to varying degrees, learning at least two languages—or more properly, a language with many levels. One of the many blessings of the proficiency movement in Arabic has been the convergence on the lower levels of the spoken and written language. Specifically what has happened is that many of us have simplified the kind of Arabic we speak with our students, as well as the kind of text we read. Consciously and unconsciously, many of us are choosing to cut down on the discrepancy between the written and the spoken language through our selection of materials.

This is pedagogically wise at the early stages of learning Arabic, but the question is: what happens as the student progresses past the Intermediate stage? Like it or not, the higher we go on the oral proficiency scale, the closer we come to language typical of more literary Arabic. Indeed, some of the functions students are expected to be able to perform at the Advanced and Superior levels described in the ACTFL Oral Proficiency Guidelines include tasks such as giving a speech and introducing a guest at a formal function. Likewise, the kind of logically elaborated argumentation found more commonly in written material is a feature students need to transfer to their speaking at the upper levels of the proficiency scale.

Whatever can be said of the earliest levels of language training, it simply cannot be claimed that all the aural/oral work students need will be accomplished through speaking and listening comprehension work. Once they reach the Intermediate stage, students need to incorporate in their speech material most readily available in the texts they are reading. Incorporation of the more stylized Arabic common in written texts should be encouraged by reading aloud in order for them to develop a sense of that register and apply it to the speaking skill. Otherwise, the likelihood of crossover among the skill areas will be reduced, especially if oral reading has been shunned from the very beginning of the course of study. Failing to encourage this cross-fertilization through oral reading contributes, in my view, to placing a ceiling on students' development of oral proficiency and exacerbates the inherent problem of diglossia in Arabic.

A second and ultimately more far-reaching consequence of eliminating oral reading is to be feared, namely the implications of this decision on the future development of our students' interests, and hence of the whole field of Arabic studies.

We all agree that the clientele we serve in first- and second-year Arabic courses is a diverse one: some students will have no more exposure to the language than these introductory courses, while those who go on in the language choose different disciplinary paths, ranging from contemporary social science studies to medieval Arabic scholarship. The question I would like to put forth is whether by neglecting the kind of close reading that breeds the precision needed for their studies, we are closing off the path to potential medievalists. While it is recognized that language teaching goals "can only be set in relation to the specific needs of a specific group" (Byrnes 1985:77), the problem we face with Arabic is that often neither we nor the students can predict the direction in which their interests will develop and what their needs ultimately will be.

Many would reply that this is absurd, that close reading out loud is not necessary for the development of precision and that, in any case, students should not be burdened with this type of reading early on since they can always develop more rigor in their reading as they advance and their interests develop. I have my doubts—not because this is not possible, but merely because it is not only psychologically, but also logistically more difficult to play this kind of catch-up after the first couple of years of study.

By the time the student reaches third-year Arabic, s/he is reading longer texts and discussing them exclusively in Arabic. There is, in fact, little time for the kind of reading training I suggest should be done in the first two years. The difficulty involved in "programming" a student for this kind of precision when s/he has been getting along without it for several years should likewise not be underestimated.

In conclusion, then, I would like to reiterate my support for the use of close reading in the first- and second-year Arabic classroom. By close reading, I do not mean the solitary rendering on the part of the student of the sounds of the Arabic text, mechanically corrected by a half-attentive teacher. Rather, what I have in mind is reading aloud that is orchestrated by the dialogue the teacher sets up with the student as s/he is reading aloud, a dialogue intended to provide "basic training" in the strategies needed to read efficiently. Meaning, the primary focus of the reading process is by no means neglected in this process. On the contrary, this technique encourages students to focus naturally on meaningful units of text and to become, using the cues provided by the language system, more skilled contextual guessers.

Done right, therefore, this type of reading fosters many of the goals of proficiency-oriented teaching, and it can be combined with other techniques currently enjoying wider acceptance for the development of reading proficiency.

The very useful techniques of scanning and skimming can be combined with close reading as a means of checking meaning and instructing students in how to isolate details that are necessary to the purposes of their reading. Reading aloud of selected sections of a text can be a useful way of responding to the question of where the needed meaning was found in the text. Employing the technique of close reading does not mean that other recognized methods of developing reading proficiency should be abandoned. Techniques such as quick in-class reading of short texts, where students are expected to identify only the main idea, are still very useful.

I am not alone in the opinion that reading needs are best served not by faithful adherence to a single approach, but rather by a combination of different methods that train students in all the needed skills. Such an eclectic approach also has the best chance of supporting the different inclinations and strengths of our diverse student clientele (Coady 1969:11).

The important role of student interaction in proficiency-oriented teaching can be well accommodated using close reading. It is very useful, for example, to break students up into groups working on a new text, where two of the students are expected to guide two others through the reading of the text in the manner employed by the teacher. The purpose of having students assume this role of "coach" to their colleagues is to ensure that they are not only responding to the questions of the teacher as they are being guided through a text, but are also internalizing the technique or program itself. It is insufficient for the student to be able to respond to the questions and leads provided by the teacher; we must also make sure s/he is internalizing reading strategies that can be put into operation during his/her own private reading.

The obvious problem of time constraints comes immediately to mind as a potential objection to this method of reading, and indeed, what I have described is a time-consuming process. It is, however, a method that pays off and actually saves time in many ways. First of all, it is my view that this method of reading should be employed as a staple during the first two years of Arabic study. During that time, it is extremely useful in helping students remember vocabulary, a problem that often slows down the pace of the class. Furthermore, what is more difficult to assess, but of which I am firmly convinced, is that this method of guided reading aloud allows the reading process a more profound impact on the other skill areas—and this integration of listening, speaking, reading, and writing is, after all, what we are after. These gains early on can only pay off not only in terms of time saved later, but also in terms of overall linguistic competency.

Afterward, it should be possible to use close reading more sparingly as a checking device or a refresher when students are getting sloppy in their reading. Omaggio goes even a step further:

> Perhaps a form of grammar-translation methodology would be useful at the higher levels of proficiency where the purpose of instruction is to fine tune students' control of the target language, especially in terms of learning to use specialized vocabulary or developing competence in written stylistics (Omaggio 1986:56).

Close reading aloud should nonetheless be used sparingly at the later stages, for it is then that this method can lead to some of the detrimental effects feared by researchers (Rivers 1981:274).

Finally, though it puts me on thin theoretical ground, I would like to suggest that there is more to this whole question of reading aloud than has been discussed here. It seems to me that the experience itself of reading Arabic aloud, especially when it coincides with the successful apprehension of meaning that this method leads to, is an experience students are entitled to enjoy. It helps the language become not just something they can manipulate, but something that is part of them, something they feel.

Reading a printed Arabic text aloud is very much like playing a musical piece from sheet music or, perhaps more precisely, like singing from printed music. The visual experience of the piece comes together with the perception of the sounds the musician is producing and both coincide with the physical sensation of producing the sounds with one's own body. The physical awareness of one's own breath and muscle activity combined with the pleasure of understanding is a powerful experience. At that moment, the language becomes not something outside the student, but rather part of him/her.

In discussing the inadequacy of traditional conceptions of cognition in describing the varieties of modes in which human knowing occurs, Bennett Reimer describes a kind of "aesthetic knowing" (Reimer 1992:27) which, I believe, is equally applicable to foreign languages.

> In experiences of meaningful form the "knowing of" them, includes, as an inseparable aspect, an internalized awareness of expressiveness—that is, feeling constituting an essential component of what is being experienced and known. Interrelations among qualities are not just noticed. They are felt, and do not reach the fullness of meaning of which they are capable unless and until they are felt (Reimer 1992:37).

I have never had a student who, no matter how much s/he had to struggle or how hard s/he had to work at reading, did not at some point experience that moment when it all comes together and the meaning just clicks into place as his/her voice brings forth the sounds of the text. Though it defies quantification, assessment and delineation, such an experience in the process of learning a language cannot be inconsequential. It is, in any case, a magic I am unwilling to deprive my students of.

REFERENCES

ABBOUD, PETER F. AND ERNEST N. MCCARUS. 1983. *Elementary Modern Standard Arabic*, vol. 1, 2d ed. New York: Cambridge University Press.

BYRNES, HEIDI. 1984. The Role of Listening Comprehension: A theoretical base. *Foreign Language Annals* 17:4. 317-29.

_____. 1985. "Teaching toward Proficiency: The receptive skills." In *Proficiency, Curriculum, Articulation: The ties that bind*, ed. by Alice C. Omaggio, 77-107. Middlebury, VT: The Northeast Conference on the Teaching of Foreign Languages, Inc.

CAZDEN, COURTNEY B. 1972. *Child Language and Education*. New York: Holt Rinehart and Winston.

CHOMSKY, NOAM. 1965. *Aspects of the Theory of Syntax*. Cambridge, MA: MIT Press.

COADY, JAMES. 1969. "A Psycholinguistic Model of the ESL Reader." In *Reading in a Second Language*, ed. by Ronald Mackay, Bruce Barkman and R. R. Jordan, 6-12. MA: Newbury House.

GREEN, DAVID AND PAUL MEARA. 1987. The Effects of Script on Visual Search. *Second Language Research* 3:2. 102-117.

HOSENFELD, CAROL. 1979. "Cindy: A learner in today's foreign language classroom." In *The Foreign Language Learner in Today's Classroom Environment*, ed. by Warren C. Born, 53-75. Middlebury, VT: The Northeast Conference on the Teaching of Foreign Languages, Inc.

KODA, KEIKO. 1988. Cognitive Process in Second Language Reading: Transfer of Ll reading skills and strategies. *Second Language Research* 4 (2): 133-56.

OLLER, J. W., JR. 1973. Cloze Tests of Second Language Proficiency and What They Measure. *Language Learning* 23:105-18.

OMAGGIO, ALICE C. 1986. *Teaching Language in Context. Proficiency oriented instruction*. New York: Heinle and Heinle.

PHILLIPS, JUNE K. 1984. Practical Implications of Recent Research in Reading. *Foreign Language Annals* 17:4. 285-297.

REIMER, BENNETT AND RALPH A. SMITH, EDS. 1992. *The Arts, Education and Aesthetic Knowing*. Chicago: The National Society for the Study of Education.

RIVERS, WILGA M. 1981. *Teaching Foreign-Language Skills*, 2d ed. Chicago: University of Chicago Press.

SAVILLE-TROIKE, MURIEL. 1979. "Reading and the Audio-Lingual Method." In *Reading in a Second Language,* ed. by Ronald Mackay, Bruce Barkman and R. R. Jordan, 24-35. MA: Newbury House.

SMITH, FRANK. 1982. *Understanding Reading.* New York: Holt, Rinehart and Winston.

8

THE GRAMMAR CONTROVERSY: WHAT TO TEACH AND WHY?

Zeinab Taha
The American University in Cairo

Teaching grammar extensively at the expense of the other language skills has been the focus of Arabic curricula in the United States as well as in the Arab world throughout the past three decades. With the emergence of the proficiency movement, the rising awareness of the learners' needs, and the shifting focus towards communicative competence, two major camps have arisen. One camp emphasizes the role of grammar in the classroom and maintains that if the students are not taught grammar formally, their linguistic skills will not develop properly. The other camp, however, emphasizes fluency and communication, and deemphasizes the formal teaching of grammar in the classroom. Each camp claims a basis in research and theory.

In dealing with the teaching of grammar inside the Arabic language classroom, a blend of the two schools' views would seem to be the best bet. The question to ask now is not whether to teach grammar in class. The question is what grammar to teach, and why. In attempting to find answers to these questions, materials and pedagogy must address the following questions: 1) what rules of grammar should be emphasized?, 2) what constitutes grammatical error, and how can it be corrected?, and 3) what are the variants used by native speakers and how can they illustrate new standards by which non-native speakers can be judged?

This chapter addresses these questions and illustrates some mismatches between our goals in the profession on the one hand, and our classroom practices on the other. This chapter also presents evidence of variation in Modern Standard Arabic (MSA) in the structure of the conditional clauses, and discusses the possible accommodation of these variations in today's MSA books.

1. Introduction

In recent years, our dominant professional discourse as teachers of Arabic as a foreign language, though not necessarily our classroom practice, has shifted from a focus on "knowledge about" language, exemplified by form and grammar-focused language instruction, to an emphasis on the need of the learners to develop the "ability to use" language through a communicative approach. The latter approach is sometimes wrongly thought to be associated with a pedagogy of non-attentiveness to accuracy, particularly grammatical accuracy. This thinking poses a dual threat to how we think about our work and how we propose to accomplish it.

In a period of shifting paradigms, our debate should not concentrate on whether to teach grammar, i.e., teach for accuracy, or not. Our inquiry cannot be phrased as an either-or-dichotomy; either the ability to use language at a higher communicative level, or with greater accuracy. Instead, we desperately need to see both parts together, presenting a program aiming at accuracy and communicative ability at the same time. Moreover, our debate should concentrate on the assumption that since well-rounded communicative ability, or proficiency, and acceptability of language use depend ultimately on accuracy, the critical pedagogical issue for our times is whether a shift toward a communicative-oriented instruction is more likely to yield for our learners the desired higher level of accurate performance than the traditional form-and-mastery-focused approaches.

Consequently, our materials and pedagogy in the 1990s must address the following questions:

1. What rules of grammar should we emphasize for the various levels, and how should we sequence them according to functions?
2. What constitutes grammatical error at each level, and how do we correct them?
3. What are the variants used by native speakers, and how can these variants illustrate new standards by which non-native speakers may be judged?

2. Problems We Must Deal With

The above questions can be dealt with in light of two problems which face our profession as teachers and curriculum designers of Arabic as a foreign language. The first problem is global and relates to the whole tradition of teaching foreign languages, while the second problem is specific and relates to the nature of the Arabic language.

As to the global problem, there seems to exist a mismatch between our goals and our means (Byrnes, forthcoming). No matter how methodologies, syllabi, or curriculum designers try to introduce Arabic through a functional or communicative approach, one which inevitably minimizes grammatical explanation in class, students are still tested and their work assessed by most standardized tests on the basis of accuracy which, for the most part, means grammatical accuracy.

It is true that grammatical accuracy is regarded as crucial only at the intermediate high level and above in the Oral Proficiency Interview (OPI), but students are still expected to try to form grammatically correct sentences as much as they can. In other words, students are expected to show a developing stream of grammatical accuracy by which they are only formally evaluated at the intermediate high level and above.

When we look at the ACTFL Generic Guidelines for assessing the productive skills, namely speaking and writing (the skills which a communicative approach to language would emphasize), we see that accuracy is one of the most important bases for assessment. The following quotations are taken from the sections on speaking and writing:

1. Speaking:
   Intermediate-High: "There is emerging evidence of connected discourse, particularly for simple narration and/or description.
   Advanced: "...narrate and describe with paragraph-length connected discourse."
   Superior: "Able to speak the language with sufficient accuracy to participate effectively in most formal and informal conversations on practical, social, professional, and abstract topics."

2. Writing:
   Intermediate-High: "In those languages relying primarily on content words and time expressions to express time, tense, or aspect, some precision is displayed; where tense and/or aspect is expressed through verbal inflection, forms are produced rather consistently, but not always accurately."
   Advanced: "Good control of the morphology and the most frequently used syntactic structures, e.g., common word order patterns, coordination, subordination, but makes frequent errors in producing complex sentences."
   Superior: "Good control of a full range of structures" (ACTFL 1986).

The implication of the previous quotations is, among other things, that grammatical accuracy is basic to any success or failure in learning a foreign language. Students are not to be placed in the intermediate-high, advanced, or superior levels unless they show evidence of their ability to use the grammar of the language they are learning.

The same kind of mismatch which exists between our goals and our means, or rather between what we preach and what we practice, is manifested in most of the books which are used to teach Arabic as a foreign language today. Most of these books start with an introduction to Modern Standard Arabic (MSA) and its features, claiming that they present such a variety with a communicative approach. However, the actual lessons proceed to display characteristics that may appear contradictory to the initially-stated goals:

1. Structures are introduced through passages or dialogues with no explanation of grammar provided, but then endless drills on structures follow. Such drills do not necessarily engage the students in communicative activities as much as they train them in the new structures.

2. Intermediate books look very different from first-year books, in that the second-year books include extensive explanation of grammar accompanied with more structural drills in every chapter. The transition from first year to second is thus perfectly abrupt.

3. Many books claim to introduce the variety of Arabic needed for communication, yet they introduce structures like *mā ajmala,* . . . . ما اجمل "how beautiful is . . . . " and *lam,* لم "did not," before they introduce present tense verbs; the conditional sentence; and *laysa,* ليس "is not." A strong argument can be made that the last three are more important than the former in terms of communication. One inevitably wonders how the students are expected to have a communicative ability when the structures are not sequenced in a way that facilitates the development of such ability.

The other puzzling phenomenon is the way we express our underlying assumptions about grammar, as well as the way these assumptions change once the students start the second-year book. Several first-year books regard the idea of explaining grammar or the inclusion of grammatical notes as being unimportant, while in second-year books the same authors seem to change their views regarding the role of grammatical notes. It is very hard to believe that Arabic language teachers should not explain any grammar at all to their first-year students, and then suddenly start by providing extensive explanations in the second year. Again, we must stop and ask ourselves whether or not what we are trying to tell the students reflects what we actually do in the classroom.

Regardless of what textbooks do with regard to grammar, the truth is that we, as Arabic teachers, *do* in fact explain grammar in class sometimes, in the first year as well as in the second. We do it because it is essential and because the students need it. It is true that our approaches have shifted toward presenting grammar briefly, then engaging students in communicative activities rather than spending the class time on reading and translating, but that does not mean that grammar is not important, nor does it mean that grammar explanation does not actually take place.

Our books, therefore, should reflect the reality of the situation. The students should be able to see a consistency in our approach from day one. We need not wait until the students have finally "grown" to give them clues about how the Arabic language works. They should be guided from the very beginning in order to develop their accuracy along with their fluency in Arabic.

The second problem that faces our profession, as I mentioned above, is specific to the diglossic nature of Arabic. Because of this feature, important questions have to be considered when we are writing proficiency-based text books. In other words, we need to take into consideration the different varieties of Arabic and the overlap between them as they relate to the different functions that students must master. This is a crucial issue when we try to deal with the question of accuracy. It is so because related to the issues of accuracy and communicative competence is appropriateness. Consequently, grammar should be understood as discourse grammar, where formal features are seen in terms of their contribution to the extended message and the intended meaning construction. Accuracy, then, is akin to appropriateness, involving multiple decisions with respect to a specific interlocutor in a specific communicative event (Gunterman 1987). Consequently, the question of which variety to teach emerges as a core issue in the profession, since we know that there are certainly situations in which it is appropriate to speak in the dialect, and others in which an elevated form of Arabic is appropriate. The issue of appropriateness is also important when we discuss the different levels of MSA and how we introduce them inside the classroom.

3. Levels of MSA

It is very well known that MSA does not constitute only one level of the Arabic language. Every book of Arabic usually includes in its introduction a vague statement about MSA in which a reference is usually made to the language of the media. Indeed, such books aim at developing the students' ability to read Arabic newspapers, but the range of structures and the vocabulary that such books provide may give the impression that MSA is in fact the same, whether it is used in formal speeches, in the media, in the mosques, or in literary works. Once again, the material presented in these books reflects our own views of what MSA is today. I do not think that clear distinctions of the different varieties of MSA exist in our pedagogy nor have complete descriptions of the features of each variety been carried out. More importantly, I do not think that the changes in the variety of MSA used in newspapers have been accounted for. There are changes that newspaper Arabic has been undergoing which the authors of Arabic textbooks have failed to address. An example of these changes is word order. Several linguists and Arabic teachers have noticed that the word order used in newspaper headlines and in several parts of the article itself is subject-verb-object, rather than verb-subject-object (Parkinson 1981 and Taha 1981). I have come across only one book that deals with this linguistic phenomenon and explains when it is likely to be used (Badawi 1987).

The fact that only one book "reveals" to the students the linguistic reality of MSA today is in itself a major defect in the Arabic language profession today. This not only represents a lack of material that is supposed to be genuine and realistic, but it also reflects our underlying views of MSA. In a nutshell: We regard MSA as what we want it to be rather than what it *is* in reality. More importantly, I think we cannot even realize that what we see today may not be the same as what we will see in the future, and it is definitely different from what we used to see in the past.

3.1 *Variation in Newspaper MSA*

The MSA that is used in the newspapers today is full of features which have not been accounted for. As a result, variation of MSA is not presented in Arabic language textbooks. Needless to say, so long as the issues of accuracy and appropriateness are concerned, accounting for variation in MSA is obviously of extreme importance.

In this respect I will present and discuss one feature of MSA variation in today's newspapers. This is the variation in conditional clauses as used by editors of the Egyptian newspaper *Al-Ahrām*, and the Saudi newspaper *Al-Sharq Al-Awsaṭ*. My preliminary study shows that the conditional particles *law*, لو "if," and *iðā*, إذا "if," are sometimes used interchangeably regardless of whether or not the situation is realistic. More striking is the variation in the response clause where *fa*, ف "so" is used sometimes with *law*, لو , rather than the particle *la*, ل "so" and where the response clause is not preceeded by any particle when *iðā*, إذا, is used.

To illustrate the findings of the study, I include below some examples of variation in MSA conditional clauses as used in some Arabic newspapers:

1. Clauses that introduce the response clause without a particle, such as

١ . اذا كان لديك مجفف الغسيل ، احرص على وضع منشفة بين
الغسيل المراد تجفيفه .

٢ . ... فان العراق اذا قام بالتنفيذ الكامل للقرارات يستطيع
ان ينضم الى المجتمعالعالمى .

٣ . واذا ذهبنا الى ابعد الفروض ، و توهمنا ان اسرائيل قد قبلت
بالانسحاب ...... ماذا سيحدث حينئذ ؟

While the above constructions are used randomly, others containing the particle *fa*, ف , are used side by side with the above constructions and sometimes even in the same paragraph, which suggests that we are actually dealing with different options in the language that may be employed to express the same idea.

2. Clauses that are introduced with *law*, لو and use the particle *fa*, ف rather than *la*, ل to introduce the response clause, such as

١ . فلو اطمأنت تلك الجالية الى ان العرب لايريدون ازالة اسرائيل فان
هذا سيسهل مهمة اقناع الرأي العام الأمريكي بذلك .

٢ . ولو نظرنا في كل هذه العناوين لرأينا ان ما يسمى بقضايا
اللاجئين هواكثر حيوية لانه يتعلق مباشرة بالانسان ......

The above evidence is significant, because if we are teaching students to communicate in Arabic, then our frame of reference should be what native speakers actually do with the language, not what we think they ought to be doing. It is also important because any description of MSA has to account for all the features that now exist in it. We should be asking ourselves whether or not such features constitute free variation, whether or not there are any choices that native speakers make under certain sociolinguistic factors, and whether or not we know why we choose one and not the other.

All MSA books, without exception, present the conditional clauses with *iðā* and *law* as having to introduce their response clauses by *fa* and *la,* respectively (when the response clause does not have a past tense verb with *iðā*). This presentation is inaccurate for two reasons. First, it is inaccurate because it is not wrong to use the clauses without the *fa* and the *la*. There are twenty-three verses

verses out of seventy-nine in the Qurʾan where *law* response clauses are not introduced with *la*. Instead, some are introduced with *fa* and others with *ma* or no particles at all. Other numerous examples are found in literary books, poetry, prose, and medieval grammar books.

Secondly, in my own view, if the variation is actually taking place now in world-wide newspapers like *Al-Ahrām* and *Al-Sharq Al-Awsat*, this fact in itself is enough reason to persuade us to present to the students a fair and complete version of the Arabic linguistic reality.

This should not be taken to mean that we are going to make new rules for the conditional clauses and make the less frequent to be our teaching model. But it should mean, however, that the students must be exposed to all the varieties and all the different combinations that did and do take place in Arabic. This also means that if the students use one of the constructions that are actually used by educated native speakers of Arabic, although not necessarily the most frequent construction in today's MSA books, we are not going to consider the students' sentences to be wrong. If we continue to present some structures of MSA as stemming from certain rules of classical Arabic—allowing no room for variation—to students of Arabic as a foreign language, we will be making the following mistakes: 1) Presenting a form of MSA that is not used by native speakers consistently, 2) not accounting for changes that are taking place in the language used in the newspapers, and 3) having unrealistic expectations of students by holding them to standards that native speakers do not keep.

4. Conclusion

I am sure that a close analysis of MSA will reveal even more features that are worth studying carefully in order to reach a comprehensive understanding of the language. A close, analytical look at MSA today will help tremendously in defining our goals as teachers and curriculum designers. It will also justify our means in so doing and relate our work to the communicative approach of teaching languages.

The important issue that is now at hand, and which will probably be of major concern to all of us in the future, is the issue of the possible marriage of accuracy and communicative language teaching. No matter how we try to achieve this goal, the issue to remember is that our ultimate goal in the profession is to expose students to all the forms of Arabic used by native speakers. The forms which native speakers actually use are those which we should be aiming for the students to acquire, and they should certainly be regarded as the most accurate forms as far as communication is concerned.

REFERENCES

Al-Ahrām Newspaper. February and March issues 1992.

ACTFL. 1986. "ACTFL Proficiency Guidelines." Hasting-on-Hudson, NY: American Council on the Teaching of Foreign Languages.

ALEXANDER, LOUIS G. 1990. "Why Teach Grammar?" in *On Language and Linguistics*, 377-383. Washington, DC: Georgetown University Round Table.

Al-Sharq Al-Awsaṭ Newspaper. February and March issues 1992.

BADAWI, SAID, ET AL. 1987. *Al-Kitāb Al-Asāsi*, vol. II. Tunis: The Arabic Organization for Education, Culture, and Sciences.

BREEN, MICHAEL. 1985. Authenticity in the Language Classroom. *Applied Linguistics* 6:1. 201-220.

BYRNES, HEIDI. Forthcoming. Proficiency and the Prevention of Fossilization—A response. *Modern Language Journal*.

GUNTERMAN, GAIL. 1987. The Issue of Grammar. *Theory into Practice* 26:4. 276-281.

MET, MYRIAM. 1985. Trends. *Educational Leadership* 48:1. 84-85.

PARKINSON, DILWORTH B. 1981. VSO to SVO in Modern Standard Arabic. *Al-ʿArabiyya* 14:24-37.

TAHA, ZEINAB. 1981. Variation in Structures of Front Page Newspapers Headlines and News Items. Master's thesis, American University in Cairo.

VALDMAN, ALBERT. 1986. Development in Linguistics and Semitics. *Language Variability and Language Teaching*, Georgetown University Round Table, 143-1100.

VALLETTE, REBECCA. 1990. "Fossils or Forests? The Challenge of Teaching for Proficiency in the Secondary Schools," in *On Language and Linguistics*, 235-244. Washington, DC: Georgetown University Round Table.

_____. 1991 Proficiency and the Prevention of Fossilization—An editorial. *Modern Language Journal* 75:325-328.

9

Learning from Gulliver: The Teaching of "Culture" in an Advanced Arabic Language Course

Samar Attar
University of Sydney

Taking as a point of departure the experiences of Swift's Gulliver, notably the notion of the relativity of "point of view," this chapter aims at suggesting a strategy for the selection of texts to teach culture within an advanced Arabic language course. The strategy is based on theoretical premises concerning the problem of intercultural communication in light of the current debate among anthropologists and ethnographers on the "representation" of the "Other." In the case of Arabic, within a tradition of problematic communication between East and West, it appears imperative that teachers and students develop a critical consciousness of their own role within a discourse fraught with assumptions that are often unstated and part of a popular unreflected knowledge. Apart from addressing the conceptual issues involved, the chapter presents a complete lesson plan, using both authentic historical texts and simulated language situations. It is argued that the learning of Arabic should aim at involving students in a cross cultural encounter, following an integrated course of communicative, literary, and interpretative skills based on social, political, and historical reflection and analysis. The study of historical documents set in a simulated, present-day context may thus become part of a learning process of contemporary students whose reading of a past text will lead to a critical reflection of their own experiences of encountering Arabic language and civilization.

To see Others not as ontologically given but as historically constituted would be to erode the exclusivist biases we so often ascribe to cultures, our own not least.[1]

—Edward W. Said

1. Gulliver and the Relativity of the Point of View

When Jonathan Swift's hero, Gulliver, a good-natured and simple Englishman, first encounters different races in the course of his travel, he often expresses his abhorrence at how they differ from him and from his race.[2] The same is true of those people who first set eye on him. They, too, are terrified, and think Gulliver to be a weird and inferior creature. But as time passes, both parties, the Englishman and the various "foreigners," come to understand each other, even to appreciate one another. This progress, however, takes place only when Gulliver learns to communicate with the people among whom he dwells. Through a study of their languages, the traveller is finally able to comprehend how different people organize their lives. Swift makes the point, to use Stephen Freeman's terminology, that "a foreign language, well learned, is a bridge of communication and contact with another people, another culture, which then becomes less foreign, more human, to the learner."[3]

Gulliver's first journey to the land of the little people teaches the English traveller that human size is relative, and that height is certainly not required for great achievements. At first, he laughs at the tiny creatures, who are not even six inches high. He thinks of them as insects. In their turn, they are shocked to look at him. But gradually, both Gulliver and the little people begin to see positive things about each other. The stranger speaks to them in as many languages as he knows: "Dutch, Latin, French, Spanish, Italian, and Lingua Franca; but all to no purpose" (25). He finds it necessary to learn their language. Learned men are appointed by the Emperor of Lilliput to teach the shipwrecked traveller their language and to instruct him in their customs and laws. As a result, Gulliver learns more about the tiny people and eventually becomes so involved with them that he offers to serve in their wars. In return, they name him a hero. Other men become jealous of him, and he is finally forced to flee the country.

Gulliver's second journey, this time to the land of the giants, confirms the philosophers' belief that "nothing is great or little otherwise than by comparison" (70). Gulliver is shocked when he sees the giants. They, too, think he is a

---

1. Said (1989:225).

2. Swift (1960). All subsequent references are from this edition. Page numbers will be cited in the text in parentheses.

3. Freeman (1968:261). Cf. Rivers (1983:136).

strange animal. A farmer's wife screams when she first sees him and runs back as "women in England do at the sight of a toad or a spider" (72). Gulliver begins to despise himself as a little creature who becomes a toy in the hand of a giant baby. Ultimately, he attempts to learn the giants' language and gradually becomes aware of the differences between the rustic phrases of the farmers and the polite style of the court. During his stay with the giants, Gulliver learns about their laws and customs, and they, too, learn about Europe, although they are not given the whole picture. Gulliver confesses to the reader that he has eluded many of the Emperor's questions, and that he has hidden "the frailties and deformities" of England and placed "her virtues and beauties in the most advantageous light" (107). Gulliver, then, decides to leave the land of the giants. He tells us he prefers to be among people of his size, for he has always been afraid of being "trod to death like a frog or young puppy" (113). But when he is picked up by an English ship he finds it very difficult to accept his own people. The sailors appear in his eyes "the most little contemptible creatures" (119) he has ever seen. When he arrives home, he observes the littleness of everything: houses, trees, cattle, and human beings. He is afraid to trample on people he meets as if they were pygmies, and he a giant.

In the course of his travels, Gulliver visits many other countries of which not the least interesting one is the land of the intellectuals. He finds the inhabitants amazingly absent-minded. Their servants, who are called the "flappers," (128) are obliged to remind them to listen and reply. A flapper simply has to touch the mouth of the intellectual who is to speak, while another flapper has to touch the right ear of the intellectual who is to listen. Swift tells us that his protagonist, by now a truly experienced language learner, manages to learn the intellectuals' language, acquiring "a tolerable proficiency" (133) in about a month's time. Lucky Gulliver, and prescient Swift, who, already more than two hundred years ago, put their fingers on the very center of the language teacher's concern, the notion of proficiency! One wonders, though, whether Gulliver had to submit to a standard proficiency test to prove his competence in the land of the intellectuals.[4]

The relativity of the "point of view" in *Gulliver's Travels* demands attention. The notion of "seeing others" and "being seen by others" might provide a point of departure for a discussion of the teaching of culture in a foreign lan-

---

4. The debate on "proficiency" in Arabic language teaching is, of course, of great importance to the future direction of our profession. However, the issues involved in this debate clearly go beyond the scope of the present chapter. For the most recent contributions to the proficiency debate, see Allen (1990).

guage course. It highlights the importance of what the German sociologist Karl Mannheim calls "perspective."[5] When Gulliver attempts to come to grips with various cultures and understand something about their laws, customs, and ways of life, he finds it necessary to learn foreign languages in order to successfully engage in intercultural communication. He stresses the significance of the "point of view." Any story has as many interpretations as there are people concerned. Gulliver learns how to listen to other points of view, and at times he even accepts them. He learns to guess from the usage of language the speakers' association with a particular class. He also becomes able to differentiate between people even within one culture. In this respect at least, Gulliver, our eighteenth century model language learner, is more clever than some of our contemporaries, including a few anthropologists, who until not so very long ago had a habit of generalizing about a given culture and its people.

2. The Theoretical Debate on Cultural Representation: An Overview

Since the sixties and seventies, in particular, with the advent of post-colonial nations demanding recognition from the West and challenging the legitimacy with which Western institutions represent them, a debate has arisen in literary, historical, and anthropological discourse. It has focused on the question of how to represent the Other. The French cultural anthropologist Michel Leiris is a very important and early contributor to this debate. His essays, most notably "L'Ethnographe devant le Colonialisme" (1950) and *Race et Civilisation* (1951), translated into English as *Race and Culture*, clearly formulate the most pertinent points in a critique of Western ethnographic writing with regard to the representation and appropriation of foreign cultures.[6]

More recently, and with particular relevance to our own case of Arabic culture, Edward Said's *Orientalism* has opened the way for a critical re-evaluation of the intercultural discourse between East and West. Said's book, first published in 1978, is a brilliant "example of a text illustrating the uses and abuses of the cultural Other by Western institutions."[7] Said's book has become a classic. No scholar dealing with cultural studies is able to ignore it, nor—I believe—can we as teachers of Arabic language and culture. The problem, of course, is how to use and incorporate Said's findings in our own work.

---

5. See Mannheim (1927, 57: 68-142, 470-95). Cf. Mannheim (1953), (1986:190).

6. See Leiris (1950:357-374) and (1958). UNESCO has also published in its series on "The Race Question in Modern Science," a valuable book by Claude Levi-Strauss, *Race and History* (1958).

7. Marc Manganaro (1990:3).

The central thesis of *Orientalism* is the controversial issue of cultural representation, "in the so-called truthful text (histories, philological analyses, political treatises) as in the avowedly artistic (i.e., openly imaginative) text."[8] The issuing problems are enormous. Is it possible to represent other people and cultures? Is the representation a creation of the scholar or poet with no corresponding reality? What is the background of the person who attempts to represent others? What are his or her aims? Why have different people with different motives seen the same material in different ways and have discussed the same culture in opposing fashion? What is the relationship between representation and power? All these questions have become central to scholars, particularly anthropologists, who are interested in the representation of the cultural Other.[9] The issues involved here have not always been recognized. In the mid sixties, for example, many American anthropologists did not seem to worry about such concerns. To give one example: in his confidently naive approach to analyzing the Arabs, in a book entitled *The Hidden Dimension*, the anthropologist Edward Hall assures us that "Arabs apparently recognize a relationship between disposition and smell. The intermediaries who arrange an Arab marriage usually take great precautions to insure a good match. They may even on occasion ask to smell the girl and will reject her if she 'does not smell nice,' not so much on esthetic grounds but possibly because of a residual smell of anger or discontent. Bathing the other person in one's breath is a common practice in Arab countries. The American is taught not to breathe on people. . . . The lack of congruence between U.S. and Arab olfactory systems affects both parties and has repercussions which extend beyond mere discomfort or annoyance."[10]

As an Arab who grew up in Damascus, Syria, my immediate reaction to a statement like Hall's is laughter mixed with anger. And yet, I suspect that Hall's intention is not devious. He tells us naively that "in spite of over two thousand years of contact, Westerners and Arabs still do not understand each other" (144). Who would disagree? In his own way, Hall is only trying to explain to us the reasons that lie behind this misunderstanding. As an American professor who served in the 1950s as a Director of the State Department's Point IV Training

---

8. Said (1978:21).

9. See, for example, Johannes Fabian (1990:753-772). Fabian argues that "the Other is never simply given, never just found or encountered, but *made*." For him, "investigations into othering are investigations into the production of anthropology's object" (755).

10. Hall (1966:47). Subsequent page numbers will be cited in the text in parentheses. Note that Douglas Brown describes Hall's books as "classic references in the field of cultural anthropology" and that they are "excellent sources written for the layperson." See Brown (1980:144). Brown fails to see that Hall's picture of other cultures is not only oversimplified, but also misleading.

Program, he tells us "little is known about cross-cultural communication. Because of this lack, much of the good will and great effort of the nation has been wasted in its overseas programs." He recommends that Americans who are sent abroad should "be carefully selected as to their suitability to work in a foreign culture. They should also be taught to speak and read the language of the country of assignment and thoroughly trained in the culture of the country."[11] But how? One wonders whether Hall has heeded his own advice, and whether he might have come to different conclusions in his anthropological work if he had.

Fortunately, many anthropologists since the beginning of the seventies have taken a very self-critical look at what they are doing. They have begun to question the issue of representation and its relationship to power. Some have noticed the close ties between anthropology and colonialism and stressed the importance of point of view or perspective. In his article "Objectivity in Anthropology," Jacques Maquet argues that it is not enough for an anthropologist to indicate that his or her object is "the social structure" of such and such people; but that "one should add: as seen by an anthropologist belonging to" a specific socio-economic and political and racial group.[12] The danger in representation here is that it is done by an anthropologist (or a subject) who determines the meaning of social phenomena. He/she is alone responsible for reading into the gestures or patterns of behavior he/she observes in their objects.

I should like to conclude my sketchy survey with a reference to a very recent contribution. The American journal *New Literary History* has devoted its winter 1992 issue to the topic "Versions of Otherness." In an article entitled "The Other's Double. The Anthropologist's Bracketed Self: Notes on Cultural Representation and Privileged Discourse," R. S. Khare argues that "if anthropology recognizes that the self is the Other's double, the anthropologist shows how, as he appropriates the Other to reconstitute his self, he learns to recognize an irreducible presence of the Other."[13] For the critic, the issue now is not simply to represent the Other but "to recognize it anew" (1). In order to do that one has to re-examine "the unresolved issues of one's own self-identity" (1). R. S. Khare concludes his argument by saying that "since representation invariably

---

11. Hall (1959:xiv).

12. Maquet (1970:264).

13. Khare (1992:1). All subsequent page numbers will be cited in the text in parentheses. Note that Khare relies heavily on Levi-Strauss who suggests that "in ethnographic experience the observer apprehends himself as his own instrument of observation. Clearly, he must learn to know himself, to obtain, from a *self* who reveals himself as *another* to the *I* who uses him, an evaluation which will become an integral part of the observation of other selves" (Levi-Strauss 1977:36). Quoted by Khare in his article (17).

raises issues of privilege and politics of self within a discourse or a text, a control of self-privileging reflexivity is doubly necessary for anthropology to move beyond its beleaguered colonial past." (14).

In case you begin to wonder about the relevance of such a debate on the teaching of culture in an advanced Arabic language course, let me say this: I think this current debate is crucial to us. I believe we should participate in it, not only because I think we have something worthwhile and unique to contribute, given our specialist roles as mediators between East and West, but also because our participation might lessen our isolation as Arabists, allowing us to contribute to a most topical and political intellectual debate, and thus bridging the gap between ourselves and the other disciplines.

3. Culture and Language Learning

But what about the teaching of culture in Arabic language programs? In an article on cultural proficiency in Arabic, published in *Foreign Language Annals*, Mahmoud Al-Batal has formulated "a catalogue" of cultural "topics" which he suggests should be included in an Arabic language course.[14] I find his list very useful and I have, indeed, come to very similar conclusions in my textbook *Modern Arabic: An Introductory Course for Foreign Students*.[15] What I should like to suggest in the following are some ideas that address the more basic issues involved in the teaching of culture within a process of intercultural communication. As a practicing language teacher, I should like to offer these suggestions in the form of a concrete proposal for a teaching unit for advanced learners of Arabic. The material collected here forms one chapter of a textbook on which I am presently working. This textbook represents a sequel to *Modern Arabic* and is intended for use in the second or third year of language instruction. The principles of text selection for this chapter follow the issues raised earlier: the example of Gulliver and his latter-day followers, the contemporary ethnographer and cultural anthropologist.

1.   In foreign language teaching and learning, particularly with regard to Arabic, it appears imperative that both teachers and students develop a critical consciousness of their role within a socially- and culturally-conditioned dis-

---

14. Al-Batal (1988:443-453). Cf. Lafayette (1975). Also consult Weber (1976) and Seelye (1976).

15. Samar Attar (1988). Also, (1991). *Modern Arabic* is a textbook on representations of one Arab city. It provides exemplary insights into aspects of ancient and contemporary Arab civilization and culture. The city of Damascus in the book is meant only as a model which could be easily substituted by or complemented with information on other Arab cities.

course that is fraught with unstated assumptions. The problem of generalization is one obvious difficulty we are confronting here. I wonder how many of us would agree that the kind of clichés, half-truths, idées recues, and misinformation that are so characteristic of earlier anthropological writings (such as Edward Hall's), are still very much part of the popular imagination that occupies the average American's concept of the Arab world. The kind of information provided by today's mass media, as well as the haphazard educational curriculum in the primary and secondary sectors, serve to perpetuate precisely the level of ignorance and semi-information that characterizes the view of Arabs and Arab culture among ordinary Americans. How are we, then, as teachers of Arabic, to address this deficit which, I assume, most if not all of our students possess initially?

To tell specialists and non-specialists alike that nations have different attitudes towards time, spatial relationships, work, sex, and learning, and to cite an example or two to back up one's argument, is to immerse oneself in generalization and absurd clichés. One cannot generalize like Hall by saying that Americans are direct and forthright while Greeks are not, and that this is the reason why American officials have difficulty with Greek officials. Or that Arabs think only God knows about the weather and the future and therefore Americans have a difficult time discussing modern agricultural methods with them.[16] I suppose there is no easy solution to this except being ever vigilant, trying to be as specific and concrete as possible, and countering so-called evidence that seems to confirm the cliché with other evidence that questions it and stresses its relativity. Perhaps we should compose a drill for us that would make it a reflex action to avoid saying "the Arabs are . . ." but instead to say "the Arabs in . . . at the time of . . . under this circumstance . . . are . . . ." And when students tell us, as they have heard on the TV news, or read in Hall's book, that the Egyptian peasants cannot understand the American agricultural adviser who asks them about their future yield because they think it is presumptuous to try to look into, or even talk about, the future, we should tell the equally true story of the faithful Muslims in Saudi Arabia who are making their own future by irrigating the desert and producing wheat for export. It is not to be understood that the faithful Muslims in Saudi Arabia are more intelligent than those peasants in Egypt. The example is meant to suggest that people with similar religious convictions can have different views about life and can react differently to existing problems, that Islam is not the reason for backwardness, or outdated agricultural

---

16. Hall (1959:xv-xvi).

methods, and that not *all* Egyptian peasants, or Saudis, for that matter, constitute one homogenous group.

2. The model of teaching Arabic culture that I am constructing here is based on the premise that it is imperative to examine each point of view in a way which allows a critical recognition of the process of "seeing others" and "being seen by others." The principle of text selection is that of a juxtaposition of texts containing an Arab and a Western perspective relating to the same or similar topic or theme. The emphasis throughout is on the notion of encounter: pieces of culture as seen from within and from without. Contrasting points of view, value judgments, political opinions, or instances of socio-cultural differences allow for a deeper, critical understanding of one own's position and that of the Other. Important is that the learner recognizes himself/herself within a given context and at the same time is forced to take into account the position of the Other.

3. A third criterion of selection is the historical dimension which should always be present. It is imperative that authentic historical documents be used, designed to contribute to a learning process of contemporary students whose reading of a past text will reflect on their present experiences encountering Arabic language and civilization. The historical perspective discourages generalizations: if we say, "this is how things are," we should add "that is how things were before" and "they will be different in the future." We also might say: "Things are changing even as we speak." We are thus giving the students a very clear signal that a static view of the world is untenable, in one's own society as well as in that of the language one studies. The historical perspective is, of course, crucial to any critical understanding of civilization. How are we to appreciate the opinions and customs of an Arab speaker if we do not recognize how these opinions and customs are products of historical development and change, and how they are conditioned by a culture that has come to be what it is as a result of a process of socio-economic and political development as well as by a projection of assumptions, plans, and wishes which extend into the future? The historical perspective also constitutes an important linking and integrative factor, thematically as well as methodologically. In my planned textbook, the chapters will be organized thematically according to different episodes of historical encounters which seem to be typical or prominent within the history of East-West relations. The period of the Crusades, which is covered in the model teaching unit that follows, is one such exemplary historical encounter, which offers students a number of examples of Westerners meeting with Arabs. The critical evaluation of the attitudes of the Crusades will allow the students to

reflect on their own. They will see themselves as only the last link in an historical chain that connects East and West, and they will realize that their expectations, values, and views are as much conditioned by the weight of the traditions
and the "pile of rubble"[17] of history as the interpretation of their expectations,
values, and views by the Arab speakers with whom these students, it is hoped,
will engage in a fruitful and enriching communicative encounter.

4.   This brings me to my last point, the experience of what R. S. Khare
has termed the re-examination of "the un-resolved issues of one's own self-
identity." I think this is the most important point, and I have no doubt that it
involves a very difficult task that will not be achieved by the critical reading of
one text or two. With regard to the learning of language and culture, intercultural communication must involve a process of reflection on the learner's own
role and motivation. The students need to examine and re-examine critically
why they want to learn Arabic and why they want to travel to the Middle East.
They must become aware of all the assumed and half-conscious reasons, emo-
tions, dreams, and fantasies that accompany their choices. In order to facilitate
this experience, the students need to be given characters, either fictional or
historical, authentic or constructed, that would allow them to define their own
position in contrast to other, similar characters with their specific, concrete
ambitions and aims, successes and failures.[18] In my text, these persons are all
travellers to the East. The history of exploration, conquest, and tourism from
Europe and North America to the Arab countries constitutes the "red thread," as
it were, which constitutes the unity of a critical investigation into Arabic culture, seen from both the visitor and the visited.

I believe that a language learning process, which integrates communicative skills with techniques of literary and socio-historical analysis, based on
such premises of a critical appropriation of intercultural encounters, offers the
chance for conducting an experiment that will eventually determine whether
cross cultural understanding and dialogue is possible. In my opinion, such a
program of language learning will help students to learn some aspects about
diverse Arab cultures as well as about themselves and their own cultures. Although our aims of teaching Arabic will always be different, we should not

17. Benjamin, "Uber den Begriff der Geschicte," (1991:698). Cf. Benjamin, "Theses on the
Philosophy of History," (1977:260).

18. Cf. Erik H. Erikson, who is known for his work in developmental psychology and who
coined the term "identity crisis." Erikson argues that personal identity is achieved through a long
process of resolving critical problems encountered at different stanges of psychosocial development. See 1959:50-100; 1963; 1968; and 1979.

forget that our primary task as teachers is to help build bridges and to facilitate social, political, and historical understanding between nations. Whether we stress grammar and structural knowledge of the language, communicative skills, literary interpretive skills, or translation, we should always present to our students texts that open up a debate on the kinds of questions I have tried to address.

The ultimate aim is a domination-free discourse leading to social, political, and historical awareness of two different, yet not dissimilar, worlds that share a common basis of human experience. Old traditional houses in Damascus usually have small undistinguished doors leading to marble floors, mosaic walls, vast courtyards, and enchanted gardens under which rivers flow. Similarly, the learning of Arabic starts by necessity from small and narrow openings but should lead to a wide vista which enchants the learners and widens their horizons. And when the students of Arabic approach closer and look into the fountains and rivers of the old Damascene house, they will also see a reflection of their self, albeit in a very new and exciting surrounding.

APPENDIX I

Cultural Representation and the Relativity of Point of View in the Teaching
of an Advanced Arabic Language Course: Sample Extracts

There are many encounters between Arabs and Westerners throughout history. One such an encounter is the confrontation of East and West in the Middle Ages. The period of the Crusades (1096-1291) provides ample materials for a course that integrates language learning and its four skills with history, architecture, fine arts, travel, and comparative literature. The examples I am suggesting here would be addressed to students who have already taken Arabic for at least two years, or to students who have a High Level of proficiency in the four skills. The material may also be suitable for graduate students who are interested in history and comparative literature in particular. The objectives of such a course will vary. But the primary purpose will always be to study different points of view of the Other and to evaluate these views.

A sample chapter which highlights the notion of "seeing others" and "being seen by others" is outlined as follows:

1. An introductory dialogue dealing with historical materials in Arabic. (A bus trip to Krak des Chevaliers.)

2. An authentic historical text in Arabic, a contemporary Arab point of view. (Usāmah Ibn Munqidh reporting on the Crusaders' medical practice in the twelfth century.)

3. An authentic historical text in English, a contemporary Western point of view. (Jean De Joinville reporting on the Muslim's medical practice in the thirteenth century.)

4. A dialogue in Arabic dealing with historical materials. (A visit to Saladin's Mausoleum in Damascus.)

5. A selection of authentic Arabic texts on Saladin and the relationship between Muslims and Crusaders, a contemporary Arab traveller's point of view. (Ibn Jubayr's observation during his last journey to the East at the end of the twelfth century.)

6.   Authentic literary texts on Saladin and other Muslims in English, a non-contemporary western point of view. (Dante's views of Saladin, Avicenna, Averroes, Mohammad, and Ali in his imaginary journey to the other world.)

7.   A commentary in Arabic based on Dante's literary text: *The Inferno.* (Dante, the Italian poet and Saladin.)

In order to illustrate the cultural and linguistic objectives of the chapter and point out some of the possible means which could be used to fulfil our goal, I will specifically deal at some length with three examples, namely, the first dialogue and the two authentic texts by Usāmah Ibn Munqidh and Jean De Joinville; then I will briefly refer to the rest of the texts.

1.   A Bus Trip to the Krak des Chevaliers

The first constructed dialogue (appendix II) is between an American tourist and a Palestinian student who are on a tour from the Syrian city of Homs to Krak des Chevaliers, the mightiest fortress of the Hospitallers and one of the Crusaders' Military Orders in the twelfth century. The tourist, whose name is James, had previously studied Arabic for four years at the University of Michigan and lived for two years in Morocco. As a child, he built and played with medieval castles and read romantic tales about Peter the Hermit and King Richard the Lion-Heart. Sawsan, on the other hand, is a graduate student at the University of Cairo; she is writing a dissertation on the Crusaders' castles in the Middle East and is very knowledgeable about the history of that particular era.

The specific cultural objectives of the introductory dialogue are:

1.   To name and locate military and aesthetic monuments in the Middle East, (such as Crusaders' castles), and be aware of their historical significance.[19]

2.   To gain insight through the study of a simple text into the history of the Arabs and the Crusades in the Middle Ages.

3.   To see the world from a different perspective and experience what it is like to belong to another racial, religious and linguistic group.

---

19. The teacher could ask the students to look at the map of the Middle East, then write the names of the following castles in their appropriate geographical locations, e.g., Kerak Castle (Qal^{c}at al-Karak), Sahyun Castle (Qal^{c}at Ṣahyūn, or Salah al-Din), Marqab Castle (Qal^{c}at al-Marqab), Krak Des Chevaliers (Qal^{c}at al-Ḥuṣn, or al-Akrād), Schaizar Castle (Qal^{c}at Shayzar), Aleppo Castle (Qal^{c}at Ḥalab), the Castle of Montfort, and the Citadel of Cairo (Qal^{c}at al-Qāhira). The students could be asked to write a paragraph or two in Arabic or English on the history of at least six castles.

4. To understand the values and viewpoints of others.

5. To learn that religious fanatics are to be found everywhere and are not restricted to any particular religion or religious group. "Holy Wars" have taken place in different regions of the world and have been fought by different races.

6. To appreciate the beauty of the Crusaders' castles all over the Middle East and to learn that ugliness and violence can sometimes yield beauty and peace after the passing of wars and enmity between nations.

The language objectives are:

1. Speaking:

   a. Reproducing and appropriately modifying patterns of spoken Standard Arabic.

   b. Discussing the historical background of monuments with sufficient accuracy and participating in formal and informal conversations on similar topics.[20]

   c. Expressing one's opinion regarding the role played by a particular group of people in history, and supporting such an opinion.

2. Listening:

   a. Developing the ability to comprehend historical terminology in spoken Standard Arabic, and understanding technical discussion in architecture.

   b. Developing awareness of the underlying tone of the oral text.

3. Reading:

   a. Reading Arabic texts that deal with historical materials with ease.

   b. Developing the ability to scan a text and perceive the main ideas accurately and at the average speed of a native speaker.

4. Writing:

   a. Writing advanced and accurate Arabic essays.

   b. Describing and narrating personal experiences.

   c. Discussing different views and substantiating them.

   d. Developing the ability to refer to historical sources and evaluate them.

---

20. Note that I am using only Modern Standard Arabic. Students should use case endings in formal Arabic, but drop them in informal conversations. No dialect whatsoever is allowed here.

Presentation and Specific Tasks

Speaking

In developing the communicative skills, a great deal of attention will be given to oral/aural exposure to, and practice of, simple and complex elements of the language. This will be achieved through class drills, conversations, debates, role play, the language laboratory, slides, television, and film documentaries. Emphasis will not be on formal grammar, but rather on learning the morphology and syntax of the language through patterns in conversational situations.

1. Class activity: Playing various roles, visiting a historical castle, describing it, telling about its history, presenting a point of view, comparing past with present events, trying to persuade others.[21]
2. Individual activity: Summing up the text in a narrative form, commenting on the speakers, and evaluating their attitudes towards history and current political events.
3. A discussion among three students: Arguing about the views expressed by the characters in the text and taking sides, commenting on what each student believes the characters are really saying.
4. A general debate: Half of the class supports the Crusades, and the other half is against the Crusades.

Writing

Individual or Group Activity:
1. Writing a dialogue in which two or more characters are involved. The topic is a visit to a historical monument.
2. Summing up the text, commenting on the characters and expressing one's point of view.
3. Writing an essay about two different views and positions of Arabs and Crusaders in the Middle Ages.

---

21. Students should be given characters, either fictional or historical, and encouraged to play various roles. They should always be reminded of the following quotation from Shakespeare's *As You Like It*:

All the world's a stage,

And all the men and women merely players:

They have their exits and their entrances;

And one man in his time plays many parts. . . (II, vii. 139-142).

Reading

1. Reading the text
2. Reading supplementary extracts about the Krak Des Chevaliers or other Crusaders' castles.

Listening

1. Listening to the text read.
2. Listening to other similar texts dealing with Crusaders' castles and their history.

2. Usāmah's Text

Usāmah Ibn Munqidh was born in Syria in 1095, and died in 1188. He was a warrior, a hunter, a gentleman, and a poet. He was acquainted with Arab and Western leaders, and travelled to the courts of Nūr al-Dīn and Saladin in Damascus, the Fatimid Caliph in Cairo, and the Zanki in Mosul. He knew Baldwin, Bohemond, Roger, Fulk, and other leaders of the first two Crusades. Usāmah lived in his castle, Shayzar, on the Orontes River and was often warring against Crusaders and Byzantine troops. At the age of ninety, he dictated his memoirs, entitled *Kītāb al-Ī'tibār*, in which he described many of the political events to which he was an eyewitness.

The extract (Appendix III) describes the impressions of a Christian Arab doctor about Western medicine and practice in the twelfth century.

The specific cultural objectives of Usāmah's text are:

1. To see how Western medicine was often based on religious and super-stitious assumptions rather than on scientific experiment during the twelfth century.
2. To realize that the Arabs were highly advanced in comparison to Europeans in medicine during the twelfth century.
3. To evaluate the testimony of Ibn Munqidh about the Franks and to judge his objectivity.
4. To describe the relationship between Arabs and Crusaders and their attitudes toward each other during peace time.
5. To analyze the characteristics and tone of the speaker in the text.

The specific language objectives of Usāmah's text are:

Speaking

1. To sum up the argument in accurate Arabic.
2. To comment on its content and express personal views in accurate Arabic.
3. To comment on the narrator and to describe his attitude and point of view.[22]
4. To speak about renowned Arab and Moslem doctors in the Middle Ages, either as an individual or a communal class activity.
5. To re-write Usāmah's text as a dramatic scene and perform it.

Writing

1. To analyze the text in accurate Arabic.
2. To comment on the speaker and his tone.
3. To evaluate the speaker's objectivity.
4. To describe the significance of the text and to express one's personal opinion in accurate Arabic.
5. To modify the Classical text into Modern Standard Arabic, and to re-write it, either as a dialogue between several characters to be performed or as a narrative form.
6. To write two short paragraphs commenting on Usāmah's language and how it differs from or resembles our Standard Arabic of today.

Reading

1. To read various extracts from Usāmah's book.
2. To become acquainted with Arabic written in the twelfth century.

Listening

1. To listen to a presentation on Usāmah's book and be able to sum up the main ideas with ease.

---

22. The teacher could introduce a variety of adjectives to the class in Arabic, e.g., objective (*mawḍūʿī*), neutral (*ḥiyādī*), ignorant (*jāhil*), fanatic (*mutaʿaṣṣib*), biased (*mutaḥayyiz*), tolerant (*mutasāmiḥ*), indifferent (*ghayr muktarith*), open-minded (*dhū ʾaql munfatih*), liberal (*ghayr mutaʿaṣṣib*), impartial (*ghayr mutaḥayyiz*), prejudiced (*mutaḥāmil, mutaḥayyiz*), extremist (*mutaṭarrif*), radical (*mutaṭarrif, radicālī*), and so on.

3. Jean De Joinville's Text

The text by Jean De Joinville is presented in appendix IV. The author, who is the son of a nobleman of Champagne, was born between 1224 and 1225. Following his family tradition, he took the cross in 1248 and went on the Seventh Crusade. He wrote his *Life of Saint Louis* in old age, as a tribute to King Louis IX of France, who was not only his lord but also his loved friend.

The extract which is taken from Joinville's book, chapter 9, "The French in Captivity, April 1250," describes briefly Arab medicine in the thirteenth century.

The specific cultural objectives of Joinville's text are:

1. To see how the Crusaders' medicine was often based on superstitious beliefs rather than on scientific experiment during the thirteenth century.
2. To realize that the Arabs were far more advanced than Europeans in medicine during the thirteenth century.
3. To evaluate the treatment of captives by the Arabs as seen in the text.
4. To judge the speaker's tone and attitude towards his captors.

The specific language objectives of Joinville's text are:

Speaking

1. To sum up the main ideas in fluent accurate Arabic.
2. To comment on the story and express one's personal views in accurate Arabic.
3. To re-write Joinville's text as a dramatic scene and perform it as a communal theatrical activity.

Writing

1. To summarize the essence of the story into accurate Arabic.
2. To comment on the story and the speaker and to express one's personal opinion about them.
3. To write a short dialogue between the captives and the captors, either as an individual or group activity.

Reading

1. To choose other extracts in English and to summarize their core argument in accurate Arabic.
2. To comment on these new extracts and evaluate them in accurate Arabic.

Listening
1. To listen to an Arabic presentation on Joinville's book and to be able to sum up the main ideas with ease.

4. A Visit to Saladin's Mausoleum in Damascus

The second dialogue (appendix V) is between a man and a woman in the city of Damascus. Michael is non-Arab and is very much interested in the history of the Crusades. He asks Rim, an Arab speaker, to go with him to Saladin's mausoleum that afternoon. She agrees. The conversation between the two characters is highly charged with political connotations. It hints at why sometimes some Arabs and some Westerners might misunderstand or even hurt each other. But the tone here is very light and amusing.

The specific cultural objectives of the second dialogue are:
1. To gain insight through the study of a simple text into the history of the Arabs in the Middle Ages.
2. To understand the values and viewpoints of others.
3. To read more about Saladin and understand why he was and still is admired by many people.

The language objectives are similar to those of dialogue 1. Students will be encouraged to perform the text, to discuss it among themselves and to write about it. However, the emphasis here will be on the significance of the hidden meanings and ambiguous tone of the speakers.

5. Ibn Jubayr on Saladin and the Arab East during the Crusades Period

Ibn Jubayr, an Arab traveller and scholar from Spain, was born in Valencia in 1145, and died in 1217. During one of his most important journeys to the East, a journey that lasted three years, from February 1182 to April 1185, he visited Alexandria, Cairo, and Damascus, among other cities, and travelled through the Crusaders' states. At that time, Saladin was the sole master of both Egypt and Syria.

Ibn Jubayr was a great admirer of Saladin, who only two years after the traveller's visit to the Kingdom of Jerusalem crushed the Frankish armies at Hittin near Lake Tiberias and reconquered Jerusalem and the greater part of the Crusaders' territories.

The four extracts (appendix VI) are taken from *Riḥlat Ibn Jubayr* "Ibn Jubayr's Travels." The first text describes the Citadel of Cairo and the Christian captives working on its fortifications. The second text praises Saladin, the just king, who abolished the unjustified taxes paid by pilgrims in Egypt on their way to Mecca. The third text describes the traveller's observation concerning the peaceful co-existence between Muslims and Franks in various towns. Ibn Jubayr marvels at the Muslim and Frankish merchants who are doing business at a time when Saladin is besieging Al-Karak, one of the greatest Crusaders' castles in the region.

Many more extracts from Ibn Jubayr's *Riḥlat* could be included in the chapter, e.g., the entries on the cities of Tyre or Acre. They all deal with this scholar's observations on the relationship between Muslims and Franks and clearly state the traveller's position vis-à-vis the conflict.

The cultural and linguistic objectives of these texts are similar to those of Usāmah Ibn Munqidh. But one might question here the apparent lack of sympathy, or more precisely the indifference, on the part of Ibn Jubayr towards the enemy captives.

6. Dante's Views of Saladin and Other Muslims: An Authentic Literary Text Written Some Sixteen Years after the Final Defeat of the Crusaders
Dante Alighieri (1265-1321)

Dante Alighieri, the celebrated Italian poet, was born in 1265, some seventy-eight years after Saladin's victory over the Crusaders and the Arab reconquest of Jerusalem. When Dante was twenty-six years old, the Sultan Khalil, son of Qalawūn, took Acre, putting an end to two centuries of Frankish presence in the Orient. The city of Acre, in particular, had extensive trade dealings with Italian ports whose welfare depended on the Eastern trade.

Before Dante's birth, Sicily and Southern Italy were important transmitters of Muslim civilization to Europe, particularly during the reign of the Norman kings. It was only fifteen years before Dante's birth that Frederick II, who ruled both Sicily and Germany besides holding the title of Emperor of the Holy Roman Empire, had undertaken a new Crusade to the Arab East. Frederick II was fluent in six languages, of which Arabic was one. Like his grandfather Roger II, who was called the half-heathen king by his critics, Frederick was very much interested in the East, its philosophy, its religion, and its learning.

During Dante's life, Arab Spain had yet to be completely reconquered and Christianized by the Spaniards. Granada was still flourishing and Arab learning was the basis for the newly established universities and scholarly institutions in the West.

Two extracts (appendix VII) are taken from Dante's *Inferno*. The first one describes Dante's encounter with "The Virtuous Pagans" who are not tormented but have no hope. Saladin is placed with them along with Aristotle, Avicenna, and Averroes. The second extract describes the severe punishment of both Mohammad and Ali in hell.

The cultural objective of these extracts is to examine Dante's views, and possibly those of his contemporaries, of Saladin, Avicenna, and Averroes in particular, and Islam as a religion in general. Students should be encouraged to search for new Western texts, preferably written in the wake of the Crusades, and report to the class in Arabic, or English, about the texts' views of Islam and its prophet. On the other hand, the teacher can use Dante's extracts to further the students' proficiency in both speaking and writing skills.

7. A Brief Commentary in Arabic Based on Dante's Literary Text in the *Inferno*

The linguistic objective of this brief commentary on Dante's text (appendix VIII) is to reinforce the students' ability to speak, write, read, and listen to Modern Standard Arabic with ease, to follow a similar discussion on a similar topic, and to venture an opinion or a possible explanation for the hostility of some Westerners towards Islam and Muslims in the Middle Ages.

Appendix II

رحلة بالباص الى قلعة الحصن

حوار بين جيمس وسوسن

(كتبت الحوار معتمدة على مصادر شتى نشرت بالانكليزية ، منها : ستيف رونسمان . تاريخ الصليبيين ، ٣ اجزاء . لندن : طبعة بينغوين ، ١٩٦٥؛ فيليب حتي . تاريخ العرب ، الطبعة العاشرة . لندن : مكميلان ، ١٩٧٠؛ أمين معلوف . الصليبيون كما يراهم العرب، ترجمه للانكليزية جون روتشيلد . لندن : الساقي ، ١٩٨٤؛ ديفيد نيكول . الحملات الصليبية ودويلات الصليبيين . لندن:دار نشر اوسبري ، ١٩٨٨؛ أندريا هوبكنز . الفرسان . لندن : كولنز وبراون ، ١٩٩٠ . كما اطلعت على كتاب ڤولڤغانغ مولر ڤينر . القلاع أيام الحروب الصليبية ، ترجمه للعربية عن الألمانية العميد الركن محمد وليد الجلاد . دمشق : مركز الدراسات العسكرية ، ١٩٨٢) .

جيمس	اسمي جيمس روبرتس .
سوسن	أنا سوسن أبو غزالة . هل أنت أمريكي ؟
جيمس	نعم . أزور الشرق الأوسط لأول مرة .
سوسن	عربيتك ممتازة . هل تتكلم العامية أيضا ؟
جيمس	لهجة مراكش وبعض الكلمات القاهرية فقط . هل أنت سورية ؟
سوسن	لا . أنا فلسطينية . هل تعلمت العربية في الولايات المتحدة؟
جيمس	نعم . درستها لمدة أربع سنوات في جامعة ميشغان، ثم قضيت سنتين في المغرب . وأنا الان مهتم بتاريخ الصليبيين ، وأنوي أن أزور عددا من قلاعهم في الشرق الأوسط .

سوسن   حقا ؟ أنا أيضا مهتمة بهذه الحقبة .

جيمس   ياللمصادفة ! هل قرأت شيئا عن قلعة الحصن ؟

سوسن   كثيرا . كنت قد درست تاريخ الصليبيين لسنوات في جامعة القاهرة . وأنا أعمل حاليا على أطروحة الدكتوراة حول القلاع الصليبية .

جيمس   ت ي . لورنس أيضا كتب عنها عندما كان يدرس في أكسفورد . لا شك أنك تعرفين ذلك . أنا لست مختصا الى هذا الحد . أنا هاو فقط . في طفولتي بنيت وخربت قلاعا كثيرة ، وقرأت قصصا رومانتيكية عن الناسك بيتر والملك ريتشارد قلب الأسد .
(ينظر لصورة قلعة الحصن في الخارطة السياحية ثم يقول لسوسن): من الصورة تبدو قلعة الحصن رائعة . أليس كذلك ؟

سوسن   لكن تاريخها دموي .

جيمس   هل هي بعيدة جدا عن مدينة حمص ؟

سوسن   لا . أعتقد حوالي لستين كيلومترا فقط .

جيمس   لا شك أنها كانت ذات موقع ستراتيجي للغاية. انظري للصورة. الجبل الذي ينحدر بحدة من ثلاث جهات . القلعة الشامخة على قمته. الأبراج الدائرية الضخمة. متى عاش فيها الصليبيون ؟ هل تعرفين ؟

سوسن   احتلها فرسان المستشفى مابين عامي ١١٤٣ و ١٢٧١ . وكان فيها حامية مكونة من ٢٠٠٠ جندي أيام السلم .

جيمس   فرسان المستشفى؟ أذكر أنني قرأت عنهم شيئا ، لكنني لم أعد أذكر التفاصيل .

سوسن   أصلهم من أمالفي في ايطاليا . بدأوا كجماعة من التجار المسيحيين المهتمين بأعمال البر والاحسان. وكان لهم نزل خاص بهم . لكنهم بعد الحروب الصليبية الأولى تخلصوا تدريجيا من سيطرة الدير والبطريرك ، وصاروا تابعين مباشرة للبابا . ففي القرن الثاني عشر قبلوا أولا بعض المسؤوليات الحربية في الدفاع

عن الحدود ، ثم صاروا فيما بعد ملزمين بالقيام بدور فعال في
الحروب بين الصليبيين والمسلمين .

جيمس   من تجار الى فرسان ، ومن متدينين الى محاربين ! سأتعلم منك
الكثير . هل ستبقين معي خلال زيارتا للقلعة ؟

سوسن   اذا شئت .

جيمس   سيكون لي الشرف بمعرفتك .

APPENDIX III

الطب عند الصليبيين

أسامة بن منقذ . كتاب الاعتبار ، تحقيق فيليب حتي . برنستون: ١٩٣٠ ،
ص . ١٧٠-١٧٢ . (راجع أيضا عبد الكريم الأشتر . من كتاب الاعتبار .
دمشق: وزارة الثقافة ، ١٩٨٠ .)

عجائب طبهم

ومن عجيب طبهم أن صاحب المنيطرة كتب الى عمي يطلب منه انفاذ طبيب
يداوي مرضى من أصحابه . فأرسل اليه طبيبا نصرانيا يقال له ثابت . فما
غاب عشرة أيام حتى عاد فقلنا له « ماأسرع ماداويت المرضى !» قال
«أحضروا عندي فارسا قد طلعت في رجله دملة وامرأة قد لحقها نشاف .
فعملت للفارس لبيخة ففتحت الدملة وصلحت . وحميت المرأة ورطبت مزاجها .
فجاءهم طبيب افرنجي فقال لهم (هذا ما يعرف شيء يداويهم) وقال للفارس
(أيما أحب اليك تعيش برجل واحدة أو تموت برجلين؟) قال (أعيش
برجل واحدة) . قال (أحضروا لي فارسا قويا وفأسا قاطعا) . فحضر الفارس
والفأس ، وأنا حاضر ، فحط ساقه على قرمة خشب وقال للفارس (أضرب
رجله بالفأس ضربة واحدة اقطعها) . فضربه ، وأنا أراه ، ضربة واحدة ما
انقطعت . ضربه ضربة ثانية فسال مخ الساق ، ومات من ساعته . وأبصر
المرأة فقال (هذه امرأة في رأسها شيطان قد عشقها . أحلقوا شعرها) .
فحلقوه . وعادت تأكل من مأكلها الثوم والخردل . فزاد بها النشاف . فقال
(الشيطان قد دخل في رأسها) . فأخذ الموسى وشق رأسها صليبا وسلخ وسطه

حتى ظهر عظم الرأس وحكه بالملح ، فماتت في وقتها . فقلت لهم (بقي لكم الي حاجة) قالوا (لا) . فجئت وقد تعلمت من طبهم مالم أكن أعرفه »٠

وقد شاهدت من طبهم خلاف ذلك . كان للملك خازن من فرسانهم يقال له برنارد ، لعنه الله ، من ألعن الافرنج وأرجسهم . فرمحه حصان في ساقه فعملت عليه رجله وفتحت في أربعة عشر موضعا . والجراح كلما ختم موضع فتح موضع . وأنا أدعو بهلاكه . فجاءه طبيب افرنجي فأزال عنه تلك المراهم وجعل يغسلها بالخل الحاذق . فختمت تلك الجراح وبرأ وقام مثل الشيطان .

ومن عجيب طبهم أنه كان عندنا بشيزر صانع يقال له أبو الفتح له ولد قد طلع في رقبته خنازير . وكلما ختم موضع فتح موضع . فدخل أنطاكية في شغل له وابنه معه . فرآه رجل افرنجي فسأله عنه فقال هو ولدي . قال « تحلف لي بدينك ان وصفت لك دواء يبرئه لاتأخذ من أحد تداويه به أجرة حتى أصف لك دواء يبرئه ؟» فحلف . فقال له « تأخذ له أشنانا غير مطحون تحرقه وتربيه بالزيت والخل الحاذق وتداويه به حتى يأكل الموضع . ثم خذ الرصاص المحرق وريه بالسمن . ثم داوه به فهو يبرئه » . فداواه بذلك فبرأ ، وختمت تلك الجراح . وعاد الى ما كان عليه من الصحة .

وقد داويت بهذا الدواء من طلع فيه الداء فنفعه وأزال ماكان يشكوه .

APPENDIX IV

The French in Captivity, April 1250

Jean De Joinville. "The French in Captivity April 1250." In *Joinville and Villehardouin: Chronicles of the Crusades*. 1963; rpt. 1987. Trans. with an introduction, M.R.B. Shaw. Harmondsworth: Penguin, pp. 244-245.

As soon as I met them [his Arab captors] they took off my hauberk; then, out of pity for me, they threw over me a scarlet wrap of my own lined with miniver, which my dear mother had given me. One of them brought me a white leather belt. I strapped this round me over the wrap, after making a hole in the latter, in order to use it as a garment. Another man brought me a hood which I put over my head. Then, because of the fright I was in, and also on account of the sickness that troubled me, I was seized with a terrible fit of trembling. So I asked for a drink, and they brought me some water in a pitcher. But no sooner had I put the pitcher to my mouth than the water spurted out of my nostrils.

When I saw this happen, I sent for my men and told them I was a dying man, since I had a tumour in my throat. They asked me how I knew it, so I showed them. As soon as they saw the water spurting from my throat and nostrils, they began to weep. When the Saracen knights saw my people in tears, they asked the man who had rescued us why these men were weeping. He replied that he understood I had a tumour in my throat and so could not hope to recover. Then one of the Saracen knights told our rescuer to bid us take comfort, for he would give me something to drink that would cure me within two days. And this, I may say, he did.

Raoul de Wanou, who was one of my following, had been hamstrung in the great battle on Shrove Tuesday and could not stand on his feet. I should like you to know that an old Saracen knight who was in that galley, used to carry him pick-a-back to the privy whenever he so required.

APPENDIX V

حول زيارة ضريح صلاح الدين الأيوبي في دمشق

(كتبت الحوار معتمدة على مصادر شتى عن حياة صلاح الدين الأيوبي .
منها : أبو الفداء . المختصر في أخبار البشر . ٤ أجزاء . استنبول ، ١٢٨٦ ،
بهاء الدين بن شداد . النوادر السلطانية: سيرة صلاح الدين . القاهرة ،
١٩٦٢ ، هاملتون جب . حياة صلاح الدين . اوكسفورد ، ١٩٧٣) .

مايكل   كنت أقرأ شيئا عن تاريخ الصليبيين منذ فترة وجيزة ،
ووجدت نفسي مهتما بتلك الحقبة التاريخية . ثم بدأت أستعير
كبا من المكاتب العامة. كبا بالانكليزية ، وبالعربية،
وبالفرنسية . وقرأت سيرة صلاح الدين الأيوبي . وعندما قررت
زيارة دمشق قلت لنفسي اني سأزور قبره قبل أي شئ .
هو مدفون هنا • أليس كذلك•

ريم   نعم. ضريحه متواضع جدا . في بيت صغير بالقرب من الجامع
الأموي •

مايكل   متى نذهب معا لزيارة الضريح .

ريم   اليوم اذا شئت . لدي مقابلة هامة قبل الظهر . ولا أعتقد أنها
ستستغرق أكثر من ساعة . بوسعنا أن نذهب بعد الظهر . الساعة
الواحدة مثلا • ما رأيك ؟

مايكل   عظيم• اتفقنا• هل لديك وقت الان لشرب فنجان قهوة معي ؟

ريم   لا . ستحدثني بلا شك عن صلاح الدين ، وعن كل الكتب التي قرأتها عنه . أليس كذلك ؟

مايكل   أنا مهووس به . قرأت عنه كثيرا . هل تعرفين أنه عندما مات لم يكن في حوزته سوى سبعة وأربعين درهما ، وقطعة واحدة من الذهب كما يروي المؤرخ الحموي أبو الفداء معاصره . بطل المسلمين وملك مصر وسورية . هل تصدقين ؟

ريم   لماذا تريد أن تغم لي قلبي هذا الصباح؟ كان صلاح الدين شاذا عن القاعدة· هل أنت غبي الى هذا الحد ؟

مايكل   (يضحك) أنا غبي جدا . هل تعرفين أن أصله كردي ؟

ريم   طبعا أعرف ذلك . ماغرضك الان ؟ صلاح الدين كان رمزا لنا جميعا . لايهم أصله وفصله ودينه . هل تريد أن تغضبني ؟

مايكل   لا . أردت أن أغيظك قليلا . أنت تغضبين بسرعة . نيتي لم تكن عاطلة كما ظننت . هل نحن أصدقاء من جديد ؟

ريم   (ضاحكة) أجل . الى اللقاء حتى الواحدة بعد الظهر .

مايكل   الى اللقاء .

Appendix VI

زيارة الرحالة ابن جبير للمشرق العربي في عهد صلاح الدين الأيوبي

ابن جبير . رحلة ابن جبير . بيروت: دار صادر ، ١٩٦٤ .

<u>قلعة القاهرة</u> ، ص . ٢٥ .

وشاهدنا ايضا بنيان القلعة وهو حصن يتصل بالقاهرة حصين المنعة ، يريد
السلطان ان يتخذه موضع سكناه ، ويمد سوره حتى ينتظم بالمدينتين
مصر والقاهرة . والمسخرون في هذا البنيان والمتولون لجميع امتهاناته ومؤونته
العظيمة كنشر الرخام ونحت الصخور العظام وحفر الخندق المحدق بسور
الحصن المذكور ، وهو خندق ينقر بالمعاول نقرا في الصخر عجبا من العجائب
الباقية الاثار ، العلوج الاسارى من الروم ، وعددهم لا يحصى كثرة ، ولا
سبيل أن يمتهن في ذلك البنيان أحد سواهم .

وللسلطان أيضا بمواضع أخر بنيان والأعلاج يخدمونه فيه ، ومن يمكن
استخدامه من المسلمين في مثل هذه المنفعة العامة مرفه عن ذلك كله ولا
وظيفة في شئ من ذلك على أحد .

<u>الحرب واتفاق النصارى والمسلمين</u> ، ص . ٢٦٠-٢٦١ .

شاهدنا في هذا الوقت ، الذي هو شهر جمادى الأولى ، من ذلك خروج
صلاح الدين بجميع عسكر المسلمين لمنازلة حصن الكرك ، وهو من أعظم

حصون النصارى ، وهو المعترض في طريق الحجاز والمانع لسبيل المسلمين على البر ، بينه وبين القدس مسيرة يوم أو أشف قليلا ، وهو سرارة أرض فلسطين ، وله نظر عظيم الاتساع متصل العمارة ، يذكر انه ينتهي الى أربع مئة قرية ، فنازله هذا السلطان وضيق عليه وطال حصاره .

واختلاف القوافل من مصر الى دمشق على بلاد الافرنج غير منقطع . واختلاف المسلمين من دمشق على كذلك . وتجار النصارى أيضا لا يمنع أحد منهم ولا يعترض . وللنصارى على المسلمين ضريبة يؤدونها في بلادهم ، وهي من الأمنة على غاية . وتجار النصارى ايضا يؤدون في بلاد المسلمين على سلعهم ، والاتفاق بينهم والاعتدال في جميع الأحوال . وأهل الحرب مشتغلون بحربهم ، والناس في عافية ، والدنيا لمن غلب .

. . . . وشأن هذه البلاد في ذلك أعجب من أن يستوفى الحديث عنه ، والله يعلي كلمة الاسلام بمنه .

عدل صلاح الدين ، ص ٣٠-٣١ .

ومن مفاخر هذا السلطان المزلفة من الله تعالى وآثاره التي ابقاها ذكرا جميلا للدين والدنيا : ازالته رسم المكس المضروب وظيفة على الحجاج مدة دولة العبيديين . فكان الحجاج يلاقون من الضغط في استيدائها عنتا مجحفا ويسامون فيها خطة خسف باهظة . وربما ورد منهم من لا فضل لديه على نفقته أو لا نفقة عنده فيلزم أداء الضريبة المعلومة ، وكانت سبعة دنانير ونصف دينار من الدنانير المصرية التي هي خمسة عشر دينار مؤمنية على كل رأس ، ويعجز عن ذلك ، فيتناول بأليم العذاب بعيذاب . فكانت كاسمها مفتوحة العين .

وربما اخترع له من أنواع العذاب التعليق من الأنثيين أو غير ذلك من الأمور الشنيعة ، نعوذ بالله من سوء قدره . وكان بجدة أمثال هذا التنكيل وأضعافه لمن لم يؤد مكسه بعيذاب ووصل اسمه غير معلم عليه علامة الأداء . فمحا هذا السلطان هذا الرسم اللعين ودفع عوضا منه ما يقوم مقامه من أطعمة وسواها ، وعين مجبى موضع معين بأسره لذلك ، وتكفل بتوصيل جميع ذلك الى الحجاز، لأن الرسم المذكور كان باسم ميرة مكة والمدينة ، عمرهما الله ، فعوض من ذلك أجمل عوض ، وسهل السبيل للحجاج . . . . فترتب الشكر له على كل من يعتقد من الناس أن حج البيت الحرام احدى القواعد الخمس من الاسلام ، حتى يعم جميع الافاق ويوجب الدعاء له في كل صقع من الأصقاع . . . . الى مكوس كانت في البلاد المصرية وسواها ضرائب على كل مايباع ويشترى مما دق وجل ، حتى كان يؤدى على شرب ماء النيل المكس فضلا عما سواه . فمحا هذا السلطان هذه البدع اللعينة كلها وبسط العدل ونشر الأمن .

حسن سيرة السلطان ، ص . ٢٧٠ .

وقد تقدم الذكر أيضا في غير موضع من هذا الكتاب عن حسن سيرة السلطان بهذه الجهات٠ صلاح الدين أبي المظفر يوسف بن أيوب ، وما له من المآثر المأثورة في الدنيا والدين، ومثابرته على جهاد أعداء الله ، لأنه ليس أمام هذه البلدة بلدة للاسلام، والشام أكثره بيد الافرنج ، فسبب الله هذا السلطان رحمة للمسلمين بهذه الجهات، فهو لا يأوي لراحة ، ولا يخلد الى دعة ، ولا يزال سرجه مجلسه ، انا بهذه البلدة نازلون منذ شهرين اثنين وحللناها وقد خرج لمنازلة حصن الكرك، وقد تقدم الذكر ايضا له ، وهو عليه محاصر حتى الان، والله تعالى يعينه على فتحه .

Appendix VII

Dante's Views of Mohammad, Saladin and Other Muslims

Dante Alighieri. *The Inferno.* 1954. Trans. John Ciardi. New York: The New American Library.

I. Canto IV, Circle One: Limbo. The Virtuous Pagans, pp. 49-54.

[The Virtuous Pagans] were born without the light of Christ's revelation, and, therefore, they cannot come into the light of God, but they are not tormented. Their only pain is that they have no hope.

With [the great poets of all time] Dante enters the Citadel of Human Reason and sees before his eyes the Master Souls of Pagan Antiquity gathered on a green and illuminated by the radiance of Human Reason. This is the highest state man can achieve without God, and the glory of it dazzles Dante, but he knows also that it is nothing compared to the glory of God.

I saw Camilla, and the Queen Amazon
....
And, by himself apart, the Saladin.

And raising my eyes a little I saw on high
Aristotle, the master of those who know,
ringed by the great souls of philosophy.

....
And I saw
....
Hippocrates, Galen, Avicenna
And Averrhoes of the Great Commentary.

2. Canto XXVIII: Circle Eight: Bolgia Nine. The Sowers of Discord, pp. 234-236.

First come the SOWERS OF RELIGIOUS DISCORD. Mahomet is chief among them, and appears first, cleft from crotch to chin, with his internal organs dangling between his legs. His son-in-law, Ali, drags on ahead of him, cleft from topknot to chin. These reciprocal wounds symbolize Dante's judgment that, between them, these two sum up the total schism between Christianity and Mohammedanism. The revolting details of Mahomet's condition clearly imply Dante's opinion of that doctrine.

A wine tun when a stave or cant-bar starts
does not split open as wide as one I saw
split from his chin to the mouth with which man farts.

Between his legs all of his red guts hung
with the heart, the lungs, the liver, the gall bladder,
and the shriveled sac that passes shit to the bung.

I stood and stared at him from the stone shelf;
he noticed me and opening his own breast
with both hands cried: "See how I rip myself!

See how Mohamet's mangled and split open!
Ahead of me walks Ali in his tears,
his head cleft from the top-knot to the chin.

And all the other souls that bleed and mourn
along this ditch were sowers of scandal and schism:
as they tore others apart, so are they torn.

Behind us, warden of our mangled horde,
the devil who butchers us and sends us marching
waits to renew our wounds with his long sword."

دانتي ، الشاعر الايطالي ، وصلاح الدين الأيوبي

(كتبت هذا التعليق معتمدة على النص الانكليزي لجحيم دانتي الذي ترجمه جون سياردي من الايطالية ، نيويورك ، طبعة المكتبة الأمريكية الجديدة ، ١٩٥٤) .

في جحيم دانتي نجد في الحلقة الأولى بموطن الأرواح وثنيين فاضلين ، لم يستنيروا بوحي المسيح ، ولهذا السبب فانهم لن يعرفوا الحضرة الالهية ، ولا النور السماوي . ولكنهم في موطنهم هذا لا يعذبون كالوثنيين الاخرين . وعقابهم فقط هو أنه ليس لديهم أمل .

يدخل دانتي قلعة العقل البشري في رحلته الى موطن الأرواح ، ويرى بعينيه أرواح العظماء الوثنيين في العصور القديمة . وهذه هي أرفع مكانة يتوصل اليها الانسان بدون الله . لكن دانتي يعرف ان لا شئ يمكن أن يقارن بعظمة الله .

ولسبب ما يضع الكاتب الايطالي الذي ولد في مدينة فلورنس في القرن الثالث عشر القائد صلاح الدين الأيوبي والفيلسوفين المسلمين ابن سينا ، وابن رشد لا في الجحيم ، بل في موطن الأرواح الوثنية مع الفلاسفة العظماء أمثال أرسطو ، سقراط ، وأفلاطون .

اما في الحلقة الثامنة ، والحفرة التاسعة في أسفل الجحيم فان دانتي يضع النبي محمد مع باذري الخلاف من أمثال علي بن أبي طالب ، ويجعل عقاب هؤلاء مماثلا لخطيئتهم . ففي رأي دانتي أن محمدا ، مثلا ، قد مزق اربا ما أراده الله أن يكون متحدا ، فتركه في الجحيم يتمزق اربا حتى ما لا نهاية بسيف ينقط دما يحمله شيطان ضخم .

REFERENCES

ALLEN, ROGER. 1990. Proficiency and the Teacher of Arabic: Curriculum, course, and classroom. *Al-ʿArabiyya* 23 (1&2): 1-30.

ATTAR, SAMAR. 1988. *Modern Arabic: An introductory course for foreign students*, 2 vols. and *Teacher's Manual*. Beirut: Librairie du Liban.

_____. 1991. *Modern Arabic: Workbook 1; Workbook 2*. Beirut: Librairie du Liban.

AL-BATAL, MAHMOUD. 1988. Towards Cultural Proficiency in Arabic. *Foreign Language Annals* 21:5. 443-453.

BENJAMIN, WALTER. 1977. *Illumination*. 2d impression. Ed. Hannah Arendt. Great Britain: Fontana/Collins.

_____. 1991. *Gesammelte Schriften*. Band 1.2. Frankfurt am Main: Suhrkamp.

BROWN, DOUGLAS. 1980. *Principles of Language Learning and Teaching*. Englewood Cliffs: Prentice-Hall.

DANTE ALIGHIERI. 1954. *The Inferno*. Trans. John Ciardi. New York: The New American Library.

ERIKSON, ERIK H. 1959. Growth and Crisis of the Healthy Personality. *Psychological Issues* 1:50-100.

_____. 1963. *Childhood and Society*. 2d ed. New York: Norton; London: Hogarth (1965).

_____. 1968. *Identity in Youth and Crisis*. New York: Norton, London: Faber & Faber.

FABIAN, JOHANNES. 1990. Presence and Representation: The other and anthropological writing. *Critical Inquiry* 16:4. 753-772.

(ABU-AL) FIDĀ. 1286. *Al-Mukhtaṣar fī Akhbār al-Bashar.* 4 vols. Constantinople.

FREEMAN, STEPHEN A. 1968. Let Us Build Bridges. *The Modern Language Journal* 52:5. 261-268.

GIBB, SIR HAMILTON. 1973. *The Life of Saladin*. Oxford: Clarendon Press.

HALL, EDWARD T. 1959; rpt. 1973. *The Silent Language*. Garden City, NY: Doubleday.

_____. 1966. *The Hidden Dimension*. Garden City, NY: Doubleday.

HITTI, PHILIP K. 1970. *History of the Arabs*. 10th ed. London: Macmillan, St. Martin's Press.

HOPKINS, ANDREA. 1990. *Knights*. London: Collins & Brown.

JOINVILLE. 1963; rpt. 1987. "The Life of Saint Louis." In *Joinville and Villehardouin: Chronicles of the Crusades*. Trans. M. R. B. Shaw. Harmondsworth: Penguin.

(IBN) JUBAYR. 1964. *Riḥlat Ibn Jubayr*. Beirut: Dār Sadir & Beirut.

KHARE, R. S. 1992. The Other's Double—The Anthropologist's Bracketed Self; Notes on cultural representation and privileged discourse. *New Literary History: A Journal of Theory and Interpretation* 23:1. 1-23.

LAFAYETTE, ROBERT C., ED. 1975. *Cultural Revolution in Foreign Languages: A guide for building the modern curriculum*. Lincolnwood, IL: National Textbook Company.

LEIRIS, MICHEL. 1950. L'Ethnographe devant le Colonialisme. *Les Temps Modernes* 6:58. 357-374.

_____. 1958. *Race and Culture*. Paris: Unesco.

LEVI-STRAUSS, CLAUDE. 1977. *Structural Anthropology*. Harmondsworth: Penguin.

MAALOUF, AMIN. 1984. *The Crusades Through Arab Eyes*. Trans. John Rothschild. London: Al-Saqi.

MANGANARO, MARC. 1990. "Textual Play, Power, and Cultural Critique: An orientation to modernist anthropology." In *Modernist Anthropology*, ed. by Marc Manganaro, 3-47. Princeton: Princeton University Press.

MANNHEIM, KARL. 1927. *Das Konservative Denken*. Archiv für Sozialwissenschaft und Sozial Politik.

_____. 1946. *Ideology and Utopia*. New York: Harcourt & Brace and Co.

_____. 1986. "Conservative Thought." In *Essays on Sociology and Social Psychology*, ed. by Paul Kecskemeti. London: Routledge & Kegan Paul.

_____. 1986. *Conservatism: A contribution to the sociology of knowledge*. Ed. by David Kettler et al. London: Routledge & Kegan Paul.

MAQUET, JACQUES. 1970. "Objectivity in Anthropology." In *Applied Anthropology*, ed. by James A. Clifton, 254-272. Boston: Houghton Mifflin Company.

MULLER-WIENER, WOLFGANG. 1982. *Al-Qilāʿ Ayyām Al-Ḥurūb Al-Ṣalībiyya*. Trans. into Arabic, Muhammad Walid Al-Jallad. Damascus: Center for Military Studies.

(IBN) MUNQIDH, USĀMAH. 1930. *Kitāb al-Iʿtibār*. Ed. by Philip K. Hitti. Princeton: Princeton University Press.

_____. 1980. *Min Kitāb al-Iʿtibār*. Ed. by Abd al-Karim al-Ashtar. Damascus: Ministry of Culture.

NICOLLE, DAVID. 1988. *The Crusades and the Crusader States*. Ed. by Martin Windrow. London: Osprey Publishing.

RIVERS, WILGA M. 1983. *Communicating Naturally in a Second Language: Theory and practice in language teaching*. Cambridge: Cambridge University Press.

RUNCIMAN, STEVEN. 1951; rpt. 1991. *A History of the Crusades*. 3 vols. London: Penguin.

SAID, EDWARD W. 1978; rpt. 1991. *Orientalism*. London: Penguin.

_____. 1989. Representing the Colonized: Anthropology's interlocutors. *Critical Inquiry* 15:2. 205-225.

SEELYE, H. NED. 1976. *Teaching Culture: Strategies of intercultural communication*. Lincolnwood: National Textbook Company.

(IBN) SHADDAD, BAHA' AL-DIN YUSUF B. RAFI'. 1962. *Al-Nawādir Al-Sulṭāniyya: Sīrat Ṣalāḥ Al-Dīn.* Ed. by Al-Shayyal. Cairo.

SHAKESPEARE, WILLIAM. 1905; rpt. 1959. "As You Like It." In *The Oxford Shakespeare: Complete works,* 217-242. London: Oxford University.

SWIFT, JONATHAN. 1960. *Gulliver's Travels and Other Writings.* Ed. by Louis A. Landa. Boston: Houghton Mifflin Company.

WEBER, HORST, ED. 1976. *Landeskunde im Fremdsprachenunterricht.* Munich: Kösel-Verlag.

10

DISCOURSE COMPETENCE IN TAFL: SKILL LEVELS AND CHOICE OF LANGUAGE VARIETY IN THE ARABIC CLASSROOM

Karin C. Ryding

Georgetown University

One of the most daunting pedagogical issues that has characterized the teaching of Arabic as a foreign language is the effect of the problem of diglossia on methodology, materials preparation, curriculum development and formulation of proficiency goals. Until recently, the Arabic teaching profession has essentially "agreed to disagree" on how to approach the problem of teaching speaking, listening, reading, and writing proficiency in a language where the written and spoken forms differ substantially.

Arabic teaching professionals who have supervised and administered training programs to U.S. government officials preparing for careers in the Arab world have come to agree that the most effective and pragmatic form of spoken Arabic to be taught is neither fully colloquial nor a spoken reproduction of Modern Standard Arabic. It is what we refer to as Formal Spoken Arabic (FSA) or Educated Spoken Arabic (ESA).

This paper is a review of the issues and also a description and evaluation of the first Formal Spoken Arabic course taught at Georgetown University.

1. Myths about Arabic

In 1959, Charles Ferguson published an article entitled "Myths about Arabic" (Ferguson 1959, 1970), in which he analyzed some of the more pervasive attitudes and beliefs of the Arabic speech community that he had encountered as a linguist over the years. He summarized them under four headings: "the superiority of Arabic, the classical-colloquial diglossia, dialect rating, and the future of Arabic." (Ibid. 375-376).

I have used this article as a starting point in courses on Arabic linguistics in order to generate discussion on these topics, which even in the 1990s retain some of their vigor. The reason I use it as an opening here is that there have been "myths" about Arabic teaching and learning that have pervaded our field for many years and which have hindered objective and critical analysis of the issues that confront Arabic teachers and learners. For instance, one pervasive myth is that Arabic cannot be "genuinely" learned as a second or foreign language, at least not to a level where a non-Arab learner would be able to claim proficiency at the "educated native speaker" level. There has been a great deal of serious discussion over whether or not a non-native speaker can ever reach the "5" level in Arabic[1] (in terms of FSI proficiency ratings), and I have even heard experienced Arabic teachers express the conviction that this level of achievement is simply not within the realm of possibility.

These myths about Arabic learnability are even more subtle and pervasive than the ones Ferguson analyzed in his article. They consist of attitudes and values on the part of native speakers and non-native speakers, laypersons and professionals, teachers as well as students, toward Arabic language and Arab culture, toward the function, usefulness, and even the feasibility of learning Arabic as a foreign language. I think it should be part of our responsibility as a profession to surface and examine these myths, and to try to clear them away so that the path in the 1990s and into the twenty-first century is more balanced,

---

1. A "5" is the top of the FSI proficiency rating scale, and is described as "functionally native proficiency." The full descriptions for speaking and reading proficiency are as follows: "*Speaking proficiency* is functionally equivalent to that of a highly articulate well-educated native speaker and reflects the cultural standards of the country where the native language is natively spoken. An S-5 uses the language with complete flexibility and intuition, so that speech on all levels is fully accepted by well-educated native speakers in all of its features, including breadth of vocabulary and idiom, colloquialisms, and pertinent cultural references. Pronunciation is typically consistent with that of well-educated native speakers of a non-stigmatized dialect." (FSI Skill Level Definitions for Speaking:3) "*Reading proficiency* is functionally equivalent to that of the well-educated native reader. Can read extremely difficult and abstract prose; for example, general legal and technical as well as highly colloquial writings. Able to read literary texts, typically including contemporary avant-garde prose, poetry, and theatrical writing. Can read classical/archaic forms of literature with the same degree of facility as the well-educated, but non-specialist native. Reads and understands a wide variety of vocabulary and idioms, colloquialisms, slang, and pertinent cultural references. With varying degrees of difficulty, can read all kinds of handwritten documents. Accuracy of comprehension is equivalent to that of a well-educated native reader" (FSI Language Skill Level Descriptions for Reading:5).

encouraging, ambitious, humane, and effective in developing communicative competence in learners of Arabic as a foreign language.

2. Linguistic Competence in Arabic

One of the reasons these myths have emerged and tenaciously prevailed has to do with the complex, culturally-contextualized linguistic competence of the native Arabic speaker, and I use "competence" here in the Chomskyan sense of "competence" versus "performance."[2] The psycholinguistic range of Chomsky's "ideal native speaker" when that speaker is an Arab is extremely broad, pluralistic, multifaceted, and difficult to describe. As a non-native speaker, I can only make a very general and superficial observation that the range of spoken "competence" covers an extraordinary spectrum of social, cultural, and geographic variants; the range of listening comprehension an even wider one that includes Classical and Modern Standard Arabic on top of the spoken forms of language; the range for the receptive skill of reading and the expressive skill of writing also covers historical and stylistic spectra that range from the Middle Ages to the present day. The day-to-day "performance" of a native Arabic speaker has him or her tapping into these vast realms of competence developed over many years and responding spontaneously to whatever the dimensions of the speech situation require.

Therefore, there is something behind the feeling or the myth that it is extremely difficult, if not impossible, to approximate the level of a native speaker of Arabic. I think I can reasonably speculate that the competence and performance of a native Arabic speaker may represent the most elaborate psycholinguistic capacity in the world today.

3. Structuring Acquisition of Arabic as a Foreign Language

Such an elaborate and culturally-bound capability cannot be approximated by non-native learners except in stages. These stages are crucially important. The sequence and content of these stages depend ultimately on the *learning goals of the students*. There is no one formula that will solve all learning problems or be the answer to every learner's quest. However, Arabic teaching professionals can and must attune themselves to the psychological and functional needs of the majority of students of Arabic.

---

2. "Competence" is essentially the speaker-hearer's unconscious knowledge of her native language; "performance" is the actual use of that language in concrete situations. (See Chomsky 1965:4.) Halliday is reported to define competence as "the range of variation available to the speaker" (Sauvignon 1992).

In the past, the American Arabic teaching establishment at the university level opted most often for extensive training in Classical and Modern Standard Arabic (MSA), with perhaps a course or two of a specific regional colloquial offered to students to "round out" their education. Whether or not it was ever explicitly stated, the assumption was that "when the student gets to the Arab world, she will 'pick up' the dialect of whatever region she visits, and develop 'fluency' on her own." We now know that what we were doing was having the students "learn" one language variant in the classroom, and expecting them to "acquire" another variant in the real world.[3] The fact that the spoken variants of Arabic were often dramatically different from MSA in structure and vocabulary was disregarded and discounted.

However, current concepts of "proficiency," "proficiency levels," and "communicative competence," when juxtaposed onto Modern Standard Arabic, have caused us to re-evaluate our assumptions, and they have not offered any simple solutions. They have simply raised our consciousness with regard to the complicated set of facts that relate to Arabic language pedagogy.

In most programs, first-, second-, and third-year Arabic are straight MSA. Even though little dialogues are sometimes introduced at the beginning, they are eventually abandoned because MSA is not an authentic dialogue language, and increasing proficiency in MSA means proficiency in reading and writing, not in negotiating meaning in a spoken context.

4. Reassessing Skill Levels

I do not need to reiterate here the frustration of generations of American students with being unable to perform at an even an elementary level in spoken skills, while they are expected to become increasingly competent in reading the literary language. What is even more curious is that while the educational establishment has for decades enforced the concept of MSA first and foremost, this is completely the reverse of the native speaker's experience with Arabic as a mother tongue. This order of learning does not reflect the natural order, which is gradually to acquire competence in everyday functions, and thus equipped, to proceed to the discipline of the literary language.[4] Of course, this reverse

---

3. For a discussion of the difference between second language "learning" and second language "acquistion," see Krashen (1985:1 and 1981:1-2).

4. Perhaps it is worth mentioning here that the ACTFL Arabic Proficiency Guidelines point out the difficulties involved in assessing proficiency levels for Arabic, and state that "at the lower levels (Novice, Intermediate, and possibly Advanced) testing be done in the form that the learner has learned [i.e., usually MSA], but that at the higher levels (Advanced High and Superior) the

approach was originally based on the fact that there were no written materials for teaching the spoken Arabic vernaculars, and when these materials gradually developed, they were not normally written in Arabic script, but in phonetic transcription. Moreover, the pervasive myth that the spoken Arabic variants were all "substandard" and had no "grammar" made it difficult for well-educated native speakers of Arabic to accept the idea that the study of a spoken form of Arabic was a legitimate academic activity.

Being a product of that traditional system, I can attest to its frustrations and its ultimate undermining of learner confidence in spoken interaction. I know the arguments—I have used them myself from time to time: learning the literary language first builds discipline; it gives the student a firm foundation on which to build speaking skills; it trains the student in the intellectual rigors of desinential inflection, diptotes, the dual, the jussive, and many other complex grammatical features, which, when she comes to study a spoken form of language, to her great relief, do not exist. In other words, do the painful part first, and the rest is easy.

It sounds good, and it even sounds virtuous to approach Arabic in this intellectually demanding way. However, the net result of this has been the early discouragement of many potential Arabic students, and for those who continue, like myself, the crippling feeling (however irrational) that one cannot attempt to speak for fear of making mistakes. We now know, thanks to Steve Krashen,[5] that this is a symptom of "monitor over-use," and that the strong initial conditioning to focus on grammatical accuracy does have the potential to disrupt and undermine the intuitive, meaning-centered instinct that learners must trust in order to acquire spoken fluency.

I think it is clear that the kinds of speaking skills defined in the U.S. government "skill level descriptions" cannot authentically be taught in MSA except at the most advanced levels. The lower level speaking skills, in order to be effective and authentic, need to be taught in a variety of spoken Arabic. For example, an S-1 (Elementary Proficiency) "can typically satisfy predictable, simple, personal and accommodation needs; can generally meet courtesy, in-

---

learner must show ability to comprehend and to communicate in both [MSA and colloquial dialect], with at least partial awareness of appropriate choice depending on the situation involved" (374). At the Superior speaking level, the guidelines state: "The Superior speaker of Arabic should have Superior-level competence in both MSA and a spoken dialect" (379). The listening skill level guidelines state that *all* levels (Novice, Intermediate, Superior) "are predicated on the assumption that reception involves the ability to comprehend either MSA or any colloquial dialect" (379).

5. See Krashen (1981:12-16) for discussion of the concept of the monitor, both overusers and underusers.

troduction, and identification requirements; exchange greetings; elicit and provide, for example, predictable and skeletal biographical information" (FSI Language Skill Level Descriptions:1). A 1+ "can initiate and maintain predictable face-to-face conversations and satisfy limited social demands." She can "satisfy most travel and accommodation needs and a limited range of social demands beyond . . . immediate survival needs" (FSI Language Skill Level Descriptions:2).

These functions are not authentic functions of MSA. It is a distinctive feature of Arabic that the most elementary and mundane spoken functions are the ones that differ most radically in their vocabulary and structure from the literary language. Not to have access to a reasonable form of spoken Arabic at these elementary levels handicaps and discourages our MSA students to a point where they feel frustrated and unequipped to deal with everyday life. When they try to use MSA with native speakers they are often dismissed as "cute" or, worse, misunderstood completely. It is this elementary level of spoken language interaction that must be tackled and taught in order for American students to acquire a sense of authenticity in their learning of Arabic. We should no longer "wait" for students to travel to the Arab world after three or four years of MSA study finally and painfully to find out how to order a meal or schedule the day's events with friends. Their interactional needs should come first, and then be consistently and constantly reinforced throughout their years of study. Moreover, the Arabic teaching profession should be exploring and teaching Arabic discourse strategies and actively researching critically important linguistic issues for Arabic such as "sociocultural parameters of intelligibility" (Nelson 1992) so that research insights can serve to inform the pedagogy of Arabic discourse competence.

5. Formal Spoken Arabic as an Option in the Classrooom

For learners whose future contexts of spoken language use are not predictable, as Widdowson (1988:7) remarks, "they need to learn a language of wider communication, a language of maximal generality or projection value. They cannot do this by concentrating on any specific set of communicative conventions and sociocultural contexts." Widdowson was discussing English as a Foreign Language, but his observations are valid for other languages, including Arabic. The Arabic sociolinguistic profile covers a wider spectrum than English, and is more difficult to characterize, but there is still something to be said for learning a form of spoken language which is "of maximal generality," and which will "activate learners to learn" (ibid.).

One tried and proven way to do this is through the use of Educated Spoken Arabic (ESA) or Formal Spoken Arabic (FSA) as a "middle" form of spoken language that will ease students into interactive skills. I have discussed the nature and reasoning behind the choice of ESA/FSA elsewhere.[6] I want to emphasize that I view it as one option for teaching spoken Arabic skills at the basic and intermediate levels; not the ultimate solution to all Arabic proficiency problems, but one viable and proven way of tackling the diglossia problem without detracting from the students' command or study of MSA.[7]

Until last year, the teaching of Formal Spoken Arabic had been the almost exclusive domain of U.S. Government agencies, and Georgetown University has been the first to introduce it into an academic setting. The course is offered for three credits at the second-year level, in addition to Intensive Intermediate MSA (six credits per semester). Students with more than one or two years of MSA may also enroll in the FSA course if they feel they need exposure to spoken Arabic. The text used is *Formal Spoken Arabic: Basic Course*, which is based on the curriculum developed at the Foreign Service Institute. The Georgetown course is now in its second year of existence, and growing in student attendance and interest.[8] A class visit and survey of the students in the spring of 1993 yielded the observations discussed below.

The course was entirely in Arabic. Students had previously taken one to three years of MSA. During this class, each student gave a brief report on a topic of interest to him or her. Some reports were personal, some were political, and some were cultural. (One student described Kurdish dancing and had all the others get up and try a dance for which she gave the directions to them in Arabic. Then they got into a general discussion of the arts, and how Americans pursue artistic interests.)[9]

The Arabic that was produced by these students was not error-free, but it was effective, comprehensible, and relatively fluent. I would judge them as a group to be at around the 2 or 2+ level in speaking (high intermediate in ACTFL terms). One of the most important things was that no English was used at all.

---

6. See Ryding (1990, 1991).

7. I would also like to emphasize that FSA is not a "replacement" in any sense for MSA, nor was it ever intended to be. It is an adjunct to it, a variant usable for teaching low-to-intermediate speaking skills.

8. One result which I feel I must mention is that for the first time in history, in 1992, an Arabic course was selected as one of the "Top-Twenty" courses at Georgetown University (by the students)—Formal Spoken Arabic.

9. My visit to the class was unscheduled, so it is certain that these students were not putting on a special performance just for me. This was their regular mode of operation.

Student comments after this class observation session included some interesting observations:

1) One student of Syrian-American background said that she had only been able to understand Syrian dialect when she began this course, but that now she found herself able to understand a wide range of Arabic dialects, including North African. She had thus expanded her comprehension through conscious awareness and focussing on the shared grammatical features of Arabic urban dialects.

2) For all of these students, FSA was the only Arabic course they were taking this semester; some were therefore concerned about keeping up their reading and writing skills in MSA. They had some suggestions on how to incorporate MSA assignments into the FSA class, including discussion and summary of MSA reading assignments and drama activities.

It therefore appears that the pedagogical goal of introducing FSA into the curriculum has been achieved. These students are able to speak on a basic level without hesitation or fear and can get across whatever they need to say. Moreover, this variety of Arabic seems to help them in a very broad sense with their comprehension skills. A final and very important point is that FSA cannot be an isolated offering; it must be grounded on good MSA skills, and should be reinforced with MSA. These two varieties of Arabic taught together enhance and complement one another and can offer a key to Arabic proficiency for the future.

REFERENCES

ACTFL Arabic Proficiency Guidelines. 1989. *Foreign Language Annals* 22:4.373-392.

CHOMSKY, NOAM. 1965. *Aspects of the Theory of Syntax*. Cambridge: MIT Press.

FERGUSON, CHARLES A. 1959. "Myths about Arabic." In *Languages and Linguistics Monograph Series, Georgetown University,* 12. Reprinted in *Readings in the Sociology of Language,* ed. by Joshua A. Fishman, 1970. The Hague/Paris: Mouton.

Foreign Service Institute Language Skill Level Descriptions. N.d. Washington: Department of State.

KRASHEN, STEPHEN D. 1981. *Second Language Acquisition and Second Language Learning.* Oxford: Pergamon.

_____. 1985. *The Input Hypothesis: Issues and implications.* London: Longman.

NELSON, CECIL L. 1992. Sociocultural Parameters of Intelligibility. Paper presented at Georgetown University Round Table on Languages and Linguistics. Washington, D.C.

RYDING, KARIN C. 1990. *Formal Spoken Arabic: Basic course.* Washington: Georgetown University Press.

_____. 1991. Proficiency Despite Diglossia: A new approach for Arabic. *Modern Language Journal* 75:2.212-218.

SAUVIGNON, SANDRA. 1992. Language, Communication, Social Meaning, and Social Change: The challenge for teachers. Paper presented at Georgetown University Round Table on Languages and Linguistics, Washington, D.C.

WIDDOWSON, H. G. 1988. Language, Context and Culture in the Classroom. *ERIC/CLL News Bulletin* 12:1.6-7.

11

An Integrated Curriculum
for Elementary Arabic

Munther A. Younes
Cornell University

If the goal of an Arabic-as-a-foreign-language program is to prepare students to function successfully in Arabic, then they should be introduced to both a spoken Arabic dialect and Modern Standard Arabic from the beginning of an Arabic course. The argument is based on time limitations, the need to be consistent with the Arabic sociolinguistic situation, and the desire to use modern methods of language instruction. It is suggested that fear of confusing students, the major objection to such an approach, should be viewed in a different light: errors involving the use of the wrong language variety need not be treated differently from errors involving grammatical structures. This approach is consistent with the principles of proficiency-based language teaching and learning in which emphasis at the lower levels of proficiency is on intelligibility rather than on accuracy, both linguistic and sociolinguistic.

0. Introduction

For an Arabic-as-a-foreign-language program to function successfully, its goals need to be clearly defined and its policies and practices must be determined in such a way as to ensure achievement of these goals. A program at a research university may set as its goal the preparation of graduate students to have a reading knowledge of Classical Arabic texts. The teaching methodology, instructional materials, and the variety of the language presented to the students in such a program will differ significantly from one whose goal is to prepare students to converse with native speakers in their mother tongue. A Grammar-Translation method of teaching, with a grammar book, a dictionary, and the *Muqaddima* of Ibn Khaldoun may achieve the desired outcome in the first instance (Allen 1992:228), but it will not in the second.

233

While the study of Classical Arabic by graduate students may have been the norm in the past, a change has clearly taken place in both the Arabic student population and students' goals (Belnap 1987, Heath 1990:34, Allen 1992:227, Al-Batal 1992:293). This change necessitates a reexamination of program policies and practices, particularly teaching methodologies, instructional materials, and the variety of Arabic to be presented to the learners. Many more students than ever before, graduate as well as undergraduate, are taking Arabic classes, with the majority interested in learning it for purposes of communication with modern-day Arabs, not as a research tool (Belnap 1987): they want to understand what Arabs say and write, and they want to speak to them and be understood. In order to communicate with Arabs, they need to learn both a spoken Arabic dialect and Modern Standard Arabic (MSA)[1]—the dialect for ordinary conversation and MSA for reading, writing, and formal speaking (Allen 1989; Heath 1990; Younes 1990; Alosh 1991, 1992; Al-Batal 1992). They will also need to develop the skill to move along a colloquial-MSA continuum as required by particular sociolinguistic situations (Blanc 1960, Badawi 1973, El-Hassan 1977, Allen 1989). To achieve these goals, three logical possibilities present themselves: first, mastering a spoken dialect and then introducing MSA; second, mastering MSA and then introducing a spoken dialect; third, introducing the two simultaneously.[2] While it is quite possible that, given enough time, these three tracks will achieve similar results, certain factors must be taken into account in determining the choice of a specific track. First is the time factor: a program that has 1500 hours to teach Arabic to students may follow a different track from one that has only 150. Second is the sociolinguistic factor: how important is it to be consistent with the way Arabic is used by native speakers? Third is the pedagogical factor: while a certain method of language teaching may be appropriate for a certain situation (e.g., the Grammar-Translation method for developing a reading skill in MSA), it may not be so for another.

---

1. A brief examination of published materials on the issue of which variety or varieties of Arabic to teach in the present North American university setting clearly shows a consensus for introducing MSA as opposed to Classical Arabic to the majority of Arabic students (Allen 1989, 1992; Heath 1990; Al-Batal 1992).

2. I am assuming here that the Arabic-as-a-foreign-language program aims to prepare its students for real proficiency in all language skills. Programs that teach only MSA or a colloquial dialect are showing their students only half the picture of the Arabic sociolinguistic situation and ignoring the other half.

1. Dealing with Diglossia in the Classroom

In this section, I will examine the three different tracks available to Arabic programs in light of these factors, showing the strengths and weaknesses of each one, and then I will present the one approach that I believe best prepares students to function in Arabic within the limitations of a typical North American university Arabic program. This approach assumes that the Arabic program has two to four semesters (150-300 contact hours) to prepare its students. It also assumes the existence of a need to be consistent with the Arabic sociolinguistic situation as well as a desire to use a communication-based approach of language instruction as opposed to a grammar-based one.

1.1 *Dialect First and MSA Later*

This approach mirrors the way native speakers of Arabic learn their language: first they learn a spoken dialect at home, and when they go to school they learn MSA (mainly for reading and writing). While this approach is consistent with the way Arabic is learned and used by native speakers and potentially allows the use of communication-based methodologies, the major problem facing it is the time limitation: students obviously do not have the time to master an Arabic dialect and then start MSA in two or four semesters. Another criticism is that the colloquial portion of the course would focus only on the listening and speaking skills, which may result in students leaving the program with no ability to read or write. Furthermore, learning the language this way would not be as efficient as a situation in which the reading and writing skills are introduced early in the course and used to reinforce the other two skills.

1.2. *MSA First and a Dialect Later*

Most Arabic-as-a-foreign-language programs follow this approach, if they introduce a spoken dialect at all. The argument most frequently used in its support is that if one learns MSA first, then he/she can easily learn any Arabic dialect afterward. This is graphically described in Al-Hamad (1983:95) where he states:

> My students who showed a desire to study a dialect found wonderful psychological relief when I gave them the analogy of the high language [being] like the peak of a mountain and the dialects like its numerous low sides, and [when] I showed them that we seek to take them to the peak because after that they could descend to the lower [sides] if they so desired. Our interest in one dialect over another makes reaching the peak difficult.

This approach is also appealing for its convenience: when the thorny issue of which variety of Arabic to teach is brought up, it emerges as a favorite alternative, at least for a while. The reasoning is that whereas the spoken dialects vary from one area of the Arabic-speaking world to another, MSA is virtually the same everywhere.

This approach, however, faces a number of problems. First, there is no attested proof in support of Al-Hamad's assertion that a transition from MSA to a spoken dialect is easier to make than one from a spoken dialect to MSA or from one dialect to another.[3] Second, if the sociolinguistic factor is taken into consideration, then an Arabic program cannot teach students to converse informally in the first part of the course, which is exactly the kind of function that should be the focus of a beginning Arabic course if the program is committed to a communication-based curriculum. Third, as Williams (1990:46) rightly argues, this situation will "deprive students of the many benefits of oral reinforcement, which early introduction of CO [the colloquial] can give." Oral reinforcement in MSA "is bound to be artificial" (Williams 1990:46). Consequently, graduates of an Arabic program using this approach may leave it with no ability to converse or understand ordinary conversation.

1.3. *MSA and a Dialect Simultaneously*

This option can be implemented in one of two ways: the two varieties of the language are either introduced in the same course or in two parallel courses, with certain hours designated for spoken Arabic and other hours for MSA. The practice of introducing the two simultaneously but separately is followed at an early stage at the Foreign Service Institute (FSI:iii).[4] A major criticism of this practice, in my view, stems from the fact that a certain amount of duplication is likely to occur in which distinctions in linguistic functions between the two

---

3. Williams (1990:46) states that in his experience students who start with a colloquial dialect find "considerable difficulty in shifting from one CO [colloquial dialect] to another." Such a statement of course remains an impression as long as it is not supported by research that shows, among other things, the degree and type of difficulty faced, at what stage it was faced, how much Arabic a student has learned, etc. Too many vague statements like this have been made, and it is most likely that the issue here is one of level of mastery of an Arabic variety: the more proficient the learner is in any variety, the easier the transition is to any other.

4. By simultaneous introduction of MSA and a colloquial dialect, I mean introduction of the two from the beginning of the Arabic course and not teaching the two simultaneously at an advanced stage in an Arabic program as is done at many institutions such as The University of Texas, Georgetown University, The University of Michigan, Ohio State University, etc., which offer a colloquial dialect as an option to students who may also be taking MSA.

language varieties are blurred, resulting in a situation that would be inconsistent with the sociolinguistic realities of Arabic. For instance, informal speaking activities may be conducted in the two portions of the course, rather than the colloquial only. This can conceivably be avoided with a syllabus that truly reflects the way Arabic is used. A more serious problem, however, is lack of reinforcement of language skills. A well-designed curriculum that truly integrates the two language varieties would include reading and writing activities, for example, that build on vocabulary and topics in the listening and speaking activities of the same lesson or unit.

With the exception of the program I will be outlining and arguing for below, no Arabic-as-a-foreign-language program exists, to my knowledge, in which the two language varieties are integrated in the same course of instruction, using the same set of instructional materials, and in which the classroom situation truly reflects the linguistic realities of Arabic.

Both versions that call for simultaneous introduction of the two language varieties described above are generally criticized as potentially overwhelming and confusing to the learner. The issue of confusion will be addressed in detail in section 2.2 below as part of the argument for the integrated simultaneous approach.

2. Discussion

In the following, I will present and argue for a program for first-year Arabic that I have developed and tried for four years, which is based on what I described above as an integrated simultaneous approach.[5] The main goal of the program is to prepare students for real proficiency in Arabic right from the beginning, including the sociolinguistic skill of using each variey of the language in its proper context. The choice of the approach was determined by the time limitation (students take two to four semesters, or about 150-300 contact hours of Arabic), a conscious decision to be consistent with the way Arabic is used by native speakers, and a desire to use a communication-based approach to language instruction, as opposed to a grammar-based one.

---

5. For more arguments in support of simultaneous introduction of a colloquial dialect and MSA, see Younes (1990) and Al-Batal (1992).

2.1 *Integration: Simultaneous Introduction of MSA and the Dialect*

The program introduces spoken Levantine Arabic[6] and MSA simultaneously, integrating them in a way that reflects native usage.[7] Emphasis in the first few hours of the program is on the familiar, concrete, and informal, for which the colloquial is particularly appropriate. Reading and writing activities, in which MSA is used, are also introduced in the first few hours, building on areas of overlap between the two language varieties such as numbers and names of people and places. MSA occupies an increasingly more prominent role in the curriculum with the move towards the less familiar, less concrete, and more formal, but integration remains an important feature of the whole program. An attempt is made to develop the four language skills simultaneously, with emphasis on the three skills of listening, speaking, and reading, in that order, in addition to the skill of moving from one Arabic variety to another. Speaking activities are conducted in the colloquial throughout the course, while reading and writing are conducted in MSA. One lesson typically involves work on more than one language skill, which results in a continuous and spontaneous movement from MSA to the colloquial and vice versa as a function of the linguistic situation that is being replicated and the language material used in this replication. Following common practice by native speakers, material presented in MSA is discussed in the colloquial, which contributes to the continuous movement between the two language varieties.

An example of a lesson that integrates the colloquial and MSA is given in appendix I. The lesson, consisting of listening, speaking, reading, and writing activities, is introduced around the fifteenth hour of the program. The listening selection (اسمع) consists of a short paragraph in which a Palestinian student from Jordan introduces himself and his family members; the speaking activity (حوار) consists of a dialogue between a student traveling to Jordan and a passport officer, which focuses on names and professions; the reading activity (اقرأ) consists of a visa application filled out by the same student; and the writing activity (اكتب) involves filling out a visa application with personal information.

The listening and speaking activities are recorded on tape for students to listen to and answer comprehension questions in English. They do not see the listening selections and the dialogues in print. (This is why only vocabulary

---

6. For a detailed discussion of the issue of which dialect to choose in an Arabic program, see Younes (1990).

7. I would like to emphasize in this context that the program does not attempt to replicate the way Arabs *learn* Arabic but rather to reflect the way they *use* their language.

items and questions in English appear under the listening and speaking activities in the students' workbook.) The dialogues are further used as a basis for creating and acting out similar dialogues in class. MSA is used in the reading and writing activities. Students are required to read and write MSA, but they are not expected to use it for speaking.

2.2 Confusion

As was pointed out above, the major criticism of this approach focuses on the fact that students may get confused. Thus Parkinson (1985:27) states that: "It is *very* difficult to incorporate the colloquial into a Standard Arabic class without leaving the students hopelessly confused. Arabic is hard enough without having to remember almost from the first day that you say 'mish' but you can't *write* it."[8] Critics of the approach also point out that students taught this way will not be able to tell which is MSA and which is the colloquial (Rammuny 1993:11).

The argument used in support of the claim that students may get confused has an intuitive appeal: how can we introduce them to both مش and ليس and expect them to use each in its proper context? However, concrete evidence based on studies of student behavior has never been produced to support this claim. Undoubtedly, errors exist, but their frequency in comparison with purely structural or grammatical errors and their effect on communication have not been systematically studied, or if they have, findings have not been published.

In the following paragraphs, I will examine the issue of confusion in some detail, offering two concrete examples as an attempt to view the risk of confusing students in more objective, rather than purely impressionistic terms. The two examples, a writing and a speaking sample, shown in Appendices II and III, were produced by the same student at the end of the second semester (after about 150 hours of classroom instruction). The writing sample was written as a homework assignment and is shown as it was handed in. The speaking sample constitutes the first half of a fifteen-minute informal interview with the student, and is presented in Roman transliteration to approximate the exact pronunciation more accurately. These two samples were selected because the student who produced them had no knowledge of Arabic or any other Semitic language or a language that uses the Arabic script before enrolling in the Arabic class. She ranked between fifth and tenth in a group of thirty-two students.

---

8. Parkinson told me that he no longer feels the same way about this issue (personal communication, June 1992).

As the samples show, errors involving the use of the wrong language variety (indicated by a circle around the incorrect form) are observed, but they generally go in one direction: using colloquial features in writing MSA. Purely MSA features are generally absent in speaking the colloquial, which may be due to two factors: first, the focus of the course is on the listening, speaking, and reading skills, with at least two thirds of the time spent on the first two skills, which are conducted in the colloquial for the most part. Second, MSA materials are generally introduced for passive recognition, mainly for reading, not to be spoken in their original forms.[9]

Sociolinguistic writing errors generally consist of using high frequency colloquial forms such as كويس, بس, and مش instead of their MSA equivalents. In some cases, a word which is used in both varieties is used in its dialectal form, without the correct case ending, for example.

Grammatical or structural errors are noted in the two samples. These are indicated by underlining the incorrect form. In the speaking sample, the correct form is provided in brackets after each error.

One important observation about both types of errors in the two examples is of particular relevance: these errors do not seem to affect the intelligibility of the linguistic message. (The composition and the conversation can be understood without much difficulty. One should also bear in mind that extralinguistic factors are involved in understanding the conversation.)

Errors, whether linguistic or sociolinguistic, are, of course, expected at this level, regardless of the approach followed. No approach can be considered error-free linguistically or sociolinguistically, due to the nature of the learning process. Another way of looking at errors and confusion relates to what can be considered a justifiable price to pay in learning a foreign language. A heavier price is paid in learning the two varieties of a language such as Arabic than in learning one accepted variety as in the case of French and Spanish, for example. But I cannot think of any justification for teaching a student to converse

---

9. By "purely MSA features," I mean forms like *laysa* "not," *ðahaba* "he went," etc. for which a completely different form is used in the colloquial. This is to be differentiated from a pronunciation like *ṣayīr* "small" instead of *ṣyīr* (which assimilates to *zyīr*), which is the form generally used in ordinary conversation. However, native speakers of Arabic frequently retain MSA pronunciations of shared lexical items when speaking the colloquial, particularly educated speakers in relatively formal speaking situations: compare, for example, MSA *ʔustāð ǰāmiʕa* with Levantine *ʔustāð ɣāmʕa*. An explanation for the acceptance of MSA pronunciations in colloquial contexts but not colloquial features in MSA contexts may be due to the prestige of MSA as opposed to the dialects and/or to the fact that MSA rules of grammar and usage have been codified and deviation from the accepted written norms is not permissible.

with a shopkeeper in MSA, even if his/her MSA was grammatically impeccable and was obtained at a reduced price.

If the emphasis in the Arabic program is on intelligibility at the lower levels of proficiency, as advocated by the proficiency movement (Allen 1989), for example, rather than on monitoring and correcting errors, then these errors and the fear of "confusion" will turn out to be less serious than they may seem at first sight. The potential for sociolinguistic errors in the integrated approach that I am advocating here is greatly diminished because the colloquial is introduced to be actively spoken, and MSA is introduced mainly to develop the skill of silent reading comprehension. Writing MSA at this stage is of minor importance and is used primarily to reinforce the other skills.

Errors resulting from an integrated approach are potentially less serious than errors from an approach that prepares students to use an Arabic variety in the wrong context. For example, students who have been taught to converse informally in MSA, a very common practice in Arabic-as-a-foreign-language programs, would be making countless sociolinguistic errors if they used this variety for informal conversation. A more confusing and misleading practice is teaching MSA and using it for ordinary conversation and also teaching a dialect to be used for the same function. Imagine teaching students to converse with a postal clerk in MSA and a few months later teaching them to converse with the same clerk in Egyptian Arabic!

A final argument for introducing spoken Arabic and MSA simultaneously is based on one presented by Williams (1990:46). He argues that "if variation is inherent in language, it is perhaps less disconcerting for the student if s/he is introduced to variation earlier rather than later." We in effect mislead students when we present them with only one variety of Arabic while we are well aware that another, probably more widely used, variety exists.

2.3 Reinforcement

Any approach that aims at preparing students to function in Arabic, be it the one that places MSA on the top of a mountain and the dialects on its sides or another that places the different varieties side by side, assumes that a certain amount of transfer takes place between the different varieties. Knowledge of one helps in learning the other. Although I am not aware of any published literature on the issue of transfer from one variety of Arabic to another, there is strong evidence in support of this assumption. Consider, for example, the case of students who grow up in an Arabic-speaking environment, but who have no exposure to MSA, to the point where they do not know the alphabet or such

typically common MSA words like قال or ذهب. Based on my own experience, these students are able to read Arabic fluently and understand newspaper
articles and short stories written in MSA in a matter of a few months. Building
on the foundation they have in an Arabic dialect, they are able to assimilate
MSA vocabulary and structures much faster than students who do not possess
such a foundation. For example, once they see that MSA q and θ correspond to
their Lebanese or Egyptian $?$ and t, the rule is generalized to other relevant
forms, a process which saves them the effort of having to learn numerous grammatical rules and thousands of new vocabulary items, which they would have
to do if they did not know the dialect.

Linguistic evidence clearly shows that most linguistic features are shared
by different varieties of Arabic, and that where differences exist many can be
explained by a limited set of rules, thus narrowing the gap between these varieties further. The bulk of the vocabulary, whose mastery is the most demanding
part of an Arabic course, is shared.[10] In an examination of the vocabulary items
introduced in the course I have developed, which number about 1250, excluding numerals and proper names, over 92% are either identical in MSA and
Levantine or can be related from one to the other through patterns of regular
correspondence. For example, when students first hear a word like مدينة pronounced *madīni*, then they hear it pronounced in an MSA context as *madīna*,
they, with enough examples of a similar type, will realize that they are two
pronunciations of the same word.

3. Conclusion

In real life in the Arab world, the two varieties of Arabic, MSA and the
colloquial, are integrated into one system of communication which fully satis-
fies the communicative needs of its users. I have argued in this chapter that if
the goal of our Arabic-as-a-foreign-language programs is to prepare students
for real proficiency in Arabic, then the varieties of the language have to be
integrated in the same course in a way that reflects native usage. Errors are
inevitable, but instead of the focus on errors, one should focus on what a student is able to do with the language when he/she leaves the Arabic program.

Fragmenting Arabic into the colloquial and MSA when they are presented
to the students is neither consistent with the sociolinguistic realities of Arabic
nor does it serve the needs of these students. How can students possibly be

---

10. Cadora (1976:253) demonstrates that the overwhelming majority of words on the Swadesh
list are shared by the thirteen dialects he studied and by MSA (an average cognation of 91% for the
dialects in comparison with MSA).

prepared to function in Arabic if they are taught to talk to a waiter or a shop-keeper in MSA, or, alternatively, if they are only taught an Arabic dialect that has been reduced to a series of dialogues (at the post office, in the restaurant, etc.) and anecdotes written in Roman transliteration? The approach advocated here considers the language as a whole with each part playing its proper role in the communication process.

The program that I am arguing for is based on descriptive rather than prescriptive principles; it aims to prepare students to use Arabic as it is used by Arabs in real life and not according to someone's idea of how it should or could be used. A key to a successful implementation of this program is to focus on intelligibility rather than on accuracy at this early stage in learning the language. It is assumed, following the ACTFL Proficiency Guidelines, that linguistic as well as sociolinguistic accuracy occupy increasingly more prominent roles in the language learning process the higher the learner progresses on the proficiency scale.

APPENDIX I

Sample Lesson

(Teacher's manual)

اسمـع

اسمي شريف. أنا طالب فلسطيني في جامعة كورنيل. أنا بادرس هندسة في الجامعة. عمري ٢٨ سنة.

عائلتي، يعني أبوي وأمّي وإخواني وخواتي، ساكنين في مدينة اربد في الأردن. عندي أخوين وأختين. اخواني هم ايمن وعبدالله، وخواتي هم مريم وسعاد.

أبوي اسمه علي سمارة وأمي اسمها حليمة أبو اللبن. أبوي عمره ٥٦ سنة. هو عنده مطعم في اربد، وأمي عمرها ٥١ سنة، وهي ربّة بيت.

حوار

موظف الجوازات	اسمك؟
دان	دانيل.
موظف الجوازات	اسم الأب؟
دان	هنري.
موظف الجوازات	اسم الأم؟
دان	اليزابث.
موظف الجوازات	اسم العائلة؟
دان	وليمز.
موظف الجوازات	العمر؟
دان	٢١ سنة.
موظف الجوازات	العنوان؟
دان	123 State Street...
موظف الجوازات	لا، لا، مش عنوانك في أمريكا، عنوانك هون في الأردن؟
دان	أه، في الأردن، فندق الأندلس، عمان.
موظف الجوازات	المهنة؟
دان	ايش يعني المهنة؟
موظف الجوازات	يعني انت طالب، معلم، مهندس، طيّار...
دان	طالب.
موظف الجوازات	مع السلامة.

(Student Workbook)

اسمـع

كلمـات جديـدة
درَس (يدرُس) to study
هنـدسة engineering
يَعني in other word
ربّة بيت housewife

أسئلة

1. What does Shareef do?
2. How old is he?
3. How many brothers does he have?
4. What is his father's name?
5. What does his father do?

حوار

كلمـات جديـدة
مـهنة profession
مـهنـدس engineer
طيّار pilot

أسئلة

1.What is Dan's father's name?
2. What is his family name?
3. What does Dan do?
4. What is his address in Jordan

اقرأ

وزارة الداخلية
تأشيرة دخول

الإسم ـــــــــــــــــــــــــــــ

اسم الأب ـــــــــــــــــــــــــــــ

اسم الأم ـــــــــــــــــــــــــــــ

اسم العائلة ـــــــــــــــــــــــــــــ

تاريخ الولادة ـــــــــــــــــــــــــــــ

مكان الولادة ـــــــــــــــــــــــــــــ

الجنسيّة ـــــــــــــــــــــــــــــ

رقم جواز السفر ـــــــــــــــــــــــــــــ

تاريخ ومكان الصدور ـــــــــــــــــــــــــــــ

المهنة ـــــــــــــــــــــــــــــ

العنوان في الأردن ـــــــــــــــــــــــــــــــــــــــ

مدّة الزيارة ـــــــــــــــــــــــــــــــــــــــ

كلمات جديدة

date	تاريخ	birth	ولادة
place	مكان	nationality	جَنسيّة
number	رقم	passport	جواز سَفر
period, duration	مُدّة	visit	زِيارة

أسئلة

1. When was Dan born?
2. Where?
3. What is his passport number?
4. How long is he staying in Jordan?

اكتب

Pretend that you are traveling to Jordan to take an Arabic summer
course that lasts two months. Fill out the following form accordingly.

اقرأ

وزارة الداخلية
تأشيرة دخول

الإسم ــــــــــــــــــــ
اسم الأب ــــــــــــــــــــ
اسم الأم ــــــــــــــــــــ
اسم العائلة ــــــــــــــــــــ
تاريخ الولادة ــــــــــــــــــــ
مكان الولادة ــــــــــــــــــــ
الجنسيّة ــــــــــــــــــــ
رقم جواز السفر ــــــــــــــــــــ
تاريخ ومكان الصدور ــــــــــــــــــــ
المهنة ــــــــــــــــــــ
العنوان في الأردن ــــــــــــــــــــــــــــ
مدّة الزيارة ــــــــــــــــــــــــــــ

Appendix II

Sample Lesson

١

جمهورية جيبوتي

جيبوتي دولة عربية صغيرة كثيراً مساحتها

٨،٩٥٨ ميل مربع (٢٢،٢٠ كم مربع) حوالي نفس

حجم ولاية ماساشوستس .

تقع جيبوتي في شمال شرق إفريقيا و

تحدها من الشمال و الغرب و الجنوب الغربي

أثيوبيا و من الجنوب الصومال و من الشرق البحر

الأحمر و خليج عدن .

عدد سكانها ٤٣٤ ألف نسمة و حوالي

نصف الناس (٢٩٠ ألف) ساكن في عاصمة

جيبوتي اسمها مدينة جيبوتي . أكثر الناس

هم عفار أو عيسى ، العفار ساكنون في

الشمال والغرب . العيسى (ناس صوماليون)

٦

ساكنون في الجنوب. (كمان) فيها ناس

فرنسيون و عرب لكن هم أَقلية.

الأرض الزراعية فيها (مش)(كويسة)(كثير.)

أكثر الأرض صحراء وقسم من الدولة جبلي.

جيبوتي مركز للتجارة و هي ميناء مهم(كثير.) أكثر

الاشياء من و لأثيوبيا تدخل بواسطة مدينة

جيبوتي لكن جيبوتي دولة فقيرة(كثير.)

الطقس في جيبوتي حار أكثر السنة.

درجة الحرارة حوالي ٨٢ °ف في يناير و ١١٠°ف

في يوايو. الناس يقولون عن جيبوتي هي

"وادي جهنم". في جيبوتي حوالي ٥ انشات

مطر في السنة.

٢

لغة جيبوتي هي اللغة العربية لكن
أكثر الناس تتكلم عفار اوصومالي بس ٪١٠
من السكان ممكن يقرأ ويكتب
كان راية جيبوتي اختار لما مستقل
جيبوتي في سنة ١٩٧٧. قبل استقلال جيبوتي
هي بلد تابعة فرنسيون

APPENDIX III

Speaking Sample
(T=Teacher, S=student)

T   ʔinti min ween?

S   ʔana min wilaayit *Massachusetts*, madiinit *Brockton*.

T   madiinit *Brockton*. madiinit *Brockton* kbiiri walla ṣɣiiri?

S   madiinit *Brockton* miš kabiiri w miš izɣiiri, wasaṭ.

T   ḳaddeeš taḳriiban ʕadad sukkaanha?

S   ʕadad sukkaanha miyyit ʔalf nasami.

T   miit ʔalf nasami? hiyyi bʕiidi ʕan *Boston*?

S   laʔ. ḳariib, ḳariib [ḳariibi] min *Boston*.

T   ḳaddeeš bissayyaara maθalan?

S   nuṣṣ saaʕa.

T   laʔayy jiha, ɣarb, januub, šamaal?

S   januub šarḳ.

T   januub šarḳ *Boston*. hiyya ʕala baḥar walla laʔ?

S   laʔ.

T   miš ʕala baḥar?

S   miš ʕala baḥar.

T   kwayyis. ʕindkum beet fi *Brockton*?

S   ʔaywa.

T   beet ikbiir walla ṣɣiir?

S   beet ṣaɣiiri. ṣaɣiiri [ṣaɣiir, ẓɣiir] kθiir.

T   yaʕni kam ɣurfit noom?

S   ɣurfit noom? θalaaθ.

T   θalaθ ɣuraf noom bass?

S   ʔaywa.

T   fii ḥadiiḳa?

S   (does not understand)

T   fii ʔarḍ ḥawl ilbeet, walla maa fii ʔarḍ? yaʕni hoon fii *Ithaca* fii beet ufii ḥadiiḳa, yaʕni ʔarḍ ḥawl ilbeet.

S   ʔaywa, ʔaywa, fii ʔarḍ.

T	kwayyis. yaʕni kbiiri walla...?
S	rubiʕ *acre*.
T	ʔintu min zamaan saakniin fi lbeet?
S	(does not understand)
T	yaʕni min kam sani ʔintu fi lbeet?
S	min θamanṭaaš.
T	θamanṭaašar sani?
S	θamanṭaašar sani.
T	wk̠abilha ween kuntu?
S	ʔana min [kunna fii] *Maryland*.
T	min *Maryland*? ween fii ʔayy madiini?
S	fii madiinit *Ellicott City*. kariib [k̠ariibi] min *Baltimore*.
T	keef iṭṭaks fii *Brockton*? miθl *Ithaca* walla byixtalif?
S	*Ithaca...Ithaca* baarid [ʔabrad] kaθiir min *Brockton*.
T	ʔakθar min *Brockton*?
S	ʔakθar min *Brockton*. ʔaywa.
T	yaʕni binzal θalǰ fii *Brockton* walla laʔ?
S	fii θalǰ. laakin miš θalǰ kaθiir.
T	wiššita baarid?
S	hallaʔ? miš baarid. laakin issana lmaadi [lmaaḍyi kaan] baarid. ʔaywa.
T	kaan baarid. yaa *Kim*, ʔinti saafarti xaariǰ ʔamriika walla laʔ?
S	laʔ.
T	ma saafarti xaariǰ ʔamriika? ɦatta *Canada* maa rufiti?
S	ʔaywa, laakin *Canada* miš xaariǰ ʔamriika.
T	laʔayy madiini fii *Canada* rufiti?
S	fii [la]*Toronto*.
T	madiinit *Toronto*? bʕiidi madiinit *Toronto* ʕan *Brockton*?
S	ʔaywa. baʕiid [baʕiidi] kaθiir. ʔitnaašar saaʕa bissayyaara.
T	ʔiṭnaašar saaʕa bissayyaara?
S	ʔaywa.
T	ʔimta rufiti la *Toronto*? ʔayy sani, ʔayy šahar?
S	haaði ssani.
T	haaði ssani, fii ʔayy šahar?
S	fi šahar yuunyu.
T	fi šahar yuunyu.
S	maʕ ṣaaɦibni [ṣaaɦibti]. wa maʕ ṣaaɦib ilʕaaʔili.[11]

---

11. It seems that what the student meant here was *ʕaaʔilit ṣaaɦibti* "my friend's family" rather than *ṣaaɦib ilʕaaʔili* "the (or a) friend of the family." If that is the case, then this is an instance of a breakdown in communication based on a grammatical error (word order and the *idafa* construction).

T	maʕ ṣaaḥib ilʕaaʔili?
S	maʕ sitt ʔana ʔaʕrif [maʕ sitt ʔana ʔaʕrifha]. walʕaaʔili ʔalsitt [waʕaaʔilit issitt].
T	ʔeeš ʔisimha ssitt?
S	ʔissitt ʔisimha Jeanine.
T	hiyya ṣaḥibtik?
S	ʔaywa.
T	ʔeeš btiʕmal?
S	hiyya daras [btidrus] fii kulliyya fii wilaayit *New Hampshire*.
T	hiyya ṭaliba hunaak?
S	ʔaywa hiyya ṭaaliba.
T	ʔinti yaa *Kim* ʔimta jiiti la *Cornell*?
S	issana lmaadi [lmaadyi].
T	yaʕni haaði ʔawwal sana fii *Cornell*?
S	la. haaði ssani θθaani [θθaanyi].
T	haaði ssani θθaanyi. kwayyis. leeš jiiti la *Cornell*? leeš ma darasti fi jaamʕit *Boston* ʔaw *MIT*?
S	ʔana baḥibb *Cornell*, ma baʕrif.
T	ʔinti yaʕni šufti *Cornell* kabil ma jiiti lahoon?
S	ʔaywa, ʔana šuftha, wa ʔana biddi daras [ʔadrus] muhandasa [handasa, handasi] wa miš mumkin. ʔana darast muhandasa sani, waaḥad sani [sani waḥadi], wa ʔana ma baḥibb daras [ma ḥabbeet ʔadrus, diraasit] lmuhandasa [lhandasa] wa halla? ʔana daras [badrus] ʔassiyaasi...
T	ʕuluum siyaasiyya.
S	lʕuluum issiyaasiyya, ʔaywa.
T	laakin leeš jiiti la *Cornell*? leeš jaamiʕat *Cornell* ʔaḥsan min jaamiʕat *Boston*?
S	ma baʕrif. ʔana ...muhandasa kalila [kulliyat lhandasa] lkaliila [lkulliyya] kwayyis [kwayysi] kaθiir.
T	kulliyat ilhandasa fii *Cornell*?
S	ʔaywa, kulliyyat ilhandasa fii *Cornell* kwayyis [kwayysi] kaθiir. wa ʔana baḥibb *Cornell*.
T	leeš yaʕni? maθalan liʔanha *Cornell* fii karyi ṣyiiri?
S	*Cornell* jaamʕa kabiiri fii karyi ṣayiiri. haaða šii kwayyis.

REFERENCES

AL-BATAL, MAHMOUD. 1992. "Diglossia Proficiency: The need for an alternative approach to teaching." In *The Arabic Language in America*, ed. by Aleya Rouchdy, 284-304. Detroit: Wayne State University Press.

AL-HAMAD, FAYIZ. 1983. "Problems in Teaching Arabic to Foreigners." In *Proceedings of the Second Annual Linguistics Conference*, ed. by Jonathan Owens and Issam Abu Salim, 81-100. Irbid, Jordan: Yarmouk University.

ALLEN, ROGER. 1989. Arabic Proficiency Guidelines. *Foreign Language Annals* 22:4. 373-392.

_____. 1992. "Teaching Arabic in the United States: Past, present and future." In *The Arabic Language in America*, ed. by Aleya Rouchdy, 222-250. Detroit: Wayne State University Press.

ALOSH, MAHDI. 1991. "Arabic Diglossia and Its Impact on Teaching Arabic As a Foreign Language." In *International Perspectives on Foreign Language Teaching*, ed. by Gerard L. Ervin, 121-137. Lincolnwood: National Textbook Company.

_____. 1992. "Designing a Proficiency-Oriented Syllabus for Modern Standard Arabic as a Foreign Language." In *The Arabic Language in America*, ed. by Aleya Rouchdy, 251-283. Detroit: Wayne State University Press.

BADAWI, EL-SAID. 1973. *Mustawayāt l-ᶜarabiyya l-muᶜāṣira fī miṣr* [Levels of Contemporary Arabic in Egypt]. Cairo: Dār al-maᶜārif.

BELNAP, R. KIRK. 1987. Who's Taking Arabic and What on Earth for? A survey of students in Arabic language programs. *Al-ᶜArabiyya* 20 (1&2): 29-42.

BLANC, HAIM. 1960. "Stylistic Variations in Spoken Arabic: A sample interdialectal educated conversation." In *Contributions to Arabic Linguistics*, ed. by Charles Ferguson, 79-161 (Harvard Middle Eastern Monograph, no. 3). Cambridge: Harvard University Press.

CADORA, FREDERIC. 1976. Lexical Relationships Among Arabic Dialects and the Swadesh List. *Anthropological Linguistics* 18:6. 235-260.

EL-HASSAN, SHAHER. 1977. Educated Spoken Arabic in Egypt and the Levant: A critical review of diglossia and related concepts. *Archivum Linguisticum* 8:2. 112-132.

_____. 1978. Variation in the Demonstrative System in Educated Spoken Arabic. *Archivum Linguisticum* 9:1. 32-57.

FOREIGN SERVICE INSTITUTE (FSI). (No date given). *Standard Eastern Arabic*, vol. 1. Washington, DC: Foreign Service Institute.

HEATH, PETER. 1990. Proficiency in Arabic Language Learning: Some reflections on basic goals. *Al-ᶜArabiyya* 23 (1&2): 31-48.

PARKINSON, DILWORTH. 1985. Proficiency to Do What? Developing proficiency in students of Modern Standard Arabic. *Al-ᶜArabiyya* 18 (1 &2): 11-44.

RAMMUNY, RAJI. 1993. Interview with Professor Ernest McCarus (in Arabic). *American Association of Teachers of Arabic (AATA) Newsletter*, February 1993.

WILLIAMS, MALCOLM. 1990. "Ordering the Teaching of Arabic". In *Diglossic Tension: Teaching Arabic for communication*, ed. by Dionisius A. Agius, 46-49. Leeds: Folia Scholastica.

YOUNES, MUNTHER. An Integrated Approach to Teaching Arabic as a Foreign Language. *Al-ᶜArabiyya* 23 (1&2): 105-122.

12

COMPUTER-ASSISTED LANGUAGE LEARNING FOR ARABIC: RATIONALE AND RESEARCH POTENTIAL*

Mahdi Alosh
The Ohio State University

The use of computer-assisted materials in Arabic programs has a two-fold value: improved language learning environments for our students and the potential of conducting research on the strategies those learners use in order to learn. Insights derived from this kind of research will augment our understanding of the learning process and feed into the design of the computer-assisted language learning (CALL) materials, rendering them a better learning tool. In the burgeoning field of Arabic CALL, we should be cautious about the design and content of the programs to avoid some pitfalls which contributed to the demise of the audio language lab and might characterize this kind of work as a technological fad. This chapter provides a rationale for the use and/or development of CALL programs, an overview of the different types of these programs, a brief description of some Arabic projects in this area, and a rather detailed description of a CALL program being developed at The Ohio State University. In order to put the study in perspective, some salient features of a computer-assisted program, such as feedback, control, and coding elements are discussed. The research potential of CALL and the contributions it can make to the theory of foreign language acquisition in general and to the learning of Arabic in particular is also discussed with examples of pertinent

*I am indebted to Michael Janapoulos, an author of CALL materials himself (*NoteTaker* with Ibtissam Alama [1993] by Research Design Associates, Commack, NY), for his careful review of an earlier version of this article.

research questions and experimental designs. Finally, a synthesis of some selected principles is presented, which, if adhered to, may be able to enhance a CALL program and increase its usefulness as a learning tool.

1. Introduction

In our quest for improved learning environments for our students, one serious consideration may be the use or development of CALL programs. Nonetheless, this effort should be grounded in a theoretical framework that bases this medium of delivery and the methodology incorporated into its design on established fundamentals in foreign language acquisition, lest the endeavor be characterized as a technological embellishment rather than a legitimate learning medium. Parkinson (1992:305) wonders whether CALL is just another passing fad or whether it has a measurable impact on the learners' proficiency. This and other research questions might be a good starting point for serious research, not only in the usefulness of CALL, but also in the ways learners learn through this medium and whether this learning is different from other kinds of learning. In the area of foreign language instruction, Arabic scholars, along with their colleagues in other less commonly taught languages, can make a significant contribution to the knowledge base in foreign language acquisition that comes from an entirely different perspective made available by their relative freedom to explore drastic alternatives to established practices, since their fields are still much less codified than those of the commonly taught languages (Ervin 1991:4). Our actions and decisions, however, should be driven and informed by, but not limited to, the research done in foreign and second language acquisition. There are a number of crucial questions with which we are grappling, such as which Arabic variety or varieties to teach and in what order (Al-Batal 1992, Alosh 1991), when and how to introduce the writing system, whether or not to teach grammar explicitly, and how to deal with the design and special technical problems relevant to Arabic CALL materials. Besides, much of the research conducted so far is done on commonly taught western European languages. It is quite possible that some answers to these and other questions will be language specific and others applicable to other languages as well. Perhaps it is we who would ultimately determine the possible generalizability of that research to other foreign languages.

2. Rationale for Using and Developing CALL Materials

The rationale for using CALL varies considerably among language programs. The two most often cited reasons for using CALL can be grouped into two major categories, one pedagogical and learner-related, and the other research-oriented.

2.1 *Pedagogical Delivery Tool*

The first category includes factors such as improved language acquisition, time savings, and freeing classroom time to allow the teacher to spend more time on communicative interactions in class. Among the aims of CALL are teaching students appropriate learning strategies (Weible 1987), flexibility so that different students can use the program in different ways (Parkinson 1992), and instructional management (Johansen and Tennyson 1984).

In addition to the above reasons, our interest in CALL in the area of Arabic language instruction emanates from the existence of a gap in proficiency level between Arabic majors and their counterparts in French and Spanish, for example. Arabic majors seem to be at a disadvantage because Arabic is much less familiar to American students than French and Spanish are. Therefore, it requires much more time for students to reach a level of proficiency similar to that achieved by French and Spanish majors. Arabic majors are also required, in principle, to reach a certain level of proficiency in the language in the same amount of time that French or Spanish majors need to reach that level. Reading is a crucial skill needed by Arabic majors and graduate students to succeed in their Arabic studies. CALL is perhaps the most appropriate medium to develop this skill via actual reading practice combined with highly structured reading comprehension, vocabulary building exercises, and immediate feedback.

Another reason which calls for the use of CALL is self-paced, or self-managed, learning where students are expected to work on their own with minimal contact with an instructor. In such an environment, well-designed CALL can fill a vacuum and render the learning process a more meaningful one by virtue of some built-in features such as immediate and informative feedback, branching, drill-and-practice, simulation, and so forth. For classroom-track students, it will also allow slower learners access to a low anxiety environment in which they can bridge the gap between themselves and faster students.

2.2 *Research Tool*

The main reason in the second category is using CALL as a research tool to understand the learning process better (Garrett 1989, 1991; Dunkel 1991). Several second and foreign language educators have emphasized the need for research in CALL because they feel that CALL is at risk due to unsubstantiated claims. They also want to avoid the fate of the language lab that was prematurely put into use without adequate research-based knowledge of how it can best serve language acquisition (Dunkel 1991, Garrett 1991, Pederson 1987). To justify expenditure on CALL programs we have to provide compelling and substantiated reasons for using or developing them, ones that are based not merely on perceptions and expectations, but rather on research findings.

Research may be designed with two different purposes, one aiming at evaluating the effectiveness of CALL and another targeting the learners' processing strategies of the language input. Currently, there is a shift away from the first type of research toward the second. In this chapter, the focus is on learner-centered research because I believe that methodological decisions should be guided and driven by knowledge gleaned from language acquisition research. Moreover, this kind of research has the potential of contributing ultimately to a theory of foreign language acquisition in general, whose research base is still confined primarily to the more commonly taught languages. It may also establish a niche for the less commonly taught languages within the wider framework of foreign language acquisition research. This is not intended to negate or question the validity of research based on comparing methods. The matter is simply one of priorities; there is currently urgent need for research on learner strategies which can provide the background for a coherent foreign language acquisition theory (this topic is discussed in greater detail in Section 8 below). CALL materials, properly programmed, may be of tremendous help in identifying the learners' language learning and processing strategies.

3. Advantages and Disadvantages of CALL

Every medium of instruction or learning has certain advantages and disadvantages, and CALL is no exception. Some of these supposed characteristics, however, are actually misconceptions about computers and CALL. One of these misconceptions is that CALL is suitable for a specific pedagogical approach whose focus is discrete structural items. We now know that computers are programmable machines with no inherent thinking capability (Ahmad et al. 1985). They perform the tasks that they are programmed to perform. Thus CALL can engage students in any type of language processing; discrete point, integrative, or even communicative based on the design of the software. Another false assumption is that a teacher who wants to develop CALL materials must turn into a programmer (Wyatt 1987). In this age of rapid developments in the field of computing, it is highly unlikely that anyone can be an expert in computer programming, instructional design, and pedagogy at the same time, let alone an expert in the target language. CALL is a collaborative undertaking, requiring the expertise of the teacher, the programmer, the instructional designer, and the content expert.

There are several advantages and disadvantages of computers and CALL programs listed by Ahmad et al. (1985) of which we should be aware. One of the most conspicuous advantages of CALL is its ability to interact with the learner. Unlike programmed instruction, which presents a lesson gradually, provides a task to be performed by the learner, reveals the correct answer, and then moves to the next item, a good CALL program should be able to evaluate the learner's response, giving feedback, branching out to other parts of the program, and making suggestions for remedial work on the basis of the response. All this can be performed very quickly and accurately. There is no room for the error or fatigue that are characteristics of humans. A good CALL program can handle a large volume of information and can accommodate variability in learner levels, styles, and desires. The speed of reading can be controlled, as can the time allowed for a response. It is also flexible. Its availability is not limited to a particular time. Students can work on their tasks at any time of the day, provided a computer is available to them.

Pederson (1987) cites an ethnographic study that found a number of positive and negative views about CALL programs. The positive views include the following: (1) the computer was a forgiving tutor, (2) it treated all students the same, (3) individualization was perceived as beneficial, (4) students stayed more on task than classroom students, and (5) students became more computer literate. The down side was that computers were too rigid and impersonal and their novelty wore off after a while.

4. CALL Program Design

4.1 *Preliminary Matters*

Although computer-assisted language learning is an offshoot of computer-assisted instruction (CAI), there is a difference between the two media that lies mainly in the last letters of the two acronyms, namely instruction and learning, entailing substantially different pedagogical approaches. But before we look at points pertinent to the design and development of CALL, we should set a number of clear-cut objectives, perhaps by asking some specific questions within a theoretical framework. Such questions would focus our attention on the purpose and expected learning outcomes of a given computer-assisted language learning program. In other words, the point is to identify an objective and then do something with the software that would produce the expected outcomes. For example, we should first of all determine the area or areas we are trying to assist. In keeping with what the acronym suggests, the focus should be on pro-moting learning rather than on attending to instruction. The designer's first step would be to identify those learning styles and strategies and design tasks that foster them. By establishing some sort of fit between instructional and learning strategies, the program might contribute to better and more meaningful learn-ing. Let's not forget, however, that such questions remain assumptions until they have been proven by empirical evidence.

Dunkel (1991) lists a number of research questions that can serve as a basis, not merely for research, but also for an informed model of CALL design. They focus our attention on such issues as which learning environment is most amenable for CALL; which kinds of CALL programs augment particular lan-guage skills; whether certain design features affect the quantity and quality of learning; and whether students' perceptions and attitudes influence their learn-ing. In the discussion that follows in this chapter, we will be able to formulate our own assumptions of the characteristics that should be obtained in a CALL program that can best serve our needs and those of our students.

4.2 Three Distinctive Qualities of CALL

There are three qualities that distinguish computers from other media of instruction and have an impact on the design of CALL programs, though they may not be directly related to the design itself (Weible 1987). The first quality is process orientation. Computers, unlike the printed media, are process-ori-ented, a feature that allows them to simulate processes, including those which simulate language usage in nearly life-like contexts. There exist programs, such as *familia* (Underwood 1984), that attempt to incorporate structural practice within a conversational framework. At a lower linguistic level, the computer can present a linguistic or orthographic process via a dynamic representation of the process, permitting the learner to observe it, analyze it, and imitate it, thus eliminating, or minimizing, the need for metalinguistic input (Weible 1987). This process also contributes to the internalization of this item due to the prob-lem-solving strategy used that promotes more lasting and meaningful learning (Ausubel et al. 1978).

The second important quality of CALL is its ability to teach learning strat-egies to the students (Weible 1987). It is assumed that learners learn not only the material presented to them through this medium, but also the methodologi-cal strategies incorporated into the design of the program. This outcome, how-ever, depends largely on the software design. For example, a program that re-sembles an electronic notebook, presenting the material serially, will have very little or no influence on the learner because of the learner's minimal or nonexistent interaction with it. A program that teaches learning strategies should incorporate certain coding options which permit learners either to control the sequence and speed of presentation, to review past items at will, to randomize the presentation of the items, or to redo an item if they are not satisfied with it.[1]

The third unique quality is the ability of CALL to individualize instruction by "learning" about users through their responses and adapting its presentation to accommodate different kinds and levels of learners. This feature makes CALL extremely useful in programs that have individualized, or self-paced, tracks. Unfortunately, most programs available today, even for the commonly taught languages, lack this important feature.

5. Types of CALL Programs

Computer-assisted programs may be classified basically into two types from the perspective of design: Frame-based systems and intelligent systems (figure 1) (Bowerman 1990). Pedagogically, however, computer-assisted language learning programs may be classified as integrated and supplementary. The former type may be viewed as a whole course of language instruction, containing all the information the student would need to learn the language. The latter type can only be a supplement to an existing course (Parkinson 1992). All Arabic CALL programs I know of are supplementary, designed either to complement a textbook or to fill gaps in the learning-teaching process.

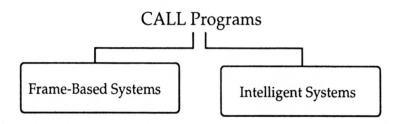

CALL Programs

Frame-Based Systems   Intelligent Systems

Figure 1. Types of CALL Programs

Systems known as frame-based are thus called because they store in a frame a set of correct and incorrect answers and match them with a student's response. Frame-based systems include three subsystems: (1) linear systems, (2) branching systems, and (3) generative systems. Started in the 1950s, linear systems

---

1. Substantial revisions sometimes occur when a student gets hints from the program, suggesting another solution.

(figure 2) are the earliest kind of CALL. They reveal the subject matter one item at a time, accept an answer, inform the learner whether or not his or her response is correct, and then proceed to the next item (Bowerman 1990). Obviously, they lack informative feedback, the ability to adapt themselves to the levels and styles of learners, and several other aspects characteristic of later, more sophisticated systems.

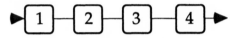

Figure 2. Linear System

In the 1960s linear systems gave way to branching, or adaptive, systems (figure 3). They consist of serial systems that are arranged into layers differentiated by level of difficulty. If a learner enters an incorrect answer, the program branches to a lower layer, and if the next answer is also incorrect, the program branches to a yet lower layer. If, however, the student enters a correct answer at the second layer, the program moves up to the first one (the diagram in figure 3 represents three correct and two incorrect answers). While this system accommodates variability in student levels, it suffers from a major drawback: the formidable task of preparing a huge set of questions for the different layers, a matching set of correct answers, and an even greater number of predictable and possible incorrect answers. Generative systems were later designed to rectify this problem. They generate a new set of questions every time the program is launched to avoid storing a huge set of questions. But they still suffer from the same shortcomings of the other two systems. They have to match a response with a number of predicted, possible responses. And since they normally follow a single predetermined instructional strategy, they are unable to adapt to individual learner needs.

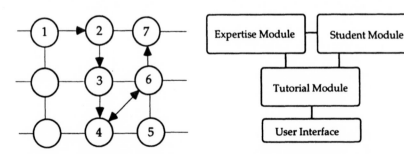

Figure 3. Branching Systems
Adapted from Bowerman (1990)

Figure 4. Architecture of an
Intelligent System

In response to these perceived defects, intelligent computer-assisted instructional systems were envisioned (figure 4). They consist of three main modules: the tutorial module, the student module, and the expertise module. There is also a user interface module that allows the user to interact with the system. All three modules can communicate with one another. The user module can communicate with the student's module only. Briefly described, the expertise module contains two subcomponents: communicable knowledge, or the system's domain knowledge, and the expert model (Wenger 1987). The student module's function is to adapt the tutoring to the individual student's abilities by keeping track of his or her progress. The tutorial module holds the system's repertoire of teaching operations (Bowerman 1990). The rationale behind intelligent systems is to enable them to respond appropriately to different learners by using the data which the system collects about individual learners to modify instruction accordingly.

Tennyson and Christensen (1988) describe an intelligent learning system that has five components: cognitive processes, learning objective, knowledge base, instructional variables, and computer-based enhancements (figure 5). Its major improvement over conventional frame-based systems is that it takes a holistic approach to the learning process. It uses different instructional strategies with different students. Thus, instead of reacting to errors, for instance, it assesses the learner's performance continuously, adapting itself to the individual learner's needs. A model of cognitive-based learning theory with instructional variables and strategies needs to be incorporated in the design in addition to the basic components of content, objectives, and coding options.

Intelligent systems, nevertheless, are still in their embryonic stage. Their development and successful use in language learning will depend in large measure on the advances made in understanding the learning process and how knowledge is represented in the mind. Most CALL programs available today fall into the frame-based category.[2]

Within the frame-based category, there are several types. Wyatt (1987) identifies fourteen different types, including drill and practice, tutorial, game, holistic practice, modeling, simulation, and so forth. He, however, classifies these types into three categories based on the interactional relationship between student and computer. These are the *instructional, facilitative, and collaborative* categories. For example, tutorial, drill and practice, and game are grouped to-

---

2. See Tennyson and Christensen (1988) for a detailed description of the Minnesota Adaptive Instructional System that fits in the category of intelligent systems.

gether because students are responders, not initiators, and they learn from the computer. In this type, the program follows a predetermined path and has a set of objectives to achieve. Figure 6 shows the three categories with a listing of the characteristics of each one as detailed by Wyatt.

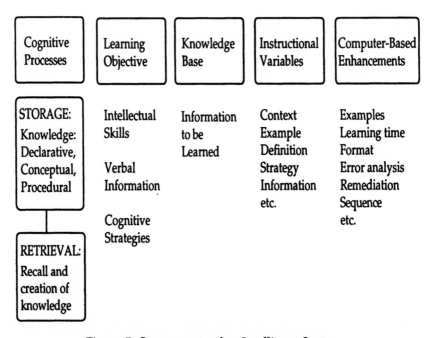

Cognitive Processes	Learning Objective	Knowledge Base	Instructional Variables	Computer-Based Enhancements
STORAGE: Knowledge: Declarative, Conceptual, Procedural	Intellectual Skills	Information to be Learned	Context Example Definition Strategy Information etc.	Examples Learning time Format Error analysis Remediation Sequence etc.
	Verbal Information			
RETRIEVAL: Recall and creation of knowledge	Cognitive Strategies			

Figure 5. Components of an Intelligent System
Adapted from Tennyson & Christensen (1988)

Similarly, Kemmis and his colleagues (1977) classified instructional computer programs into four major types on the basis of theoretical assumptions about how learning and teaching occur (see also figure 6) (Higgins 1988). They labeled them *instructional, revelatory, conjectural,* and *emancipatory*. Each category corresponds to a differentiated role for the learner.

It may be the case that more than one program type can be adopted by one CALL program, particularly those which address different learning levels[3] despite the sharp contrast that exists between them. For instance, the instruc-

---

3. The Arabic CALL program *Ahlan wa Sahlan* adopts more than one type. It has drill and practice features at the phonological and morphological levels, and it also has higher-level cognitive processing features when dealing with texts at the sentence and discourse levels.

tional type focuses on discrete points of language, while the focus in the collaborative type is clearly on the process of learning, the functions of language, meaning, and communication.

Another classification of CALL programs is based on the more familiar continuum of foreign language learning activities, ranging from mechanical to communicative (Chun and Brandl 1992). The paradigm represented in figure 7 classifies the CALL software into three categories. The first and third categories represent the two extremes of the continuum. The middle category is called *meaning enhancing*, and it corresponds to the so-called meaningful activities. They enhance the meaning aspect by providing a rich context for the activity, utilizing the information gap principle.[4]

Wyatt's Classification		Kemmis's Classification	
Instructional Tutorial; drill and practice; games	- Students are responders - Low/high-level objectives - Predetermined learning path	Instructional programmed instruction	- Learner as absorber - Make statements and check for recall
Collaborative Modeling; discovery; simulation; adventure reading; annotation	- Students are initiators partially responsible for their learning - High-level learning objectives - No preset learning path - Discovery learning	Revelatory Simulation	- Learner as experiencer - Provide structured experience and check for assimilation
Facilitative	- Students are initiators entirely responsible for their learning - Learning objectives and paths not specified - Computer as tool	Conjectural Discovery learning	- Learner as explorer - Set open-ended tasks - Provide facilities - Provide rich feedback
		Exploratory Word Processor	- Learner as practitioner - Provide tool to facilitate relevant learning activity

Figure 6. Two Classifications of Computer Program Types

The message conveyed by the above paradigms is that computers themselves are unimportant. What really matters is the design of the software that organizes instruction in some fashion to create a varied and rich language learning environment. Wyatt (1987) emphasizes the distinction between the medium itself and the methodology employed in the design of a particular program. He

---

4. The information gap principle is discussed in detail by Johnson (1982).

maintains that the computer, as a machine, is not associated with a particular methodology. It can be potentially used with either a grammar-based approach or a communicative, meaning-based one.

Form Restricted	Meaning Enhancing	Meaningful Communication
Grammar based Not contextualized Discrete points	Guided Communication Contextualized Discourse level (edited)	Free communication Fully contextualized Authentic discourse
Learner's input: letters, words	Learner's input: sentences	Learner's input: unrestricted

Figure 7. Classification of CALL Programs According to Learner
Tasks. Adapted from Chun & Brandl (1992)

6. Elements of CALL Programs

In mediated instruction, there are three central variables: the learner, the learning task, and the coding elements (Pederson 1987). Thus, CALL programs must address all three variables by integrating them into the design of the program. The software can be designed to serve a specific pedagogical need or to produce a desired outcome through the interaction of a particular design characteristic with specific learner traits. This can be accomplished by incorporating in the design one or more CALL design elements, such as informative feedback, error correction, degree of control by student and computer, sequencing, rate of presentation, and so on. The interaction of these design elements with the three main variables is believed to produce meaningful learning. Three elements will be discussed in this study: feedback, control, and coding options.

6.1 Feedback

Feedback can be one of three major types: (1) confirmation feedback, (2) correct response feedback, and (3) explanatory feedback (Schimmel 1987). The first type simply confirms the learner's response, be it correct or incorrect. Correct response feedback discloses the correct answer. This may be done in conjunction with confirmation. Explanatory feedback provides either an explanation of the specific point directly related to the response or a general review of the topic. If this type of feedback can adapt itself to individual differences and provides instruction that helps in preventing learner error, it can be considered part of an intelligent CALL system. Explanatory feedback need not be extensive, for research has shown that providing lengthy explanations about incorrect responses was no more useful than providing minimal information (Hendrickson 1978, Kulhavy 1977).

In many CALL programs, most feedback is of the error-signaling or corrective variety. It may be auditory, visual, or both. In CALL activities, this sort of feedback is fairly frequent, particularly in the practice and drill type. Robinson (1987), however, cautions against what is known as *cue salience*, i.e., those error signals that tend to be remembered more frequently than other cues. Learners might have an exaggerated sense of the frequency or proportion of these error signals in their minds, and consequently develop a feeling of failure at the task. Robinson cites research in the psychological literature, arguing that "people seem to weigh negative information more heavily than they do positive information" (157). Obviously, the message to the CALL software designers is to seek alternative ways to minimize the negative effect of error feedback. Immediate feedback, though, is necessary in CALL. But instead of being of the corrective or confirmation types, it may be informative. Learners get suggestions or hints either in their first language or in the target language, depending on their level of proficiency, which might help them to rectify their own errors. Such informative feedback may not only contribute toward accomplishing the task at hand, but it may also reinforce learning and enhance comprehension. Empirical research in this area can provide valuable evidence as to which kind of feedback is most appropriate for which kind of learner.

A more promising alternative may be found in intelligent learning systems discussed briefly above. One major advantage of intelligent systems over conventional CALL systems is the manner in which they handle learning failures. On the one hand, regular systems react to errors when they detect a discrepancy between the student's knowledge and the program's knowledge base. On the other hand, intelligent systems use corrective error analysis and remediation within a cognitive-based learning theory and an instructional theory. For example, if a learner fails to respond or if he/she provides an incorrect response, the program presents information directly associated with the item. This information can either be in the form of graphics, sound, or an expository description of this area of the knowledge base.

6.2. *Control*

Higgins (1988) uses a metaphor to describe two roles that the computer can perform: the *magister*, or the rigid, unimaginative instructor, and the *pedagogue*, or the obedient slave. This analogy pertains to the degree of control given in CALL either to the program itself or to the user of that program. This is known as internal control versus external control. But instead of being either internal or external, control extends rather over a continuum, on one extreme of which is the learner and on the other the program. The concept of control represents the ability to manage the sequence of instruction. While many CALL designers believe that giving control to the learner improves learning, some researchers argue to the contrary. Robinson (1988) distinguishes between being *in control* and being *in charge*. She contends that these terms are not synonymous. A learner can be in charge of instruction, but may not be in control of it if he or she lacks adequate knowledge in the field. Bandura (1977) has identified six requisite conditions that must be met before learners are given control of their learning. These conditions can be summarized as follows:

1. Learners must perceive the task as relevant and expect to perform a similar one.
2. Learners must perceive the person modeling the task as similar to themselves.
3. Learners must be exposed to multiple trials with guided participation.
4. Learners must observe positive consequences to their attempts at performing the tasks.
5. Learners need to be exposed repeatedly and gradually to tasks.
6. Learners must be convinced that they can do the task (Bandura 1977, adapted in Robinson 1991).

Weible (1987) identifies another form of control, indirect control, where the learner can have control of program variables, such as sequencing, level of difficulty, and length of study. Sequencing, however, is a crucial variable that should not be made available to learners until they have developed an adequate familiarity with the program's knowledge base. These are some of the options which the software developer can incorporate into the program in order to enhance instruction. The control of some of them, though, can be relinquished to learners at a fairly early stage, including speed of presentation of a reading passage and passage availability during a comprehension check.

6.3 *Coding Elements*

Coding elements are the potential capabilities of a medium to store and deliver instruction. They are utilized to effect variation in the use of a specific medium. Examples of these elements in CALL include display color, graphics, rate and timing of presentation, format, random access, delayed display, reading passage availability during the response, and so forth. Coding elements are found to affect cognitive subskills in learners, such as focusing and highlighting (Salomon 1979). For example, in the course of presenting instruction on how Arabic letters are combined, removing the cues from the screen will activate these subskills during drill and practice. In the *Ahlan wa Sahlan* Arabic software (Alosh and Alama 1992), two coding options, categorization and randomization, have been used with favorable reactions from the students. Although the domain of tasks that use categorization is primarily vocabulary items, they are believed to develop higher-level cognitive processing, such as drawing inferences, because learners within this context would not be looking at words as discrete, isolated items, but rather as collocations of semantic items that share at least one particular attribute. This sort of task seems to be cognitively at a higher level than filling in the blanks, for example. Pederson (1987:113) advises CALL designers to use "coding elements that learners perceive to help them to perform well."

Efficient use of coding elements in a CALL program may be able to stimulate necessary metacognitive strategies, such as strategic competence, the acquisition of vocabulary through listening, and raising the level of cognitive processing (Pederson 1987). CALL software developers should take into account learner variables, coding elements, and tasks in order to produce effective programs. They should also ascertain, perhaps through empirical research, that a selected coding option, predicted to activate a certain cognitive strategy, is task-related.

7. Status of Arabic CALL

7.1 *Overview*

The field of Arabic in the United States is not totally impoverished in CALL. There exist several software packages developed at various institutions whose main objective is to enhance and facilitate formal classroom learning. However, they differ widely in design, level, and content.[5] Some of them will be

---

5. The purpose in this article is to give a brief, general description of some CALL programs with no intention to critique or evaluate any of them. The CALL program developed at Ohio State, however, will be described in greater detail.

272 • MAHDI ALOSH

briefly described here. The pioneering Arabic CALL program was developed by the late Victorine Abboud at the University of Texas at Austin in the 1970s (copyrighted in 1985). It is based on *Elementary Modern Standard Arabic.*[6] It was originally developed for the IBM mainframe and was later adapted to the IBM-PC system. It features Arabic script and phonology, structural drills, and reading passages. Although the program does not use digitized voice, it synchronizes the display with a special audio unit so that students can listen to the pronunciation of selected syllables and words. Some reading passages contain unfamiliar words with no meanings provided. Some of them are accompanied with exercises, and some are not. The program has also a testing component. There is a test after every three lessons and a cumulative test after every five lessons.

The package developed at the University of Massachusetts by Mohamed Jiyad for the Macintosh addresses the affective domain in learners by offering them game-like programs. The rationale seems to be that once a program triggers the interest of the learner, the opportunity for learning is enhanced significantly. Also, the learner will spend more time on the task, trying to beat the computer and at the same time processing the language input necessary to play the game successfully. Jiyad's twelve programs provide practice in Arabic at the word, phrase, and sentence levels, and they check the recognition and production abilities of the users. They cover several aspects of the language, such as vocabulary, morphology, syntax, culture, and even grammatical terminology. They are independent of any particular textbook, making them usable in any Arabic language program.

Another program for the Macintosh has been developed at the University of Chicago by Lynn Killean which follows a more formal approach in presenting the sound and writing systems of Arabic. It utilizes the computer's sound, color, and graphics capabilities.

In 1987, Roger Allen at the University of Pennsylvania supervised the development of a HyperCard[7] program for the Macintosh. It is a reading comprehension program, using authentic texts and spanning all proficiency levels. Learners select and read a given text suitable for their level and then type in answers in English to open-ended questions, which serve as comprehension checks. The instructor can access these answers to correct or comment on them on the disk itself for the learners to review. In 1989, Allen supervised another

---

6. By Abboud et al., Cambridge University Press, 1983.
7. Personal communication.

CALL program for the IBM personal computer and compatibles accompanied with two video discs based on *Arabic for the Media*. The programming was done in the *Tool Book*, a powerful object-oriented application. All the reading passages are organized according to topic. Learners view the passage and, if desired, he or she wishes, they can read the passage intensively word by word or sentence by sentence with the help of an English translation. They can go back and forth between the two versions as many times as they wish.

Dilworth Parkinson, Kirk Belnap, and others have developed a set of programs for the Macintosh at Brigham Young University to reinforce learning in the areas of the script and phonology, vocabulary, reading, and grammar, using a digitized native-speaker voice. These programs include (1) a vocabulary tutor which displays words in either Arabic or English first with various response types (e.g., multiple choice, typed answer, oral answer)[8] and (2) a text tutor that helps students study reading passages, featuring an on-line glossary with voice accessed by clicking on individual words. What is noteworthy about Parkinson's programs is that they were conceived and developed to respond to specific, observed student needs.

7.2 *The Ahlan wa Sahlan CALL Program*

This program has been developed at The Ohio State University by the present writer and Ibtissam Alama, as programmer, through a grant from the OSU Center for Teaching Excellence. The project started in 1989 and is still in progress. The rationale provided for the project was centered on the potential of CALL to free classroom time for more interactive learning, leaving such tasks as learning the script and phonology, practicing the vocabulary and structure, and doing reading comprehension exercises for outside the class. Other goals include introducing and drilling the Arabic sound system in conjunction with its graphemic representation; word recognition; vocabulary practice; reading comprehension; and teaching learners some effective learning strategies, especially in the area of vocabulary.

The program's language content is based on the vocabulary and language functions contained in the textbook series *Ahlan wa Sahlan* (Alosh 1989-1992), though the two media have different contents, i.e., the textbook's passages or dialogues are not replicated in the computer program. This program is based on HyperCard, whose language, HyperTalk, provides easy and powerful programming. The material is presented not in a rigid, linear fashion but in a manner

---

8. Personal communication.

that allows the learner to access any part of the program at will. In other words, the learner is not compelled to do any task that he/she does not wish to do. However, since the computerized tests integrated in the program are part of the course requirements, and since success in them hinges mainly on developing familiarity with the drills and exercises, many students have quickly come to realize the importance of doing the drill-and-practice component.

7.2.1 *Structure of the program*

The program is designed to guide the beginning learner gradually through the basics of the sound and writing systems, vocabulary, functional phrases, and later through reading comprehension passages. The structure of the first three stages[9] is somewhat different from the latter stages because they contain segments which present and drill the script and phonology of Arabic in addition to drills and exercises. Basic reading exercises are provided for stage 3. In fact, this is a misnomer, since these exercises involve more than reading. One type of exercise involves viewing a picture of an item. The learner has the choice of listening to the pronunciation of this word and then selecting it from four alternative words on the screen. In another type of reading exercise, the learner listens to a phrase expressing a language function. He or she then selects the sentence that correctly represents it from four alternatives. Another type of exercise represents an exchange. The stem is the first part of the exchange and one of the four alternative phrases represents the response.

The software is thus divided into stages, each one containing a number of tasks. In addition to the Stage Menu, which allows the learner to navigate through the entire first-year material comprising fifteen stages, there is a main menu for each stage. From stage 4 upward, individual stage main menus display the content of a particular stage, which is made up of two main components, namely the reading passages (called Text 1, Text 2, etc.) and the test. Each Text contains four sections: (1) the reading passage (e.g., Text x), (2) vocabulary review, (3) grammar[10] and (4) exercises. The chart in figure 8 illustrates the structure of the *Ahlan wa Sahlan* software.

7.2.2 *Design of the Ahlan wa Sahlan program and coding elements*

First of all, this program is designed to be as user friendly as possible, allowing learners to move throughout the program at will. The menus and

---

9. The term *stage* is an arbitrary designation which refers to the amount of material, or units, the learner covers in ten contact hours of classroom instruction.

10. The grammar component is not complete yet.

submenus help them to find their way to what they want to do. They can even take a test without doing the drill-and-practice part, although they are alerted by a message to the importance and usefulness of practice. Once they are ready to begin a task, a list of instructions pertinent to the task is displayed to which they can return at any time at the click of a button. The program keeps a record of each student taking a test. The information gathered includes name, Social Security number, the time the user started the test and the time he/she finished it, the date, and the score on the test. The students can obtain a hard copy of the test answers with the score if they wish to do so.

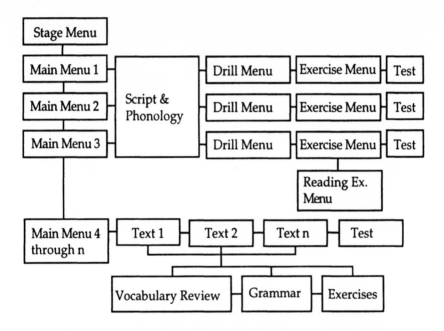

Figure 8. A Schematic Representation of the Software Structure

In keeping with the principles of the instructional approach adopted for *Ahlan wa Sahlan*, which stresses "learning by doing," the students do things in order to perform a task. For instance, they click on the appropriate shapes of letters to form words, play a sound and then select a matching word, or highlight a word and click on a matching one. Also, instead of looking at a gloss of words, they click on a certain word in the text itself to view the English meaning of that particular word, which appears in a pop-up field along with its pronunciation if it is provided, thus minimizing the need to go through a list of meanings every time they need to refer to the glossary. Such coding elements inculcate in learners appropriate learning strategies (Weible 1987).

Highlighting is used in several exercise types, e.g., matching, categorization, and scrambled sentences, in order to show the learner which items have already been done and which items need to be attended to. Another important coding element is randomization. It is used in order to preserve the validity of a test or an exercise if the student decides to retake it. Not only are the items in an exercise or a test randomized automatically when the learner selects the exercise or the test, but so are the alternatives within each item. Feedback is provided in all the tasks except in tests. Although the familiar "correct/wrong" feedback is used particularly in drills, the informative type is also used. This is done in the form of hints, suggestions, or through direct reference to the correct choice, though the correct answer itself is not provided. For example, the learner might receive messages such as these to guide them in performing a given task correctly:

(1) Such-and-such is not the capital of X.
(2) So-and-so has two sisters only.
(3) Look for the independent shape of "waw."

As noted above, the role which coding elements play is not restricted only to the design and delivery of instruction—they also have an impact on the way the learners process the language input. In other words, learners learn certain strategies through the performance of tasks employing these elements.

7.2.3 *Content*

In order to account for the learners' different learning styles and strategies, the language content is presented in multiple formats and levels (e.g., word, sentence, and paragraph levels) to maximize the opportunity for learning. The content ranges from the sounds and letters of Arabic to reading passages. The content, however, is not as crucial as what the learner will do with it, i.e., the learning tasks. In addition to the presentation of the vocabulary either in glossary[11] or on-line formats, there are multiple-choice, matching, and categorization exercises as well as vocabulary reviews. The first three exercise types activate different cognitive subskills in learners as they attempt to do these exercises. Multiple-choice makes learners view a word in a linguistic context, matching lets them look at lexical items as pairs which share at least one semantic

---

11. Glossaries are now being phased out in favor of on-line lexical reference.

trait, and categorization makes them view words as collocations which have some common function in the language. Such cognitive exercises improve learning due to the re-organization of lexical items which they cause learners to make in their cognitive structures. Carroll (1971:56) maintains that "questions are most effective when they cause not only mental search but also cause some sort of re-organization of memory traces and associations." The reviews in this program, however, resemble electronic flashcards with frills. The student can control the speed of presentation, display the Arabic word or the English word first, and listen to the pronunciation of the Arabic word simultaneously.

At the sentence level, learners "unscramble" words to form meaningful sentences. They also use sentence builders[12] to form sentences. At a still higher level, i.e., the paragraph, learners read scrambled sentences and try to reconstruct the paragraph. Of course, sequence and time indicators are built into each sentence to make the reconstruction of a coherent paragraph possible. All tasks are accompanied with English language instructions either at the top of the screen if they are brief or on a separate screen that can be called up quickly and easily.

7.2.4 *Methodology*

The affinity between coding elements and methodology is rather strong. If methodology is the art, or science, of delivering instruction, coding elements are the instruments of delivery. The methodology used supports a functional, interactive, communicative, semantic approach. Obviously, it should focus on meaning and function, and this is what the coding elements try to accomplish. First, they make learners do something in order to perform the task. Second, they make them process the linguistic items in certain ways that stimulate different cognitive processes. The assumption is that the more varied the modalities are, the more permanent and meaningful the learning will be. It should also be noted that the various exercise types used are level related. This means that certain exercises target abilities assumed to be characteristic of learners at particular levels of proficiency. For instance, an exercise on naming objects is provided at the Novice[13] level, whereas exercises on categorization, scrambled sentences, and scrambled paragraphs appear at the Intermediate level.

---

12. These are tables with columns containing words or phrases that can form sentences if they are strung in the right sequence.

13. ACTFL Guidelines.

7.2.5 *Testing component*

The *Ahlan wa Sahlan* Arabic software is accompanied by a testing component. Each stage has a test (see figure 8) which makes an assessment of how much of the material covered in a given stage the learner has controlled. To a great extent, the test format resembles the format of the exercises with the exception of feedback. In the early stages, learners are tested on listening, basic reading, and word and phrase recognition. At later stages, reading comprehension is emphasized. At the conclusion of the test, a raw score is displayed. If students wish to see printouts of their answers to go over the details by themselves or with their instructor, they can do so easily.

7.2.6 *Evaluation*

Over the duration of this project, we have conducted formative evaluation on a continuous basis with the purpose of identifying strong and weak points in the program. Most users, particularly first-year students, fill out a questionnaire on the CALL program. In addition to the questionnaire, the students are unobtrusively observed almost on a daily basis in the Arabic Learning Center where the computers are housed in order to find out where they are having trouble. Face-to-face interviews with selected students are also used to obtain further, in-depth information about the program. Numerous changes and modifications, some of them quite substantial, have been made based on the feedback obtained from the students. Some features were dropped altogether and others were incorporated. For example, a drill that displayed the process of forming a word automatically where the letters connected to each other slowly was dropped because of the lack of interaction and control on the part of the learner. Although a button was later added that gave the learner control by enabling him/ her to redo the process and display a letter at a time, no learners used this feature. The conception was based primarily on the theory that simulating the process leads to better learning (Salomon 1979). This was replaced by two types of drill in which learners played a more active part. In the first type, learners select appropriate shapes of a string of letters to form a word. In the second, they listen to a word and then select appropriate shapes to form that word. In both cases, they have full control over the formation process. These two types received positive feedback from the students.

7.3 *Projected Plans*

This program was initially envisioned as a complete, self-contained program of computer-assisted Arabic language learning in which learners would be able to find all that they need in order to control the material in a given course. In reality, however, no one modality is adequate for successful learning for all students, nor can one methodology achieve the objectives for all students. Thus the role which the program has played so far is a complementary one in the areas where the computer can be of utmost benefit, such as vocabulary practice and reading comprehension exercises. Interaction with native-speaker instructors and fellow learners, for example, cannot be replicated on the computer, but drilling the vocabulary and structures used in such interactions can be done efficiently. CALL is perhaps well suited for doing structural drills and exercises as well as presenting conceptual information about the language (Garrett 1986). Currently, only a limited number of verb conjugations are included, which is inadequate for learners who are beyond the Novice range. The future plans, therefore, include an on-line grammar component with explanations and exercises. The items missed in a given exercise will be pooled for further practice. The feedback learners receive will be of the remedial type. If learners, for example, make the wrong choices among alternatives, the program will provide them with brief explanations and refer them to the appropriate section for more detailed explanations.

8. Research Agenda

8.1 *Research Areas*

Arabic CALL-based research can contribute significantly to research in foreign language acquisition in general and to the Arabic research base in particular. First of all, it is important to determine what it is that we want to investigate. Obviously, the interest in this chapter is in computer-assisted language learning materials which can also be used as an appropriate research tool to investigate factors that may have an impact on Arabic language learning. This kind of research, however, has three main purposes: (1) to substantiate claims about the effectiveness and usefulness of CALL programs, (2) to find out which design elements are best suited for which learner traits, and (3) to identify and evaluate language learning strategies.

This emphasis on learner-centered research is perhaps a direct consequence of what Swaffar (1991) calls "the new paradigm in language learning," which has entailed a shift in research emphasis from the *product* of learning to its *process*. For instance, learner errors are accepted in the new paradigm as manifestations of the evolving new language system. A galaxy of other learner variables, including affective and background factors, cognitive processes, and so forth, have increasingly become the focus of research designs.

Learner-centered research within the CALL environment yields data of two basic types, behavioral and linguistic:

(1) The behaviors learners exhibit during the process of completing a task
(2) The linguistic product (Chapelle 1994)

With regard to the first type, Chapelle identifies three subordinate categories of data. The first one is related to the *choices* the learners make while processing language input, including consulting the on-line dictionary, grammar notes, or whatever coding elements are made available to the learner. The second type is the *duration* of processing language input measured in real time. The third type is the learners' *editing* of their linguistic output, or the changes they make in their responses. The linguistic product may be in the native language of the learners if the focus is primarily on the meaning of a text. The researcher's interest in this case is probably not in surface structure items, but rather in the functional, pragmatic propositions of the text that can be conveyed more effectively in the native language, especially for elementary learners.

Chapelle suggests that interpretation of the data and inferences drawn from them be informed by "a theory which hypothesizes the factors affecting observed behavior and language" (Ibid:2). These factors comprise two categories: learner factors and contextual factors. Learner factors are the components of *communicative language ability* (Bachman 1990), which includes language knowledge, fundamental (i.e., cognitive) processes, and metacognitive strategies, which involve thinking about, planning for, and monitoring learning. The latter category pertains to a theory of how a specific context of a language interaction constrains the choice of linguistic elements. Chapelle finds the theory of context advanced by Halliday and Hasan (1989) as an appropriate theory for research within the CALL paradigm. The reason is that the theory accounts for the participants in a language interaction and their relationships and objectives, the topic in a particular language act, the setting in which language is used, the modality employed, and the genre of the language used in that context.

8.2 *Media Comparison and Learners' Product Studies*

With regard to the first type of research, one might ask the following research questions about the computerized medium vis-à-vis the conventional medium:

(1) What are the most effective ways to teach grammar?
(2) Is computer-assisted learning better than classroom learning?

(3)   Can reading tutorials teach reading better than the teacher?
(4)   Is CALL good for learning vocabulary?

These and similar simplistic research questions entail the elicitation of language product from two groups of learners, a control group that learns through traditional methods and an experimental group that receives a "treatment." The two sets of language product are then analyzed and statistically compared. Nevertheless, Garrett (1991) sees fundamental problems with research designs that collect and analyze learners' product. She believes that such methodological comparisons are of questionable validity for several reasons. First, there are too many uncontrollable variables, in the learners, in the teachers, and in the design of the materials. Second, the learners' product consists of misproduction or nonproduction of language forms which are analyzed in terms of rules that are applicable to native speaker product. Third, the research based on product analysis tells us nothing about the process that yielded the product. Fourth, learners' forms may be correct for the wrong reasons. Moreover, what militates against media comparison research and product research findings is that learners normally avoid what they do not control (Blake 1992). Pederson maintains that media comparison research is incapable of providing generalizable results for several reasons (1987). First, it is impossible to replicate exactly the conditions of the experiment. Second, it is difficult to ascribe with confidence the results to the independent variables which supposedly caused learning. Third, such studies are not usually based on language learning theory, and therefore it is impossible to integrate the results into the research base of foreign language acquisition theory, nor can we use them to improve instructional methodology.

Reservations about the validity of media comparison research are also based on the contention that the research questions asked in such a context tend to give centrality to the medium rather than to the content, the delivery methodology, or the learner (Dunkel 1991). In other words, neither the medium nor the technology should be made the independent variable that influences learning. Before we can make any sense of the learners' production data, we must have an understanding of their interlanguage rules.

8.3 *Learner Traits and Coding Elements*

The message conveyed by the section above is that neither media comparison research nor learners' product research have the potential to yield the findings we need in order to contribute to or develop a viable theory of how Arabic, or any other foreign language for that matter, is learned by nonnative speakers. One of the alternative ways of investigating learning within the CALL paradigm is to examine certain design characteristics and their effects on and interaction with specific learner traits. Pederson finds problems with research that tries to attribute learning gains to the computer rather than to "the way the medium was manipulated to affect achievement" (1987:104). She recommends the kind of research which investigates the interaction of psycholinguistic processes with the way instruction is delivered, or its coding elements.

Pederson relies on Salomon's (1979) theoretical base which takes into consideration the three most important variables of CALL: the learner, the learning task, and the coding elements. CALL-based research, therefore, must account for learner differences and their interaction with different coding options. For instance, some of the interactions we are trying to examine, using the *Ahlan wa Sahlan* software, is unlimited access to meanings, text availability during answering reading comprehension questions, and the effect of categorization on vocabulary learning in different learners.

8.4 *Investigating the Language Learning Process*

Garrett identifies four kinds of theories of learner language, which are so distinct that we need to establish priorities among them before we can develop any kind of a coherent foreign language acquisition theory (1991). The first kind of learner language theory is idiosyncratic form-meaning mapping, or processing ability. Such study investigates the cognitive processes and meaning-form associations made by individual learners within the constraints of either the classroom situation or mediated instruction, such as CALL. The study must consider what the forms mean to individual learners and why they create such meaning-form connections. It must also recognize cognitive and affective factors of different learners in specific situations.

The second type of theory is language knowledge. It is the realm of pure linguistic inquiry which tries to provide an understanding of the relationship between form and meaning. Garrett argues that, contrary to the beliefs of many in the field, language knowledge develops only when the ability to process language becomes stable (1991). She firmly believes that "what a learner acquires is not bits of knowledge about how the abstract language system works, but mapping or processing ability" (78) and that performance is really the basis for competence. She urges us to discard the notion that internalizing linguistic rules is the basis for expressing meaning. We should recognize that "communication is based on the use of psycholinguistic rules" (78).

The third domain is language use in speech acts, or the ability to map meanings onto forms in interpersonal communication. Garrett distinguishes two processes within this domain. The first process involves accessing, processing, and producing meaning-form connections held in memory. The other concerns the appropriateness of these connections in a particular communicative situation (1991). The first process is cognitive and the second is sociocultural.

The fourth area is language acquisition. It refers to the learner's gradual development of the ability to map meanings onto forms, access these connections in real time, and produce them according to the demands of the communicative situation (Garrett 1991). Garrett concludes that research "for investigating idiosyncratic mapping at any one point in time is therefore essential to and must precede acquisition research" (1991:83). It must consider what idiosyncratic meaning the meaning-form connections produced by a learner may mean in the learner's interlanguage and why they are created.

Several researchers agree on giving priority to investigating the process rather than the product (Dunkel 1991, Noblitt and Bland 1991, Blake 1992, Pederson 1987). Noblitt and Bland study the real-time processing strategies used by their students learning French. They recognize certain benefits of the data generated by their research. These include the study of real-time processing strategies, enhanced reference materials, error analysis, possible instruction in learning strategies, and finally the formulation of developmental research questions for further research. Blake (1992) also looks into reading processing strategies of students reading Spanish passages on the computer. He uses the tracking capability of the computer to keep a log of records for each student, showing every card opened, every button clicked, and every question answered. Computers are suitable media to collect such data; they can capture processing strategies, or the learner's interaction with text, as they occur in real time. They allow us to see how learners form grammatical concepts and what these concepts are.

8.5 *Investigating Reading Strategies in Arabic*

In an experiment reported elsewhere (Alosh 1994) are the results of a CALL-based reading experiment the purpose of which is to identify and evaluate reading strategies that are difficult to investigate in reading print. The subjects' task is to read and understand a set of four Arabic passages and then provide a recall protocol in English for each of them. Access to meaning is provided instantaneously in a pop-up field when a word is clicked. This has been found to be faster and more efficient than calling up a dictionary and searching for the appropriate word. The process of clicking a word and comparing it with the glossed form and its English meaning is, in fact, a coding element with two functions. The first function, of course, is accessing the English meaning. The second one helps us evaluate the learner's ability to construct overall meaning by analyzing the forms, since the clicked word does not necessarily match the glossed word in form. All verbs, for example, appear in the gloss in the third person masculine singular, and nouns are listed in the third person masculine singular form. The degree of success in morphological analysis will certainly have pedagogical and design implications.

This type of research, unlike research on linguistic output where learners produce what they think they control and avoid what they think they do not, provides us with data about what learners actually do in order to process aspects of the linguistic input and output which they may not fully control. As noted above, one of the objectives of the experiment is to find out how successful beginning students are in morphological analysis with no formal instruction in Arabic morphology available to them. The research questions which this experiment attempts to answer include the following:

(1) Do learners with different levels of proficiency use similar processing strategies?
(2) Does unlimited access to the glossary have a positive effect on reading comprehension?
(3) Does text availability when doing the exercises positively affect reading comprehension?
(4) Does the time spent on reading a passage have a positive effect on comprehension?

The tracking capability of CALL is utilized in this experiment to generate records for each learner taking the experiment. The program first elicits the name and Social Security number of the learner as well as the number of foreign languages he or she has learned and the duration of study of each. Then it automatically and invisibly records the date and time the student started the experiment, the time each search lasted, and the number of searches for each passage. It must be noted that each passage is coded differently. The first passage provides unlimited access to the glossary and the text window is available during the response; the second has unlimited access to the glossary, but the window is unavailable; the third has limited access to the glossary with the window available during the response; and the fourth has limited access to the gloss and the window is unavailable.

Further CALL research is surely needed to determine the usefulness of some aspects of software design, such as the degree of learner control over the program, the effectiveness of CALL for certain language skills rather than others, the effect of voweling in texts on comprehension (in the case of Arabic), the type of feedback that is more effective than others, the way learners form grammatical concepts in the absence of formal grammar instruction and how close these concepts are to the native-speaker norm, and so forth. These and other research questions, when answered, will certainly enhance the design of Arabic CALL programs and applications as well as our theory of Arabic learning.

9. Principles of CALL Program Design

Throughout this chapter, indirect reference has been made to several principles associated with different topics of CALL design. In this section, a list of these principles will help to focus them and make them more readily accessible. They are by no means exhaustive, but are deemed relevant to the topic of this chapter and can be considered as a handy checklist to be used either when developing CALL programs or when evaluating them (see also Hubbard 1987, and Curtin and Shinall 1987 for detailed CALL evaluation forms and criteria).

(1) Well-defined objectives for each instruction should be formulated.

(2) Advance organizer(s) to attract the attention of the learner and relate the content to his/her cognitive structure should be presented.

(3) The objective should be presented either implicitly or explicitly.

(4) Prerequisite skills for each instruction should be available.

(5) Feedback in the practice component should be provided.

(6) A match between classroom instructional strategies and CALL strategies should be established. A discrepancy would result in a confused mind set as to which objectives are more important.

(7) Coding elements rather than the medium itself affect cognition. Research has shown that programs should be based on known human processing capabilities, rather than on computer potentials (Lesgold and Reif 1983).

(8) Different learners are affected differently by a certain coding element.

(9) A coding element interacts with task and learner variables.

(10) Meaningful practice is possible and preferable in CALL.

(11) A CALL program must be related to acquisition theories.

(12) CALL software should not be identified with any single approach or methodology (Wyatt 1987).

(13) The target learner must be identified.

(14) A CALL program requires careful programming, thoughtful instructional design, good sense, intuition, and sensitivity to student needs (Pederson 1987).

(15) Feedback should be mostly of the informative type.

(16) Discrepancy between aims and practice should be eliminated.

(17) Most tasks should address higher-level cognitive processing.

(18) A CALL program should not try to be cute, funny, or entertaining, though it should be interesting. The reward to the learner is success at the task.

(19) The target language should be used whenever possible. This will depend on the level of proficiency of the learner to a large extent. Responses, however, should always be in the target language. When testing single skills, sometimes test makers resort to English (or the common first language of the learners) to check comprehension. This should be minimized and restricted to testing only.

(20) A CALL program should be flexible, responding to individual needs of learners. Branching at will to any part of the program, or exiting it completely, is perhaps one way of accommodating learner differences.

(21) A CALL program should not duplicate what a textbook can do.

10. Conclusion

The use of computers in education was initially envisioned as a means for maximizing efficiency by standardizing and mechanizing the learning process (Pennington 1989). Learner differences were thought of by the proponents of this view as gaps in knowledge or performance to be filled in. In a sense, the intention was to use computers to minimize or eliminate learner variation. Fortunately, most CALL developers today recognize learner variability as a normal human attribute and consider it an important variable in the foreign language learning process. It is in this area where computer-assisted learning and research can play a significant role.

CALL software is only one part of the foreign language learning environment. It is designed for the purpose of facilitating the learning of some aspects of the target language, usually the literacy skills, and it delivers such instruction in an interactive mode. Good programs should accommodate learner differences and should be adaptable to different learners by varying the rate and sequence of presentation. It is important to note that this adaptive feature shifts the responsibility of managing learning to the learners themselves. Therefore, CALL program developers should account for learner variability, design a variety of tasks to match several known learning strategies and styles, and use coding elements appropriate for that purpose.

CALL can also provide language programs with a bonus in addition to facilitating and reinforcing learning. It can serve as an invisible research tool to track learner activities in the process of learning. This feature alone has the potential of enriching research in foreign language acquisition significantly.

REFERENCES

AHMAD, KHURSHID, GREVILLE CORBETT, MARGARET ROGERS, AND ROLAND SUSSEX. 1985. *Computers, Language Learning and Language Teaching.* London: Cambridge University Press.

AL-BATAL. MAHMOUD. 1992. "Diglossia, Proficiency, and the Teaching of Arabic in the U.S.: The need for an alternative approach." In *The Arabic Language in the U.S.,* ed. by Aleya Rouchdy, 284-304. Detroit: Wayne State University Press.

ALOSH, MAHDI. 1991. "Arabic Diglossia and Its Impact on Teaching Arabic as a Foreign Language." In *International Perspectives on Foreign Language Teaching,* ed. by Gerard L. Ervin, 121-137. Lincolnwood, IL: National Textbook Company.

_____. 1989-92. *Ahlan wa Sahlan: A course for teaching Modern Standard Arabic to speakers of English.* Columbus, OH: Ohio State University Foreign Language Publications.

_____. 1994. *Learner, Text, and Context in Foreign Language Acquisition.* Work in progress.

ALOSH, MAHDI AND IBTISSAM ALAMA. 1992. *Ahlan wa Sahlan: Computer-assisted materials for Arabic.* Unpublished software. Columbus, OH: The Ohio State University (Arabic Program).

AUSUBEL, DAVID P., JOSEPH D. NOVAK AND HELEN HANESIAN. 1978. *Educational Psychology: A cognitive view.* New York: Holt, Rinehart and Winston.

BACHMAN, LYLE F. 1990. *Fundamental Considerations in Testing.* Oxford: Oxford University Press.

BANDURA, ALBERT. 1977. *Social Learning Theory.* Englewood Cliffs, NJ: Prentice-Hall.

BLAKE, ROBERT J. 1992. Second-Language Reading on the Computer. *ADFL Bulletin* 24.1:17-22.

BOWERMAN, CHRIS. 1990. ICALL: An underview of the state of the art in CALL. *Computer Assisted Language Learning* 3:45-54.

CARROLL, JOHN B. 1971. Learning from Verbal Discourse in Educational Media: A review of the literature. *Research Bulletin.* Princeton, NJ: Educational Testing Service.

CHAPELLE, CARL A. 1994. "Theoretical Bases for Human-Computer Interaction Research in CALL." Paper presented at the CALICO Symposium, Flagstaff, AZ.

CHUN, DOROTHY AND KLAUS BRANDL. 1992. Beyond Form-Based Drill and Practice: Meaning enhancing CALL on the Macintosh. *Foreign Language Annals* 25.3: 255-267.

CURTIN, CONSTANCE O. AND STANLEY L. SHINALL. 1987. "Teacher Training for CALL and Its Implications." In *Modern Media in Foreign Language Education: Theory and implementation*, ed. by William Flint Smith, 255-285. Lincolnwood, IL: National Textbook Company.

DUNKEL, PATRICIA. 1991. "The Effectiveness Research on Computer-Assisted Instruction and Computer-Assisted Language Learning." In *Computer-Assisted Language Learning: Research issues and practice*, ed. by Patricia Dunkel, 5-36. New York: Newbury House.

ERVIN, GERARD. 1991. "International Perspectives on Foreign Language Education: A synopsis." In *International Perspectives on Foreign Language Teaching*, ed. by Gerard L. Ervin, 1-5. Lincolnwood, IL: National Textbook Company.

GARRETT, NINA. 1991. "Foreword." *Computer-Assisted Language Learning: Research issues and practice*, ed. by Patricia Dunkel, xii-xvi. New York: Newbury House.

_____. 1989. "The Synergism of Technology and Theory in Classroom Second Language Acquisition Research." In *Language Teaching, Testing, and Technology: Lessons from the past with a view toward the future*, ed. by James Alatis, 288-294. Washington, DC: Georgetown University Press.

_____. 1986. The Problem with Grammar: What kind can the language learner use? *The Modern Language Journal* 70:133-148.

HALLIDAY, MICHAEL A. K. AND RUQAYA HASAN. 1989. *Language, Context, and Text: Aspects of language in a social-semiotic perspective*. Oxford: Oxford University Press.

HENDRICKSON, JAMES M. 1978. Error Correction in Foreign Language Teaching: Recent theory, research, and practice. *The Modern Language Journal* 62:387-398.

HIGGINS, JOHN. 1988. *Language, Learners and Computers*. London: Longman.

HUBBARD, PHILIP L. 1987. "Language Teaching Approaches, the Evaluation of CALL Software, and Design Implications." In *Modern Media in Foreign Language Education: Theory and implementation*, ed. by William Flint Smith, 227-254. Lincolnwood, IL: National Textbook Company.

JOHANSEN, KJELD AND ROBERT D. TENNYSON. 1984. Effect of Adaptive Advisement Perception in Learner-Controlled, Computer-Based Instruction using a Rule-Learning Task. *Educational Communication and Technology* 31:226-236.

JOHNSON, KEITH. 1982. *Communicative Syllabus Design and Methodology*. Oxford: Pergamon.

KEMMIS, STEPHEN, RODERICK ATKIN AND ELEANOR WRIGHT. 1977. *How Do Students Learn? Working Papers on Computer-Assisted Learning: UNCAL evaluation studies*. Norwich, England: Centre for Applied Research in Education.

KULHAVY, RAYMOND W. 1977. Feedback in Written Instruction. *Review of Educational Research* 47:211-232.

LESGOLD, ALAN AND FREDERICK REIF. 1983. *Computers in Education: Realizing the potential. Chairman's report of a research conference*. Washington, DC: Office of Educational Research and Improvement.

NOBLITT, JAMES S. AND SUSAN K. BLAND. "Tracking the Learner in Computer-aided Language Learning." In *Foreign Language Acquisition Research and the Classroom*, ed. by Barbara F. Freed, 120-131. Massachusetts: D. C. Heath and Company.

PARKINSON, DILWORTH B. 1992. "Computers for Arabic Teaching: The promise and the reality." In *The Arabic Language in the U.S.*, ed. by Aleya Rouchdy, 284-304. Detroit: Wayne State University Press.

PEDERSON, KATHLEEN. 1987. "Research on CALL." In *Modern Media in Foreign Language Education: Theory and implementation*, ed. by William Flint Smith, 99-131. Lincolnwood, IL: National Textbook Company.

PENNINGTON, MARTHA C. 1989. "Preface." In *Teaching Languages with Computers: The state of the art*, ed. by Martha C. Pennington, vii-ix. La Jolla, CA: Athelstan.

ROBINSON, GAIL L. 1987. "Effective Feedback Strategies in CALL: Learning theory and empirical research." In *Computer-Assisted Language Learning: Research issues and practice*, ed. by Patricia Dunkel, 155-167. New York: Newbury House.

SALOMON, GAVRIEL. 1979. *Interaction of Media, Cognition, and Learning*. Washington, DC: Jossey-Bass.

SCHIMMEL, BARRY J. 1987. "Providing Meaningful Feedback in Courseware." In *Instructional Designs for Microcomputer Courseware*, ed. by David H. Jonassen, 183-195. Hillsdale, NJ: Lawrence Erlbaum Associates.

SWAFFAR, JANET K., KATHERINE M. ARENS, AND HEIDI BYRNES. 1991. *Reading for Meaning: An integrated approach to language learning*. Englewood, NJ: Prentice Hall.

TENNYSON, ROBERT D. AND DEAN L. CHRISTENSEN. 1988. "MAIS: An intelligent learning system." In *Instructional Designs for Microcomputer Courseware*, ed. by David H. Jonassen, 247-274. Hillsdale, NJ: Lawrence Erlbaum Associates, Publishers.

UNDERWOOD, JOHN. 1984. *Linguistics, Computers, and the Language Teacher: A communicative approach*. Rowley, MA: Newbury House.

WEIBLE, DAVID M. 1987. "Toward a Media-Specific Methodology for CALL." In *Modern Media in Foreign Language Education: Theory and implementation*, ed. by William Flint Smith, 67-83. Lincolnwood, IL: National Textbook Company.

WENGER, ETIENNE. 1987. *Artificial Intelligence and Tutoring: Computational approaches to the communication of knowledge*. Morgan Kaufmann.

WYATT, DAVID H. 1987. "Applying Pedagogical Principles to CALL Courseware Development." In *Modern Media in Foreign Language Education: Theory and implementation*, ed. by William Flint Smith, 85-98. Lincolnwood, IL: National Textbook Company.

13

COMPUTERS AND PROFICIENCY GOALS: FACING FACTS

Dilworth B. Parkinson
Brigham Young University

Computers are slowly but surely entering into the arsenal of tools which we utilize to teach Arabic. Several institutions have labs with computers, and a fairly large number of computer assisted language instruction (CALI) programs have been developed which are at use in various institutions. In this chapter, I first attempt to discuss the "proficiency" related rationale for these programs and why teachers of Arabic are justifiably excited about them. I then try to explain what kind of a thing computers are, and what kind of an activity language learning is, and then look for matches between the two descriptions. I discuss some specific programs and types of programs which have been developed for teaching language, as well as some problems which users of these programs have encountered which are not usually recognized and which might tend to dampen our enthusiasm. I will then end with an appeal for realism in our expectations and a more effective attempt to match the strengths of the computer to what we expect it to accomplish for us, as well as a more concentrated effort to develop a kind of consensus about curriculum in the field as a whole, so that the fruits of our efforts can be more widely and usefully shared with others.

1. Proficiency Goals

1.1 *Near Unanimity of Goals*

I take it as a given that despite disagreements about methods, materials, emphases, and definitions, all of us want our students to become proficient readers and speakers of Arabic (and probably listeners and writers as well, if we had enough time). I am using the word "proficient" here in its non-technical sense, so that I can also have the agreement of those who consider themselves outside the proficiency camp. All of us would be thrilled if our students could pick up a piece of Arabic prose and deal with it comfortably, with ease, without pain. Who of us would complain if our students could turn on the Arabic News and then discuss it with us intelligently in Arabic without the least bit of linguistic discomfort? No matter what our position on the "official" proficiency movement, I think we can all agree that the idea of proficiency, when injected into the language teaching situation, is a powerful concept which helps us clearly define our goals for that situation. It is the notion of proficiency which forces us to ask specifically what the expected outcomes of our programs are in terms of our students' actual ability to read, speak, write, and listen to authentic Arabic.

1.2 *Native Speaker Model*

The natural model of any proficiency-based approach is the native speaker/ user of the language, and this fact alone creates enormously high, impossible goals for us. We cannot help but notice that little Arab children, presumably no smarter than the students in our college classes, are born into the world, and within a few years, with no formal instruction, and no overt knowledge or learning of anything linguistic (be it vocabulary, morphology or syntax), and with apparently little effort, become native speakers, "5's," in one of the Arabic dialects. Many of them then go to school for a few years and receive formal instruction in their standard language, and are able to read Arabic prose with incredible ease, write effortlessly, and understand media broadcasts in their formal language without obvious problems. Why doesn't this happen very often to our students, sometimes even after years of serious work in the language?

1.3 *Frustration with Results*

There are two possible types of answers to this question, and both are probably right. The first is that we simply do not have enough time in the college setting to reasonably be able to accomplish the goal of getting a learner to a proficient state. Although some learners spend as much as five years in our classrooms without achieving the proficiency of a five-year-old native speaker, we find that when we compare contact hours, the five-year-old comes out far ahead. We rarely have more than an hour a day with our students, five days a week, while the native speaker is immersed in the language for all of her/his waking hours. Further, the five-year-old, while quite proficient, certainly is not a "5" in the technical sense. Developing adult competency takes many more years than that, including years of formal education in a setting where the language is used. We can never hope to match that number of contact hours. In short, proficiency provides us the model of the native speaker, but then makes it quite clear that we have to try to push our students toward this model without anywhere near the time that "nature" takes to create one. This is a frustrating result of our interest in developing proficiency.

The second type of answer to the question, of course, is that it is possible that we are not as successful as we might be because our methodologies are inappropriate. Since the native speaker is our model, many theorists point to the way children learn language, claiming that for us to be effective we need to model our programs after them. This means, among other things, less emphasis on grammar explanations and drills, and much more time spent on communicative practice, and in general in providing a rich communicative setting where the students will hear or be exposed to a lot of language with a lot of contextual support so that meaning can be inferred.

If we put these two types of answers together, we get an ideal proposed solution to our problem. Being only somewhat facetious, I suggest that we send our students to Middlebury for two or three summers, and then to CASA for a full year, because these programs combine the two features needed: since they are intensive programs, unlike almost all college programs, they have the time to really immerse students in the language and see the fruits of that immersion, and they also have the time and resources to provide an enormous amount of communicative practice and activities for the students. Although I have not done a study, few would disagree with me that our former Middlebury and CASA students are our most proficient students (and graduates of other intensive programs as well). [Caveat: I realize that there may be some self selecting going on here, and that these students would probably have been our best students even if they had not attended these programs. But we still see the enormous impact these programs have on these students' proficiency.]

This fact makes us feel that we are on the right track in our ideas about proficiency, but it still leaves us frustrated. We are frustrated because these types of experiences are only available to our very best, or very richest, students, and we know that the huge majority of our students, many of whom only stay with us for one or two years, will simply never have the opportunity to have an intensive experience with Arabic, and most will never develop much in the way of proficiency with Arabic. We try to apply the methods of CASA and Middlebury in our own programs, and they help some, but we are still frustrated. We notice how quickly a fifty-minute class period goes by when communicative activities are introduced and how little else we get done; we have trouble figuring out ways to get students to spend time with Arabic outside of class, and we all feel a certain amount of pressure to simply get through the material, whatever materials we are using, simply because this is a college class and must be evaluated with timely exams, assignments, etc. In short, we find that because of our lack of time, the communicative methods do not seem to work as well as they do for the intensive programs.

2. The Promise of CALI

I believe that this is the reason why so many of us have placed such hope in technological solutions. We felt that computers (together with video machines, sound, etc.) might be able to provide that rich communicative setting, those authentic language situations, and enough pizzazz to keep the students interested and involved outside of class, that they would double our students' exposure to Arabic from what could be accomplished in a class period. Computers could provide access to a wide variety of native speakers, to situations that would be difficult or impossible to simulate in class, and in general would provide something like the immersion experience which Middlebury and especially CASA students get by living in an environment where Arabic is spoken. The expectation was, and is, therefore, that using computers in teaching Arabic would help us in many ways reach proficiency goals for our students that we are not able to reach without them.

2.1 *Video Courses*

The ideal computer program, from this point of view, is the video course. This typically involves short movies of survival situations, such as getting a hotel room, ordering a meal at a restaurant, or of more complicated ones, such as having car trouble or a family discussion. The students usually are given control of the movie with an on-screen version of start, stop, and rewind buttons, so that they can watch it as many times as they want, or concentrate on any particular part of it. The program then typically provides a whole series of helps for the student. These might include the option of watching the movie with the words of the dialogue displayed on the screen as they are said, an electronic dictionary for any of the words in the dialogue which the student may be unfamiliar with, a series of cultural explanations that give the student background information s/he may need to understand the movie, and some even provide grammatical explanations of difficult constructions that occur in the text of the movie. The program then typically provides a number of exercises for the student. These include comprehension checks, vocabulary drills, structure drills, reading passages using the same vocabulary as the movie, etc. As far as I know, no such programs have been developed for teaching Arabic, but a number have been developed for English as a Second Language, Spanish, and German. They are frankly quite exciting to watch and play with, and language teachers who see them become justifiably envious of programs that can afford the computers and video systems in their labs necessary to run these programs.

2.2 *Other Arabic CALI Programs*

Because such programs are extremely expensive and time consuming to develop, developers of Arabic software to this point have set their sights on less ambitious programs, with correspondingly less promise and excitement, but still with at least some of both. These programs present texts, gloss words, do comprehension checks, play games, drill vocabulary and structure, give various levels of feedback, present cultural information, and if nothing else, provide a way for students to be involved with Arabic outside of class, other than doing drills from a book, memorizing lists of words, etc. In the bibliography of this paper I have provided a list of Arabic CALI programs.

2.3 *Congratulations to Developers*

Before I begin to evaluate these programs, both the video kind and the less ambitious kind, I want to state that I applaud all developers. Anyone who has had the courage to stick his or her neck out and actually come up with something at this primitive stage of the field has my total admiration and encouragement to continue on. I would hope that anything I say here will not be taken as criticism of any individual effort, but rather of the generic class of programs I am discussing.

3. **How Computers Are**

Computers are machines; they are not people and they do not think like people. Computers do not understand language, and they are not close to understanding language. Although there have been some successful machine translation projects, these have been for mainly cognate languages, and for very limited areas of meaning (for instance, programs for the translation of weather forecasts). There have been many attempts to do more than this, but to this date most would have to be described as interesting experiments rather than successes.

For example, one might wonder why there are no spelling checkers currently available for Arabic word processors. The answer is that the process of extracting roots from words on a printed page, done so naturally and almost effortlessly by native speakers and even by good students, turns out to be immensely more difficult for a computer than anyone could have imagined. This turns out to have important implications for Arabic CALI. For example, when development started on ARABCARD, a program that presents a wide variety of authentic texts with reading aids, the developers wanted students to be able to look up any word of the many texts they presented electronically simply by clicking on the word. Besides showing them the definition, the program would also give the sentence and paragraph of any other occurrence of that word in the texts currently on line. The students could then, if they desired, thumb forward and backward in the electronic dictionary from that point and see forms closely related to that word and the usage of those forms. This would allow the student to study the word in context, and would have many theoretical and pedagogical advantages for the student. When the problem of extracting roots showed itself to be beyond their abilities and resources at that time, the developers decided that words in texts would simply be organized according to how they appeared in the text. For English words this would be a reasonable solution. For example, you would find the form "writes" right after the form *write*, and *written* would not be far away. For Arabic, it turns out to be a nightmare. Perfect forms of the verb show up fairly close to each other, but the imperfect forms are scattered around the dictionary, with /yaktubu/ under *yaa²* and /taktubu/ under *taa²*, etc. Further, the form /wayaktubu/ ends up under *waaw* instead of *yaa²*, /liyaktuba/ ends up under *laam*, etc. Two things resulted. First, the person inputting the definitions has three times or more the work than s/he would have for an English system of the same type; and second, a student clicking on a form like /wayaktubu/ gets much less informative help than s/he would in another language. Believe it or not, the computer does not care.

Computers really understand only instructions that can be given them in the most basic and explicit of forms (ultimately in the form of series of zeros and ones). The computer can do only what the designer can write an extremely explicit set of instructions for. I have recently given seminars in computer assisted instruction, and my impression is that the biggest problem beginners have is that they seem to feel the machine is magic. They explain to me that they want it to do some high-level discrimination operation based on what the students have responded to in their input. I tell them that unless they can write out the steps of that operation in excruciating detail, they can probably not get the computer to do it. For example, they may ask the student an open-ended question, and let the student type in his answer. They want the computer to evaluate that answer and respond appropriately. To a human it is reasonable to give the instruction: "Find out what's wrong with the answer, and respond appropriately." A machine, however, will have no idea what you are talking about. The programmer has to either program the computer to actually parse the sentence and compare it to an internal grammar programmed into the computer (a task that currently is beyond even the most talented programmer) or list all possible answers and appropriate responses. Since open-ended questions have a large number of possible variant answers, even this task becomes close to impossible, given time and budget constraints. It should be becoming clear that the nature of the machine provides certain constraints, both theoretical and practical, on the types of programs we can have. Many programmers simply learn to avoid open-ended questions altogether so that the problem does not arise. Others use open-ended questions, but only provide individual feedback for those answers they consider to be likely. Others may simply react to a student's answer in one way, but provide other helps so that students who have given other correct answers might have a way of finding that out. The important point here is that the machine is constrained, by its very nature, as to the kinds of input it can deliver and the kinds of feedback it is capable of giving. It is inappropriate to think of the computer as a patient private tutor sitting next to the student, figuring out where the student is coming from and providing appropriate input and feedback for that student's needs. This is a machine, and no matter how subtle the programming or how fine the design, the student will be constantly reminded that this is no human being s/he is dealing with.

4. How Language Learning Is

There is not one hundred percent agreement on how students might best learn a language, but we can at least see patterns and consistencies in the variation. I would like to suggest here that there are commonalities which can be derived from all approaches to language teaching. Specifically, all approaches must somehow:

1) *Present the details of the language to the students at some specified rate.*

By details of the language, I mean the sound system, the vocabulary, the morphological paradigms, and the syntactic structures which the language makes use of. The crux of the disagreements about how to present these facts to students revolves mainly around how much of this material we should present and talk about directly, and how much should be simply intuited by the students through exposure to authentic, holistic language. For example, all approaches must somehow get the students to acquire vocabulary. Some are willing to simply provide vocabulary lists for the students, with English meanings attached, while others try to present the words in a "rich" enough context so that this is not necessary. For morphological patterns, some approaches simply provide the students with the paradigm, talk about it, and ask them to practice it and commit it to memory, while others never present the paradigm per se, although it is latent in the language they present to the students, and the hope is that they will figure it out, at least on some level. There is also disagreement as to whether we should protect students from authentic language at the first, and dole out vocabulary and structures in measured and pre-planned units, or whether we should simply provide authentic language from the beginning, and deal with whatever vocabulary and structures appear in that language. I would like to point out that whatever the approach, we are still doling out language to students at a specific rate. Even if we begin with totally authentic language and stick with it, even if we present no planned vocabulary lists, morphological paradigms, etc., still, in the context of a college language class where we are severely limited as to time, we have no choice but to present only a certain number of texts, listening passages, and other activities with the language to the students, and they are therefore getting their exposure to vocabulary and structure at a specifiable rate.

2) *Provide opportunities for the students to practice using what they are trying to learn, enough so that eventually the vocabulary, morphological patterns, syntactic structures, etc., become automatic and fluent. This, of course, is the basis of proficiency.*

Again, there are disagreements about what kind of practice is appropriate and effective. Some are willing to key on specific vocabulary items, morphological paradigms, and syntactic structures with relatively uncontextualized drills that are overtly related to the item being practiced, while others prefer to design activities and communicative drills that ultimately allow students to practice the same vocabulary, morphological patterns, and syntactic structures, but in a less direct and more communicatively authentic way. Others, of course, use a combination of the two approaches. The point, again, is that no matter what the approach, we all agree that students must practice reading Arabic if they are ever to be proficient readers, that they must practice speaking and listening if they are to become effective oral communicators, etc. We do not know a lot about the process of making language features automatic, but we have quite a bit of evidence that it does not happen by mere exposure to a language fact. ESL students in a study needed to see a word in context an average of eleven times before they remembered it consistently,[1] and numerous studies discuss the importance of "spiraling" through topics in terms of vocabulary and structure,[2] the idea being that students need to come back to things again and again before those things finally sink in in a permanent way.

3) Prepare the students, either immediately or eventually, to deal with authentic language, language that has not been prepared specifically for them, but which is "lifted," so to speak, directly from the speech community that uses the language natively.

Again, some approaches take a gradualist approach to this, starting out with greatly simplified language and gradually adding more complex vocabulary, structure and idiomatic usage until they get students to the point where they feel they are ready for the "real thing." Other approaches start out with the "real thing" from the very beginning, although as I stated above, the nature of the college classroom provides some constraints at least on the quantity of authentic language students can reasonably be exposed to (compared to what they might get if dropped into the country where the language is spoken) and usually on the type. No matter how much a teacher might believe in using totally authentic language, I believe it would be rare to find a sensitive teacher who did not, if only subconsciously, simplify the language used in class at least somewhat, since teachers are typically very sensitive to levels of student understanding, and the more authentic the language, the richer and more diverse the vocabulary and structures used, the more likely you are to have students with absolutely blank looks on their faces and no ability to follow what is going on in class. The point here is, again, that despite the differences of approach, all of us have to make adjustments, first, to the current level of our students, and second, to the actual way Arabic is used in Arabic-speaking communities.

What I am trying to demonstrate here is that beneath all our diversity of practice in language teaching, there are three threads, or organizing ideas, which are common to us all: initially, we have to present the resources of the language to the students somehow, then we have to find ways of letting the students practice using those resources enough that they begin to become "deep-wired" or automatic, without which proficiency is impossible, and finally, we have to move the students in the direction of authentic language.

---

1. Cheryl Brown, personal communication.
2. See any of the ACTFL training materials.

There are two other aspects of language teaching I would like to point out here. Both are the results of many years of research in the field, and are based on the results of numerous studies.

4) Recognize that students bring differing basic abilities, different learning styles, and even more importantly, different motivations, to the language classroom, and these abilities, styles, and motivations are critically important to the ultimate success of their personal language learning enterprise.

Although no one can definitely state that "language ability" is more than a theoretical construct, it is a convenient way of talking about what every language teacher knows intuitively: there are good language learners, average ones, and bad ones, and methods that work well for the good ones may be only somewhat effective for the medium ones, and may be totally ineffective for the bad ones. Educational research in general has shown that there are different preferred learning styles, and it has been the experience of many that no matter what method is used, from the very grammatical to the very communicative, some in the class will love it and learn a lot, while others will be annoyed by it, or even alienated, and eventually learn very little, if anything. Theorists assume that one of the most important reasons that second language learners almost never acquire a native accent while all native children do, is that the native children are also acquiring a personal identity, and that they are therefore very strongly motivated to mimic precisely what people in their group do, while our students come to us already possessing an identity, and they are thus not able to mimic so closely. Research in Canada (Swain 1982) has clearly shown that students who have positive attitudes toward the group that speaks the language they are learning are likely to learn better than students who have negative attitudes towards that group. And it is obvious in every classroom that some students have decided that they really care about learning Arabic, for career, social, or other reasons, and are therefore willing to put a lot of time into working on it, while other students almost seem to have fallen into our classrooms by mistake, and while they may like the idea of learning Arabic they are not really committed to it and are not willing to spend much time working on it. The point here is that no matter what the methodology or the quality of the materials and the teaching, or even no matter how theoretically sound our practice, all of us can expect widely varying outcomes of our work, simply because of these factors which are entirely beyond our control.

5) *Recognize that students need to be exposed to language in context, not just isolated examples of language.*

Authentic language out in the community is incredibly redundant, or as some put it, it is performed in an extremely rich context. It is because of this context that it is easy to guess the meaning of unknown forms or figure out what was said even when it was only partially heard. Some even believe that it is this context which makes progress in language acquisition possible. Many studies have shown that the more context provided by a test, activity, reading passage, etc., the better students do and the more they learn. Much of the push toward more authentic language in the proficiency movement generally can be considered an effort to provide a richer context in which the students can practice the target language.

5.   Computers and Language Learning: The Match

I have described both computers and language learning in this much detail for the purpose of comparing the two and determining where the best fit between the two is. I will begin with a number of anecdotes about specific CALI programs which point out certain problems in the relationship, and I will then attempt a more systematic comparison.[3]

5.1 *Teaching for Mastery*

The very first lecture I attended on CALI, given by a man who later became one of the founders of Computer Assisted Language Instruction Consortium (CALICO), involved a demonstration of an ESL computer course which he and a team of researchers had developed for a main frame computer system. It is hard not to be impressed with such programs. They are large and complex, they take an enormous amount of time to develop, and they provide the student with numerous options and a great deal of practice. However, in the introduction to his presentation, he presented to us what he called the "Teaching for Mastery" Model. The program, based on this model, presents material to students, provides various kinds of drill and practice, as well as numerous helps, and then tests the student to determine if s/he is ready to go on. If the student passes the test at the 80% level, s/he is considered to have mastered the material, and the computer goes on to the next lesson. If the student gets below 80% on the test, the student is considered not to have mastered the material, and the computer routes her/him back through the presentation and practice sections of

---

3. One of the best reviews of this match is to be found in Garrett (1991).

the lesson until s/he is ready to take the test again. Does the "Teaching for Mastery" Model match what we know about language learning? Not at all. We have seen that the process of moving language material towards automaticity is a fairly long-term process involving a number of exposures to the same vocabulary or structure. It is absurd to think that once a student has had the lesson on Form IV verbs, and has done the drills and passed a quiz at the 80% level on them, s/he is now "done" with Form IV verbs, having acquired them as part of her/his knowledge of the language, and that they can now be considered part of the "given" of the student's competence. Why then would a major researcher base his program on such a model? I did not find the answer to this question until years later when I started developing programs on my own. The answer is not that anyone thinks that this model fits language learners. Rather it is that the model fits the machine. It is straightforward, easy to interpret, and most importantly, can easily be reduced to a set of excruciatingly detailed instructions. There are other ways of figuring out where students are so as to route them through programs more sensitively, but these ways require an enormous investment of time and resources to "overcome," in a sense, the nature of the machine. "Learning for Mastery," on the other hand, fits the machine perfectly, is very cost effective, and is easy to program. The point is that the machine itself, with its limitations, lures developers into a myriad of such errors, and developers find themselves, unconsciously, designing machine appropriate programs, rather than people-appropriate programs.

5.2 The Three-Million-Dollar Program

Another researcher I know was given three million dollars by a Japanese company to design an ESL program for Japanese students who wanted to learn to deal with survival situations when traveling in English-speaking countries. The program was designed to be "free-standing," not to be used in conjunction with a class, for example. The resulting program was very impressive. You could see videos of a Japanese person getting a hotel room, ordering meals at a restaurant, getting a rental car, etc., and it included many of the features I described when discussing video programs above. When demonstrating the program the researcher said with a touch of pride: "And all the student ever has to do is click." The implications of this take a while to sink in. All the student ever has to do is click. Is this appropriate language-teaching practice? What would happen if one of these Japanese students arrived in San Francisco and actually had to get a hotel room? Would s/he be able to click his/her answers? Does this match with what we know about the language learning process? It means that the student clicks to start and stop the video, to choose various options when playing the video, to do matching, multiple choice, true/false and similar exercises, and to take whatever tests or evaluations are provided. Again, the program was specifically designed to be appropriate to the machine rather than to the learner. If the program had been designed to take real student answers into account, it would have cost much more than three million dollars. This is not to say that it is not a useful program, but this view helps us become more honest about what kind of program it is, what kinds of practice it provides, and thus what kinds of abilities it is likely to engender in our students.

5.3 *The Apples Where Are?*

Specifically to avoid problems like those I have been mentioning, many designers go to incredible lengths to allow students to answer and respond freely, and then get the machine to try to analyze and respond to the students' input. A program to teach Japanese to American students was designed in this way. Since no program exists that allows the computer to actually understand Japanese, parse the sentences, etc., thousands of hours were spent trying to anticipate student answers, from simple spelling errors, to grammatical errors, to misunderstanding errors, etc. However, once the program was finished and was being tested by a group of students, one of the first things the evaluators noticed is that a student typing the Japanese equivalent of "The apples where are?" was told that this was an excellent answer. In other words, it really is impossible to anticipate every student error by "brute force," trying to list every individual possibility with its appropriate response. If you do not believe me, ask *anyone* who has ever tried.

5.4 *The Neglect of Programs*

It is a sad but true fact, not just with Arabic programs but with most CALI programs I am aware of, that they are not used as much as one might expect, and that as time goes on they are used less and less. More specifically, they are used most by students of the person who designed the program and at the institution where it was designed. I have heard anecdotal reports from every institution with programs, including my own, that other teachers and TA's are much less successful in getting students to use the programs than the original designer of the program is. Why might this be? The major reason seems to be that others do not see the direct relevance of the program to what they are trying to accomplish in the class. It seems peripheral to their main concerns, and so they give it only peripheral attention. It is, of course, just as true that the limitations of computer programs are noticed much more by those who were not involved in developing the programs.

5.5 The Non-Integration of Programs

Another sad but true, and very common, fact, is illustrated by the Chinese CALI programs at Brigham Young University. Because of a happy coincidence of personnel, and particularly because we have a language acquisition master's degree program that attracts students from the People's Republic of China every year, we are starting to accumulate quite a large number of CALI programs designed to help teach Chinese. When we hired a new professor this last year, however, and gave him responsibility for the basic Chinese language courses, he had the lab log use of these programs and discovered that almost none of them are used at all, even though some seem to be very useful and interesting. The problem appeared to be that most of the programs were conceived of as being supplemental to courses, rather than core parts of them, and they were not at all integrated into the overall vision of the Chinese program curriculum at BYU, either at the level of the individual course or at the program level. Eleanor Jorden has frequently pointed out that universities with individual professors teaching individual courses with absolutely no coordination between them do not have a language program. An effective program requires an overall vision, overall coordination, and some kind of articulation between stages. The same principle applies to CALI programs, apparently. They are not likely to be used in a particular language program unless there is a real language program, i.e., someone who has a vision of the overall curriculum and the place of these computer programs in it. Further, CALI programs are more likely to be used the more they are integrated into the curriculum as core elements rather than merely as supplemental activities.

5.6 Student Hatred of Programs

This brings us to an even sadder but true fact of life with CALI: despite all attempts to make the programs interesting, to add color, varied responses, games, and general "pizzazz," a certain percentage of the students come to hate the programs, and almost refuse to use them. This admittedly occurs with some programs more than others, but it is still a general rather than a specific phenomenon. This hatred has several causes. Most programs do have frustrating aspects to them; these are almost unavoidable and usually result from decisions to make a program easier to program rather than easier to use, because of limited resources and ability. If students become focused on the frustration, they can miss the good the program might do for them. Some students really do seem to have a general fear of and aversion to computers, no matter what the program. Others get headaches after more than a few minutes in front of a screen. To them it seems bizarre, for example, that they should spend time reading and answering questions about Arabic text on a fuzzy screen, when they could be reading the same text and answering the same questions on a clearly printed page, in good lighting, and without the accompanying headache and physical discomfort. But in most cases, it simply appears that the learning style built into a specific program does not (indeed cannot) match the learning style of all students. The same students who feel threatened and "afloat" in a communicative language class often feel the same way with communicative computer programs, and on the other hand, students who love communicating but despise drills, grammar, and the nitty-gritty aspects of language, may also despise computer programs that key into these aspects and work with them. And finally, it must be said that college students are extremely busy. They often take a full course load, work, and may have family duties. They simply cannot give time to something they do not see as essential. Many of these students begin to see working on the computer as an imposition on their time. They have to sign up, wait their turn, deal with computer problems and in the end come to resent the computer for what it is doing to the rest of their lives.

5.7 A Systematic Comparison

Despite the clear drawbacks indicated by these anecdotes, a comparison of the basic ideas or principles of language teaching with the nature of the machine clearly reveals that there are areas of close match. We will deal with them one at a time, following the general principles of language learning outlined above, first mentioning the computer's strengths in a particular area, and then pointing out its weaknesses.

5.7.1 Initial presentation of material: Positive factors

Computers can be fairly effective at making the initial presentation of language material to students. This is true whether the material to be presented is keyed into specific vocabulary or structures, or whether it is simply a dialogue or other text that includes the language data to be presented. It is extremely easy to get the computer to do what a textbook already does: bring up a dialogue on the screen, show its translation, or a translation of any part of it, bring up a grammatical explanation, show the meaning of a word, display a word list, etc. It is even quite easy to link these features more tightly than they are linked in a book, so that a student can get from a sentence to an associated grammar point, or from a word in a text to the same word in a vocabulary list, in one intuitive click. Because it is becoming easier to integrate sound, graphics, text, and video into a program, it is doable, if not easy, to provide a much richer "meaningful" context for all of these materials on the computer than any book could do. To see a dialogue in video adds the context of the physical surroundings, as well as the associated body movements, which can only aid in student understanding. Vocabulary items can be associated with graphics and sound to make them more memorable. Grammatical explanations can be linked to familiar texts which could be made to highlight the construction under consideration so the student can see it in actual, non-decontextualized use. To what extent a particular program actually is able to do this is dependent partly on the time and resources available for development and partly on the creativity and persistence of the developers.

5.7.2 *Initial presentation of material: Negative factors*

On the other hand, there certainly are many aspects of the presentation of language to students that are either entirely inappropriate, or not effective, on computers. One aspect of reading proficiency is the ability to deal with text in various printed formats, with various fonts, on various qualities of paper, etc. The computer can mimic this variety only to a very limited extent. After that, students should be dealing with actual printed texts at least some of the time. It makes sense to introduce some texts on the computer where all the helps and aids are available, but students can become so dependent on those aids that they fear real texts. Since one gets good at what one does, it makes sense to do some real reading of unfamiliar texts in their original setting. The same thing can be said for listening activities, where the benefits of the computer are so palpable for some students that they might become dependent. More than reading, listening activities are of two types, matching two modes of listening in the real world. The first is non-interactive, and involves extracting information from TV and radio, from public speeches, and the like; these activities are quite appropriately transferred to the computer. The second type, however, depends on interaction, and must be closely related to speaking and face-to-face interaction. The computer is quite good at presenting such dialogues between two actors, but is quite bad at involving the students in them. Since most of us want our students to become proficient at the language in face-to-face interaction, we would almost certainly not want to relegate this aspect to a computer program, although a computer program might supplement it. The introduction of interactive kinds of language material is probably best done in a classroom, involving face-to-face interaction between teacher and students.

5.7.3 *Practicing language: Positive factors*

The computer can also be a very useful tool in the "practice" phase of language learning. However, it is much better at some kinds of practice than others. It is very good at any kind of practice where the student's response is relatively limited or set or predictable. With a certain amount of creativity, this can cover a lot. It is common, after reading or listening exercises, for example, to do comprehension checks which both practice the language involved and guide the student in understanding the passage better. If these checks can be formulated in multiple choice, true/false, matching, or any other straightforward format with a limited set of possible answers, the machine works like a charm. In fact, it can work much better than the equivalent exercises on paper, since the machine can be made to give added helps, to replay key sections on demand, and to make more extensive use of graphics and sound. Computers are also very good at traditional drilling of various types, and again they can be made to improve on machine-less methods. Vocabulary tutors can be made like flash card programs, but with the addition of sound, graphics, and a host of ways to drill words that students on their own probably would never think of. With creativity, the computer can be made to add context to these programs, a huge step ahead of paper flash cards. Text programs can be developed for memorizing or becoming familiar with basic texts. These programs can generate automatic cloze exercises, they can mix up the sentences and wait to be put back together, they can drill the vowels of a text, and other such activities which are possible to prepare on paper but which most of us do not take the time to do consistently. Grammar exercises are also easily done on the computer; again, these may be put in a limited answer format, or they may be constructed such that the students give their own answers and then compare them with the right answer and decide for themselves if their answers are really wrong or simply variants of the right answers. Again, these exercises can have advantages over similar paper and pencil or classroom grammar drills. Most important, the computer provides instant feedback to each question, whereas students often wait days for their homework to be corrected by hand. They also allow every student to do every question, whereas when a drill is done in class, some students will tune out unless it is their turn. Further, the computer can provide helps so that the student understands the exercise better. For example, many grammatical exercises are constructed so that students can march through them without understanding the sentences. The computer can provide instant translations of the prompt and the answer on demand or use other means to make the experience more meaningful. Specific questions (or even specific wrong answers) can also be keyed to specific explanations of the grammatical point involved so the student does not have to thumb through the book to find it explained somewhere.

5.7.4 *Practicing language: Negative factors*

On the other hand, there really are many kinds of practice which are inappropriate or ineffective on the computer. Even with reading and listening checks, we find that with overuse, multiple choice and similar exercises lose their effectiveness, because students can key in on the exercise without paying much attention to the passage they read or heard. Since we are trying to work towards real reading and listening proficiency, most teachers would want to vary these with open-ended discussion questions which really do take the students back into the passage and help them understand it better. Computers are not very good at dealing with such activities. In general, while a computer can be an excellent tool for presenting a text and providing helps for students to deal with it, they are only somewhat effective in "discussing" the text, in finding out to what degree a student has understood it, and in leading him or her to a deeper understanding of it. Further, while the computer can be fairly good at the receptive skills, reading and listening, it has definite problems with the productive ones, speaking and writing. Some CALI programs try to include the student by leaving out half of a dialogue and letting the student fill it in, but they usually provide no feedback at all on the student's performance. Others tell the student to type in what s/he would say, and then try to analyze it with all the above-mentioned problems involved in that process. Others limit the student to multiple choice answers and the like. The claim here is not that these things cannot be useful—they can. However, they can by no stretch of the imagination replace the face-to-face interactive practice that is necessary to develop fluency—proficiency—in speaking. In fact, the most useful thing a computer can do in this regard is a positive: it can take care of so many other things so well that the teacher feels comfortable spending more class time on interactive practice. In other words, if the computer can be made to present the material well, and provide the vocabulary and structure practice that the teacher feels is necessary, all outside of class, the teacher will be much more motivated to devote large portions of class time to interactive practice, which the computer is not able to simulate very well at all. The writing skill is in a similar situation. Although one could use the computer for word processing, even that is probably not a good idea all the time, at least in the first couple of years, because students need constant feedback on their handwriting in order to bring it into line gradually with native norms. Even in traditional drilling of morphological patterns, vocabulary, etc., although clever design and a lot of hard work can make computer programs more varied and interesting than similar drills done in class, a look at available programs suggests that this is not always put into practice, and that many actual computer drills are more constrained, repetitive, boring, and just plain ill-designed and ill-thought-out than one might hope. It is important, therefore, to recognize not only what the computer does well but also what it does not do well. Programs will be less frustrating both for the developers and the users if we bring our expectations for them in line with the strengths and weaknesses of the machine. We then need to exploit the machine for its possibilities and not be content with easy solutions which are dictated more by the nature of the machine than by student needs.

5.7.5 *Authentic language: Positive factors*

Computers can be very good at providing students access to authentic language. With the use of authentic videos and audio, for example, the student can be exposed to a much larger sample of language than a teacher would be able to manage by himself/herself in class. This is particularly true for Arabic, where it would be very nice to see a program that exposed students to various dialects and accents. Advanced reading programs with authentic texts (like ARABCARD) have been quite successful in exposing students to a broad range of materials in a relatively painless context, simply because the help the computer provides for the students to deal with these texts is so extensive that the students become less afraid and more willing to launch into them in a holistic, rather than a word by word, manner.

5.7.6 *Authentic language: Negative factors*

The same caveats about the productive skills mentioned under language practice apply here: students can hear and read authentic interchanges between others, but sometimes they need to participate in authentic interchanges themselves, and computers are not good at that.

5.7.7 *Different abilities, learning styles, and motivations: Positive factors*

CALI programs, with good design, can be made somewhat sensitive to different abilities, learning styles, and motivations of students. For example, some programs offer students a choice between short easy or long technical explanations, and many programs continually test students' understanding and retention of the material, sending them back for more help when needed. Programs can also be created for specific students in mind. For example, quick students may have no trouble learning the vocabulary of a lesson on their own, but slow students may be truly grateful for a simple vocabulary drilling program that, if nothing else, provides them ways of drilling that they would not do on their own. Students who are frustrated by a communicatively oriented class, and who demand more verb paradigms, for example, can be given access to a program that presents the paradigms and drills them ad nauseam, thus satiating these students and making them more willing to participate in the classroom activities. And some students, who like computers and games, but who do not particularly like to study, really do spend more time with the computer programs than they ever would with the book, particularly if the programs are moderately entertaining.

5.7.8 *Different abilities, learning styles, and motivations: Negative factors*

On the other hand, no matter how sensitive programs are made to be, they can never be made as sensitive as a good, live teacher. Teachers tend to have a good sense of where their students are coming from, and are able to adapt to varying needs and abilities, whereas computer programs are able to do this only to a limited extent. And just as programs may be appropriate for only one type of student, they may also be inappropriate for one type. Students who are afraid of computers, who get frustrated easily, or who simply do not like a particular program for whatever reason can become very alienated in a course that relies on it. Teachers need to use their natural sensitivity to shield these students from the computers, providing alternate ways of getting the same material and practice to avoid having a hard core "hate" gallery associated with all their programs.

5.7.9 *Providing context*

We have already mentioned that computers can be very good at providing extra context, although this possibility is not always exploited, since the more one sets out to add such things, the more the cost of the program goes up.

5.7.10 *Time and integration*

To be completely hard-headed and practical, we need to add one further point. Students are busy, and they are not going to use our programs, no matter how much time we spent on them, unless they see a point to doing so. There are several ways of helping them to see the point. We can lecture them about the efficacy of outside, holistic language experiences, we can keep track of the time they spend in the lab and count it as part of their grade, we can beg, cajole, and even cry. The most effective method, however, would be to integrate the CALI programs directly into the curriculum, getting the students to understand that these are not supplementary activities, but rather a core part of the class, and that if they do not do the programs they will have missed something significant. We then need to work on our programs to make sure that this is indeed true.

5.8 *Summary*

To summarize, it seems clear that we have a very valuable tool on our hands, but that because of its characteristics, it is easy to misuse this tool, or to use it so inappropriately that in fact it does not get used. Some of the programs I talked about, for example the three-million-dollar program, are wonderful for what they do, but are inappropriate for what they are expected to do. To make appropriate use of this technology, we need to have a clear idea of what we want to accomplish in a class, what we want to present, and what kinds of practice we want the students to engage in. We then need to evaluate which of these things are best done in class, and which are best done by computer, and design our programs, both CALI and classroom, to match these needs. We then need to be careful to make the programs friendly, interesting, as flexible as possible, as helpful as we can afford, not annoying or frustrating, and in short, useful in an obvious way for real students who are trying to build proficiency in Arabic. We also need to design them in such a way that the time constraints of our students, and the physical and time constraints of our computer labs are kept in mind. A wonderful program will not be effective if the lessons are so long that no student can finish them in a reasonable time, or if the lab is not open long enough or does not have enough computers to allow all students an opportunity to use the program. Yes, it seems obvious, but it really needs to be said: do not design a CALI program without carefully considering who will use it and how and in what teaching and physical context it will be used.

This last point also needs to be extended to the field as a whole. Because developing computer programs is labor and resource intensive, we would all be much better off if programs were developed that had broad applicability and could be adapted to several types of Arabic programs. To the degree that a consensus about curriculum exists in the field, or even a partial consensus, programs should be designed with that consensus in mind so that sharing becomes feasible.

6. Conclusion

There is enormous promise in this field. We have a right to be excited. I will always remember coming into the lab unnoticed behind one of my slower students right after I had developed the simplest program imaginable. This student was far behind the other students, and I wondered if he should not simply drop the class. I stood there and watched as a light came on in his head and he really started to get it for the first time, mainly because the computer was patient with him and let him take as much time as he needed, and gave him the feedback as often as he wanted it. I got a strong feeling that this program, simple as it was, had been able to use the strengths of the computer to provide just what this student needed at that time.

However, we need to temper our excitement with a good dose of realism and learn to use this new technological tool in an appropriate manner as one of a large number of techniques to enhance our students' proficiency. The promise is that if we enter this area cautiously and with our eyes open we can start to make advances in the direction of our proficiency goals. The danger is that if we rush into it with our eyes closed we will be so disappointed because of the natural limitations of the medium that it will end up, along with so many other technologies, on the trash heap of language learning history, its promise unfulfilled.

APPENDIX I

Partial List of Available Arabic CALI Programs

ABBOUD, VICTORINE
"The Texas Programs"
IBM PC
1. Writing and Sound System Program (shown to greatly reduce the time it takes to master Arabic script)
2. Vocabulary and Reading Comprehension Programs, designed for use in conjunction with *EMSA*, although it may be used independently. Each unit requires 1 to 1 1/2 hours at the computer. Each unit contains a basic text, a list of new words, vocabulary associations, exercises, a test, and a dictionary lookup option. The program monitors student progress.
3. Vocabulary and Reading Comprehension Programs, designed for use in conjunction with *IMSA*, although it may be used independently. Each cycle consists of 5-6 lessons, a new word list, word associations, drills, a vocabulary expansion section, a reading comprehension passage and tests. Each requires 2-2 1/2 hours to complete. These programs recylce all the vocabulary from the Elementary programs, and all the vocabulary of *IMSA*. Students are also trained to read intelligently by skimming and scanning. Dictionary lookup is provided.
4. Verb Derivation and Conjugtion Program, designed to be used in conjunction with *EMSA*. It helps students master the conjugations of strong verbs in all persons of the imperfect and perfect, active and passive, and the imperative. It also includes the participles and verbal nouns. A program for weak verbs is currently being prepared.
Availability: contact Peter Abboud, Director, Computer-Assisted Instruction Laboratory, Center for Middle Eastern Studies, University of Texas at Austin, 2601 University Avenue, Austin, TX 78712, (512) 471-1365.

ALLEN, ROGER

MAC II

Reading comprehension texts which have been scanned into computer so that original format is maintained, along with comprehension exercises. For beginning and intermediate levels.

IBM PC

1. Grammar and vocabulary programs to accompany *Let's Learn Arabic*, beginning and intermediate levels. Programs for each lesson.
2. Videodisk programs for listening comprehension, using Microsoft Windows and a program called "Toolbook" that operates the videodisk and provides an environment for informational back-up to the disk.
3. Programs for teaching Arabic script and typing (transcription keyboard). Item 2 is not available due to copyright restrictions. Other items can be made available by arrangement with Roger Allen at the University of Pennsylvania. They are linked to the syllabus *Let's Learn Arabic*, but can be used independently. Costs normally involve materials and postage only.

ALOSH, MAHDI

MAC

Script, Phonology, Vocabulary and Reading comprehension exercises for first two quarters of Arabic, using *Ahlan Wa Sahlan*.

Available from Mahdi Alosh at Ohio State University.

15 double-sided diskettes, $100 for whole package.

BISHAI, WILSON

IBM PC and MAC

1. Computerized Arabic-English dictionary $245.00
2. Arabic Morphology, grammar and drills 45.00

Must order both together.

Available through Wilson Bishai at Harvard University.

Price: $245.00 + 45.00 = $290.00.

BELNAP, KIRK

MAC

Sun Moon Letters Program

2 Map reading programs for beginning Arabic readers

Available from: Department of Asian and Near Eastern Languages, Brigham Young University, 4052 JKHB, Provo, Utah 84602.

Price: $10.00 each

Under development: politeness expressions and responses program.

JIYAD, MOHAMMED
MAC
A variety of verb, vocabulary, proverb and other language and culture programs.

KILLEAN, CAROLYN
MAC
Electronic Al-Arabiyya, for first-year students, on CD rom. Has:
Arabic Verb Forms
First Challenges in Arabic:
>   recognizing similar words
>   giving correct stems
>   pronunciation of article
>   linking words together
>   spelling the hamza

Available from: Corsortium for Language Teaching, 111 Grove Street, New Haven, CT 06520.
$100.00 with site license included.
Under development: Program with Quicktime video to teach Arabic gestures.

PARKINSON, DILWORTH AND BELNAP, KIRK
MAC
1. Grammar, Text, Phonology, Script, Vocabulary, Listening and Reading programs for Macintosh. These are "template" programs for use with any (mainly beginning level) materials. They are sold without the data inserted. Price: Whole package of templates with instructions for use and some training: $1000.00, includes site license for language lab.
2. The above programs with *EMSA* part 1 data inserted for Vocabulary, Text and Grammar, and *A Programmed Course in Modern Literary Arabic Phonology and Script* data for Phonology and Script portions: $50.00 per package.
3. Six Suras and the Call to prayer, a program drilling the suras, with sound: $50.00.
Available from: Department of Asian and Near Eastern Languages, Brigham Young University, 4052 JKHB, Provo, Utah 84602.

RAMMUNY, RAJI AND PARKINSON, DILWORTH
MAC
Computer Programs to accompany the *Arabic Islamic Reader*, introduction to script and beginning reading and Quran for children in Islamic Sunday Schools. Available from: Department of Asian and Near Eastern Languages, Brigham Young University, 4052 JKHB, Provo, Utah 84602.
Price: $500 + media and postage.
Packages of 5 or 6 extra Suras will be made available for $25.00 each.

UNIVERSITY OF DURHAM, ENGLAND
MAC
ARABCARD, extensive readings of computerized texts with dictionary and other aids and exercises.
Available from: University of Durham, Centre for Middle Eastern and Islamic Studies, South Road, Durham DH1 3TG, England (Telephone: 44+91-374 2820, Fax: 44+91-374 2830).
Price: Base Package, $95, Text packages, $95 each, with sound available on some packages for extra. Also discounts for volume buyers.

REFERENCES

BUSH, MICHAEL D. 1991. Hardware for Language Training: Coping with confusion. *Applied Language Learning* 2:2. 77-91.

GARRETT, NINA. 1991. Language Pedagogy and Effective Technology Use. *Applied Language Learning* 2:2. 1-14.

PUSACK, JAMES C. 1991. Software for Language Training: Directions and opportunities. *Applied Language Learning* 2:2. 61-76.

SPOLSKY, BERNARD. 1989. *Conditions for Second Language Learning: Introduction to a general theory.* Oxford: Oxford University Press

SWAIN, MERRILL. 1982. *Evaluating Bilingual Education: A Canadian case study.* Vol. 9. Clevedon, Avon, England: Multilingual Matters.

14

INCORPORATING VIDEO
IN TEACHING ARABIC

Ahmed Ferhadi
New York University

This chapter is a description of a personal technique whose aim is to increase a language learner's fluency without imperiling accuracy. It consists of an oral presentation given by each student in front of the classroom while being videotaped by means of a camcorder and a subsequent conference involving the teacher and the presenter for the purpose of thoroughly discussing the latter's performance on the macro and micro levels, both linguistically and paralinguistically.

1. Overview

Stempleski and Tomalin (1990) contend that "the introduction of a moving picture component as a language teaching aid is a crucial addition to the teacher's resources." According to Jack Lonergan (1984), video presents complete communicative situations which are "dynamic, immediate and accessible."

Furthermore, Axelson and Madden (1990) believe that bringing the video into the classroom provides the teacher with opportunities to focus on, review, and discuss the salient issues of language and culture of the classroom. However, among the problems that teachers confront in attempting to incorporate video into their classrooms, Richards and Rodgers (1987:56) mention "lack of a well-established set of methodological principles for the use of video materials."

This chapter addresses the issue of how to incorporate using video in teaching Arabic as a foreign language by developing the oral skills of the individual learner (and in the process the aural ones of his or her audience). It demonstrates how to use video presentations interactively and how to elicit class participation on the basis of the "methodological principles" of the communicative approach. It shows how video recordings of the learner's performance can be used both cross-sectionally and longitudinally.

2. Rationale

In teaching foreign languages today, the importance of the aural/oral skills and their "natural" precedence over the graphic skills, i.e., reading and writing, are emphasized.[1] Both ACTFL's Oral Proficiency Interview (OPI) and the Center for Applied Linguistics' Simulated Oral Proficiency Interview (SOPI) measure fluency in terms of whether the speaker is capable of talking in paragraphs yet.

In a situation where the foreign language learner has hardly any contact with Arabic outside the classroom, his need for help from the teacher to develop aural/oral skills is even greater. Horowitz et al. (1986:126) specified speaking and listening as "the most frequently cited concern of the anxious foreign language students needing help" (cf. Young 1990 and Koch and Terrell 1991).

2.1 *Fluency vs. Accuracy*

As teachers, we would like our students to acquire both fluency and accuracy in a speedy manner. But oftentimes, honing one takes place at the expense of the other, at least in the initial stages when students' communicative skills are not adequately developed. Teachers are faced with two choices: suppress the learners' continuity by correcting their errors as they make them—under the pretext that they are still fresh in their minds and can be remedied—and thereby inhibit their fluency, or let the student continue in a somewhat erroneous discourse, engendering in the student as well as in her/his classmates the impression that he/she did not err, or that the errors are permissible. But this dilemma can be solved with the help of a camcorder by taking care of fluency first but by no means at the expense of accuracy which will be dealt with later.

2.2 *Background*

I have been using the camcorder in my language teaching with positive results since I first tried it in teaching EFL at the Center for Research and Edu-

---

1. According to Dr. Ann Schneider, who administers the U.S. Department of Education's Title VI grant which funds many Arabic language programs in the country (private communication, April 21, 1993), the Department stresses a performance-based (formerly known as Proficiency-Based, then Competency-Based) approach to foreign language teaching. Even though the Department's nomenclature has undergone changes, the underlying principle remains the same, i.e., emphasizing the oral skill.

cational Development (CRED), University of Michigan, in the summer of 1987. While teaching an advanced English language course for visiting executives from Francophone Africa, I had each student give a presentation about his/her area of expertise. The idea behind the presentation was to allow each student to speak in paragraphs and display any potential for fluency without being interrupted. When I later privately met with those students, on an individual basis, to discuss their performance and to point out their errors, I realized they had already forgotten many of them. It occurred to me then to videotape their presentations so they could subsequently see their errors for themselves.

I have continued to use the concept while teaching Arabic at the elementary through advanced levels at New York University. In the summer of 1991, I introduced the idea to the Middlebury College's School of Arabic while teaching an advanced Arabic course there. It was quite gratifying then and in the ensuing summers to see many colleagues adopt the technique at different levels in that school.

3. Procedure

Each student is asked to give an oral presentation on a topic of choice in the classroom on a regular basis. Students usually choose topics they are comfortable with and areas in which they want to enrich their vocabulary. It is not farfetched that two students select the same topic or current event, but this can be beneficial, too. By having two talks on a related topic, the same or pertinent vocabulary will be further reinforced both by the presenters as well as by their audience.

3.1 Preparation

We often do not know how to say something out of not knowing what to say. The preparation that an oral presentation requires helps alleviate this problem. Choosing their own topics encourages the students to prepare, and as a result, they learn lexical items related to the topic not covered in the textbook or class. They will use the dictionary and check with their teacher, whose office hours they make use of more often, as well as with their classmates and colleagues in higher-level classes when preparing for the exercise.

For the presentation, a student may, according to his or her ability, choose a narrative and/or descriptive, or, in the case of advanced students, an argumentative style. Presentations need not be restricted to a monologue format. In order to encourage group work, students may pair up and present dialogues. "Dialogues provide students with an invaluable opportunity for acquisition through listening comprehension by helping them build their stock of patterns, routines, set phrases and sentences" (Tschirner 1992:507).

Students may also form groups and use a "Nightline" or "Jeopardy" format, for instance. In this way, students become producers. This "may involve scripting, speaking, interviewing, reporting—in fact, a wide range of interesting, highly motivating activities that a learner can identify with" (Lonergan 1984:6). Students usually are creative in selecting their topics. Some topics successfully presented in my classes include: "Astrology," "American Women Hitchhiking in Syria," "Elvis and Graceland," "Horoscope," "A Jilting Girlfriend," "Preparing Hummus," "Square Dancing," "The King of Greece and I" (from a student who actually met the former monarch), and "Flirting in the Church," to name but a few. In an advanced class, the "Nightline-like" format recently comprised a moderator and three engaging characters with opposing views debating the U.S. policy towards the Bosnian plight. There were even some intermittent breaks for commercial advertising.

3.2 Presentation

Turning into a non-hegemonic "silent" cameraman in the class, the teacher uses a camcorder to videotape the students' presentations, preferably each on a tape provided by the presenter who will be in the limelight. "In recent years there has been much interest in the student-centered, proficiency-oriented classroom" (Moeller and Reschke1993:75). This technique puts the student in center stage. And because the student is in the spotlight with everyone listening, the presentation provides a psychological boost.

Video technology has advanced and become common and simple in the past decade or so since Lonergan (1984:10) noted the existence of "so many apparent pitfalls," when many teachers doubted "their competence to handle a camera in the language classroom." TAFL teachers can rest assured today that introducing this aid into the classroom adds a positive rather than a daunting element (cf. ibid.:91).

The student has the floor without interruption for the duration of the presentation, which lasts from a minimum of three to four minutes to about thirty minutes or more depending on the student's level of proficiency in Arabic and on class size.

Lest the presentation be relegated to a mere "reading aloud" drill, the presenter may not be allowed to read except brief notes occasionally.[2] Students are

---

2. For quicker and easier reference, index cards with few notes on each are more practical than sheets full of text.

encouraged to maintain eye contact with the audience to make the talks more effective and also to lessen the students' dependence on the written script.

While videotaping, the teacher also jots down his or her comments on the performance because the camera, which is focused on the speaker almost all the time, cannot capture the whole scene as the teacher can.

Students give their presentations without being interrupted for correction or feedback as they make mistakes because this enables them to maintain continuity and lets them speak in larger chunks rather than in halting sentences. Moreover, they are more confident when they are not interrupted because they assume what they are saying is mostly correct. They are, therefore, more willing to show how competent they are.

In the case of intermediate and advanced students, there should be time to take questions from the audience following the presentation. This adds a level of spontaneity to a presentation that has involved much preparation and rehearsal. In the meantime, it turns the exercise into a more active process for the audience. As a result, the presentation is not "just one-way, to an unresponsive audience" (Lonergan 1984:6).

3.3 Feedback

After the presentation, the teacher meets individually with every student to discuss his or her performance. Video "is particularly suited for assessing fluency and communicative ability in specific situations" (Lonergan 1984:117). The tape could be given back to the student for viewing. The students are encouraged to view their tapes in advance and indicate what they would like to have done differently.[3] In my experience, students come prepared to tell me about certain problems: they could not remember a word at the time but now they do; they had never realized how close their /q/ sound was to a /k/; or that they mispronounced a pharyngeal.

There is no denying the importance of instant feedback for a language learner. For instance, my students who use computer-aided Arabic instruction claim that among the features they like is "the way the computer gives them instant feedback" (Ferhadi 1993:11). Axelson and Madden (1990:1) state that "video can provide direct and fast feedback on the performance of participants." Even though the teacher refrains from providing feedback while the presentation is in progress, with the help of the recorded videotape, s/he can still provide a sort of instant feedback, because her/his comments come directly after

---

3. This was originally suggested by Abbas El-Tonsi, when we were team-teaching an AFL class together at Middlebury College.

reviewing the tape bit by bit. For example, the teacher may play back a small chunk of the presentation on a VCR, then stop the tape, pointing out an error, say, in pronunciation. If the student does not understand what the error was, the tape may be rewound to replay the same section. In this way, the replaying of the tape becomes as dynamic and interesting a process as was giving the presentation.

The process is an active one for both student and teacher as the teacher may catch mistakes or achievements not noticed while the student was giving the presentation. One of my students, for example, usually pronounced her /ʕ/ accurately, but she and I both discovered that this was not the case when the sound occurred word finally, e.g., *lam yarjiʕ* "did not return."

Either the entire presentation or a portion of it may be reviewed, depending on how long it was and how much time both the teacher and the student have for the review.[4] Even when there is no time to review the whole tape, the notes the teacher has taken during the presentation can still be effectively shared with the student.

Not every mistake need be corrected. For beginners, only major errors are pointed out, especially "patterns" (see 4.1). With very good or advanced students, a teacher can go over most or all of the errors because there may not be too many. "Videotapes can be used in the same way as audio tapes to capture the learner's language for analysis and correction. The most obvious features concern pronunciation, choice of lexis and errors of syntax" (Lonergan 1984:116).

3.4 *Paralinguistic Features*

In addition to comprehensibility based on grammar, vocabulary choice, and intelligible pronunciation, paralinguistic features are also discussed, such as gestures, eye contact, speed, hesitation, the use of visual aids, etc. According to the American psychologist Robert Merabian's estimate, "as much as eighty percent of our communication is non-verbal. Our gestures, expressions, posture, dress and surroundings are as eloquent as what we actually say.[5] Video allows us to see this in action and to "*freeze* any moment in detail" (Stempleski and Tomalin 1990:4).

---

4. The teacher can simply use the pause button on the VCR after viewing a portion of the tape before resuming the process.

5. This is evident in how telephone conversations can cause uneasiness for a language learner because they are so bereft of all those non-verbal communication tools.

To make their presentations more effective and to add some flavor to them, many students use audiovisual aids. This makes a big difference, especially with longer presentations.

4. Discussion

Inasmuch as students generally like to save their performances, both student and teacher are provided with evidence of progress made between previous presentations and new ones. But rather than reviewing a past presentation, the teacher can simply save and consult her notes on it. That way she can see if the student has taken care of problems from earlier presentations in part or in whole.

Successive presentations by one language learner are good tools to measure progress in a "longitudinal" study spread across one or a number of semesters. As a result, the teacher will know the strengths and weaknesses of that student and can accurately assess how he/she develops. The tapes can also be used for a "cross-sectional" study to compare the performance of a student to the performance of his/her classmates or peers within the same group. Various presentations from the same level could be compared to each other for this purpose.

4.1 *Error Analysis*

Teachers can apply to video presentations the same principles of error analysis and correction that they use in other situations. However, video is particularly suited for assessing fluency and communicative ability in specific situations (Lonergan 1984:117).

In discussing and analyzing the student's errors, the teacher can pursue a macro/micro dichotomy, depending on the circumstance. On the macro level it could be pointed out, for instance, that the student's speech is not intelligible because of pronunciation problems. The student does not, for instance, distinguish short vowels from long ones and needs to finesse that. On the micro level this could be further narrowed down to telling her how she pronounces a *fatḥa* like an *alif* or how the emphatics sound like their non-emphatic counterparts, e.g., her /ṣ/ sounds like /s/, or her /ṭ/ sounds like /t/. This could be narrowed down even further by pointing out in what particular context the phenomenon occurs (cf. a student's word-final /ʕ/ in 3.3). A pattern emerges here.

It is important that the teacher look for "patterns" in the student's performance. In a recent presentation, a student repeatedly used *lā* instead of *lam* to negate the perfect verb in **lā kānū* "they were not," **lā kānat* "she was not," *lā fahimtu "I did not understand." Another consistently failed to use the definite article al with the noun following the demonstrators hāðā and hāðihi in examples like *fī hāðihi qarya "in this village." Some have not comprehended the noun/adjective versus iḍāfa relationship and mix them up, e.g., al-madīna(tu) (a)l-qarība(tu) "the big city" vs. madīnat(u) dimashq "Damascus City" or rather "the City of Damascus," resulting in erroneous outcomes like: madīna dimashq, al-madīna dimashq or al-madīna(tu) dimashq.[6]

A pattern denotes a "competence" error which emanates from lack of knowledge (underlying grammar) about the issue; whereas a "performance" error may only be isolated, situation-related, or ascribable to, say, "a slip of the tongue" or the like. Once the student is made aware of the pattern and why it is unacceptable, he or she will be able to apply the same principle to that whole "domain."

4.2 Caveats and Rewards

This technique can prove to be time consuming, especially for the teachers of big classes as it entails holding individual conferences with the students after each presentation. On such occasions, it could be done less frequently.

Some students are camera shy. They can still give their presentations but without the camcorder rolling. I personally have had only two such students so far; one changed her mind after her first presentation and wanted to be videotaped after that.

When people with inadequate language communicate with each other, they may feel less uncomfortable or less threatened but may not learn much. When the student makes certain errors which are not corrected on the spot, the audience may think that they are not erroneous. However, the teacher can jot down common errors as well as salient ones in the students' performances and on another day discuss them in the class without using names to avoid identifying the erring presenter(s). The presenters often recognize and learn from their errors. In the meantime, the whole class also gets a rectification of errors that were not corrected during the presentations. When many students make the same mistakes, it helps the teacher pinpoint what areas or items he or she had not been able to convey to them adequately or properly.

The technique creates competition. Since the presentation is made in the context of classmates in the same level, the interest of the other students is aroused. The presenter is being watched by all his or her peers, as opposed to sitting in the back of class, safely ensconced. Class members look at the pre-

---

6. This should not be confused with al-madīnatu dimashq "The city is Damascus," which is grammatical.

senting student as their peer and therefore think they should be equally good and similarly able to know the vocabulary used. However, this may be daunting at times when a well-prepared presentation is eclipsed by an outstanding performance of another classmate's. A student needs to be reminded that his/her performance is measured up against his/her previous one(s); not someone else's.

Moreover, this technique helps the teacher understand what interests the students. Thus, the teacher will know, for instance, what newspaper clippings and other additional materials to select for the class later on.

The presentations also provide tactile "memory hooks" for class members to learn new vocabulary. Students may bring in various props, especially for presentations in which they demonstrate a process. One of my students demonstrated how to bake a cake, pointing to the ingredients as she talked about them. Another student who liked to comment on the parallels between organic chemistry (her major) and Arabic grammar, demonstrated how mixing certain solutions together produced liquids of varying colors.[7] In such presentations, the audience is given visual reinforcement of the words.

The creativity of the students in selecting a wide range of topics is always a matter of interest for both teacher and class. When done in intervals, the exercise breaks the monotony of only the teacher teaching the class. Students temporarily are taught by their peers which adds a different flavor to the atmosphere.

Without falling into the trap of false modesty,[8] I can say that, in their evaluations, most students say that video presentation has been a highlight of their language learning experience. Some students save each performance for reviewing or get together with other classmates to watch each other's tapes and reminisce about studying Arabic.

5. Conclusion

This has been the gist of a personal experience with a technique fruitfully utilizing the virtues of a reasonably-priced and easy-to-use piece of equipment, i.e., a camcorder in TAFL. It enables the teacher to accelerate the movement of the student to the stage of "speaking in paragraphs" and thereby enhancing her or his fluency without compromising accuracy.

An oral presentation conducted in this manner is an enormous incentive for the student to prepare for and, in the process, tightens many loose ends in

---

7. She was in a class that my colleague, Kristen Brustad, was teaching.

8. The phrase is borrowed from Noam Chomsky in the 1992 documentary film, "Manufacturing Consent."

her command of the target language, be it linguistic or paralinguistic. It also promotes group work among the students in the case of joint presentations and, as a result, further helps with their communicative skills.

Students' video presentations can serve as an excellent source and record for both cross-sectional as well as longitudinal studies of the performance of groups and individuals. They also help the teacher pinpoint areas of strength, weakness, interest, and general performance of one or a class of students.

The technique flexibly lends itself to modification to accommodate the specific needs of the teacher and/or student(s) according to level, class structure, and similar variables.

REFERENCES

ALTMAN, RICK. 1989. *The Video Connection: Integrating video into language teaching.* Boston: Houghton Mifflin.

AXELSON, ELIZABETH AND CAROLYN MADDEN. 1990. Video-Based Materials for Communicative ITA Training. *IDEAL Journal* 5:1-11.

FERHADI, AHMED. 1993. Computers in Foreign-Language Instruction: Enhancing the teaching and learning of Arabic. *Academic Computing and Networking at New York University* 3:2.8-11.

HOROWITZ, ELAINE, MICHAEL HOROWITZ AND JO ANN COPE. 1986. Foreign Language Classroom Anxiety. *Modern Language Journal* 70:125-32.

KOCH, SUSAN AND TRACY TERREL. 1991. "The Effect of the Natural Approach on the Affective Filter." In *Language Anxiety: Anxiety reactions in foreign and second language learning and performance*, ed. by E. Horwitz and D. J. Young. New York: Prentice Hall.

LONERGAN, JACK. 1984. *Video in Language Teaching.* Cambridge: Cambridge University Press.

MOELLER, ALEIDINE J. AND CLAUS RESCHKE. 1993. Graded or Nongraded Communicative Activities—What is the Answer?—An Update. *Foreign Language Annals* 26:1. 75-80.

RICHARDS, JACK AND THEODORE RODGERS. 1987. Through the Looking Glass: Trends and directions in language teaching. *RELC Journal* 18:45-73.

STEMPLESKI, SUSAN AND BARRY TOMALIN. 1990. *Video in Action.* London: Prentice Hall.

TSCHIRNER, ERWIN. 1992. From Input to Output: Communication-based teaching techniques. *Foreign Language Annals* 25:6. 507-518.

YOUNG, DOLLY J. 1990. An Investigation of Students' Perspectives on Anxiety and Speaking. *Foreign Language Annals* 23:6. 539-553.

FURTHER READING

ALLAN, MARGARET. 1986. *Teaching English with Video.* London: Longman.

BRUMFIT, CHRISTOPHER, ED. 1983. *Video Applications in Language Teaching.* Oxford: Pergamon Press.

BRUMFIT, CHRISTOPHER. 1984. *Communicative Methodology in Language Teaching.* Cambridge: Cambridge University Press.

GEDDES, MARION AND GILL STURTRIDGE. 1982. *Use of Video in Language Learning.* London: Heinemann.

LONERGAN, JACK. 1982. "Video Recordings in Language Teaching." *Journal of the British Council* 15:1.

OMAGGIO, ALICE. 1986. *Teaching Language in Context: Proficiency-oriented instruction.* Boston: Heinle & Heinle.

OWEN, D. AND M. DUNTON. 1982. *The Complete Handbook of Video.* Harmondsworth: Penguin.

REVELL, J., ET AL. 1982. *Teacher Training Video project: Dealing with errors.* London: British Council.

TOMALIN, BARRY. 1990. *Video in the English Class* (a training video). London: BBC English.

WRIGHT, D. 1980. "Role-Play, Simulations, and Video in TEFL: Where are we now and where do we go from here?" In *Perspectives in Academic Gaming and Simulations* 5. London: Kogan Page.

15

THE ARABIC SPEAKING PROFICIENCY TEST AND ITS IMPLEMENTATION

Raji M. Rammuny
University of Michigan

This chapter describes the history, structure, and early testing and train-ing of the Arabic Speaking Proficiency Test (AST), one of the four compo-nents of the New Arabic Proficiency Test. The test emphasizes the usage of the type of Arabic (Modern Standard vs. dialect) which is linguistically and socially appropriate to the situation presented by each exam question.

The exam has a long and a short form, either of which can be used de-pending upon the testing situation. The long form consists of warm-up, pic-ture-based, topical, and environmental questions. The exams are scored using a special rating system that assigns each student an overall rating ranging from Novice Low to Superior.

Both versions were field-tested and carefully screened by the working committee prior to final approval, and field research continues to the present day. In addition, two free workshops were held in the United States in 1992 and 1993 to train teachers in the exam techniques. The author notes that the exam may be used for a variety of purposes, and that the detailed components of the exam and its rating system ensure a high degree of reliability.

1. Introduction

The Arabic Speaking Proficiency Test (AST) is one of four components of the Arabic Proficiency Test (APT) which is mainly designed to measure gen-eral proficiency of examinees in literary Arabic in reading and writing, and spoken standard Arabic in listening and speaking. The APT is intended for ex-aminees at proficiency levels from Novice High to Superior according to the ACTFL Arabic Guidelines, which were prepared by a team of professors of Arabic on the basis of the generic 1986 ACTFL Proficiency Guidelines (ACTFL

1986). The APT was developed in 1991-92 by Raji M. Rammuny and Mahmoud E. Sieny in consultation with John Clark (Defense Language Institute), Ernest McCarus (University of Michigan), Charles Stansfield and Dorry Kenyon (Center for Applied Linguistics) through a grant from the U.S. Department of Education.[1]

The AST is a tape-mediated test of oral proficiency in Arabic. It is intended to evaluate the examinees' ability to speak Arabic fluently and accurately. Directions are given in English, both in the test booklet and on the tape. The examinees are instructed to listen carefully to a series of instructions on a tape and record their responses on a different tape. They are requested to say as much as they can and to speak clearly and loudly enough to have their responses properly recorded.

During the test, the examinees are asked to put themselves into various situations in the Arab world. They are reminded not to accommodate Arabic to the geographic dialects of the different Arab countries but rather to use the type of Arabic which is *linguistically* and *socially* appropriate for each situation.

Within each part of the test, the speaking tasks range in difficulty from easy to considerably more challenging. The examinees are not expected to be able to answer all questions with equal facility. However, they should try to speak as much and as well as possible in response to each question.

The amount of time provided for each response varies depending on the complexity of the question or situation. The examinees are free to stop talking when they feel they have given a complete response. Two times are indicated in parentheses at the end of each item. The first time is the amount of time given to the examinees to think about each question. When that time is up, the examinees hear a question or statement in Arabic, and they may then begin to speak. The second time in the parentheses indicates the amount of time the examinees have to respond to the question. The test takes approximately fifty minutes.

2. Content and Format of the AST

There are two forms of the AST, form A and form B.[2] Each form consists of four parts.

Part one is a warm up, the purpose of which is to help the examinees relax and get used to speaking in response to a master tape. It includes simple personal background questions. For each question asked by the Arabic speaker, the

---

1. The author wishes to thank Eric Thurston, a graduate research assistant, who helped in many ways, including typing, proofreading, suggesting topics, and formatting the test materials.
2. The author plans to develop two more forms (C and D) in the future.

examinees are required to listen carefully and answer during the pause immediately following the question. They have between five and twenty-five seconds to respond, depending on the information requested. They are reminded to say as much as they can in response to each question. The following are sample questions:

س : صباح الخير .

س : تكلم لنا عن حياتك الدراسية .

Part two includes picture-based questions. The examinees look at a picture or series of pictures in the test booklet and speak in response to spoken/written instructions. The tasks include such undertakings as giving directions, describing a place or activities in a familiar setting, or telling a story. In some cases the picture guides the response; in others it serves as a source of ideas for the examinees. For each question in Parts two through four, the examinees have fifteen to thirty seconds to prepare their answers and between one minute to one minute and forty-five seconds to respond, depending on the complexity of each question.

Part three contains topic questions. In this part, the examinees are instructed to talk about five different topics. They hear the topics on the tape, in English, and also read them in the test booklet. The topics require the examinees to organize information. The examinees are placed in a situation in which they have to describe personal preferences, explain a process step by step, state advantages and disadvantages, hypothesize on a formal topic or speak to persuade, and support an opinion. For example:

> An Arab student named Hamdi, who has recently arrived in the United States, asks you how to go about opening a checking account in a bank. You will have fifteen seconds to prepare your response. Then, after Hamdi asks his question you will have one minute and fifteen seconds to *suggest where he might begin to get information and people he might want to contact.*

Part four consists of situation questions. Five descriptions of real-life situations are identified. In each case, the examinees are asked to imagine that they are actually in that situation and to respond in a linguistically and socially appropriate manner. The situations include making polite conversation, offering an apology, giving advice, making a formal introduction, and making simple requests. For example:

You are attending a conference on "Ways to improve business and trade relations between the Arab world and the United States" in Cairo. At the end of the conference you are invited to have dinner with an Egyptian business-man named Mr. Badawi and his family at their home. Before you leave their home, you want to thank the Egyptian family for their invitation and generos-ity. After Mr. and Mrs. Badawi thank you for coming to dinner, *tell them that you have enjoyed the evening and learned a lot about Arab customs during your short visit with them.*

(For an overview of the structure of the AST, see Appendix I.)

3. Field Testing

After all items for the two forms of the AST were developed, draft versions of the forms, including the audio tapes,[3] were carefully reviewed by members of the working committee. Suggested revisions were incorporated into the forms and tapes. During the summer of 1991, form A was field tested on fifty-nine examinees from various levels of Arabic instruction. Form B was field tested on eighty-six examinees in the fall of 1991. Examinees participating in the field testing also completed a questionnaire eliciting their personal evaluations of the test and their suggestions for improvement. After the results of the field testing were statistically analyzed and the questionnaire responses read, tallied, and summarized, the two test forms were further revised using the information collected from the field testing. These revised forms were again carefully re-viewed by members of the working committee before the final versions of the test forms were printed.

4. Scoring the AST

The AST is a criterion-referenced test. This means that the rating that an examinee receives is determined according to a fixed set of criteria, or stan-dards, not by how the performance of one examinee compares to that of an-other. As mentioned in the Introduction, the set of standards used for the AST is the Speaking Proficiency Guidelines of the American Council on the Teaching of Foreign Languages (ACTFL), published in 1986, and the ACTFL Guide-lines for Arabic which are based on the ACTFL Proficiency Guidelines.

The AST has been carefully designed to elicit a representative sample of an examinee's speech in a short period of time. Trained raters listen to the speech sample and assign it one of nine proficiency ratings: Novice Low, Novice Mid,

---

3. The AST was recorded in the recording studio of the Language Resource Center, Uni-versity of Michigan.

Novice High, Intermediate Low, Intermediate Mid, Intermediate High, Advanced, Advanced High, or Superior.

The AST master tape begins with a warm-up. The rater choose not to listen to the warm-up if he/she wishes, but instead can skip ahead to the fifteen tasks that make up the test: five pictures, five topics and five situations. The rater rates the examinee on each task, using a Rater Evaluation Sheet/Form (see appendix II). During the rating process, the rater is guided by the Rater Training Manual which contains discussions of the fifteen tasks in some detail, describing performance on each task at each level (see sample in appendix III) and Rammuny's Arabic Rating Scale, which is an adaptation of the Foreign Service Institute (FSI) interview scale (Reschke 1978) and both the Bartz and the Schulz studies described in Bartz's publication (1979) (see appendix IV).

In general, the examinee's global rating is the highest level at which he or she performs consistently on tasks at that level. Thus, once the rater has rated an examinee on each task on the AST, he/she must determine the highest level on the scale where the examinee's ratings match the level of the task. The examinee's global rating is at the level where he or she does this consistently.

The Rater Training Manual includes decision rules for assigning global ratings.[4] The rater is instructed to follow these rules step-by-step beginning with step 1, but to stop as soon as he/she assigns an examinee a rating. These decision rules are summarized in table 1.

5. AST Workshops

Two free workshops were held to train Arabic language teachers in the administration and scoring of the Proficiency Arabic Speaking Test. The first workshop was held May 23 and 24, 1992, at the University of Michigan in Ann Arbor. It was sponsored by the University of Michigan Center for Middle Eastern and North African Studies (CMENAS) and the Center for Applied Linguistics (CAL) in Washington, D.C. Fourteen teachers representing fourteen Arabic programs in the nation participated in this workshop. The second workshop, which was sponsored by the Center for Applied Linguistics and Eastern Michigan University (EMU), was held March 27-28, 1993, at the EMU Conference Center in conjunction with the EMU Eleventh Annual Conference on Languages and Communication for World Business and the Professions. This workshop was attended by eleven teachers of Arabic.

---

4. These decision rules were developed by Charles Stansfield and his staff at the Center for Applied Linguistics.

Table 1
Decision Rules for Assigning Global Ratings

Step 1: <u>Examine the three Superior level tasks</u>
    a. If 2 or more ratings = **S**, and,
       if applicable, the third = **AH**   then global rating = **S ***
    b. If 2 or more ratings = **AH or higher**, and,
       if applicable, the third = **A**   then global rating = **AH ***
    c. Otherwise,   **go to Step 2 —>**

Step 2: <u>Examine the three Superior level tasks and the seven Advanced level tasks together</u>
    a. If 7 or more ratings = **A or higher**,   then global rating = **A ***
    b. If 7 or more ratings = **IH or higher**,   then global rating = **IH ***
    c. Otherwise,   **go to Step 3 —>**

Step 3: <u>Examine the seven Advanced level tasks and the five Intermediate level tasks</u>
    a. If 8 or more ratings = **IM or higher**,   then global rating = **IM ***
    b. Otherwise,   **go to Step 5 —>**

Step 4: <u>Examine the five Intermediate level tasks</u>
    a. If 3 or more ratings = **IM or higher**,   then global rating = **IM ***
    b. If 3 or more ratings = **IL or higher**,   then global rating = **IL ***
    c. Otherwise,   global rating = **NH or lower**

    *   =   Stop and record global rating.

Each participant received a packet of test materials necessary for training at the workshop and also for administering and scoring the AST at their own institutions. These materials included copies of the Examinee Handbook, Examinee Test Booklet (form A), Master Test Tape (form A), Rater Training Manual, Rater Evaluation Sheet/Form, Arabic Rating Scale, Security Agreement, AST Order Form and Workshop Evaluation Questionnaire (see appendix V).

Each workshop consisted of four sessions. The first session, which was conducted by Charles Stansfield, Director of the Division of Foreign Language Education and Testing at CAL, was a general introduction to the Simulated Oral Proficiency Interview (SOPI) and to the ACTFL Proficiency Guidelines. The participants were provided with training in rating a few samples of examinees' responses in English at the end of the session. Raji Rammuny conducted the second and third sessions. The second session familiarized the participants with the format and structure of the AST in detail and how to administer it. During the third session, the participants were provided with opportunities to practice rating responses recorded by students of Arabic, ranging from Novice through Superior level of proficiency, using the Rater Training Manual together with the Arabic Rating Scale prepared by Raji Rammuny. Charles Stansfield conducted the conclusion session, which discussed assigning global ratings followed by practice.

At the end of each workshop, the participants were given an evaluation questionnaire to fill out. The results obtained from the questionnaire were also utilized in revising the AST.

6. Uses of the AST

The Arabic Speaking Test, together with its sister components of the New Arabic Proficiency Test (i.e., listening, reading, and writing) is intended to provide data on the examinees' general proficiency in Arabic. Such a rating may be useful for a variety of purposes:

a. admission to an Arabic study program
b. placement within an Arabic study program
c. certification of Arabic language proficiency for employment
d. selection of candidates for scholarship
e. measurement of students' programs during academic or summer study
f. evaluation of Arabic instructional programs

7. Rationale for Use of the AST

Unlike the ACTFL Oral Proficiency Interview (OPI), which must be individually administered by trained and certified interviewers, the AST can be administered to a group of examinees in the language laboratory by any individual teacher, teaching assistant, or language laboratory technician. Secondly, the OPI takes between twenty and twenty-five minutes to administer and produces about ten to fifteen minutes of examinee speech, whereas the AST lasts for fifty minutes with a total of about twenty-five minutes of examinee speech. According to Stansfield, "the more extensive sample may contribute to a more valid assessment" (1989:2). Thirdly, the AST contains a fixed series of fifteen tasks in addition to the warm-up; therefore, it offers the same quality of interview to each examinee and a standardized approach to oral proficiency testing. Finally, by recording the examinee's responses on tape for later scoring, with the aid of the Rater Training Manual and Rammuny's Arabic Rating Scale, we ensure high reliability. This is especially true since both the Rater Training and Rammuny's Arabic Rating Scale contain detailed profiles, discussion, and checklists which would help the rater to focus on all aspects of speech; namely, comprehensibility, fluency, amount of communication, quality of communication including linguistic accuracy and cultural appropriateness.

8. Research on the Simulated Oral Proficiency Interviews

In his report entitled "Simulated Oral Proficiency Interviews," Charles Stansfield (1989) reported that "in five studies involving different test development teams and different languages, the SOPI has shown itself to be a valid and reliable surrogate of the OPI." The studies carried out by Clark and Li (1986) on Chinese showed the correlation between the SOPI and the OPI to be .93. The results of the studies conducted by Stansfield and Kenyon (1988) on Portuguese showed a correlation of .93. These results were also supported by the most recent study of Stansfield and Kenyon (1989) on the development and validation of SOPI's in Indonesian and Hausa. The correlation between OPI and SOPI in the Indonesian study was .95 and in the Hausa study was .91. The investigator, in collaboration with Mahmoud al-Batal, Director of the School of Arabic at Middlebury, plan to administer the two forms of the AST, together with the OPI, to forty students of Arabic who will participate in the 1995 Arabic Summer Program at the University of Michigan and at Middlebury College. The results of the scores on the two different tests (i.e., AST and OPI) will be statistically correlated in order to report on the validation of the two forms of the Arabic AST or SOPI.

Appendix I

(Structure of the AST: Form A)

Key: I = Intermediate
A = Advanced
S = Superior

Item	Intended Level	Speaking Tasks
Warm-up	I	Answer personal questions
Picture 1	I	Give directions
Picture 2	I	Describe a place
Picture 3	A	Narrate in present time
Picture 4	A	Narrate in past time
Picture 5	A	Narrate in future time
Topic 1	I	Make suggestions/State preferences
Topic 2	A	Explain a process
Topic 3	A	State advantages and disadvantages
Topic 4	S	Hypothesize on a professional topic
Topic 5	S	Support an opinion
Situation 1	I	Give a description of a personal nature
Situation 2	A	Give an apology
Situation 3	A	Give advice
Situation 4	S	Make a formal introduction
Situation 5	I	Request information

Appendix II

(Sample of AST Rating Form)

Name of Rater: _____

Date of Rating: _____

Examinee Name: _____

Testing Location: _____

Examinee Rating: _____

AST Form (*please circle*):   A   B

Segment Rating Profile (*please circle*):

Warm-up	NL	NM	NH	IL	IM	IH	A	AH	S	Notes
P1(I)	NL	NM	NH	IL	IM	IH	A	AH	S	
P2(I)	NL	NM	NH	IL	IM	IH	A	AH	S	
P3(A)	NL	NM	NH	IL	IM	IH	A	AH	S	
P4(A)	NL	NM	NH	IL	IM	IH	A	AH	S	
P5(A)	NL	NM	NH	IL	IM	IH	A	AH	S	
T1(I)	NL	NM	NH	IL	IM	IH	A	AH	S	
T2(A)	NL	NM	NH	IL	IM	IH	A	AH	S	
T3(A)	NL	NM	NH	IL	IM	IH	A	AH	S	
T4(S)	NL	NM	NH	IL	IM	IH	A	AH	S	
T5(S)	NL	NM	NH	IL	IM	IH	A	AH	S	
S1(I)	NL	NM	NH	IL	IM	IH	A	AH	S	
S2(A)	NL	NM	NH	IL	IM	IH	A	AH	S	
S3(A)	NL	NM	NH	IL	IM	IH	A	AH	S	
S4(S)	NL	NM	NH	IL	IM	IH	A	AH	S	
S5(I)	NL	NM	NH	IL	IM	IH	A	AH	S	

COMMENTS:

Rater's Signature: _____

Center for Applied Linguistics
1118 22d Street, NW
Washington, DC 20037

.

APPENDIX III

(Sample of Rater Training Manual)

PICTURE 5: NARRATE A SEQUENCE OF ACTIVITIES IN THE FUTURE

This task is at the Advanced level, since it involves the narration of specific, concrete events in the future. The examinee is asked to talk about a planned trip to some Arab countries. In rating an examinee's performance on this task, raters should focus on the following elements.

• Communicative task: Would a listener who is not familiar with the events and who is not looking at the drawings develop an understanding of the kind of activities that should occur?

• Accuracy: Does the examinee have the ability to express future activities that will or should occur through the use of appropriate verb tenses (i.e., simple future, subjunctive). Does the examinee have appropriate vocabulary to express the content?

An Advanced level speaker should perform this task at the Advanced level. A speaker whose proficiency is higher than Advanced will probably carry out this task at least at the Advanced level. An Intermediate High speaker will have significant features of the Advanced level in his/her performance, but the performance will not be consistently at the Advanced level. Intermediate Mid and Low level speakers will usually fall far short of Advanced level performance.

PROFILE: INTERMEDIATE LOW PERFORMANCE

The performance at this level is not adequate to handle the task due to insufficient vocabulary and structure. The performance will exhibit a skeletal outline, with a number of the activities omitted. Each major activity might be reduced to a simplistic verbal phrase or a somewhat flawed sentence. Miscommunication arises due to frequent mispronunciation and broken sentences. However, the language produced shows evidence of creating with the linguistic forms, rather than reciting memorized and formulaic phrases.

PROFILE: INTERMEDIATE MID PERFORMANCE

The examinee cannot accomplish the task satisfactorily. The response will exhibit one or more of the following features:

- difficulty in communicating some of the plans
- a lack of fluency
- inadequate vocabulary
- use of English: beach . . . أم . . . أم . . . إلى وسنذهب tent سنزور

PROFILE: INTERMEDIATE HIGH PERFORMANCE

An Intermediate High performance is one that is below the Advanced level in quality, although it exhibits significant features of the Advanced level performance. The examinee may attempt to organize the response through a pre-organizer, but the response will not fully come across as a well-organized narration. Instead, parts of the response will be more like a series of discrete activities, (نستمع إلى موسيقى، نزور الجامعة الأردنية). The limitations in vocabulary will interfere at times with the effectiveness of the overall response and occasionally with fluency.

In practice, the rater would likely find one or more of the following characteristics:

- attempts to link sentences for organization though unsuccessful at times
- a lack of the precise vocabulary, thus using more general terms such as:

سنشاهد حياة البدو في الصحراء بدلاً من « سنحضر حفلة غناء وموسيقى
شعبية »

PROFILE: ADVANCED LEVEL PERFORMANCE

An Advanced level performance is one that accomplishes this task quite adequately. This means that most of the information given in the pictures, and perhaps other information as well, is included in the response. The response presents the information in a logical order, and the examinee may describe some activities not included in the drawings. The examinee's vocabulary is adequate to express the ideas. The examinee should be able to make the response sound like a narration or a connected series of planned activities. The examinee may begin by using a pre-organizer about the planned trip. The examinee may also sequence the remaining information, beginning with something like "First, I am going to...". The examinee may also indicate why he/she is planning to do something, which may elicit a verb in the subjunctive. Such a response tends to confirm that this is narration. Some of the following features may be found in such a performance:

- opening with a background, explaining why the trip is planned
- consistently doing the future planning using simple future or subjunctive: نريد أن ، سنشاهد
- varied vocabulary, including السباحة ، ركوب الجمل ، الأهرام and descriptions of some detail, fluency of delivery, and accuracy of pronunciation and structures

PROFILE: ADVANCED HIGH PERFORMANCE

The examinee can accomplish the task in an impressive way. He or she demonstrates a knowledge of precise vocabulary while communicating about the activities which have been planned. In addition, the examinee may mention the reasons for making many of the visits. The examinee makes use of some less frequent words and phrases, such as الدفّ ، العزف على الآلات الموسيقية للراحة والاستجمام ، المزمار ، .

PROFILE: SUPERIOR PERFORMANCE

The Superior level performance of this task will be characterized by a consistent performance of all the features enumerated at the Advanced High level; in particular, it will demonstrate fluency, accuracy, and a good organization. In addition, the response will contain elaborate description of the people and places in each picture. For example, when talking about picture 2 in the series of pictures given for this task, the response may contain some detailed description, such as:

وفي قطر سنحضر حفلة وموسيقى شعبيّة يحييها ستة فنّانين قطريين يرتدون ملابسهم الوطنية ويعزفون على الآلات الموسيقية العربية كالكمنجة والدف والمزمار والعود والقانون ، إلخ .

The response should also display control of a larger and precise vocabulary and grammatical structures.

APPENDIX IV

(Rammuny's Arabic Rating Scale)

A/S tasks	I tasks	
		أ . مَدى وضوح فهم الاستجابة Comprehensibility
N	NL	١ . فهم بعض الكلمات والعبارات المتناثرة هنا وهناك
IL	NM	٢ . فهم بعض العبارات القصيرة غير المترابطة مع بعضها البعض
IM	NH	٣ . فهم أجزاء قليلة من الكلام
IH	IL	٤ . فهم أجزاء كثيرة من الكلام
A	IM	٥ . فهم معظم الكلام
AH	IH	٦ . فهم جميع الاستجابة المطلوبة
S	A	٧ . فهم الاستجابة المطلوبة ومعلومات اضافية
		ب . الطلاقة في الحديث Fluency
N	NL	١ . استعمال كلمات وعبارات مع التكرار والترّدد باستمرار
IL	NM	٢ . استعمال بعض العبارات مع التكرار والترّدد في حالات كثيرة
IM	NH	٣ . استعمال جمل بسيطة مع التكرار والترّدد في معظم الحالات
IH	IL	٤ . محاولة ربط الجمل البسيطة مع التكرار والترّدد احياناً
A	IM	٥ . ربط الجمل وتنسيقها مع التكرار والترّدد في بعض الحالات
AH	IH	٦ . إجابة عاديّة مع استعمال ادوات الربط وقلة التكرار والترّدد
S	A	٧ . إجابة عاديّة سَلِسة مع تكرار أو ترّدد طبيعي
		ج . كمّية المعلومات المطلوبة في الاستجابة Quantity
N	NL	١ . كلمات قليلة جداً
IL	NM	٢ . جزء صغير من المعلومات

IM	NH	٢ . بعض المعلومات
IH	IL	٤ . قِسم لا بأس به من المعلومات
A	IM	٥ . معظم المعلومات
AH	IH	٦ . جميع المعلومات المطلوبة
S	A	٧ . استجابة كاملة مع بداية ونهاية وتفاصيل وتعليقات اضافية

د . نوعيّة الاستجابة (النواحي اللغوية والحضاريّة) (Accuracy (Linguistic & Cultural))

N	NL	١ . عدم القدرة على اختيار المفردات والتعبيرات المناسبة وصياغة التراكيب الصحيحة واستعمال الأسلوب والنطق السليمين
IL	NM	٢ . كثرة الأخطاء في اختيار المفردات والتعبيرات المناسبة وصياغة التراكيب الصحيحة واستعمال الأسلوب والنطق السليمين
IM	NH	٣ . استعمال بعض المفردات والتعبيرات المناسبة والتراكيب الصحيحة والأسلوب والنطق السليمين
IH	IL	٤ . استعمال المفردات والتعبيرات المناسبة والتراكيب الصحيحة والأسلوب والنطق السليمين في معظم الحالات
A	IM	٥ . كثرة استعمال المفردات والتعبيرات المناسبة والتراكيب الصحيحة والأسلوب والنطق السليمين
AH	IH	٦ . نُدرة وجود أخطاء في اختيار المفردات والتعبيرات والتراكيب الصحيحة واستعمال الأسلوب والنطق السليمين
S	A	٧ . سلامة اللغة المستخدمة من جميع النواحي اللغوية والحضارية

APPENDIX V

(Participant Feedback Form)

This feedback form contains questions about the general introductory and conclusion sessions (Friday and Saturday afternoons) and the language specific workshops (Friday evening and Saturday). We are interested in finding out how we can improve future SOPI workshops, both by altering the workshop format and by retaining its most helpful characteristics. Please respond to the following questions about the SOPI rater training workshop.

PLEASE RETURN THE COMPLETED FORM TO YOUR LANGUAGE TRAINER AT THE CLOSE OF THE SATURDAY SESSION. THANK YOU!

Which language session did you attend? Please circle: AST, CST, JST, PST

PART I: General Introductory Workshop Sessions

1. What did you find most valuable about this part of the workshop?

2. What did you find least valuable about this workshop? How could this be improved?

3. Do you have any other comments on any aspect of this training session?

PART II: Language-Specific Workshop

1. What did you find most valuable about your workshop?

2. What did you find least valuable? How could part of your workshop be improved?

3. Do you plan to use the SOPI in your language program? Why or why not?

4. To what extent do you now feel prepared to use the SOPI in your language program?

PART III: General Comments

Please use the space below to comment on any other aspects of the workshop.

REFERENCES

ACTFL. 1986. ACTFL Proficiency Guidelines. *Foreign Language Annals* 22:4. 373-92.

BARTZ, WALTER H. 1979. *Testing Oral Communication in the Foreign Language Classroom.* Language in Education Series: Theory and Practice 17. Washington, DC: Center for Applied Linguistics.

CLARK, J. L. D. AND Y. LI. 1986. *Development, Validation, and Dissemination of a Proficiency-Based Test of Speaking Ability in Chinese and an Associated Assessment Model for Other Less Commonly Taught Languages.* Washington, DC: Center for Applied Linguistics (ERIC Document Reproduction Service No. ED 278 264).

RESCHKE, CLAUS. 1978. "Adaptation of the FSI Interview Scale for Secondary Schools and Colleges." In *Direct Testing of Speaking Proficiency: Theory and application,* ed. by John L. D. Clark, 77-88. Princeton, NJ: Educational Testing Service.

STANSFIELD, CHARLES W. 1989. Simulated Oral Proficiency Interviews. *ERIC Digest,* 1-2. Washington, DC: Center for Applied Linguistics.

STANSFIELD, C. W. AND D. M. KENYON. 1988. *Development of the Portugese Speaking Test.* Washington, DC: Center for Applied Linguistics (ERIC Document Reproduction Service No. ED 296 586).

_____. 1989. *Development of the Hausa, Hebrew, and Indonesian Speaking Tests.* Washington, DC: Center for Applied Linguistics (ERIC Document Reproduction Service, forthcoming).

INDEX

352 • *Index*

Printed in the United States
205047BV00002B/79-525/P

9 780962 153099